NIH CLASS LIBRARY DISTRIBUTION KIT

The NIH Class Library distribution kit is available on MS-DOS 5-1/4″ high-density diskettes containing UNIX shell archive files. This software requires R2.0 of the AT&T C++ compiler, or a R2.0 compatible C++ compiler. The distribution kit has been tested on Sun-3/SunOS 3.5 and Sun-3/SunOS 4.0 systems. Most of the classes should port easily to other UNIX systems.

The diskettes contain a source code distribution kit including the NIH Class Library, library test suite, all the example programs described in this book, release notes, and an installation guide.

Order the NIH Class Library distribution kit *today*, priced £11.50 including VAT/$16.95 from your computer store, bookseller, or by using the order form below.

Gorlen et al.: NIH Class Library distribution kit—2 diskettes

Please send me .... copies of the **NIH Class Library distribution kit** at £11.50/$16.95 (includes VAT) each.

ISBN 0 471 92752 X

POSTAGE AND HANDLING FREE FOR CASH WITH ORDERS OR PAYMENT BY CREDIT CARD
☐ Remittance enclosed .... Allow approx. 14 days for delivery
☐ Please charge this order to my credit card (All orders subject to credit approval)
Delete as necessary:—AMERICAN EXPRESS, DINERS CLUB, BARCLAYCARD/VISA, ACCESS/MASTERCARD
CARD NUMBER ☐☐☐☐☐☐☐☐☐☐☐☐☐☐☐ Expiration date ....
☐ Please send me an invoice for prepayment. A small postage and handling charge will be made.
Software purchased for professional purposes is generally recognized as tax deductable.
NAME/ADDRESS ....
....
....
OFFICIAL ORDER NUMBER .... SIGNATURE ....

If you have any queries please contact:

Helen Ramsey
John Wiley & Sons Limited
Baffins Lane
Chichester
West Sussex
PO19 1UD
England

Customer Service Department
John Wiley & Sons Limited
Shripney Road
Bognor Regis
West Sussex
PO22 9SA
England

DATA ABSTRACTION AND OBJECT-ORIENTED PROGRAMMING IN C++

DATA ABSTRACTION AND OBJECT-ORIENTED PROGRAMMING IN C++

Keith E. Gorlen,
National Institutes of Health
Maryland, USA

Sanford M. Orlow,
Systex, Inc.
Maryland, USA

Perry S. Plexico,
National Institutes of Health
Maryland, USA

B. G. TEUBNER
Stuttgart

JOHN WILEY & SONS
Chichester · New York · Brisbane · Toronto · Singapore

Published in 1990 by John Wiley & Sons Ltd,
Baffins Lane, Chichester,
West Sussex PO19 1UD, England

Reprinted October 1990
Reprinted with corrections March 1991

Other Wiley Editorial Offices

John Wiley & Sons, Inc., 605 Third Avenue,
New York, NY 10158-0012, USA

Jacaranda Wiley Ltd, G.P.O. Box 859, Brisbane,
Queensland 4001, Australia

John Wiley & Sons (Canada) Ltd, 22 Worcester Road,
Rexdale, Ontario M9W 1L1, Canada

John Wiley & Sons (SEA) Pte Ltd, 37 Jalan Pemimpin 05-04,
Block B, Union Industrial Building, Singapore 2057

UNIX is a registered trademark of AT&T
Sun is a registered trademark of Sun Microsystems, Inc.
Ada is a trademark of the Ada Joint Program Office, Department of
Defense, United States Government

Library of Congress Cataloging-in-Publication Data:

Gorlen, Keith E.
    Data abstraction and object-oriented programming in C++ / Keith E.
Gorlen, Sanford M. Orlow, Perry S. Plexico.
        p.   cm.
    Includes bibliographical references.
    ISBN 0 471 92346 X (pbk)—ISBN 0 471 92751 1
    1. C++ (Computer program language)   2. Abstract data types
(Computer science)   3. Object-oriented programming (Computer
science)   I. Orlow, Sanford M.   II. Plexico, Perry S.   III. Title.
QA76.73.C153G68 1990
005.1—dc20   90-31720
                                                        CIP

British Library Cataloguing in Publication Data:

Gorlen, Keith E.
    Data abstraction and object-oriented programming in C++.
    1. Computer systems. Programming languages: C language
    I. Title   II. Plexico, Perry S.   III. Orlow, Sanford M.
    005.133

    ISBN 0 471 92346 X pbk
    ISBN 0 471 92751 1

Printed in Great Britain by Courier International Ltd, Tiptree, Essex

CONTENTS

List of Figures   xiii

List of Tables   xv

List of Examples   xvii

Preface   xix

1 Introduction   **1**
- 1.1 DATA ABSTRACTION 1
- 1.2 OBJECT-ORIENTED PROGRAMMING 2
- 1.3 THE C++ LANGUAGE 3
  - 1.3.1 How C++ differs from C 3
  - 1.3.2 C++ and object-oriented programming 4
  - 1.3.3 Ways of using C++ 5
- 1.4 THE NIH CLASS LIBRARY 6
- 1.5 EXAMPLE PROGRAMS 6
  - 1.5.1 Source code distribution kit 7
  - 1.5.2 Programming environment 7
  - 1.5.3 Programming conventions 7

I   PROGRAMMING WITH ABSTRACT DATA TYPES IN C++   **9**

2 Data Abstraction in C++   **11**
- 2.1 INTRODUCTION 11
- 2.2 AN EXAMPLE OF PROCEDURAL PROGRAMMING IN C 12
  - 2.2.1 Example problem 12
  - 2.2.2 A solution using C and a procedure library 12
- 2.3 AN EXAMPLE OF DATA ABSTRACTION IN C++ 14
  - 2.3.1 Specifications and implementations 16
  - 2.3.2 Encapsulation 16
- 2.4 OVERVIEW OF C++ SUPPORT FOR DATA ABSTRACTION 17
- 2.5 CHAPTER SUMMARY 18

3 An Example Specification   **19**
- 3.1 INTRODUCTION 19
- 3.2 SPECIFICATION OF CLASS `BigInt` 19

	3.2.1	Classes	20
	3.2.2	Encapsulation	20
	3.2.3	Member functions	21
	3.2.4	Function argument type checking	22
	3.2.5	Function name overloading	23
	3.2.6	Default function arguments	24
	3.2.7	Calling member functions	24
	3.2.8	Constructors	25
	3.2.9	Default constructors	26
	3.2.10	Constructors with more than one argument	26
	3.2.11	Constructors for static class instances	26
	3.2.12	Constructors and type conversion	27
	3.2.13	Constructors and initialization	28
	3.2.14	Operator overloading	29
	3.2.15	Destructors	30
3.3		CHAPTER SUMMARY	31

4 An Example Implementation   **33**
4.1		INTRODUCTION	33
4.2		IMPLEMENTATION OF CLASS `BigInt`	33
	4.2.1	The `BigInt(const char*)` constructor	33
	4.2.2	The scope resolution operator	34
	4.2.3	Constant types	35
	4.2.4	Constant member functions	36
	4.2.5	Casting constants	37
	4.2.6	Implicit member variable and function references . . .	37
	4.2.7	The new operator	38
	4.2.8	Declarations in blocks	38
	4.2.9	The `BigInt(unsigned)` constructor	39
	4.2.10	The `BigInt` copy constructor	39
	4.2.11	Reference types	39
	4.2.12	The `BigInt` addition operator	41
	4.2.13	The `BigInt(char*,unsigned)` constructor	42
	4.2.14	Class `DigitStream`	43
	4.2.15	Class-based as opposed to object-based encapsulation	44
	4.2.16	Friend functions	45
	4.2.17	The keyword `this`	45
	4.2.18	The semantics of return	46
	4.2.19	The `BigInt` assignment operator	46
	4.2.20	The member function `BigInt::print()`	47
	4.2.21	The `BigInt` destructor	47
	4.2.22	Inline functions	48
4.3		CHAPTER SUMMARY	50

5 Applications for Abstract Data Types   **51**
5.1		INTRODUCTION	51
5.2		STREAM I/O	51
	5.2.1	The stream package header file	52
	5.2.2	Writing to the standard output stream	52
	5.2.3	Reading from the standard input stream	54
	5.2.4	Extending stream output operations to a new C++ class	54
	5.2.5	Extending stream input operations to a new C++ class .	55
	5.2.6	Associating an I/O stream with an open file	58
	5.2.7	Summary for I/O streams	59
5.3		DYNAMIC CHARACTER STRINGS	59
	5.3.1	A simple string application	60
	5.3.2	`String` operators	61

	5.3.3	A `String` abstract data type.	62
	5.3.4	Substrings.	64
	5.3.5	Private classes	65
	5.3.6	Forward references to class declarations	66
	5.3.7	Assignment to references.	67
	5.3.8	Overloading constant member functions.	67
	5.3.9	Casting away `const`-ness	68
	5.3.10	Mixing `Strings` and `Substrings` with C strings	69
	5.3.11	Implicit type conversion	69
	5.3.12	ADT design issues	69
	5.3.13	Summary for class `String`	71
5.4	ABSTRACT DATA TYPES FOR DATES AND TIMES	72
	5.4.1	An abstract data type for dates	72
	5.4.2	A simple date application	74
	5.4.3	An abstract data type for times	76
	5.4.4	Summary for classes `Date` and `Time`	77
5.5	REGULAR EXPRESSIONS	77
	5.5.1	Functionality of class `Regex`.	77
	5.5.2	Implementation of class `Regex`	79
5.6	NUMERIC DATA TYPES	81
	5.6.1	Extensions of fundamental arithmetic.	82
	5.6.2	Complex numbers	82
	5.6.3	Vectors	83
	5.6.4	Matrices	88
	5.6.5	The automatic derivative as an ADT	90
	5.6.6	A practical application for automatic derivatives	93
5.7	CHAPTER SUMMARY	97

II   OBJECT-ORIENTED PROGRAMMING IN C++   **99**

6   Object-oriented Programming Concepts   **101**
6.1	INTRODUCTION.	101
	6.1.1	Derived classes.	102
	6.1.2	Virtual member functions	102
	6.1.3	The `switch` statement considered harmful	104
6.2	GEOMETRY EXAMPLE.	104
	6.2.1	Class `Point`	104
	6.2.2	Class `Line` and class `Circle`	105
	6.2.3	Class instances as member variables	106
	6.2.4	Class `TransformStack`	107
	6.2.5	The member function `move()`	108
	6.2.6	The member function `draw()`	108
	6.2.7	Class `Shape`	109
	6.2.8	Class `Picture`	110
	6.2.9	Type compatibility	112
	6.2.10	Pure virtual functions	113
	6.2.11	Subpictures	114
6.3	IMPROVED GEOMETRY EXAMPLE	114
	6.3.1	Object initialization	116
	6.3.2	Object finalization	119
	6.3.3	Calling virtual functions from a base class constructor. . . .	119
6.4	OBJECT-ORIENTED PROGRAMMING TERMINOLOGY.	120
	6.4.1	Single and multiple inheritance	120
	6.4.2	Abstract classes	120
	6.4.3	Protected members	121

| | 6.4.4 | Polymorphism . . . . | 122 |
| 6.5 | CHAPTER SUMMARY . . . . | 122 |

7 An Introduction to the NIH Class Library   123
7.1	INTRODUCTION.	123
7.2	GEOMETRY EXAMPLE USING NIH LIBRARY CLASSES	123
	7.2.1	NIH Library class `Point`	124
	7.2.2	NIH Library class `Stack`	124
	7.2.3	NIH Library class `OrderedCltn`.	125
	7.2.4	Deriving a class from class `Object`	125
	7.2.5	Implementation of class `Picture` using class `OrderedCltn`	126
7.3	COPYING OBJECTS	127
	7.3.1	Implementation of `shallowCopy()`	131
	7.3.2	Implementation of `deepCopy()`	132
	7.3.3	Summary of object copying	134
7.4	OBJECT I/O	134
	7.4.1	Object output	134
	7.4.2	Class `OIOout`	137
	7.4.3	Object input	138
	7.4.4	Class `OIOin`	140
	7.4.5	Static member functions	140
	7.4.6	Object input and polymorphism	140
	7.4.7	Object I/O summary	141
7.5	CHAPTER SUMMARY	141

8 Programming with the NIH Container Classes   143
8.1	INTRODUCTION.	143
	8.1.1	Class `Object`	143
	8.1.2	Identifying and testing an object's class.	144
	8.1.3	Comparing objects	146
	8.1.4	Printing objects	149
8.2	CLASS `Patient`.	149
8.3	THE NIH CLASS LIBRARY CONTAINER CLASSES	151
	8.3.1	Class `Collection`	152
	8.3.2	Class `Iterator`.	152
	8.3.3	Class `SeqCltn`	156
	8.3.4	Class `OrderedCltn`	157
	8.3.5	Class `SortedCltn`	160
	8.3.6	Classes `KeySortCltn`, `LookupKey`, and `Assoc`. .	161
	8.3.7	Class `LinkedList`	169
	8.3.8	Class `Set`.	173
	8.3.9	Class `IdentSet`.	176
	8.3.10	Class `Dictionary`	177
	8.3.11	Class `IdentDict`	182
	8.3.12	Class `Nil` and the `Nil` object	185
8.4	GUIDELINES FOR USING CONTAINER CLASSES	186
	8.4.1	Specializing container classes.	186
	8.4.2	Managing memory correctly	187
	8.4.3	Modifying objects while in containers	189
8.5	CHAPTER SUMMARY	190

9 Designing Library Classes   193
9.1	INTRODUCTION.	193
9.2	OBJECT-ORIENTED DESIGN	194
	9.2.1	When to use classes.	195

9.2.2 Organizing classes 196
9.2.3 Member instances as opposed to member pointers to instances 204
9.2.4 Member functions 209
9.2.5 Member variables. 213
9.2.6 Member accessibility 215
9.3 CHAPTER SUMMARY 218

10 An Example NIH Library Class **219**
10.1 INTRODUCTION. 219
10.2 WRITING THE SPECIFICATION 219
10.2.1 Including header files and preventing multiple definitions 221
10.2.2 Declaring NIH Class Library members 222
10.2.3 Member variables of class ArrayOb. 222
10.2.4 Private member functions of class ArrayOb 222
10.2.5 Object I/O member functions of class ArrayOb 223
10.2.6 Public member functions of class ArrayOb. 223
10.3 WRITING THE IMPLEMENTATION 225
10.3.1 Include files 225
10.3.2 THIS and BASE 226
10.3.3 BASE_CLASSES, MEMBER_CLASSES, and VIRTUAL_BASE_CLASSES 226
10.3.4 DEFINE_CLASS preprocessor macro. 227
10.3.5 DEFINE_ABSTRACT_CLASS preprocessor macro 228
10.3.6 Symbolic error codes 228
10.3.7 ArrayOb constructors 228
10.3.8 ArrayOb assignment operator 229
10.3.9 ArrayOb::operator==() 229
10.3.10 ArrayOb::species() and isEqual(). 230
10.3.11 ArrayOb::hash(). 234
10.3.12 ArrayOb::deepenShallowCopy() 234
10.3.13 ArrayOb::addContentsTo() 234
10.3.14 ArrayOb::compare() 235
10.3.15 Interface to class Iterator. 235
10.3.16 ArrayOb::at() 236
10.3.17 size() and capacity() 236
10.3.18 ArrayOb::reSize(). 236
10.3.19 ArrayOb::removeAll() 237
10.3.20 ArrayOb::allocSizeErr() 237
10.3.21 ArrayOb::indexRangeErr() 237
10.3.22 Stream object I/O. 238
10.3.23 File descriptor object I/O. 238
10.4 CHAPTER SUMMARY 239

11 Lightweight Processes **241**
11.1 INTRODUCTION. 241
11.1.1 The lightweight process data type 241
11.1.2 Lightweight processes in the NIH Class Library 242
11.2 CLASSES Process, StackProc, AND HeapProc. 244
11.3 CLASS Scheduler 247
11.4 CLASS Semaphore 250
11.5 CLASS SharedQueue 256
11.6 CHAPTER SUMMARY 258

12 An Object-Oriented Application **261**
12.1 INTRODUCTION. 261
12.1.1 Background and design goals 261

       12.1.2   A model of the backup system   261

   12.2   THE OBJECT-ORIENTED DESIGN   262
       12.2.1   Lightweight processes   265
       12.2.2   Resource management   266
       12.2.3   The backup database   266

   12.3   AN IMPLEMENTATION BASED ON THE NIH CLASS LIBRARY   267
       12.3.1   Data records   268
       12.3.2   Data object containers   269
       12.3.3   Data flow containers   271
       12.3.4   Specialized objects   272
       12.3.5   Lightweight process objects   273
       12.3.6   The dynamics of the backup system   276

   12.4   IMPLEMENTING A DATABASE WITH THE NIH CLASS LIBRARY   279
       12.4.1   Backup State database   281
       12.4.2   Residence Registry database   283
       12.4.3   Tape Catalog database   283
       12.4.4   Tape Registry database   285
       12.4.5   Implementation of the backup database   285

   12.5   CHAPTER SUMMARY   290

13 Multiple Inheritance   **293**

   13.1   INTRODUCTION   293

   13.2   MULTIPLE INHERITANCE AND MODULAR PROGRAMMING   293
       13.2.1   What is modular programming?   293
       13.2.2   Practicing "modular programming" in C++   294
       13.2.3   Class `NIHCL` as a "module"   295
       13.2.4   Private base classes   297

   13.3   MULTIPLE LINKED LIST EXAMPLE   297
       13.3.1   Inheritance diagrams   299
       13.3.2   Improved vehicle linked lists   300

   13.4   RESOLVING AMBIGUITIES   302

   13.5   VIRTUAL FUNCTIONS AND MULTIPLE INHERITANCE   304

   13.6   VIRTUAL BASE CLASSES   305
       13.6.1   Changes to class `Vehicle`   305
       13.6.2   Classes `LandVhcl` and `WaterVhcl`   305
       13.6.3   Classes `StopLightQ` and `DrawBridgeQ`   305
       13.6.4   Class `AmphibVhcl`   306
       13.6.5   Virtual base class constructors   307
       13.6.6   Virtual base class example   308

   13.7   VIRTUAL BASE CLASSES AND VIRTUAL FUNCTIONS   312

   13.8   OBJECT INITIALIZATION AND MULTIPLE INHERITANCE   314
       13.8.1   Object finalization   316
       13.8.2   Calling virtual functions from a base class constructor   316

   13.9   PROGRAMMING WITH VIRTUAL BASE CLASSES   318
       13.9.1   Static method for eliminating multiple function calls   318
       13.9.2   Dynamic method for eliminating multiple function calls   322
       13.9.3   Summary of programming with virtual base classes   324

   13.10 MULTIPLE INHERITANCE AND THE NIH CLASS LIBRARY   325
       13.10.1 `Object` as a virtual base class   328
       13.10.2 Downward casts from a virtual base class   328
       13.10.3 Multiple inheritance and `deepCopy()`   334
       13.10.4 Multiple inheritance and object I/O   337
       13.10.5 Methods for resolving ambiguous downward casts   343
       13.10.6 Summary of multiple inheritance and the NIH Class Library   345

   13.11 CHAPTER SUMMARY   346

14 Future Directions **349**
14.1 INTRODUCTION 349
14.2 EXCEPTION HANDLING 349
    14.2.1 A hypothetical exception handling mechanism for C++ 350
    14.2.2 Exception handling in the NIH Class Library 352
14.3 PARAMETERIZED TYPES 353
    14.3.1 A hypothetical parameterized type facility for C++ 354
    14.3.2 Parameterized types in the NIH Class Library 358
    14.3.3 Summary of parameterized types 361
14.4 GARBAGE COLLECTION 361
    14.4.1 Counted pointers 361
    14.4.2 Garbage-collecting versions of `malloc()` 365
14.5 DYNAMIC LINKING 367
14.6 CHAPTER SUMMARY 369

Appendix A NIH Class Library Hierarchy **371**

Appendix B NIH Class Library Template Files **373**

Appendix C Tips for C Programmers **381**

References **393**

Index **395**

LIST OF FIGURES

1.1   The heritage of C++.   4

2.1   Combining specification and implementation in a client program.   16

3.1   An instance of class `BigInt` representing the number "654321"   21
3.2   Access to private member variables via public member functions   22

6.1   A class hierarchy   103
6.2   Class hierarchy for Example 6-1   109

7.1   Operation of `shallowCopy()`   129
7.2   Operation of `deepCopy()`.   130
7.3   The data structure created by Example 7-2.   131

8.1   `LinkedList` with direct links   170
8.2   `LinkedList` with indirect links   171
8.3   `Dictionary` containing three associations   179

9.1   Single inheritance container hierarchy for class `ArrayOb`   201
9.2   Multiple inheritance container hierarchy for class `ArrayOb`   202
9.3   Container class hierarchy with `ArrayOb` as member variable   202

11.1 State transitions for an NIH Class Library lightweight process.   243

12.1 NIH workstation network.   263
12.2 Model of backup system   264
12.3 Request scheduling operations   277
12.4 Backup scheduling operations   278
12.5 Backup staging operations   278
12.6 Backup taping operations   279

13.1 Class `Vehicle` inheritance DAG for Example 13-1.   300
13.2 Inheritance DAGs for `StopLightQ` and `DrawBridgeQ` in Example 13-4 .   306
13.3 Class `AmphibVhcl` Inheritance DAG for Example 13-4.   307
13.4 Class `C` inheritance DAG for Example 13-5   312

13.5 Inheritance DAG for Example 13-6. 316
13.6 Inheritance DAG for Example 13-7. 318
13.7 Inheritance DAG for Example 13-9. 327
13.8 Non-virtual `Object` inheritance DAG for Example 13-9. 329

LIST OF TABLES

9.1 Member function call execution overhead 211

11.1 The states of a Semaphore 251

12.1 Backup system operations and resource requirements 266
12.2 Classes representing backup resources 269
12.3 Containers transmitting data between lightweight processes 271
12.4 Classes derived from class Process representing backup operations 274
12.5 Data types from the backup system 280
12.6 Key/value associations for the backup database 281
12.7 Class libraries in the backup application 291

LIST OF EXAMPLES

2-1   Add ints.   12
2-2   Add multiple-precision integers using *mp* library   13
2-3   Add instances of class `BigInt`.   14

5-1   Writing to the standard output stream   52
5-2   Reading from the standard input.   54
5-3   Writing a `BigInt` to the standard output   55
5-4   Reading a `BigInt` from the standard input   57
5-5   Opening a stream for a file.   58
5-6   String substitution   60
5-7   Find dates of working days.   74
5-8   Vector operations.   83
5-9   Matrix algebra with class `Matrix`   89
5-10 Automatic derivatives with class `AutoDeriv`.   92
5-11 Using automatic derivatives to solve systems of equations   96

6-1   Geometry class hierarchy   105
6-2   Improved geometry class hierarchy   115
6-3   Order of construction of base and member classes   117
6-4   Calling a virtual function from a base class constructor   119

7-1   Geometry class hierarchy using NIH Class Library   124
7-2   Improved geometry class hierarchy using NIH class library.   127
7-3   Object I/O `readFrom()`   138

8-1   Description of a `Patient` object   151
8-2   Use of an `Iterator` with container for objects of unknown class   153
8-3   Nested `Iterators`.   154
8-4   Incorrectly modifying a container during iteration   155
8-5   Modifying a container during iteration   156
8-6   Sequential access to `Objects` in an `OrderedCltn`   158
8-7   Sorting `Patient` records by name   160
8-8   Sorting `Patient` records with a `KeySortCltn`   165
8-9   Sorting on multiple keys with `ArrayOb` and `KeySortCltn`   167
8-10 Linking into a `LinkedList`.   172

8-11 Test if date falls on a weekday   174
8-12 Binary `Set` operators   175
8-13 Comparison of classes `Set` and `IdentSet`.   177
8-14 A `Dictionary` of `Patient` records keyed by name   180
8-15 Comparison of classes `Dictionary` and `IdentDict`.   182
8-16 Property list   183

9-1   Class `ArrayOb` example   194
9-2   Incorrect handling of member pointers to class instances.   204
9-3   Correct handling of member pointers to class instances   205
9-4   Virtual inline function calls.   212

10-1 Variations of `isEqual()`   230

11-1 Scheduling lightweight processes in the NIH Class Library.   248
11-2 Managing N resources with a `Semaphore`   252
11-3 Protecting a critical section of code with an `AutoSignal`.   255
11-4 LWP communication with a `SharedQueue`   256

13-1 Class `Vehicle` with multiple links   298
13-2 Improved vehicle linked lists   300
13-3 Virtual functions and multiple inheritance   304
13-4 Class `AmphibVhcl` with virtual base class   308
13-5 Virtual base classes and virtual functions   313
13-6 Order of construction of base and member classes   314
13-7 Calling a virtual function from a base class constructor   317
13-8 Static method for avoiding multiple calls to members of virtual base. . . .   319
13-9 Multiple Inheritance with the NIH Class Library   325
13-10 Multiple Inheritance and object I/O `readFrom()`   342
13-11 Limitation of object I/O   345

14-1 Exception handling in the NIH Class Library   352
14-2 Counted pointers   362

PREFACE

This book is about the C++ programming language and how to use it to write abstract data types and object-oriented programs. An abstract data type is a programmer-defined data type that encompasses data elements along with the operations that can be performed on them. Object-oriented programming (O-OP) extends the concept by organizing abstract data types and exploiting their common features to reduce programming effort. The computing community has no agreement on what kind of programming environment supports data abstraction and object-oriented programming. Some claim that they can be done in almost any programming language, while others claim that only a few languages qualify as supporting these programming techniques. We hold the more restrictive view, as shown in the following table:

Language	Procedural Programming	Modular Programming	Data Abstraction	O-OP
C	Yes	No	No	No
Pascal	Yes	No	No	No
Modula-2	Yes	Yes	No	No
Ada	Yes	Yes	Yes	No
Smalltalk-80	No	No	Yes	Yes
C++	Yes	No	Yes	Yes

As the table shows, only Smalltalk-80 and C++ from among this group of well known programming languages accommodate both data abstraction and object-oriented programming. Smalltalk-80, one of the pioneers among object-oriented programming languages, is a complete standalone programming environment combining language, user interface, and operating system. It excels at experimentation and fast prototyping, but it does so apart from general purpose environments that include operating systems like UNIX. C++, because it is derived from C with its concomitant association with UNIX, offers wide appeal. C++ supports object-oriented programming in that it lets us define abstract data types and use them to build object-oriented programs. But we cannot simply sit down and write such a program because C++ doesn't include a built-in set of basic classes for us to use.

This book grew out of a project, on which the authors continue to work at the time of this writing, to make UNIX-based workstations more useful to biomedical scientists at the National Institutes of Health (NIH). We became convinced that object-oriented programming and C++ offer opportunities for better programs that are easier to write, easier to understand, and easier to maintain, yet retain the compactness and efficiency of C programs. The NIH

Class Library that we describe evolved from our experience and adds the class library that C++ lacks. We modeled it after Smalltalk-80, so that it provides much of the functionality of Smalltalk-80's basic, non-graphical classes. The NIH Class Library consists of over 60 C++ classes written in 275K bytes of source code. We have used it in the examples especially prepared for this book and in a number of object-oriented applications including the one described in Chapter 12. Based on this experience, we think that the NIH Class Library and C++ taken together yield a programming environment that combines many of the strengths and overcomes most of the weaknesses of Smalltalk-80 and C++.

We wrote this book for experienced programmers who have some knowledge of the C programming language and who wish to learn about its successor, C++, and what it can do. Much of the book follows a tutorial style by introducing concepts and then illustrating their application in examples, but it is not a primer: it does not cover features that C programmers are familiar with, such as syntax, meaning of declarations and control structures, and the C library. Nor is it a reference manual since it does not cover all of the features of C++. Rather, this book presents our experience in developing the NIH Class Library, and object-oriented applications based on it. We hope that the techniques and examples we present are clear and accessible to C programmers as well as sufficiently advanced to interest even those fluent in C++.

We organized the book around the concepts of data abstraction and object-oriented programming, then threaded the conceptual structure with practical illustrations of how to write good C++ programs using these tools. Chapter 1 differentiates C++ from C and highlights the features that suit C++ to write abstract data types and object-oriented programs. Part I (Chapters 2–5) then deals with abstract data types, focusing mainly on their use in conventional procedural programs. Chapters 2–4 define and explain "abstract data type", develop a motivation for using data abstraction, and trace the development of both the specification and the implementation of an example abstract data type. Chapter 5 concludes Part 1 by describing several abstract data types representing familiar data units and structures that almost all programmers will have encountered.

Part II (Chapters 6–14) turns to object-oriented programming concepts. Chapter 6 describes object-oriented programming and explains some of its advantages. Following the tutorial style of Chapters 2–4, it then develops a complete object-oriented programming example. Next, Chapter 7 shows how we can exploit reusable software components from class libraries to simplify and generalize program development, and it introduces the NIH Class Library, developed by the authors and made available with this book.

Chapter 8 discusses the NIH Class Library container classes—classes that represent common data structures encountered in many applications, and which account for most of the more complex library classes. Chapters 9 and 10 explain how to extend the NIH Class Library with other, user-supplied classes using template files and illustrate this by presenting a complete specification and implementation for a particular class.

Chapter 11 describes the NIH library classes that help to support multiprogramming using coroutines.

Chapter 12 contains a case study of the object-oriented design and implementation of a large software system based on the NIH Class Library, and addresses many of the design issues that arise in building such a system.

Chapter 13 explores multiple inheritance, a recent addition to C++ that lets a class inherit the characteristics of multiple base classes.

Finally, Chapter 14 investigates some potential areas of further development, both for C++ and the NIH Class Library.

Programmers who want an overview of C++, object-oriented programming, and class libraries may find that the first seven chapters satisfy their needs. C++ programmers who expect to apply object-oriented programming concepts and the NIH Class Library to write their own programs should read Chapters 6, 9, and 10, as well. They may also wish to study Chapter 12 to gain some insight about how to associate classes with conceptual design objects, particularly in complex software systems where the association is not obvious. Chapters 11 and 13 deal with advanced topics that primarily will interest those who need to use them in specialized applications. The last chapter will interest all readers, but will be of most value to serious C++ and NIH Class Library users.

We hope this book will motivate you to apply the object-oriented style of programming, using C++ and the NIH Class Library, to some real problems, and we hope that by making the full NIH Class Library available with the book, we will speed and simplify your venture into this exciting area of software development.

ACKNOWLEDGMENTS

We are grateful to Alan Demmerle, Chief of NIH's Computer Systems Laboratory, for his motivating influence and his support. Without the organizational support and backing that Al secured and assured for us, we could not have written this book.

Bjarne Stroustrup deserves much credit for inspiring the book because of the encouragement and the help he provided to one of the authors (Keith) during the early development work on NIH Class Library.

We thank others of the Computer Systems Laboratory's staff for their valuable support: Ted Persky for his work on the NIH Class Library `Date`, `KeySortCltn`, and `Vector` library classes, and his careful reading and constructive criticism of early drafts of the book; Don Jansen for producing the drawings seen throughout the book; Connie Eppich for her work on the `String` class; and Nurul Hamseth whose diligent reading of the manuscript uncovered errors hidden in the index.

Keith Gorlen
Sandy Orlow
Perry Plexico
National Institutes of Health
Summer 1989

1
INTRODUCTION

Data abstraction and object-oriented programming together represent a style of programming that offers opportunities for improved software productivity. While other modern programming techniques like modular programming are similarly motivated, they often are used in concert with conventional procedural programming. They tend to emphasize ways to overcome particular problems with widely used programming practices, and thus offer incremental improvements to the art of computer programming. Because of its close association with object-oriented programming, we discuss data abstraction—the use of abstract data types—in considerable detail in this book. As we shall see, data abstraction similarly offers substantial benefits when used with conventional programming styles. More important, though, is the value of data abstraction as a necessary stepping stone to object-oriented programming. Object-oriented programming, with data abstraction as a necessary foundation, differs greatly from other programming styles and methodologies in that it requires a different way of thinking, in essence, a different approach to problem solving using computers.

Our first task in this chapter is to present a bird's eye view of data abstraction and object-oriented programming and to specify their place in computer programming. Next, we will look at the similarities and differences between C++ and C, then turn to the new features of C++ and how they aid data abstraction and object-oriented programming. In this introduction, we will neither define the vocabulary nor treat the details of our subjects but will concentrate of a summary exposition of these topics.

1.1 DATA ABSTRACTION

Programmers have long recognized the value of organizing related data items in program constructs like Pascal RECORDs or C structs, and then treating the resulting data structures as units. Data abstraction extends this organization to encompass a set of operations that can be performed on a particular instance of the structure. Usually, the data elements and the implementation of the operations that can be performed on them are held private or *encapsulated* to prevent unwanted alteration. Instead of accessing data elements directly, user code, often called *client programs*, must invoke the permissible operations to achieve results. To do this, clients have access to a client interface or *specification* by which they can know how to invoke the operations.

When we encapsulate data structures and their operations in this way, we can make them behave analogously to the built-in or *fundamental* data types like integers and floating point numbers. We can then use them simply as black boxes which provide a transformation between input and output. We need not understand or even be aware of their inner workings, just as we do not need to know exactly how a compiler treats a fundamental data type. Data abstraction, in essence, lets us create new data types, giving rise to the idea of calling them *abstract data types*. In later chapters, we will show how to use abstract data types to represent many familiar data structures like character strings, dates, complex numbers, and matrices. You will even see how to use them for graphical constructs and input–output streams.

Programming languages that support data abstraction provide a language construct—called a *class* in C++ and in some other languages—which we can use to encapsulate the abstract data type's data elements and operations. Although they are not precisely the same, we often will use the terms "class" and "abstract data type" interchangeably.

1.2   OBJECT-ORIENTED PROGRAMMING

Object-oriented programming is not new; its concepts date back some two decades. The origins of object-oriented programming stem from the Simula 67 programming language [5] and from the Smalltalk [7] research begun at Xerox Palo Alto Research Center in the early 1970s. What *is* new is the recent spate of interest in this important and promising methodology—interest that has arisen in part because a new language, C++, for the first time gives us the programming tools and resources to write efficient object-oriented programs for a general-purpose computing environment. We have said that object-oriented programming differs so greatly from more familiar programming styles that it requires a different approach to problem solving, but just what is object-oriented programming, and what makes it so different?

When doing object-oriented programming, a programmer specifies *what* to do with an object rather than focusing on the conventional procedural aspects of *how* something gets done. Simply stated, object-oriented programming deals with the manipulation of objects. An object, in turn, can represent almost anything—a number, a string, a hospital patient record, or a graphic construct like a rectangle or some other geometric shape. In essence, an object comprises the data elements or the data structure needed to describe the object, together with the set of permissible operations on the data. This description bears remarkable similarity to the one we gave for an abstract data type. In fact, we will see that an object is nothing more than a particular instance of an abstract data type that we have designed according to a particular set of rules.

Much of the value of object-oriented programming results from *inheritance*—the idea by which a programmer starts with a library of already-developed object types, or classes, and extends them for a new application by adding data elements or operations to form new classes. In other words, instead of developing a new application by writing code from scratch, a client inherits data and operations from some useful *base* class, and then adds new functionality by describing how the new class differs from the base class. When adding new data elements or functions, the programmer need not modify the base class at all, thus giving rise to one of the benefits of object-oriented programming: *code reusability*.

Another idea integral to object-oriented programming is that of *dynamic* or *late binding*, which helps to make programs more general by letting each class of a related group of classes have a different implementation of a particular function. Client programs can apply the function to an object without needing to know the specific class of the object. At execution time, the run-time system will determine the specific class of the object and invoke that class's implementation of the function.

Just what does all this mean? To start to comprehend these new concepts, consider a program that manipulates data structures representing various geometric shapes. Perhaps we would start with a `Shape` abstract data type to represent general shapes. Through inheritance, we could design new classes to represent more specific `Shapes`, like `Circles` or `Squares`, and implement these simply by dealing with how a `Circle`, for example, differs from other `Shapes`. When the program manipulates `Circles`, it will in many instances use inherited variables or functions that work for all `Shapes`.

By contrast, we might encounter situations in which we need a program that, instead of operating on specified data structures like `Circles`, can deal with generic `Shapes` whose particular types we do not know when we write the program. For example, we might want the program to draw a set of `Shapes` comprising `Circles`, `Triangles` and `Rectangles`. When the program executes, the run time system will determine the particular class for each `Shape`, and, using dynamic binding, invoke the appropriate `draw()` function for it.

Most programmers will want some clear understanding of the advantages of object-oriented programming before they invest the time and effort to learn how to do it. The technique, indeed, offers advantages, particularly in terms of potential productivity improvements. The principal ones are reusability and reliability. We can design classes that are reusable because others either can use them directly or can add functionality by making them more specific to a given task through inheritance. Dynamic binding lets us make programs very general, thereby also contributing to reusability. Because programmers often will need only to put a framework around a large volume of already-developed, tested software, their programs should be easier to debug and should behave more reliably when they are completed.

1.3   THE C++ LANGUAGE

The C++ programming language was designed and implemented by Bjarne Stroustrup of AT&T Bell Laboratories as a successor to C. While borrowing several key ideas from the Simula 67 and Algol 68 programming languages, C++ retains compatibility with existing C programs and the efficiency of C. Figure 1.1 illustrates the heritage of C++.

C++ also adds many powerful new capabilities, making it suitable for a wide range of applications from device drivers to artificial intelligence. C++ will interest serious software developers because of its intimate relationship with C, and for its potential use for building graphical user interfaces, for systems programming, and for supporting large-scale software development.

The definitive book on C++ is Stroustrup's *The C++ Programming Language* [23], which gives a detailed description of the language and contains many examples and exercises. It also includes the C++ reference manual, a concise, more formal definition of the language.

1.3.1   How C++ differs from C

Most programmers will agree that C, while it is a compact and efficient language, offers more than its fair share of ways to commit programming errors. C++ overcomes many of these problems and provides many new features as well.

For example, C provides only limited compile-time type checking, and does not type check function arguments at all. Moreover, C suffers from its exclusive reliance on a treatment of

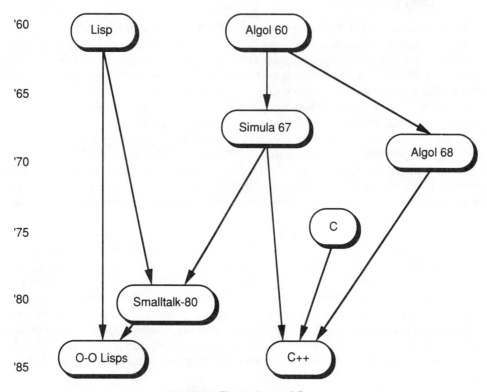

Figure 1.1 The heritage of C++

function arguments known as *call by value*. Whenever we need to pass a function argument by reference, we must resort to the rather obscure and error prone approach of passing a pointer to the argument.

C++ addresses both of these problems. Its type checking features strongly encourage a programmer to declare the types of the arguments of all functions. For example, when we declare a function, we can write

```
fcn(int p1, char* p2);
```

and the compiler will check for inconsistent argument types when the function is called, thereby eliminating many bugs at an early stage. C++'s syntax allows variables to be declared as references. When a function has a reference as a formal argument, the C++ compiler knows that it must pass an address to the actual argument when the function is called.

1.3.2   C++ and object-oriented programming

Why is C++ important to a discussion of object-oriented programming? Why can we not do object-oriented programming in plain old C, or Pascal, or some other familiar language? In his article "What is Object-Oriented Programming?" [27], C++ designer Stroustrup explains it this way: a "language *supports* a programming style if it provides facilities that make it convenient (reasonably easy, safe, and efficient) to use that style."

If, on the other hand, a language requires you to have uncommon ability or to expend excessive effort to write programs using a given style, then that language only *"enables"* the style. For example, it is easy and effective to write structured programs in Pascal. You can also write structured programs in FORTRAN 77, but it is a difficult, thankless task.

C++ not only corrects most of C's deficiencies, it also introduces many completely new features that were designed into the language to provide support for data abstraction and object-oriented programming. Here are some of the more prominent new features:

- *classes*, the basic language construct for creating programmer defined data types that we call abstract data types;

- *member variables*, which describe the data in abstract data types, and *member functions*, which define the permissible operations on the data type;

- *operator overloading*, which lets us give additional meaning to most operators so that we can use them with our own data types, thereby making those data types easier to use, and *function name overloading*, similar to operator overloading, which lets us reduce the need for unusual function names, making code easier to read;

- *programmer-controlled automatic type conversion*, which lets us blend our own types with others and with the fundamental data types provided by the C++ language;

- *derived classes*, which inherit member variables and member functions from their base classes, and can be differentiated from their base classes by adding other member variables and member functions;

- *virtual functions*, which let a derived class redefine member functions inherited from a base class. We can then write very general programs that are oblivious to the specific classes of the objects they manipulate; through *dynamic binding*, the run time system will choose the function appropriate to a particular class.

We shall show in succeeding chapters how to apply these new tools provided by C++ to create data types that are suitable for particular applications, and then to combine those abstract data types into object-oriented programs.

1.3.3 Ways of using C++

C++ is compatible with C, and because C++ uses the fundamental data types—int, float and so forth—in the conventional way, it does not force the object-oriented paradigm on programmers. You can continue to write conventional procedural programs just as you did in C, and still take advantage of many of C++'s new features.

You can go a step farther and use some of C++'s new features to build your own data types that are suitable for your application. Often you will find that the resulting programs will be easier to write and debug, and, once written, easier to read and maintain. That is because the new abstract data types, since you can use them almost like the built-in data types, add a sense of naturalness to programs, making them more sensible and more readily understandable.

Finally, by using still more new C++ features and by building abstract data types in a particular way, you can do object-oriented programming. It is these last two ways of using C++ that we will concentrate on in this book.

1.4   THE NIH CLASS LIBRARY

We must, however, emphasize at this point that for all its new features and its power, C++ is not an object-oriented programming language in the sense of Smalltalk-80. Instead, it provides the tools to let us do object-oriented programming, within limits, if we choose.

For example, C++ does not treat all data types uniformly: since it handles fundamental data types the same way that C does, we can make abstract data types behave similarly but not identically to the built-in types. Conversely, fundamental types are not classes, so they cannot inherit functionality from other classes. Nor is it possible to redefine the meaning of built-in operations that C++ provides for the fundamental types.

More importantly, however, C++ lacks a class library so that users can not easily take full advantage of its object-oriented features; thus we have developed the NIH Class Library [8], a library of classes that extends functionality similar to that provided by some of the basic Smalltalk-80 classes to programs written in C++.

The NIH Class Library implements abstract data types that have been designed to simplify object-oriented programming using C++. It contains generally useful data types, such as String, Date, and Time, and it provides a set of classes similar to the Smalltalk-80 collection classes, including OrderedCltn (indexed arrays), LinkedList (singly linked lists), Set (hash tables), and Dictionary (associative arrays). Classes Process, Scheduler, Semaphore, and SharedQueue implement multiprogramming with coroutines. The set of Vector classes and a handful of others such as Random (random number generator) and Range (range of integers) assist in various kinds of arithmetic and mathematical problems. NIH Library classes are organized into the inheritance hierarchy shown in Appendix A.

The NIH Library includes an object I/O facility in its class implementations which can make program- and machine-independent representations of arbitrarily complex data structures comprising NIH Library and user-defined objects. Client applications can then save these representations on disk files or move them between programs running on the same or different (via a network) machines.

As you will see, you can often develop new, application-specific classes that manipulate complex data structures by writing only a small amount of code that combines several classes from the NIH Library. The NIH Library classes then do most of the real work—storage management, searching, string comparison, and the like.

1.5   EXAMPLE PROGRAMS

We have included many example programs in this book to illustrate the concepts and programming techniques we describe. We have tried to give examples that are pertinent, concise, realistic, practical, and deal with application areas that are likely to be familiar or useful to the reader. This is a tall order to fill, so no example program meets all of these ideals.

Unlike the examples in many contemporary books on computer programming, many of the examples in this book will not compile and run if you type them in from the text. This is because they depend upon the NIH Class Library environment or because we have omitted details that we felt were irrelevant to the discussion at hand. We have indicated those places in the example programs where we have omitted code with an ellipsis comment:[1]

```
// ...
```

1.5.1   Source code distribution kit

We believe that having working example programs to try out and experiment with is critical to learning how to program, so we have arranged with the publisher to distribute the source code in machine-readable form for all the example programs in this book together with the NIH Class Library. This software is in the public domain and may be freely copied and used, except for a few files which may be copied subject to the terms and conditions set forth in the copyrights they bear. Each example program in this book begins with a comment indicating the name of the file in the distribution kit that contains the complete, working example. For instance

```
// ex1-1.c

main()
{
    int a = 193;
    int b = 456;
    int c;
// ...
    c = a + b + 47;
    printf("%d\n",c);
}
```

indicates that you will find the complete code for this example program in the file named `ex1-1.c`.

Some examples require, in addition to NIH library classes, classes designed especially for the examples. The distribution kit includes these as well in their own specification and implementation files named, for example, `Patient.h` and `Patient.c`.

1.5.2   Programming environment

We compiled and tested the example programs contained in the Source Code Distribution Kit using Release 2.00 of the AT&T C++ Language System with the UNIX operating system running on several varieties of 32-bit workstations.

1.5.3   Programming conventions

We used the following conventions when writing the example programs.

Preprocessor symbols and compilation constants are written in all upper case:

---

[1] In C++, comments that begin with a // extend to the end of the line.

```
#ifdef DEBUG
const unsigned EXPANSION_FACTOR = 2;
```

Names of classes are written in mixed upper and lower case and begin with an uppercase letter:

```
class BigInt { // ...
```

Variables names are written in mixed upper and lower case and begin with a lowercase letter:

```
char* digits;
```

Function names are also written in mixed upper and lower case and begin with a lowercase letter:

```
float abs(float);
```

However, when we use the name of a function in the text, we always write it with () at the end to make it clear that it is a function. When we write a function name this way, the empty parentheses do *not* necessarily mean that the function has no arguments; for example, the preceding declaration declares the function abs().

While we would have preferred to adhere to these conventions religiously, we occasionally deviate, sometimes for historical reasons, and at other times because we describe software written by others who do not follow the same conventions.

Part I
PROGRAMMING
WITH ABSTRACT
DATA TYPES

2

DATA ABSTRACTION
IN C++

2.1 INTRODUCTION

In this chapter we begin our discussion of *data abstraction*, which is the programming technique of inventing new data types that are well suited to an application, thereby making it easier to program. Data abstraction is a powerful, general-purpose technique which, when properly used, can result in shorter, more readable, more flexible programs.

Most programming languages treat program variables and constants as *instances* of a *data type*. A data type provides a description of its instances that tells the compiler such things as how much memory to allocate for an instance, how to interpret the data in that memory, and what operations are permissible on that data. For example, when we write a declaration such as float x in C or C++, we are declaring an instance named x of the data type float. The data type float tells the compiler to reserve, for example, 32 bits of memory, to use the machine's floating point instructions to manipulate this memory, and that operations such as "add" and "multiply" are permissible, whereas operations such as "modulus" and "shift" are not. We do not have to write this description of the float type—the author of the compiler did that for us and built it into the compiler. Data types that are built in to a compiler in this way, such as int, char, and float in C and C++, are known as *fundamental data types*.

Some programming languages have features that allow us to effectively extend the language by adding our own data types. A programmer-defined data type is called an *abstract data type* (ADT) to distinguish it from a *fundamental data type*. The term "abstract" refers to the way in which a programmer abstracts some concepts from a mass of programming detail and unifies these concepts to create a new data type.

In the C++ language we can implement our own abstract data types by declaring C++ *classes* and we can operate on them as if they had been built into the C++ language. This language extension feature of C++ allows programmers to become, in effect, language designers. Being able to design and implement our own data types gives us a lot of power—power that we can use to cope with programming large, complicated applications. But along with this comes the responsibility to exercise good judgement when designing ADTs and the need to master a few, more sophisticated language features.

To establish the motivation behind data abstraction, we will first present a conceptually simple programming problem, and show how it is typically approached in C using procedural programming techniques. We will examine this solution and point out its shortcomings. Next, we will present a C++ program that solves the same problem in a more elegant fashion using data abstraction, and describe the language features necessary to support data abstraction. We will then introduce the concept of splitting an ADT into a specification and an implementation, and describe how encapsulation enforces this division. Finally, we will present a brief overview of the language features C++ has to support data abstraction.

2.2 AN EXAMPLE OF PROCEDURAL PROGRAMMING IN C

The best way to learn about data abstraction in C++ is to write a program, and that is what we will do in this and the following two chapters. Let us start in familiar territory by taking a look at a simple program written in ordinary C:

```
// ex2-1.c - Add ints

main()
{
    int a = 193;
    int b = 456;
    int c;
    c = a + b + 47;
    printf("%d\n",c);
}
```

This program declares three integer variables named a, b, and c, initializing a and b to the values 193 and 456, respectively. The integer c is assigned the result of adding a and b and the constant 47. Finally, the standard C library function printf() is called to print out the value of c. The quoted string "%d\n" tells how to print the result: %d prints c as a decimal number, and \n adds a newline character. If we compile and execute this program, it prints out the number 696 and exits.

2.2.1 Example problem

Now suppose we wish to perform a similar calculation, but this time a and b are big numbers, like the US national debt expressed in dollars. Such numbers are too big to be stored as ints on most computers, so if we tried to write int a = 25123654789456 the C compiler (we hope!) would give us an error message and fail to compile the program. Big integers have many practical applications, such as cryptography, symbolic algebra, and number theory, where it can be necessary to perform arithmetic on numbers with hundreds or even thousands of digits, so it is worth our effort to construct a convenient way to handle such numbers.

2.2.2 A solution using C and a procedure library

To gain an appreciation for the power of data abstraction, let us first write a program to perform arithmetic on big numbers in C, which restricts us to using procedural programming techniques. Fortunately, we can take advantage of *mp*, an existing C library for performing multiple precision integer arithmetic available under Berkeley 4.3 UNIX [32], so most of the work has already been done.

The *mp* library is a typical C language procedure library. It defines a struct called MINT for representing big integers, and it provides a variety of functions for operating on MINT-type variables. The functions from the *mp* library that we need for this example are:

- MINT* itom(n), which creates a new MINT initialized to the value of the (small) integer n, and returns a pointer to it;

- madd(a,b,c), which adds the MINTs pointed to by a and b and returns their sum in the MINT pointed to by c;

- mult(a,b,c), which multiplies the MINTs pointed to by a and b and returns their product in the MINT pointed to by c;

- mout(a), which prints the MINT pointed to by a;

- mfree(a), which frees the MINT pointed to by a.

To use the *mp* library to solve our problem, we also need to write a function to convert a big integer constant into a MINT, since the library does not provide a way to do this. The function MINT* dtom(d) takes a big integer written as a character string constant, and converts it into a MINT one digit at a time.

Here is a C language version of a program using the *mp* library to solve the big integer problem:

```
/* ex2-2.c - Add multiple-precision integers using mp library */

#include <mp.h>

MINT* dtom(d)
char *d;
{
    MINT *t, *ten;
    t = itom(0);
    ten = itom(10);
    while (*d) {
        MINT *u;
        u = itom(*d++ - '0');
        mult(t,ten,t);
        madd(t,u,t);
        mfree(u);
    }
    mfree(ten);
    return t;
}

main()
{
    MINT *a, *b, *c, *t;
    a = dtom("25123654789456");
    b = dtom("456023398798362");
    c = itom(0);
    t = itom(47);
    madd(a,b,c);
```

```
        madd(c,t,c);
        mout(c);
        printf("\n");
        mfree(a); mfree(b); mfree(c); mfree(t);
    }
```

The main point to notice is that, although the problem of adding big integers is conceptually similar to that of adding small integers, the two example C programs are very different. In Example 2-2, we become so involved in the details of programming with MINTs that we lose sight of the essence of the problem we are trying to solve, making the program difficult to write and understand. The evidence for this is that the program in Example 2-1 ran correctly the first time we ran it, whereas the program in Example 2-2 required debugging.

What details does the procedural programming model force us to deal with in Example 2-2? Specifically, we had to do the following:

- initialize MINTs in separate statements, for example, c = itom(0) in main()— failing to do this is a frequent source of errors;

- handle temporary variables, such as the variable t in main();

- convert small integers to MINTs, as in the statement t = itom(47) in main();

- use functions with distinctive names, like madd() and mult(), instead of the traditional arithmetic operators; and,

- manage storage, as in the calls to mfree() in main().

C++ is not magic—code to perform operations on big integers and to handle the details of initialization, temporary variables, type conversion, storage management, and so on must still be written. The important difference is that in C++, we can package this code as an ADT such that the programmer who codes the ADT, or *provider*, handles the complexities, while those who use the ADT, the *clients*, find it as convenient to use as a built-in data type.

2.3   AN EXAMPLE OF DATA ABSTRACTION IN C++

Using C++ and making the big integer software an ADT called BigInt instead of a procedure library has a dramatic effect on writing a program to solve our example problem. Notice how similar the C program in Example 2-1 is to the C++ program in Example 2-3 which performs a similar calculation using BigInts instead of ints:

```
// ex2-3.c - Add instances of class BigInt

#include "BigInt.h"

main()
{
    BigInt a =  "25123654789456";
    BigInt b = "456023398798362";
```

```
    BigInt c;
    c = a + b + 47;
    c.print();  printf("\n");
}
```

Obviously, this C++ version is more compact and easier to understand than its C counterpart in Example 2-2.

Most other programming languages currently in widespread use, such as BASIC, C, COBOL, FORTRAN, Pascal, and Modula-2 make it difficult to practice data abstraction well. This is because data abstraction requires special language features not available in these languages. To get an idea of what these features do, let us analyze the C++ program in Example 2-3.

The first three statements in the body of the main() program declare three type BigInt variables, a, b, and c. The C++ compiler needs to know how to create them—how much space to allocate for them and how to initialize them.

The first and second statements are similar. They initialize the BigInt variables a and b with big integer constants written as character strings containing only digits, so the C++ compiler must be able to convert character strings into BigInts.

The fourth statement is the most complicated. It adds a, b, and the integer constant 47 and stores the result in c. The C++ compiler needs to be able to create a temporary BigInt variable to hold the sum of a and b. It must then convert the int constant 47 into a BigInt and add this to the temporary variable. Finally, it must assign this temporary BigInt variable to c.

The fifth statement prints c on the standard output, and the last statement calls the C library function printf() to print a newline character. C programmers are probably familiar with printf(), but c.print() may look a bit strange. It is a call on a special kind of function available in C++ known as a *member function*. We will talk more about this later, but for now just think of it as a function that prints out a variable of type BigInt.

Even though the body of main() contains no more statements, the compiler is not finished yet. It must destroy the BigInt variables a, b, and c and any BigInt temporaries it may have created before leaving a function, such as main(). This is to assure that the storage used by these variables is freed.

Let us summarize what the C++ compiler needs to know how to do with BigInts to compile the example program:

- *create* new instances of BigInt variables

- *convert* character strings and integers to BigInts

- *initialize* the value of one BigInt with that of another BigInt

- *assign* the value of one BigInt to another

- *add* two BigInts together

- *print* BigInts

- *destroy* BigInts when they are no longer needed

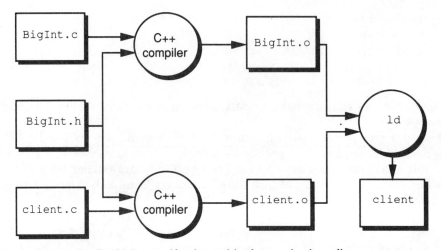

Figure 2.1 Combining specification and implementation in a client program

2.3.1   Specifications and implementations

Where does the C++ compiler obtain this know-how? From the file `BigInt.h`, which is included by the first line of the example program. This file contains the *specification* of our `BigInt` abstract data type. The specification contains the information that programs that *use* an abstract data type, called *client programs* or simply *clients*, need to have to be successfully compiled. Most of the details of *how* the abstract data type works, known as the *implementation*, are kept in another file. In our example, this file is named `BigInt.c`. It is compiled separately, and the object code produced from it is linked with the program that uses the abstract data type. Figure 2.1 shows how the specification and implementation of an abstract data type are combined with the source code of a client program to produce an executable program.

We separate the code for an abstract data type into a specification part and an implementation part to hide the implementation details from the client. We can then change the implementation and be confident that client programs will continue to work correctly after they are relinked with the modified object code. This is useful when a team of programmers work on a large software project. Once they agree on the specifications for the abstract data types they need, each team member can implement one or more of them independently of the rest of the team.

A well designed abstract data type also hides its complexity in its implementation, making it as easy as possible for clients to use.

2.3.2   Encapsulation

While it is possible to hide implementation details in almost any programming language, many modern programming languages such as Modula-2 [33], Ada [1], and C++ explicitly support it by providing mechanisms to prevent clients from accessing data and operations that are supposed to be hidden. The provider of a C++ ADT, for example, can specify *private* data and operations, so that if a client program attempts to use them, the C++ compiler issues an error diagnostic. We call this enforcement of the separation between the specification and implementation *encapsulation.*

Encapsulation is an extremely important feature, because without it we must rely on clients to cooperate by observing the separation between the specification and the implementation. Experience tells us that this is not practical, particularly on large software projects involving more than a few programmers. Somebody inevitably forgets the rules or succumbs to the temptation to use an implementation-dependent optimization, and the guarantee of being able to change an implementation without causing client programs to malfunction is gone.

In C++, the specification file (the `.h` file) almost always contains some implementation details. It usually contains the declarations for the data portion of an ADT, for example. Although the provider of an ADT can prevent client programs from accessing these data by making them private, the programmers who write client programs can nevertheless learn some of the implementation-dependent details of an ADT by reading its specification file. Languages such as Modula-2 and Ada support a stronger form of encapsulation by providing features to prevent client programmers from even *seeing* any implementation details, in addition to preventing client programs from depending upon them.

2.4 OVERVIEW OF C++ SUPPORT FOR DATA ABSTRACTION

C++ provides the *class* declaration for defining ADTs. A C++ class is similar to a C `struct`, but it allows you to associate both variables and functions with the name of a data type.

The variables and functions that belong to a class are called *members.* You can make a member either *public* or *private.* Any program can use the public members of a class, but only other member functions of the same class can use its private members. You can practice encapsulation in C++ by declaring classes with all member variables private so that clients can access or modify them only as permitted by the class's public member functions.

Unlike C, C++ requires you to specify the number and type of all a function's arguments. You can then use the same function name for more than one function, as long as the number and/or type of the functions are distinctive. We call this *function name overloading.* It eliminates the need to use different function names when you wish to define the same operation on different data types.

An extension of this idea is *operator overloading,* which enables you to give new meanings to most of C++'s operators when you use them on instances of ADTs. We used operator overloading to define the meaning of + when applied to `BigInt`s in Example 2-3, for example.

C++ classes may have two special kinds of member functions called *constructors* and *destructors.* Constructors create a new instances of ADTs and are responsible for initializing them correctly. Since C++ automatically uses a constructor to initialize any instances of ADTs required by client programs, this feature eliminates this common programming error.

C++ can also use constructors to automatically perform type conversion. For example, if we define a constructor for the `BigInt` ADT that has an argument of type `int`, C++ will use it automatically whenever it needs to convert a variable of type `int` to a `BigInt`.

Destructors destroy instances of ADTs, and we can use them together with constructors to hide the details of managing storage for ADTs from client programs.

We will describe these features and others in detail in the next two chapters.

2.5   CHAPTER SUMMARY

In this chapter we introduced the concept of a data type, which is a description of the data and operations applicable to the variables and constants of the data type, called instances. There are two kinds of data types: fundamental data types, such as `float` and `int`, which are built into the C++ language, and abstract data types (ADTs), which are data types invented by C++ programmers to simplify the programming of an application. Data abstraction refers to the process of designing ADTs.

The example problem of performing simple arithmetic on big integers demonstrates how data abstraction can make programming easier, and how it requires special language features available in C++, but not in most other common programming languages. These features enable the provider of an ADT to describe its data and operations, and handle details such as instance creation, initialization, type conversion, and storage management.

We introduced the idea of breaking up an abstract data type into its specification, which contains the information that the user, or client, needs to know to use the abstract data type, and its implementation, which hides the details of how the abstract data type works so that it may be programmed independently by a member of a programming team and be easily maintained. We then discussed how C++ supports encapsulation, which enforces the division between the specification and the implementation.

Finally, we gave a brief overview of the features C++ provides to support data abstraction: classes, member variables and functions, private class members, function argument type checking, function name overloading, operator overloading, and constructors and destructors.

3

AN EXAMPLE SPECIFICATION

3.1 INTRODUCTION

In this chapter we will take a detailed look at the specification for the `BigInt` abstract data type that we introduced in Chapter 2. We will introduce the concept of a class, and discuss member variables and functions, encapsulation, function argument type checking, function name and operator overloading, default function arguments, constructors and destructors, and type conversion.

3.2 SPECIFICATION OF CLASS `BigInt`

As you may recall from Chapter 1, the first line in the example C++ program was:

```
#include "BigInt.h"
```

This statement includes the specification of the `BigInt` abstract data type from the file named `BigInt.h` into the example C++ program so that we can use `BigInt`s in the program. Here is the contents of `BigInt.h` (note that in C++, // begins a comment that extends to the end of the line):

```
// BigInt.h - Multiple-precision integer class

#include <stdio.h>
// ...

class BigInt {
    char* digits;          // pointer to digit array in free store
    unsigned ndigits;      // number of digits
// ...
public:
    BigInt(const char*);              // constructor function
    BigInt(unsigned n =0);            // constructor function
    BigInt(const BigInt&);            // copy constructor function
    void operator=(const BigInt&);    // assignment
    BigInt operator+(const BigInt&) const;  // addition operator
                                            // function
    void print(FILE* f =stdout) const;      // printing function
    ~BigInt()    { delete digits; }         // destructor function
// ...
};
```

C programmers will understand little of this, except perhaps for the first line, which includes the standard I/O header file, but we will explain it as we cover some of the features of C++ in the rest of this chapter.

3.2.1 Classes

This is an example of one of the most important features of C++, the `class` declaration, which specifies an abstract data type. It is an extension of something C programmers should already be familiar with: the `struct` declaration.

The `struct` declaration groups together a number of variables, which may be of different types, into a unit. For example, in C (or in C++) we can write:

```
struct BigInt {
    char* digits;
    unsigned ndigits;
};
```

We can then declare an *instance* of this structure by writing:

```
struct BigInt a;
```

The individual *member variables* of the `struct`, `digits` and `ndigits`, can be accessed using the dot (`.`) operator; for example, `a.digits`, accesses the member variable `digits` of the `struct a`.

Recall that in C we can also declare a pointer to an instance of a structure

```
struct BigInt* p;
```

in which case we can access the individual member variables by using the `->` operator; for example, `p->digits`.

C++ classes work in a similar manner, and the `.` and `->` operators are used in the same way to access a class's member variables. In the example, class `BigInt` has two member variables named `digits` and `ndigits`. The variable `digits` points to an array of bytes (`char`s), allocated from the free storage area, that holds the digits of the big integer, one decimal digit per byte. The digits are ordered beginning with the least significant digit in the first byte of the array, and are binary numbers, not ASCII characters. The member variable `ndigits` contains the number of digits in the integer. Figure 3.1 shows a diagram of an instance of this data structure for the number 654321.

However, the C++ `class` can do much more than the `struct` feature of regular C. We will now look at these extensions in detail.

3.2.2 Encapsulation

In C++, a client program can declare an instance of class `BigInt` by writing:

```
BigInt a;
```

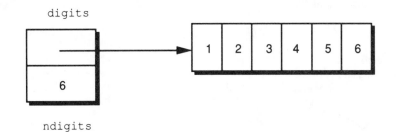

Figure 3.1 An instance of class BigInt *representing the number "654321"*

Now we have a potential problem: the client program might try, for example, to use the fact that a.ndigits contains the number of digits in the number a. This would make the client program dependent on the *implementation* of class BigInt—after all, we might wish to change the representation of BigInts to use hexadecimal instead of decimal arithmetic to save storage. We need a way to prevent unauthorized access to the member variables of the instances of a class. C++ provides this by allowing the use of the keyword public: within a class declaration to indicate which members can be accessed by anyone and which have restricted access. The initial members declared in a class declaration (that is, before the public: keyword) are *private*, as are digits and ndigits in this example, so C++ will issue an error message if a client program attempts to use them.

Protecting the members of a class in this manner is known as *encapsulation*. It is a good programming practice because it enforces the separation between the specification and the implementation of abstract data types that we are trying to achieve. This guarantees that (correct) changes to the implementation will not cause client programs to malfunction, makes modification easier because the code that manipulates the protected member variables is localized, and it helps when debugging programs. For example, if we find that ndigits has the wrong value in some situation, those parts of the program that do not have access to the variable are probably not at fault.

3.2.3   Member functions

How does a client program interact with the private member variables of a class? Whereas a struct allows only variables to be grouped together, the C++ class declaration allows both variables and the functions that operate on them to be grouped. Such functions are called *member functions*, and the private member variables of the instances of a class can be accessed only by the member functions of that class.[1]

Thus, a client program can read or modify the values of the private member variables of an instance of a class indirectly, by calling the public member functions of the class, as shown in Figure 3.2.

The example class BigInt has two private member variables, digits and ndigits, and seven public member functions. The declarations of these member functions will look unusual to C programmers for several reasons:

---

[1] Strictly speaking, friend functions can also access the private members of a class, as we will describe later in Section 4.2.16.

Instances of Class `BigInt`

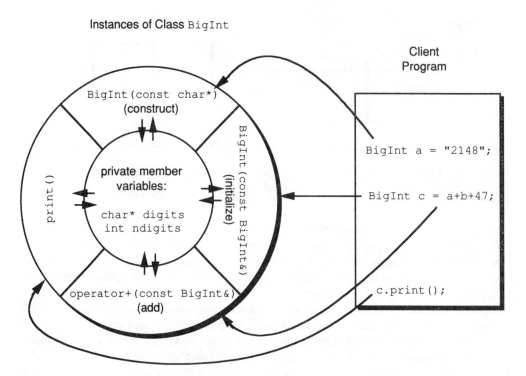

Figure 3.2 *Access to private member variables via public member functions*

- the types of the arguments of the functions are listed within parentheses in the function declarations

- three of the functions declared have the same name, `BigInt`

- the function names `operator=`, `operator+` and `~BigInt` contain characters normally not allowed in function names.

3.2.4 Function argument type checking

C++ strongly encourages a programmer to declare the types of the arguments of all functions. This makes it possible for C++ to check for inconsistent argument types when a function call is compiled, and can eliminate many bugs at an early stage. For example, the C statement

```
fprintf("The answer is %d",x);
```

will compile with no problem. However, when this statement is executed the program will abort with a cryptic error message. The problem is that the standard C library function `fprintf()` expects the first argument to be a pointer to the stream to which the output is to be written, not a format string as it is here. On the other hand, in C++ we can declare the argument types of `fprintf()`

```
extern int fprintf(FILE*, const char*,...);
```

so the compiler can give us an error message when we try to compile the incorrect function call, noting the discrepancy in the argument types. Conveniently, the argument types for most standard library functions are declared in system header files that you can include in your programs so that you do not have to write all these common declarations yourself.

Note that the C++ function declaration

```
extern int f();
```

declares a function with *no* arguments[2], while the declaration

```
extern int f(...);
```

declares a function with *any number* of arguments of *any type*. This is one of the incompatibilities between C++ and C: you must rewrite a C function declaration like f() as f(...) to mean the same thing in C++.

3.2.5 Function name overloading

Listing the types of all of a function's arguments in its declaration has a second benefit: we can define several functions with the same name, as long as each requires a different number and/or type of arguments. For example, in C++ we can declare two functions with the name abs:[3]

```
int abs(int);
float abs(float);
```

We can then write:

```
x = abs(2);
y = abs(3.14);
```

The first statement will call abs(int), and the second will call abs(float)—the C++ compiler knows which abs to use because 2 is an int and 3.14 is a float. When more than one function has the same name like this, the name is said to be *overloaded*. Overloading reduces the number of function names a programmer must remember, and it also eliminates "funny" function names. The standard C library has many examples of groups of functions that would benefit from name overloading if C had this feature. The math library functions abs() and fabs() return the absolute value of an int and a double, respectively, so they could both be named abs(). The functions execl(), execle(), execlp(), execv(), execve(), and execvp() execute processes in various ways and could all be named exec(). The prefix str could be eliminated from all of the string functions: strcat() and strncat() could be named concat(), strcmp()

---

[2] For compatibility with ANSI C, C++ also accepts extern int f(void) as a declaration of a function with no arguments.

[3] Versions of the AT&T C++ Translator earlier than Release 2.0 and other C++ compilers based on these early versions require the name of a non-member function to be specified in an overload declaration before the function name is overloaded. Thus, in this example you would need to place the declaration overload abs; before the first declaration of abs().

and `strncmp()` could be named `compare()`, `strlen()` could be named `length()`, and so on. Of course, we cannot change the names of the standard C library functions if we wish to remain compatible with C, but C++ programmers can take advantage of function name overloading when writing new libraries of C++ functions.

Note that, unlike some programming languages such as Ada, C++ considers only the number and type of *arguments* to distinguish between functions with the same name, not the type of the return value. So you cannot overload `float sqrt(float)` and `complex sqrt(float)`, for example.

3.2.6   Default function arguments

Looking back at the specification for the `BigInt` data type, the function declarations

```
BigInt(unsigned n =0);              // constructor function
```

and

```
void print(FILE* f =stdout) const;       // printing function
```

require further explanation. In addition to declaring the types of the arguments, both of these statements declare *default function arguments*. If you call either of these functions without arguments, C++ uses the expression to the right of the = sign by default; for example, the function call `print()` is the same as `print(stdout)`. Specifying reasonable defaults for function arguments can make function calls shorter and easier to read. It can also reduce the number of functions you need to write. In this example, declaring `print()` with a default argument of `stdout` gives us a single function that has the brevity of the standard C library function `print()` and the flexibility of the library function `fprintf()`, which a C programmer uses to print on something other than `stdout`.

You can specify default function arguments for only the trailing (i.e. rightmost) arguments of a function; thus, the declaration

```
unsigned maximum(unsigned a, unsigned b, unsigned c=0,
     unsigned d=0);
```

is legal, but declarations such as

```
unsigned maximum(unsigned a, unsigned b =0, unsigned c);
```

and

```
unsigned maximum(unsigned a=0, unsigned b, unsigned c);
```

are not.

3.2.7   Calling member functions

Getting back to the `BigInt` example and the discussion of member functions, we can now explain the next-to-last line in the first C++ program which is:

```
c.print();
```

Member functions are called in a manner analogous to the way member variables are normally accessed in C; that is, by using the . or -> operators. Since c is an instance of class BigInt, the notation c.print() calls the member function print() of class BigInt to print the current value of c. Similarly, if we declared a pointer to a BigInt

```
BigInt* p;
```

then the notation p->print() would call the same function. This notation ensures that a member function can only be called to operate on an instance of a class for which it is defined. We speak of this as *applying* a member function to an instance. In this example, we can apply the member function print() only to instances of class BigInt.

In C++, several different classes may all have member functions with the same name, just as in regular C several different structs may all have member variables with the same name. This lets us use simple function names, like print, rather than distinctive names, like print_bigint, without worrying about naming conflicts. We could add a new class, say BigFloat, to a program that also used BigInts, and we could also define print() as a member function of class BigFloat. Our program could contain the statements

```
BigInt a = "2934673485419";
BigFloat x = "874387430.3945798";
a.print();
x.print();
```

and the C++ compiler would use the appropriate print() in both cases.

3.2.8 Constructors

As you will recall, one of the things the C++ compiler needs to know about the BigInt abstract data type is how to create new instances of BigInts. We can tell C++ how we want this done by defining one or more special member functions called *constructors*. A constructor function is one which has the same name as its class. When a client program contains a declaration such as

```
BigInt a = "123";
```

the C++ compiler reserves space for the member variables digits and ndigits of an instance of class BigInt and calls the constructor function a.BigInt("123"). It is our responsibility as providers of the BigInt data type to write the function BigInt() so that it initializes the instance correctly. In the example, we will have BigInt("123") allocate three bytes of dynamic storage, set a.digits to point to this storage, set the three bytes to {3,2,1}, and set a.ndigits to three. This will create an instance of class BigInt named a that is initialized to 123.

If a class has one or more constructor functions (constructor functions may be overloaded), C++ *guarantees* that one will be called to initialize every instance of the class that is created. A user of an abstract data type such as BigInt does not have to remember to call an initialization function separately for every BigInt declared, thus eliminating a common source of programming errors.

3.2.9   Default constructors

A class may have a constructor function that requires no arguments, or it may have a constructor function with defaults for all its arguments. We call such a constructor the *default constructor* for a class. This is the constructor that C++ calls to initialize the variable declared in a declaration such as:

```
BigInt a;
```

C++ also uses the default constructor to initialize the individual elements of an array of class instances. For example, if you write

```
BigInt a[10];
```

C++ will call class `BigInt`'s default constructor 10 times, once for a[0], a[1], ... , a[9][4].

3.2.10   Constructors with more than one argument

You can also write the declaration

```
BigInt a = "123";
```

using an argument list to specify the constructor's arguments:

```
BigInt a("123");        // same as BigInt a = "123";
```

In fact, you must use an argument list to declare an instance of a class that you wish to initialize with a constructor that requires more than one argument. For example, if we had a class `BigComplex` that had a constructor

```
BigComplex(BigInt re, BigInt im);
```

we would declare an instance of a `BigComplex` named x and initialize it to (12,34) with:

```
BigComplex x(12,34);
```

3.2.11   Constructors for static class instances

A useful feature is that C++ arranges to call constructors to initialize even static instances of classes; that is, class instances that are declared as `static` or external variables. If, for

---

[4] Some C++ compilers, most notably R2.1 and earlier releases of AT&T's C++ Translator, cannot utilize a constructor with defaults for all its arguments to initialize an array of class instances as in this example. For such compilers, you must explicitly define a constructor with no arguments for classes which will be used as array elements. Prior to R2.1, an array of class instances could *only* be initialized by the constructor with no arguments. Beginning with R2.1, you can initialize an array of class instances with constructor calls specified in an initializer list in the array declaration.

example, we write a C++ program containing the declaration

```
static BigInt c = "29979245800";
```

C++ will automatically arrange to execute the statement c.BigInt("29979245800") at the beginning of the main() routine, before any other C++ statements are executed. A constructor for a static or external instance of a class is called a *static constructor*. Static constructors are useful for initializing static data in library routines, for example.

The term "static constructor" does not refer to any special type of constructor, but rather to the *use* of any constructor to initialize a static class instance. Thus, when writing the constructor functions for a class, you do not need to do anything special to make them useful as static constructors—C++ takes responsibility for this, so a client may use any (public) constructor of a class to initialize a static instance of the class.

3.2.12 Constructors and type conversion

Recall that to compile Example 2-3, C++ needs to know how to convert something that is a character string, such as "25123654789456", or an integer, such as 47, to a BigInt. Constructors are also used for this purpose. When the C++ compiler sees a statement like

```
BigInt c = a + b + 47;
```

it recognizes that the int 47 must be converted to a BigInt before the addition can be done, and so checks to see if the constructor BigInt(unsigned) is declared. If so, it creates a temporary instance of BigInt by calling BigInt(unsigned) with the argument 47. If an appropriate constructor is not declared, the statement is flagged as an error. We have defined BigInt(char*) and BigInt(unsigned) for class BigInt, so we may freely use character strings or integers wherever a BigInt can be used, and the C++ compiler will automatically call our constructor to do the type conversion. This is an important feature of C++ because it lets us blend our own abstract data types with others and with the fundamental types built into the language.

You can also call a constructor explicitly to force a type conversion. For example, C++ would normally process the declarations

```
unsigned long i = 4000000000;
BigInt c = i + 1000000000;
```

by first adding i to the constant 1000000000, then converting the result to a BigInt to initialize c. Unfortunately, the sum of i and 1000000000 will probably overflow and be quietly truncated before being converted to a BigInt. We can, however, avoid this problem by explicitly converting either i or 1000000000 to a BigInt:

```
BigInt c = BigInt(i) + 1000000000;
```

or

```
BigInt c = BigInt(1000000000) + i;
```

In either case, C++ will create a temporary BigInt to hold the left operand, convert the right operand to a BigInt stored in a second temporary, add the two temporary BigInts, and use the result to initialize c. C++ destroys the temporaries it creates by the end of the brace-enclosed block in which they were generated, or earlier if it can determine that they are no longer needed.

Equivalently, we can write this using the C and C++ *cast* operator:

```
BigInt c = (BigInt)i + 1000000000;
```

or

```
BigInt c = (BigInt)1000000000 + i;
```

The constructor call notation is a little more suggestive of what is really happening than the cast notation, and it is also more general since you can use it to invoke constructors that require more than one argument. For example, if we had a class `Complex` that represented a complex number type we could write

```
Complex i(0,1.0);  // the square root of -1
Complex c = Complex(3.1415,1.0) + i;
```

to construct a `Complex` temporary with the value `(3.1415,1.0)`.

3.2.13 Constructors and initialization

Compiling Example 2-3 also requires C++ to know how to initialize a `BigInt` with the value of another `BigInt`, as is required by a statement such as:

```
BigInt c = a + b + 47;
```

The `BigInt` c must be initialized with the value of a temporary `BigInt` that holds the result of the expression `a + b + 47`.

We can control how C++ initializes instances of class `BigInt` by defining the special *copy constructor* function `BigInt(const BigInt&)`.[5] In the example, this constructor allocates storage for the new instance and makes a copy of the contents of the argument instance.

When programming in C++, it is important to understand the distinction between *initialization* and *assignment*. Initialization occurs in three contexts:

- declarations with initializers (such as the one just described)
- formal function arguments
- function return values

Assignment occurs in expressions (not declarations) that use the = operator.

For example, if you write the declaration

```
BigInt c = a + b + 47;
```

---

[5] The argument `BigInt&` is an example of a C++ reference, which we will describe in Section 4.2.11.

a call to the constructor BigInt(const BigInt&) *initializes* the variable c as described earlier in Section 3.2.12. However, if you instead write

```
BigInt c;
c = a + b + 47;
```

a call to the constructor BigInt(unsigned n=0) *initializes* the variable c to 0, and the second statement *assigns* value of a temporary BigInt that holds the result of the expression a + b + 47 to c. Assignment is performed by the member function operator=(), which we will describe in Section 4.2.19.

3.2.14 Operator overloading

C++ must also be able to add two BigInts and assign the value of one BigInt to another in order to compile Example 2-3. We could just define member functions named add and assign to do these, but then writing arithmetic expressions would be awkward. C++ lets us define additional meanings for most of its operators, including + and =, so we can make them mean "add" and "assign" when applied to BigInts. This is known as *operator overloading*, and is similar to the concept of function name overloading.

Actually, most programmers are already familiar with this idea because the operators of most programming languages, including C, are already overloaded. For example, in C we can write:

```
int a,b,c;
float x,y,z;
c = a+b;
z = x+y;
```

The operators = and + do quite different things in the last two statements: the first statement does *integer* addition and assignment and the second does *floating point* addition and assignment. Operator overloading is simply an extension of this.

C++ recognizes a function name having the form operator@ as an overloading of the C++ operator symbol @. We can overload the operators + and =, for example, by declaring the member functions[6] named operator+ and operator=, as we have done in the example class BigInt:

```
void operator=(const BigInt&);        // assignment
BigInt operator+(const BigInt&);      // addition operator function
```

We can call these functions using either the usual notation for calling member functions or by using just the operator:

```
BigInt a,b,c;
c = a.operator+(b);
c = a + b;
```

The last two lines are equivalent.

---

[6] Binary operators such as + are usually not defined as member functions because automatic conversion of types is not done for the left operand. See the discussion of friend functions in Section 4.2.16 for further details.

Of course, if we overload an operator, we do not change its built-in meaning, we only give it an additional meaning when used on instances of our new abstract data type. The expression 2+2 still gives 4. We also cannot alter the precedence of an operator; for example, in the expression

```
x + y*z
```

C++ will perform the operation y*z before performing the + operation even if x, y, and z are instances of a class for which we have overloaded operator*() and operator+().

We can overload any of the C++ operators except for the structure member operator (.), and the conditional expression operator (? :).

We recommend using operator overloading sparingly and only when the operator strongly suggests the function it performs—do not overload + to perform subtraction, for example!

3.2.15   Destructors

The last thing we said was that C++ needed to know how to destroy instances of BigInts once it was finished with them. We can tell the C++ compiler how to do this by defining another special kind of member function called a *destructor*. A destructor function has the same name as its class, prefixed by the character ~. For class BigInt, this is the member function ~BigInt(). Since ~ is the C++ and C complement operator, this naming convention suggests that destructors are complementary to constructors.

We must write the function ~BigInt() so that it properly cleans-up, or *finalizes*, instances of class BigInt for which it is called. In the example, this means freeing the dynamic storage that was allocated by the constructor.

If a class has a destructor function, C++ *guarantees* that it will be called to finalize every instance of the class when it is no longer needed. Once again, this relieves users of an abstract data type like BigInt from having to remember to do this, and eliminates another source of programming errors.

Unlike constructors, destructors have no arguments, and so cannot be overloaded. Thus, a class can have at most one destructor.

Static destructors are the counterpart to static constructors, which we described earlier in Section 3.2.11. C++ arranges to call destructors to finalize static instances of classes; that is, class instances that are declared as static or external variables. For example, for the declaration we used earlier:

```
static BigInt c = "29979245800";
```

C++ will automatically arrange to execute the statement c.~BigInt() just before the program exits (when exit() is called), thereby freeing the dynamic storage used to hold the digits.[7] This is not really useful in this particular case since the entire dynamic storage area will cease to exist when the program terminates, but static destructors can perform actions that have lasting effects, such as flushing data out to a disk file or resetting the input mode of a terminal device, that make them very useful.

---

[7] Static destructors are *not* called if a program terminates by calling abort(), however.

3.3 CHAPTER SUMMARY

In this chapter, we have seen how using the technique of data abstraction can lead to more reliable, more readable, and more flexible programs, and we have introduced many of the features of C++ that help us practice data abstraction:

- *classes*, the basic language construct for defining new abstract data types;

- *member variables*, which describe the data in a class, and *member functions*, which define the operations on a class;

- *encapsulation*, which lets us restrict access to certain member variables and functions;

- *function argument type checking*, which helps to ensure that functions are called with proper arguments;

- *function name overloading*, which reduces the need for using unusual function names and helps to generalize code;

- *default function arguments*, which make function calls shorter and eliminate the need for some functions;

- *constructors and destructors*, which manage the storage for an abstract data type and guarantee that instances of an abstract data type are initialized and finalized;

- *user-defined implicit type conversion*, to let us blend our abstract data types with others and with the fundamental data types of the language; and,

- *operator overloading*, to let us give additional meaning to most of the existing operators when used with our own abstract data types, making our new data types easier to use.

4
AN EXAMPLE
IMPLEMENTATION

4.1 INTRODUCTION

Chapters 2 and 3 described a client C++ program that used the `BigInt` abstract data type and the specification for this abstract data type. Now we turn our attention to the implementation of the `BigInt` abstract data type, where all the *real* work is done. As we describe the implementation, we will encounter and explain several more new features of C++: the scope resolution operator, constant types, constant member functions, implicit member references, the `new` and `delete` operators, references, friend functions, and inline functions.

As we said earlier, the implementation of an abstract data type consists of the C++ code that embodies the details of *how* the data abstraction works. For this example it is kept in a separate file named `BigInt.c`.

4.2 IMPLEMENTATION OF CLASS `BigInt`

The implementation requires the information kept in the specification, so the first line in `BigInt.c` is:

```
#include "BigInt.h"
```

Since both the implementation and client programs are compiled with the same specification, the C++ compiler ensures a consistent interface between them.

4.2.1 The `BigInt(const char*)` constructor

Class `BigInt` has three constructors, one to create an instance of a `BigInt` from a character string of digits (a `char*`), one to create an instance from an unsigned integer (an `unsigned`), and one to initialize one `BigInt` from another. We need to be able to create a `BigInt` from a string of digits because this is the only way we can legally write very large integer constants in C++. Creating a `BigInt` from an `unsigned` is provided as a convenience, so we can write small integers in the usual way. Here is the implementation of the first constructor:

```
BigInt::BigInt(const char* digitString)
{
    unsigned n = strlen(digitString);
    if (n != 0) {
        digits = new char[ndigits=n];
        char* p = digits;
        const char* q = &digitString[n];
        while (n--) *p++ = *--q - '0';   // convert ASCII digit
                                         // to binary
    }
    else {                              // empty string
        digits = new char[ndigits=1];
        digits[0] = 0;
    }
}
```

If the character string is empty we treat this as a special case and create a `BigInt` initialized to zero.

C programmers will find this code quite recognizable, with a few exceptions that we will explain in the next few sections.

4.2.2   The scope resolution operator

The notation `BigInt::BigInt` identifies `BigInt` as a member function of class `BigInt`. In Section 3.2.7 we mentioned that several C++ classes can have member functions with the same names. When it is necessary to specify exactly *which* class member we are dealing with, we can prefix the member name by the class name and the `::` operator. The `::` operator is known as the *scope resolution operator*, and it may be applied to both member functions and member variables. Thus, `BigInt::print()` refers to the member function named `print()` that is a member of class `BigInt`, and `BigInt::digits` refers to the member variable named `digits` that is a member of class `BigInt`.

You can also use the scope resolution operator without a class name to specify an identifier at global or file scope. For example:

```
int a;          // a global (external) identifier

void f()
{
    int a;      // a local identifier
    a = 0;      // the "a" local to this block
    ::a = 0;    // the global "a"
}
```

Well written programs do not use many global variables, so the following example arises more frequently in practice:

```
class X {
    void print(char*);
};
extern void print(char*);
```

```
void X::print(char* s)
{
    print(s);        // this is a recursive call on X::print()!
    ::print(s);      // this calls the global print()
}
```

The pitfall is that if you forget to use the : : to distinguish the global function from the member function with the same name and argument list, you will be creating an infinite recursion.

4.2.3   Constant types

C programmers will be familiar with use of the type `char*` for arguments that are character strings, but what is a `const char*`? In C++, you can use the keyword `const` to indicate that a variable is constant, and therefore may not be modified by the assignment (=) operator. When used in an argument list as it is above, it prevents the argument from being modified by the function. Thus, if we tried to add a statement such as

```
digitString[0] = 'x';
```

to the preceding constructor, the C++ compiler would issue an error message. This protects against another kind of common programming error.

We recommend using `const` for pointer (and reference) function arguments[1] that are not supposed to be modified by the function:

```
extern char* strcpy(char* d, const char* s);  // copy string s to d
extern int printf(const char* f,...); // print with format string f
```

Conversely, if you have a function pointer (or reference) argument that is not declared `const`, C++ will not allow you to pass a constant as that function argument; for example, with the declaration of `strcpy()` just given, the following

```
char buf[10];
strcpy("abcdef", buf);  // error - "abcdef" is const char*
```

will not compile because `"abcdef"` is a character string literal constant (type `const char*`), but the first argument to `strcpy()` must be a `char*`.

It is also a good idea to use `const` instead of `#define` to declare *symbolic constants*:

```
const double PI = 3.14159265358979323;
```

The advantage is that you can localize the definitions of such symbolic constants to a class, block, or function definition, whereas `#define` C preprocessor symbols are effective from their point of definition through the end of the file in which they appear.

Declaring global, static, or member variables, or function return values as `const` must be done whole-heartedly. You may find that you need to propagate the `const` attribute to many more declarations than you originally anticipated because C++ prevents such things

---

[1] Declaring function arguments that are not pointers (or references) as const is not significant because changes made by a function to arguments passed by value are not seen by the caller, as we will describe in Section 4.2.11.

as assigning the address of a `const` to a non-`const` pointer and passing the address of a
`const` as an non-`const` pointer argument to a function:

```
const int limit = 10;
int* p;
extern int f(int*);
p = &limit;         // illegal!
f(&limit);          // illegal!
```

4.2.4   Constant member functions

In the class declaration for class `BigInt` shown in Section 3.2 you may have noticed that
the keyword `const` appears after the argument list in the declarations for the member
functions `operator+()` and `print()`

```
BigInt operator+(const BigInt&) const;
void print(FILE* f =stdout) const;
```

and later, in Sections 4.2.12 and 4.2.20, you'll see that the definitions of these two member
functions follow the same pattern:

```
BigInt BigInt::operator+(const BigInt& n) const
// ...

void BigInt::print(FILE* f) const
// ...
```

What does this signify? In Section 3.2.7 we explained that member functions are always
applied to an instance of their class[2] by using the `.` or `->` operators, for example:

```
BigInt c ="29979250000";    // velocity of light (cm/s)
c.print();
BigInt* cp = &c;
cp->print();
```

The `const` keyword after a member function's argument list tells the C++ compiler that the
member function is a *constant member function*: a member function that does not modify
any of the member variables of the instance it is applied to, so that it is permissible to apply
it to a `const` instance:

```
const BigInt c ="29979250000";  // velocity of light (cm/s)
c.print();
const BigInt* cp = &c;
cp->print();
```

The C++ compiler would flag these calls to `print()` as illegal if we omitted the `const`
keyword after the argument list in the declaration and definition of `print()`.

---

[2] You can also apply a member function to an instance of a class `derived` from the one it is a member of, as
we will explain in Chapter 6.

Furthermore, when the C++ compiler encounters the definition of a member function, it checks to make certain that the function declaration and its definition agree—the const keyword must appear in both or in neither—and in the case of a constant member function, the compiler further checks that it does not modify any member variables of the instance it is applied to. So, for example, if the definition of the constant member function BigInt::print() contained the statement

```
ndigits--;
```

it would be flagged as an error since it changes the value of one of the member variables of class BigInt.

4.2.5   Casting constants

When you declare a variable or function return value const, the C++ compiler does a thorough job checking your code to be sure that it does not change something that is supposed to be a constant. Occasionally, however, you may have reason to do so. In the tradition of its predecessor C, C++ permits the use of a cast to remove the const-ness of a variable. In Section 4.2.3 we gave this example:

```
const int limit = 10;
int* p;
extern int f(int*);
p = &limit;        // illegal!
f(&limit);         // illegal!
```

We can use a cast to make the assignment and function call legal as follows

```
const int limit = 10;
int* p;
extern int f(int*);
p = (int*)&limit;    // OK
f((int*)&limit);     // OK
```

and then we can change the value of limit via the pointer argument to the function f() or by dereferencing p:

```
*p = 42;
```

Of course, this subverts the C++ compiler's attempts to keep constants from changing, so you do not want to do this very often; however, Section 5.3.9 gives an example where casting away the const-ness of a variable is justified and useful.

4.2.6   Implicit member variable and function references

Throughout the body of the member function such as BigInt(const char*), you will notice that we are able to reference the member variables of the instance to which the function is applied without using the . or -> operators, as we did for example in the statement:

```
digits = new char[ndigits=n];
```

This is also true for function calls. If we added the statement

```
print();
```

to the implementation of `BigInt(const char*)`, for example, this would call the member function `BigInt::print()`.

Since member functions reference the member variables and functions of their class frequently, this provides a convenient, short notation.

4.2.7   The `new` operator

We used the C++ `new` operator to allocate the dynamic storage needed to hold the digits of a `BigInt` from the free storage area. In C, we would call the standard C library function `malloc()` to do this. The `new` operator has two advantages, however. First, it returns a pointer of the appropriate data type. Thus, to allocate space for the member variables of a `struct BigInt` in C we would write

```
struct BigInt* p;
p = (struct BigInt*)malloc(sizeof(struct BigInt));
```

whereas in C++ we can write simply:

```
BigInt* p;
p = new BigInt;
```

The second advantage is that if we use `new` to allocate an instance of a class having a constructor function (such as `BigInt`), the constructor is called automatically to initialize the newly allocated instance. In this example, the expression `new BigInt` allocates sufficient storage to hold the member variables of a `BigInt`, `digits` and `ndigits`, and also calls the default constructor `BigInt(unsigned n =0)` to initialize them. The result is more readable, less error-prone code.

4.2.8   Declarations in blocks

C programmers may have noticed that the declaration of p seems to be "misplaced"

```
if (n != 0) {
    digits = new char[ndigits=n];    // a statement
    char* p = digits;                // a declaration!
```

since it appears *after* the first statement in a block. In C++, declarations may be intermixed with statements as long as each variable is declared before its first use. The declaration is effective until the end of the block in which it occurs. You can frequently improve the readability of a program by placing variable declarations near the place where they are used.

4.2.9   The `BigInt (unsigned)` constructor

Here is the implementation of the `BigInt (unsigned)` constructor, which creates a `BigInt` from a positive integer:

```
BigInt::BigInt(unsigned n)
{
    char d[3*sizeof(unsigned)+1];     // buffer for decimal digits
    char* dp = d;                     // pointer to next
                                      // decimal digit

    ndigits = 0;
    do {                              // convert integer to
                                      // decimal digits
        *dp++ = n%10;
        n /= 10;
        ndigits++;
    } while (n > 0);
    digits = new char[ndigits];       // allocate space for
                                      // decimal digits
    for (register i=0; i<ndigits; i++) digits[i] = d[i];
}
```

This constructor works by converting the integer argument to decimal digits in the temporary array d. We then know how much space to allocate for the `BigInt`, so we allocate the correct amount of dynamic storage using the new operator, and copy the decimal digits from the temporary array into it.

4.2.10   The `BigInt` copy constructor

The job of the copy constructor is to copy the value of its `BigInt` argument into a new instance of `BigInt`:

```
BigInt::BigInt(const BigInt& n)
{
    unsigned i = n.ndigits;
    digits = new char[ndigits=i];
    char* p = digits;
    char* q = n.digits;
    while (i--) *p++ = *q++;
}
```

This function makes use of a *reference*, an important C++ feature we have not yet described.

4.2.11   Reference types

The argument type of the member function `BigInt (const BigInt&)` is an example of a C++ *reference type*, also called just a *reference*. Reference types address a serious deficiency of C: the lack of a way to pass function arguments by reference.

To understand what this means, suppose we wish to write a function named `inc()` that adds one to its argument. If we wrote this in C as

```
void inc(x)
int x;
{
    x++;
}
```

and then called `inc()` with the following program

```
int y = 1;
inc(y);
printf("%d\n",y);
```

we would discover that the program would print a 1, not a 2. This is because in C the *value* of y is *copied* into the argument x, and the statement x++ increments this copy, leaving the value of y unchanged. This treatment of function arguments is known as *call by value*.

To do this correctly in C we must explicitly pass a pointer as the argument to `inc()`:

```
void inc(x)
int* x;
{
    *x++;
}
```

```
int y = 1;
inc(&y);
printf("%d\n",y);
```

Notice that we had to change the program in three ways:

- the type of the function argument was changed from an `int` to an `int*`;

- each occurrence of the argument in the body of the function was changed from x to `*x`; and,

- each call of the function was changed from `inc(y)` to `inc(&y)`.

The point is that passing a pointer as a function argument requires consistency in every usage of the argument within the function body and, worse yet, in every call of the function made by client programs. This, combined with C's lack of function argument type checking, results in ample opportunity for error.

Using a C++ reference type, we can write the function `inc()` as follows:

```
void inc(int& x)
{
    x++;
}
```

```
int y = 1;
inc(y);
printf("%d\n",y);
```

This requires changing only the argument type from int to int&.

In the function inc(), we need to pass the argument x using a reference because its value is modified by the function. But efficiency is another reason for passing arguments by reference. When the value of an argument requires a lot of storage, as in the case of BigInts, it is less expensive to pass a pointer to the argument even though its value is not to be changed. That is why we declared the argument to BigInt as const BigInt&— the reference BigInt& causes just a pointer to the argument to be passed, but the const prevents that pointer from being used to change the argument's value from within the function.

You can also think of a reference type as being a pointer that C++ automatically dereferences whenever you use it, and you can declare variables that are references. That is, if we have

```
int i;
int* p = &i;      // a pointer to i
int& r = i;       // a reference to i
```

then you could use r anywhere in place of *p and &r anywhere in place of p—*except* that:

- you must initialize a reference in its declaration;[3] and,

- you cannot modify a reference to point to something other than what it was initialized to point to.

Thus:

```
int j;
*p = 1;           // sets i to 1
j = *p;           // sets j to 1
r = 2;            // sets i to 2
j = r;            // sets j to 2
p = &j;           // sets p to point to j
&r = &j;          // illegal
```

So we see that references are just special-purpose pointers—there is nothing you can do with a reference that you cannot do with a pointer—but they provide some safety and notational convenience.

4.2.12 The BigInt addition operator

Let us take a look at a first draft of the constant member function operator+(), which implements BigInt addition. We will encounter a few problems in this first attempt, as

---

[3] See Section 6.3.1 for an example of how to initialize a constant or reference member variable.

indicated by comments in the code, which we will deal with later in Sections 4.2.13 and 4.2.14.

```
BigInt BigInt::operator+(const BigInt& n) const
{
    unsigned maxDigits =
        (ndigits>n.ndigits ? ndigits : n.ndigits)+1;
    char* sumPtr = new char[maxDigits];
    BigInt sum(sumPtr,maxDigits);    // must define this constructor
    unsigned i = maxDigits;
    unsigned carry = 0;
    while (i--) {
        *sumPtr = /*next digit of this*/ + /*next digit of n*/
                    + carry;
        if (*sumPtr >= 10) {
            carry = 1;
            *sumPtr -= 10;
        }
        else carry = 0;
        sumPtr++;
    }
    return sum;
}
```

We add two `BigInt`s by using the paper-and-pencil method we all learned in school: we add the digits of each operand from right to left, beginning with the rightmost, and also add a possible carry in from the previous column. If the sum is greater than or equal to ten, we subtract ten from the result and produce a carry.

4.2.13   The `BigInt(char*,unsigned)` constructor

We ran into a couple of problems when writing the addition function. The first is that we need to declare an instance of `BigInt` named `sum` in which to place the result of the addition, which will be left in the array pointed to by `sumPtr`. We must use a constructor to create this instance of `BigInt` from `sumPtr`, but none of those we have defined thus far are suitable—`BigInt(const char*)` expects an argument that is a character string consisting of digit characters, most significant digit first. The variable `sumPtr` is a byte array of digits in binary form, least significant digit first; so, we must write another constructor to handle it.

This new constructor takes a pointer to an array containing the digits and the number of digits in the array as arguments and creates a `BigInt` from them. We do not want our client programs to use such an unsafe and implementation-dependent function, so we will declare it in the private part of class `BigInt` where it can only be used by member functions. Thus, we add the declaration

```
BigInt(char*,unsigned);
```

just before the keyword `public:` in the declaration of class `BigInt` in the file `BigInt.h`, and we add the implementation of this constructor to the file `BigInt.c`:

```
BigInt::BigInt(char* d, unsigned n)
{
    digits = d;
    ndigits = n;
}
```

4.2.14   Class DigitStream

The second problem we encountered is that scanning the digits of the operands in the statement

```
*sumPtr = /*next digit of this*/ + /*next digit of n*/ + carry;
```

becomes complicated because one of the operands may contain fewer digits than the other, in which case we must pad it to the left with zeros. We would also face this problem when implementing BigInt subtraction, multiplication, and division, so it is worthwhile to find a clean solution. Let us use an abstract data type!

We define a new class, called DigitStream, to keep track of which digit in a BigInt we are currently processing. Class DigitStream has a constructor that takes a reference to a BigInt as an argument and initializes a DigitStream for it. We also define a member function that returns the next digit of the BigInt each time it is called, beginning with the rightmost (least significant) digit. Here is the declaration for class DigitStream and the implementation of its member functions:

```
class DigitStream {
    char* dp;                    // pointer to current digit
    unsigned nd;                 // number of digits remaining
public:
    DigitStream(const BigInt&); // constructor
    unsigned operator++();       // return current digit and advance
};

DigitStream::DigitStream(const BigInt& n)
{
    dp = n.digits;
    nd = n.ndigits;
}

unsigned DigitStream::operator++()
{
    if (nd == 0) return 0;
    else {
        nd--;
        return *dp++;
    }
}
```

We can now declare an instance of a DigitStream for each of the operands and use the ++ operator when we need to read the next digit.

With these two problems solved, the implementation of the `BigInt` addition operator looks like:

```
BigInt BigInt::operator+(const BigInt& n) const
{
    unsigned maxDigits =
        (ndigits>n.ndigits ? ndigits : n.ndigits)+1;
    char* sumPtr = new char[maxDigits];
    BigInt sum(sumPtr,maxDigits); // allocate storage for sum
    DigitStream a(*this); // more about the variable "this" later!
    DigitStream b(n);
    unsigned i = maxDigits;
    unsigned carry = 0;
    while (i--) {
        *sumPtr = (a++) + (b++) + carry;
        if (*sumPtr >= 10) {
            carry = 1;
            *sumPtr -= 10;
        }
        else carry = 0;
        sumPtr++;
    }
    return sum;
}
```

Note that when you overload `operator++()` and `operator--()` for a class, C++ makes no distinction between the prefix and postfix forms of these operators[4]. We could equally well have written:

```
*sumPtr = (++a) + (++b) + carry;
```

4.2.15   Class-based as opposed to object-based encapsulation

Notice that `operator+()` can access the private members of *any* instance of class `BigInt`, not just the specific instance it was applied to. In this case, `operator+()` accesses the private member variables of the `BigInt` to which it is applied (its left operand) by referring to `digits` and `ndigits`, and it accesses the private member variables of the `BigInt` argument n (its right operand) by referring to `n.digits` and `n.ndigits`. Other programming languages, such as Smalltalk-80, are more restrictive in this respect—a member function (called a *method* in Smalltalk-80) can access the member variables only of the specific object to which it is applied. To access the member variables of any other instance, even if it is an instance of the same class, a method must employ another method as though it were an ordinary client program. Thus, we say that encapsulation in C++ is *class-based* or *type-based*, in contrast to some other languages in which it is *object-based*.

---
[4] The proposed ANSI C++ language *will* distinguish between the prefix and postfix forms of the increment and decrement operators. The unary operator functions `operator++()` and `operator--()` will define the prefix forms, and the binary operator functions `operator++(int)` and `operator--(int)` will define the postfix forms. The unused argument to the postfix forms will be 0 when invoked by a postfix ++ or -- operator.

4.2.16   Friend functions

The abstract data type DigitStream looks quite elegant, but you may be wondering how the constructor DigitStream(const BigInt&) is able to access the member variables digits and ndigits of class BigInt. After all, digits and ndigits are private, and DigitStream(const BigInt&) is not a member function of class BigInt. In fact this is not possible. We need a way to grant access to these variables to just this one function. C++ provides us with a way to do this—we can make this constructor a *friend* of class BigInt by adding the declaration

```
friend DigitStream::DigitStream(const BigInt&);
```

to the declaration of class BigInt.

We can also make *all* of the member functions of one class friends of another by declaring the entire class as a friend. For example, we can make *all* of the member functions of class DigitStream friends of class BigInt by placing the declaration

```
friend DigitStream;
```

in the declaration of class BigInt.

Although we have not done so in the BigInt example, you usually define binary operators like operator+() as non-member friend functions when you wish to use fundamental types (such as ints) as operands. This is because the C++ compiler does not perform automatic type conversion for left operands of operator member functions. For example, if the member function operator+(const BigInt&) is defined, C++ interprets the expression a + 47 as a.operator+(47) and recognizes that it can use the constructor BigInt(unsigned) to convert the unsigned integer 47 to a BigInt before calling operator+(). Thus, C++ compiles the expression a + 47 as:

```
a.operator+(BigInt(47))
```

However, C++ also interprets the expression 47 + a as 47.operator+(a), which is an error because 47 is not an instance of a class and therefore has no member functions that can be applied to it. Defining the non-member function

```
friend operator+(const BigInt&, const BigInt&)
```

solves the problem because the C++ compiler then interprets the expression 47 + a as a call of this non-member friend function

```
operator+(BigInt(47),a)
```

thus automatically performing conversion of the left operand to a BigInt.

4.2.17   The keyword this

Going back to the implementation of the function BigInt::operator+(), you may be wondering where the pointer variable this came from in the declaration:

```
DigitStream a(*this);
```

C++ automatically declares a local variable named `this` in each and every (non-static) member function of a class and initializes it to point to the instance of the class to which the member function was applied. Thus, in the member function `operator+()` of class `BigInt`, this is implicitly declared as

```
BigInt* this;
```

and when `operator+()` is called by writing an expression like b+47, where b is a `BigInt`, this is initialized to point to b. Thus, the effect of the declaration `DigitStream a(*this)` in the function `operator+()` is to create an instance of `DigitStream` for the left operand of `operator+()`, in this case b.

Similarly, when a member function such as `BigInt::print()` is called by an expression c.print(), where c is a `BigInt`, this is initialized to point to c.

4.2.18   The semantics of `return`

The last statement in the function `BigInt::operator+()` is:

```
return sum;
```

Since `operator+()` returns an instance of a class, in this case a `BigInt`, the `return` statement initializes an area of memory provided by the function's caller to contain the class instance returned by the function. The `return` statement initializes the returned instance using the copy constructor, which we described in Section 3.2.13, if the class defines one. Thus, the `return` statement in the function `operator+()` (1) calls the copy constructor `BigInt::BigInt(const BigInt&)` to initialize the returned instance in the caller's memory from the local variable sum, then (2) calls the destructor `BigInt::~BigInt()` to destroy sum before returning control to the caller.

It is critical to define the copy constructor for classes such as `BigInt` that have member variables that are pointers. If you do not define one, then a `return` statement will simply copy the pointer from the instance local to the function to the returned instance, then destroy the local instance, *deallocating the memory that the pointer points to*. This leaves the pointer in the instance returned from the function pointing to deallocated memory, which will undoubtedly cause problems when it is reallocated later on in the program and used for another purpose, thus creating a "time bomb" bug that can be extremely difficult to track down.

4.2.19   The `BigInt` assignment operator

The purpose of the assignment (=) operator is to copy the value of one `BigInt` (the right argument) into another (the left argument). Although the assignment operator's function is similar to that of the copy constructor `BigInt(const BigInt&)`, there is an important difference: the copy constructor copies the value into an *uninitialized* instance of `BigInt`, while the assignment operator copies the value into an *initialized* instance of `BigInt`, that is, one that already contains a proper value.

```
void BigInt::operator=(const BigInt& n)
{
    if (this == &n) return;      // to handle x = x correctly
    delete digits;
    unsigned i = n.ndigits;
    digits = new char[ndigits=i];
    char* p = digits;
    char* q = n.digits;
    while (i--) *p++ = *q++;
}
```

Notice that, except for the first two additional statements, the body of the function operator=() is identical to that of the copy constructor BigInt(const BigInt&). The first additional statement checks to see if the address of the left argument of operator=() is the same as that of the right argument. If so, we have used operator=() to assign the value of a BigInt to itself, so there is nothing to be done but return. Otherwise, we free the storage for the digits of the left argument by calling delete before copying the value of the right argument (we'll explain delete in more detail in Section 4.2.21). The check that the first statement performs is not just an optimization, but is necessary to prevent deleting the very information we are attempting to copy!

4.2.20   The member function BigInt::print()

The implementation of the constant member function print() is straightforward:

```
void BigInt::print(FILE* f) const
{
    for (int i = ndigits-1; i >= 0; i--) fprintf(f,"%d",digits[i]);
}
```

It loops through the digits array from the most significant through the least significant digits, calling the standard C library function fprintf() to print each digit.

4.2.21   The BigInt destructor

The only thing that the BigInt destructor function ~BigInt() must do is free the dynamic storage allocated by the constructors:

```
BigInt::~BigInt()
{
    delete digits;
}
```

This is done using the C++ delete operator, which in this case frees the dynamic storage that is pointed to by digits. The delete operator does what is usually accomplished in C by calling the standard C library function `free`, but in addition, if we use `delete` to deallocate an instance of a class having a destructor function, the destructor is called automatically to finalize the instance just before its storage is freed. For example

```
BigInt* a = new BigInt("98345928710");
// ...
delete a;
```

will automatically execute `a->~BigInt()`, which will deallocate the storage pointed to by `digits` before deallocating the storage for the member variables of the instance of class `BigInt`. The `delete` operator is thus the inverse of the `new` operator, and should only be applied to a pointer initially obtained from `new`.

There is another form of the `delete` operator which we must use when we deallocate an array of instances of a class having a destructor. For example, if we allocated an array of `BigInt`s with `new`

```
BigInt* a = new BigInt[10];
```

we must specify the size of the array again when we deallocate it because we have defined the destructor `~BigInt()`:

```
delete[10] a;
```

We must do this so that C++ knows how many class instances the array contains so it can call the class's destructor for each instance in the array[5].

4.2.22 Inline functions

By now you may be thinking that the overhead of calling all of these little member functions must make C++ inefficient. This would be unacceptable for a proper successor to C, which is renowned for its efficiency! So C++ allows us to declare a function to be *inline*, in which case each call of the function is replaced by a copy of the entire function, much like the substitution performed for the `#define` C preprocessor command. This entirely eliminates the overhead of calling a function, avoids the pitfalls of using the `#define` preprocessor command, and makes encapsulation practical.

To make a function such as `~BigInt()` inline, we must move its implementation from the file `BigInt.c` to the file `BigInt.h` and add the keyword `inline` to the function definition:

```
inline BigInt::~BigInt()
{
    delete digits;
}
```

The function definition must be in `BigInt.h` because it will be needed by the compiler whenever a client program uses a `BigInt`, and client programs `#include` the `.h` file, not the `.c` file.

---

[5] The proposed ANSI C++ language will *not* require the size of an array to be specified when it is deleted, so the statement `delete [] a;` would be used to delete the array a in this example.

Small functions make the best candidates for inline compilation. C++ gives us a convenient shorthand for writing inline functions: we can include the function body in the function declaration within the class declaration. Thus, we can also make ~BigInt() inline by writing

```
~BigInt()    { delete digits; }
```

in the declaration of class BigInt.

Besides short functions, functions with many arguments but little code are also good candidates for inline compilation, for example:

```
inline int f(int a, int b, int c, int d, int e)
{
    aa = a;
    bb = b;
    cc = c;
    dd = d;
    ee = e;
}
```

The rationale for this is that it takes about as much code to pass the arguments to the function when it is compiled out-of-line as it does to expand the body of the function inline.

We recommend extra care when declaring constructor functions inline—you should do this only for trivial constructors. Many C++ compilers are actually *translators* which generate C code, which is then compiled by a conventional C compiler. The constructors of derived classes (a C++ feature we will describe in Chapter 6) may make deeply-nested calls to other constructors. If you declare such constructors inline, the generated C code may become too complicated for some C compilers.

In contrast to a non-inline function, you must recompile all the client programs that call an inline function when you change its implementation, because the C++ compiler must compile a copy of the new implementation at each place where a client program calls it. This can be time-consuming on large software projects.

Here is a complete version of BigInt.h showing appropriate functions made inline:

```
#include <stdio.h>

class BigInt {
    char* digits;              // pointer to digit array in free store
    unsigned ndigits;          // number of digits
    BigInt(char* d, unsigned n) {   // constructor function
        digits = d;
        ndigits = n;
    }
    friend DigitStream;
public:
    BigInt(const char*);            // constructor function
    BigInt(unsigned n =0);          // constructor function
```

```
        BigInt(const BigInt&);           // copy constructor function
        void operator=(const BigInt&);   // assignment
        BigInt operator+(const BigInt&) const;  // addition operator
                                                // function
        void print(FILE* f =stdout) const;      // printing function
        ~BigInt()   { delete digits; }          // destructor function
    };


    class DigitStream {
        char* dp;                  // pointer to current digit
        unsigned nd;               // number of digits remaining
    public:
        DigitStream(const BigInt& n) {  // constructor function
            dp = n.digits;
            nd = n.ndigits;
        }
        unsigned operator++() {             // return current digit
                                            // and advance

            if (nd == 0) return 0;
            else {
                nd--;
                return *dp++;
            }
        }
    };
```

4.3 CHAPTER SUMMARY

This completes the example abstract data type BigInt. Let us review the C++ features presented in this chapter:

- the *scope resolution operator*, which allows us to specify which class we mean when one or more classes have member variables or functions with the same name;

- *constant types*, and *constant member functions* which we can use to protect variables or function arguments from unintended modification;

- *implicit member variable references* and the keyword this, which are used within member functions to access the instance for which the function is called;

- the new and delete operators, which manage the free storage area and call class constructors/destructors if present;

- *references*, which we can use to conveniently pass pointers to instances as function arguments instead of the instances themselves;

- *friend functions*, which give us a way to grant access to the private member variables and functions of a class to other functions and classes; and,

- *inline functions*, which make data abstraction in C++ efficient and practical.

APPLICATIONS FOR ABSTRACT DATA TYPES

5.1 INTRODUCTION

In this chapter, we give examples to show how we can develop diverse abstract data types that we can employ as reusable software components in many different programming applications. While these abstract data types vary widely in terms of the kinds of programming problems they are intended to solve, they all share the characteristics common to data abstraction as a programming technique. Each data type performs some generally useful operations on its member variables, which are usually fundamental data types. Each data type encapsulates its operations so that a client program using the data type becomes independent of implementation details and free of implementation complexities. Most importantly, each of these abstract data types can be reused readily by other C++ programs to which their operations are relevant.

Some of the data types described here may someday become "built-in" to a computer language. Others, or implementations like them, may find their way into run-time libraries for C++ programming. For example, the I/O stream package is distributed with AT&T's C++ compiler, while the NIH Class Library includes String, Date, Time, Regex, and Vector classes similar to the ones we discuss here. However, they all illustrate the value of abstract data types as tools to solve problems by computer programming.

Most readers should give careful attention to the next two sections of this chapter. Section 5.2 discusses AT&T's stream I/O, which probably will become the I/O method of choice for most C++ programs. Moreover, it explains how you can add stream I/O capability for ADTs that you write yourself. Section 5.3, which deals with dynamic character strings, not only describes an eminently useful ADT, but also illustrates a number of C++ concepts and programming techniques that you will find useful in designing your own ADTs.

The remaining abstract data types in this chapter are much more specialized. Some, like the one that implements automatic derivatives, are quite complex and could require considerable time and concentration to absorb thoroughly. We suggest you simply scan the rest of the chapter and give your attention to those ADTs that deal with programming applications in which you are interested.

5.2 STREAM I/O

C++, like C, contains no special built-in input or output statements. Instead, the language design of C++ makes it possible to develop an input/output facility using only the language features available to every programmer. AT&T offers one way to accomplish this by distributing with its C++ compiler a stream I/O package that is intended to be used instead of the standard C-language I/O library. This I/O package includes the classes `istream` and `ostream` which take the place of the standard I/O data type `FILE` in doing formatted I/O. An application can use member functions of class `ostream` to do formatted output with fundamental data types such as `int`, `char*`, and `double` instead of using standard I/O function calls such as `printf()` or `fprintf()`. Similarly, member functions of class `istream` take the place of `scan()` and `fscanf()` in doing input operations.

The stream I/O package helps to promote good C++ programming practice in several ways. Unlike the functions `fprintf()` and `fscanf()`, an `istream` or `ostream` will always properly encode or decode any supported data type. The stream classes support all fundamental data types and provide facilities that let C++ programmers easily extend I/O support to user-defined abstract data types. This section summarizes these features and gives some simple examples of how to use the I/O stream package. See [21] for more complete examples.

5.2.1   The stream package header file

To use the basic I/O stream package, an application program must contain the line

```
#include <iostream.h>
```

in place of the usual

```
#include <stdio.h>
```

used in C programs. The header file, `iostream.h`, contains the class declarations for classes `istream` and `ostream` and the external declarations for standard stream objects that all parts of the program can use for doing I/O.

Classes `istream` and `ostream` encapsulate the details needed to format and buffer file I/O. The I/O stream package also provides related classes that allow a program to attach a stream object to an open file descriptor or a named file. The stream objects referred to by the identifiers `cin`, `cout`, `cerr` are attached to the standard input, standard output, and standard error of the host process, and replace the data types `stdin`, `stdout`, and `stderr` of the standard I/O package. We can reassign these identifiers to redirect I/O to any file or device.

5.2.2   Writing to the standard output stream

With proper use, the C++ I/O stream package can help us to write simple, easy-to-read code for I/O operations. For example, we can write the following code segment:

```
// ex5-1.c - Writing to the standard output stream

#include <iostream.h>

main()

{
    float x = 1.2;
```

```
    int i = 3;
    char* prog = "myprogram";

    cout << prog;
    cout << ":";
    cout << endl;

    cout << "at step " << i << ", x = " << x << endl;
}
```

This program prints to the ostream cout, which is connected to the standard output (unless it was previously redirected). It will print:

```
myprogram:
at step 3,   x = 1.2
```

C++ interprets the statement

```
cout << prog;
```

as a call to the function

```
cout.operator<<(prog)
```

which, when executed, will print the string myprogram on the standard output. The next statement prints the string ":". In the next statement, the identifier endl is declared in the I/O stream package as a *manipulator*: a function which will perform some side effect during the I/O operation. The endl manipulator sends a newline to the output stream and flushes the stream buffer.

The last statement of Example 5-1 shows how several items can be sent to the output ostream in a single program statement. The effect of these program statements may seem mysterious until we examine the overloaded definition for the left shift operator<<():

```
ostream& ostream::operator<<(ostream& strm, int val)
{
//   ... code to write val to the file to which strm is attached ...
     return strm;
}
```

Note that operator<<() returns a reference to an ostream as its first argument. This makes it possible for the compiler to translate the statement cout << "at step " << i, by left-to-right parsing, into the composite function call:

```
(cout.operator<<("at step ")).operator<<(i)
```

We can nest these operators to make compound output statements possible.[1] By overloading operator<<() for all the fundamental data types the I/O stream package makes many combinations of output possible in this style. Each of these overloaded operators knows how to encode its own argument type for the output ostream.

---

[1] The C compiler will impose a limit on the depth of nesting: our compiler refused at 35.

5.2.3   Reading from the standard input stream

We can use `operator>>()` with the standard input `istream cin` in a way similar to the way we use `operator<<()` with the standard output `ostream cout`. For example:

```
// ex5-2.c - Reading from the standard input

#include <iostream.h>

main()
{
    float x;
    int i;
    char* prompt = "Enter [float int]?";

    cout << prompt << flush;
    cin >> x >> i;

    cout << "x=" << x << " i=" << i << endl;
}
```

When we run this program, the resulting session looks like this at a terminal:

```
enter [float int]? 1.2   3
x=1.2 i=3
```

The prompt is flushed to the standard output by the *manipulator* `flush`. How did the C++ program read the values `1.2` and `3` that the user typed? C++ interprets `cin >> x` as a call to `cin.operator>>(x)`. The function `operator>>()` returns a result of type `istream&` so that C++ can interpret `cin >> x >> i` as:

```
(cin.operator>>(x)).operator>>(i)
```

The I/O stream package overloads the function `operator>>()` for all the fundamental data types, and each operator knows how to decode its fundamental type from the input `istream`.

5.2.4   Extending stream output operations to a new C++ class

The C++ operator overloading mechanism makes it easy to extend any operator to a user defined class. For example, we can extend operations on an output `ostream` to the `BigInt` class that we introduced in Chapters 3 and 4. First, we need a member function that can write a `BigInt` object to an `ostream`:

```
void BigInt::printOn(ostream& strm) const
{
// Write each digit as data type int
```

```
    for (register i = ndigits-1; i >= 0; i--)
        strm << (int)digits[i];
}
```

Using this member function, a program can send a `BigInt` object to an `ostream`:

```
BigInt b = "1234567890";
b.printOn(cout);
```

However, this programming style is not compatible with the style already in place for fundamental data types. We can achieve compatibility by overloading `operator<<()`:

```
ostream& operator<<(ostream& strm, const BigInt& b)
{
    b.printOn(strm);
    return strm;
}
```

Now we can send a `BigInt` object to an `ostream` as:

```
// ex5-3.c - Writing a BigInt to the standard output

#include <iostream.h>
#include "BigInt.h"

main()
{
    BigInt b= "1234567890";
    cout << "The BigInt is " << b << endl;
}
```

Note that we have implemented `operator<<()` as a nonmember function because we cannot modify class `ostream`. As a matter of programming style, we chose to retain `BigInt::printOn()` as a member of class `BigInt`, rather than implement the output code directly in a function `operator<<()` declared as `friend` of class `BigInt`.

This method of writing output completely respects the encapsulation of class `BigInt`. Should the implementation of class `BigInt` change for some reason—for example, an improved internal storage mechanism or a more efficient method for some member function—we will not have to change application code that includes this kind of output statement. We may not even have to recompile the application program if the declaration for class `BigInt` did not change.

5.2.5   Extending stream input operations to a new C++ class

We can also extend stream input to class `BigInt`, but this is a good deal more complicated than the method for extending output. As with output, we first define a member function that decodes input data coming from the `istream`. For class `BigInt`, such a function will have to read whatever number of digits the input value contains. How can the function know how much memory to allocate to hold the digits? One way requires the user to first specify the number of digits so the program can allocate the proper amount of memory. However, this would create a problem when reading from the standard input: a user working at a terminal may not realize what the program expects him to do. A better solution provides a method to expand memory allocation dynamically for the member variable, `digits`, as shown in function `scanChunk()`:

```
// BigInt.c - implementation of BigInt::scanChunk(istream&)

char* BigInt::scanChunk(istream& strm)
{
    const unsigned CHUNKSIZE = 3;     // read CHUNKSIZE digits
                                      // at a time
    char chunk[CHUNKSIZE];            // buffer to hold digits read
    register char* p = chunk;         // pointer to digit buffer
    register char* q;                 // pointer to BigInt
                                      // object digits
    register i;                       // digits read in this chunk
// read a chunk of digits until eof or non-digit
    for (i=0; i<CHUNKSIZE; i++) {     // read a chunk of digits
        strm.get(*p);                 // get next character
        if (!strm.eof() && isdigit(*p))
            *p++ -= '0';              // convert to digit
        else {                        // encountered eof or non-digit
            ndigits += i;             // now we know the number
                                      // of digits
            if (ndigits != 0) {       // save digits just read
                q = digits = new char[ndigits];
                for (; i>0; i--) *q++ = *--p;
                return q;             // q now points after
                                      // last digit
            }
            else {                    // failed to find any digits,
                                      // so set istream state to fail
                strm.clear(strm.rdstate() | ios::failbit);
                return NULL;
            }
        }
    }
// At his point we have read CHUNKSIZE digits into chunk, and
// there may still be digits left on the input stream, so
// call scanChunk() recursively to read the next chunk.
    ndigits += i;                     // add no. of digits just read
    q = scanChunk(strm);              // q now points after
                                      // last digit
    if ( q==NULL ) return NULL;
```

```
    for (; i>0; i--) *q++ = *--p; // add digits just read
    return q;                     // q now points after
                                  // last digit
}
```

Function scanChunk() allocates memory for the input buffer in the local array variable, char chunk[CHUNKSIZE]. The advantage of this approach is that memory allocation and deallocation are handled by the C++ compiler. Function scanChunk() calls itself recursively until the end of the digit stream is found; only then does it allocate memory on the heap for the digit buffer. When the function returns from each recursive call, it transfers digits backwards from the input buffers to the digit buffer.

We can now write a scanFrom() function

```
void BigInt::scanFrom(istream& strm)
{
    delete digits;
    ndigits = 0; digits = NULL;
    strm >> ws;        // skip leading whitespace
    scanChunk(strm);   // scan for digits in chunks
}
```

which we might use in the following way:

```
BigInt b;
b.scanFrom(cin);
```

Thus, data scanned from an input stream overwrites an existing BigInt. We can make this look nicer by overloading the function operator>>() to comply with our style for input of fundamental data types:

```
istream& operator>>(istream& strm, const BigInt& b)
{
    return b.scanFrom(strm);
}
```

Now, we can write a program such as the following, which prompts for and reads two BigInts and prints out their sum:

```
// ex5-4.c - Extending stream I/O for class BigInt

#include "BigInt.h"
#include <osfcn.h>

main()
{
    BigInt a,b;
    while ( cin.good() ) {
        cout << "Enter a: "; cin >> a;
        if (cin.fail()) break;
```

```
            cout << "Enter b: "; cin >> b;
            if (cin.fail()) break;
            cout << "a+b=" << (a+b) << endl;
        }
        cout << endl;
}
```

Here is a sample run of this program:

```
Enter a: 01234567899
Enter b: 98765432101
a+b=100000000000
Enter a:
```

5.2.6   Associating an I/O stream with an open file

An application program can construct a stream object associated with files other than the standard I/O files. When opening a a file, a program must:

- take corrective action in case the named file is not successfully opened

- allocate and deallocate memory for I/O buffering

The I/O stream package provides a class `ofstream` for output and class `ifstream` for input. These classes implement error detection and buffer allocation and are easy to use in an application program.

The following sample program shows how to open an output file:

```
// ex5-5 - Opening a stream for a file

#include <fcntl.h>
#include <osfcn.h>
#include <libc.h>
#include <fstream.h>

const char* fname = "ex5-5.1.out";
const char* fdname = "ex5-5.2.out";

main()
{
    // open ofstream attached to
    // file on default directory
    ofstream ostrm(fname,ios::out|ios::nocreate);

    //   since ios::nocreate is set
    // construction fails when file doesn't already exist
    if ( !ostrm.good() ) {
        perror("ofstream");
        exit(1);
        }
```

```
    ostrm << "output to ofstream attached to named file"
        << endl;

    // old-style open to get open file descriptor
    int fd;
    if ( (fd=open(fdname,O_WRONLY,0644)) <0 ) {
        perror("open");
        exit(1);
        }

    // close ofstream and
    // reattach to open file descriptor
    ostrm.close();
    ostrm.attach(fd);
    ostrm << "output to ofstream reattached"
        << " to open file descriptor"
        << endl;
}
```

In this example, we first construct an `ofstream` instance from the file `fname` and an argument indicating the mode of the open operation. The list of valid modes includes `ios::in` (read), `ios::out` (write), and `ios::app` (append), `ios::nocreate` (file must exist), and `ios::noreplace` (file must not exist). To check for an error in opening the file the program uses the function `good()` which returns a non-zero value if the stream has not had a previous error or end of file. If the file opens successfully, anything the program sends to the `ofstream` `ostrm` will be written to the attached file named by `fname`. Since the `ios::nocreate` flag has been set, the construction of the `ofstream` will fail when the named file does not already exist.

The sample program also shows how to reattach an `fstream` to any open file descriptor. The program first uses the function `close()` to close the file currently attached to the `fstream`, and then uses the function `attach()` to attach the `ofstream` to a file descriptor which was opened using the old-style `open()` function call. Thus the sample program writes to two different named files using the same `ofstream` instance.

5.2.7 Summary for I/O streams

The I/O stream package, which is distributed with the AT&T C++ compiler, lets us write simple, easy-to-read code for I/O operations. It provides built-in support for I/O with fundamental data types. And it lets us extend I/O stream operations to abstract data types so that we can use a consistent style of I/O programming both for fundamental types and for programmer-defined classes. Finally, the I/O stream package gives us ways to open and close files and to redirect I/O to files or devices.

5.3   DYNAMIC CHARACTER STRINGS

Character strings find many uses in computer programming applications. Virtually all practical programs use character strings in one way or another, often to represent data items in a human-readable form. The ability to handle complex string operations efficiently is particularly crucial to systems programs like text editors and compilers. However, most programming languages—C and C++ among them—do not have built-in facilities that handle strings very well. For example, the `strcpy()` routine from C's string manipulation library limits the length of a target string to that of the destination string. The same is true of C++ as it comes "in the box." Unlike C, however, C++ contains features that let us define a dynamic (i.e., variable length) character string abstract data type that works like the string variables in languages such as BASIC.

5.3.1 A simple string application

To see how we can do this, let us consider a simple program that searches for all occurrences of one character string (a substring) in a longer string, and replaces each occurrence with another substring:

```
// ex5-6.c - String substitution

#include "ExString.h"

String replace(const String& target,
               const String& oldss,
               const String& newss)
{
    if (oldss.length() == 0) return target;     // if old is empty
    String result(target.capacity());
    unsigned i=0;        // start position for
                         // next substring comparison
    unsigned j=0;        // start position of
                         // last unmatched substring
    while (i+oldss.length() <= target.length()) {
        if (target(i,oldss.length()) == oldss) {
            result &= target(j,i-j) & newss;
            j = i += oldss.length();
        }
        else i++;
    }
    if (j != target.length())
        result &= target(j,target.length()-j);
    return result;
}

main()
{
    String orig, substr, replacement;
    while (1) {
        cout << "Enter target string: ";  cin >> orig;
        if (cin.eof()) break;
```

```
            cout << "    Replace: ";  cin >> substr;
            cout << "    With: ";  cin >> replacement;
            cout << "    replace(" << orig << ',' << substr << ','
                 << replacement << ") = ";
            cout << replace(orig, substr, replacement) << endl;
    }
    cout << endl;
}
```

Based on the description of BigInt in Chapters 3 and 4, you probably need only a few hints to read this program. The program relies on a String abstract data type. It reads three variables of type String and then invokes a function called replace() which does most of the work.

Interacting with this program might look like this:

```
Enter target string: axxxb
    Replace: xxx
    With: yyy
    replace(axxxb,xxx,yyy) = ayyyb
Enter target string: axxxb
    Replace: xxx
    With: z
    replace(axxxb,xxx,z) = azb
Enter target string: axxxb
    Replace: xxx
    With:
    replace(axxxb,xxx,) = ab
Enter target string:
```

5.3.2 String **operators**

Let us assume that we have designed our String abstract data type to overload the operators & and &= to concatenate character strings. We can also overload the relational operators <, <=, ==, and so on, to compare character strings, and overload the array subscript operator [] to address the individual characters of a string. We can also define the overloaded function call operator

```
operator() (int position, int length)
```

to perform substring extraction and replacement. The statement

```
result &= target(j,i-j) & newss;
```

from the replace() function illustrates the application of several of these operators. It first extracts a substring, target(j,i-j), comprising the i-j characters starting with the j*th* character of the original string, target. It then concatenates the substring with a string, newss. The operator &= combines assignment and concatenation, so the last step replaces the string result with the outcome of the previous operation concatenated with result itself.

5.3.3   A `String` **abstract data type**

Now we will see how we can design a `String` abstract data type that lets us write programs like Example 5-6. Recall that an abstract data type's specification, in this case contained in the file `ExString.h`, embodies its client interface. As we saw in Section 4.2.22, functions that require only brief implementations have them included in the specification so that the compiler can expand them inline:

```
// ExString.h - Dynamic character strings
#include <string.h>
#include <iostream.h>
const unsigned EXTRA = 7;   // default # characters extra
typedef int bool;
class String;
class SubString {
    char* sp;                // substring pointer
    unsigned sl;             // substring length
    SubString(const String&, unsigned, unsigned);
    SubString(const SubString&);        // private copy constructor
    friend String;
public:
    void operator=(const SubString& from);
    bool operator==(const String&) const;
    String operator&(const String&) const;
};
class String  {
    char* p;            // pointer to character string
    unsigned len;       // length of string
    unsigned alloc;     // amount of storage allocated
    friend SubString;
public:
    String(unsigned extra=EXTRA);   // construct an empty String
    String(const char* cs, unsigned extra=EXTRA);
                                    // construct from C string
    String(const String&);          // construct one String
                                    // from another
    String(const SubString&);       // construct from a SubString
    ~String() { delete(p); }
    operator const char*() const { return p; }
                                    // convert to a C string
    SubString operator()(unsigned pos, unsigned lgt);
    const SubString operator()(unsigned pos, unsigned lgt) const;
    char& operator[](unsigned pos) {
//      if (pos >= len)  error
        return p[pos];
        }
    char operator[](unsigned pos) const {
//      if (pos >= len)  error
```

```
                return p[pos];
            }
        void operator=(const String&);
        bool operator==(const String& s) const {
            return strcmp(p, s.p) == 0;
        }
        String operator&(const String& s) const;
        void operator&=(const String& s);
        unsigned length() const    { return len; }
        unsigned capacity() const { return alloc-1; }
        void printOn(ostream& strm) const;
        void scanFrom(istream& strm);
};

inline SubString::SubString(const String& s,
                            unsigned pos, unsigned lgt)
{
    sp = &((String&)s)[pos];
//  if (pos+lgt >= s.len)   error
    sl = lgt;
}

inline SubString::SubString(const SubString& ss)
{
    sp = ss.sp;   sl = ss.sl;
}

inline void SubString::operator=(const SubString& from)
{
    strncpy(sp, from.sp, sl);
}

inline bool SubString::operator==(const String& s) const
{
    return strncmp(sp, s.p, sl) == 0;
}

extern ostream& operator<<(ostream&, const String&);
extern istream& operator>>(istream&, String&);
```

File ExString.c contains the corresponding implementation code for class String. As was the case for class BigInt, each of the function implementations is relatively concise and easy to understand. We have omitted ExString.c from the text because of its simplicity, and because we do not need to examine many of the implementation details here.

When we look about one-quarter of the way through ExString.h, we find that our declaration for class String looks something like this:

```
class String  {
    char* p;                // pointer to character string
    unsigned len;           // length of string
    unsigned alloc;         // amount of storage allocated
    friend SubString;
public:
// ... declarations of functions to manipulate Strings
};
```

We represent an instance of class String as a pointer to an ordinary C string, kept on the free store, and the integer length of the string. We also include a second integer to define the amount of storage (which must be at least as great as the length) allocated to the string. Although technically unnecessary, this provides some measure of improved performance for operations like concatenation that act to increase the string's length.

5.3.4   Substrings

This String class declaration by itself does not, however, provide a convenient way to keep track of short character sequences within a longer String. How can we define the substring extraction function

```
operator() (int position, int length)
```

that was central to our example program? Let us declare another class, called SubString, that does the job for us:

```
class SubString {
    char* sp;                       // substring pointer
    unsigned sl;                    // substring length
    SubString(String&, unsigned, unsigned);
    SubString(const String&, unsigned, unsigned);
    SubString(const SubString&);        // private copy constructor
    friend String;
public:
    void operator=(const SubString& from);
    bool operator==(const String&) const;
    String operator&(const String&) const;
};
```

Class SubString has a constructor that lets us initialize a SubString from a String by providing as arguments a reference to the String and the position and length of the substring within it that we are interested in. It also provides other member functions that will replace one SubString with another, compare a SubString to a String, and concatenate a String with a SubString. Our SubString class gives us the convenient notation we were seeking:

```
String s = "abcdefghi";
String t;
String u = "xyz";
int length1 = 3;
int length2 = 4;
s(position1,length1) = u; // replace substring
t = s(position2,length2); // extract substring
```

In this code segment, the characters "xyz" replace the three characters starting at position1 of String s. The last statement sets String t to the four characters it extracts starting at position2 of String s. Assuming position1 = position2 = 4, String t will contain "xyzh" (recall the indexing here is zero-based) after the last statement has executed.

5.3.5   Private classes

We define substring replacement by the SubString member function:

```
SubString::operator=(const String&)
```

whereas substring extraction requires that we define a class String member function:

```
String::operator()(unsigned position, unsigned length)
```

which we can implement in the following way:

```
SubString String::operator()(unsigned pos, unsigned lgt);
// Extract a SubString from a String
{
    return SubString(*this, pos, lgt);
}
```

Notice that this implementation causes us to construct a SubString from whatever String we are dealing with. We can do this even though our SubString constructor is a private member function, unavailable to client programs, because we have made the private member variables and functions of class SubString accessible to all of the member functions of class String by including the statement

```
friend String;
```

in our specification for class SubString. Incidentally, we should similarly make class SubString's member functions friends of class String because some of them will need to access String's private member variables. Interestingly, unlike other classes we have examined, class SubString does not have a destructor function. Since it only constructs an association with an existing String, and does not place any new data on the free store, it does not need one. We call a class with the characteristics of class SubString—one which is introduced solely to provide convenient notation and which has only private constructors—a *private* class.

Why should any class have all constructors private? One reason has to do with good programming practices—with issues of encapsulation and data hiding. Client programs do not need to create instances of these private classes, and therefore should not be able to do so as a matter of principle. There are, however, pragmatic reasons as well. For example, were our SubString constructor not private, we might write a program that creates a String, makes a SubString from it, then destroys the String, thereby inadvertently leaving the SubString associated with garbage on the free store.

Our need to make classes like SubString private uncovers a potential trap that we must take care to avoid when we design abstract data types using C++. If a client program tries to use a constructor where a copy constructor normally is required, and the class's author did not provide one, then C++ will generate one. Moreover, it will make the generated copy constructor public. This would permit a client program to create a named instance of our supposedly private class as follows:

```
String s = "abcdefgh";
SubString ss = s(2,4);
```

Unless we take steps to prevent it, the compiler will generate a public copy constructor to create the SubString ss, thereby subverting our true intent when we made class SubString a private class. To prevent this from ever happening for class SubString, we have included a private copy constructor of our own:

```
SubString::SubString(const SubString&);
```

You always should include a similar private copy constructor for any class that you want to make private to ensure the C++ compiler will not generate an unwanted public constructor for that class.

5.3.6   Forward references to class declarations

Our class String illustrates several other details and concepts that we have not encountered before. When we look back at ExString.h, we see that, although it combines the declarations for String and for SubString, it precedes both with the construct:

```
class String;
```

This statement simply identifies the name String to the compiler; without it, we could expect the compiler to complain when it encountered

```
friend String;
```

in the declaration for class SubString.

5.3.7 Assignment to references

While we all have seen a function result used as a component of an expression, using one on the left side of an assignment is a bit rarer. Yet we can use the String member function

```
char& operator[] (unsigned pos)
```

on the left side of an assignment because it returns a *reference* to a value. In C++, we can use a reference in the same way as the value it refers to. A reference carries address information with it. For example:

```
int x = 1;        // integer
int* px = &x;     // pointer to integer
int& rx = *px;    // reference to x
int y = rx + x;   // y = 2
rx = y;           // x is now 2 also
```

So whenever we use a reference on the left of an assignment, the compiler actually makes the assignment to the object referred to. This lets us write code such as the following:

```
String s = "abcdef";
s[1] = 'X';
cout << s;        // prints "aXcdef"
```

5.3.8 Overloading constant member functions

What if we attempt to use a reference to a constant object on the left side of an assignment? Obviously, we would not want a program that contains

```
const String s = "abcdef";
s[1] = 'X';
```

to compile because running it would change the constant. On the other hand, we would expect a program containing a code fragment like

```
const String s = "abcdef";
char c = s[1];
```

to compile and to work properly. If we had to rely only on the character index function

```
char& operator[] (unsigned pos)
```

the former code fragment would fail to compile because C++ will not allow a non-constant member function to be applied to a constant operand, in this case the String s. However, the latter will not compile either, for the same reason. To remedy this and similar situations, we can overload member operators and functions with respect to const-ness, just as we can overload them to accept parameters of different types. In ExString.h, we have declared operator[] () as both a non-constant and constant member function:

```
char& operator[] (unsigned pos)        // used for non-const Strings
char operator[] (unsigned pos) const // used for const Strings
```

When we index a non-constant `String`, the compiler will use the non-constant
`operator[]()`, which returns a reference to a character (a `char&`) that we can use
either as a value or on the left of an assignment, as we described in Section 5.3.7. However,
when we index a constant `String`, the compiler selects the constant `operator[]()`,
which returns a `char` that can only be used as a value. Thus, the second fragment will
compile and work as desired, but the first will not compile because a function return type
of `char` is not permitted on the left side of an assignment.

5.3.9 Casting away `const`-ness

As we pointed out in Section 4.2.5, circumstances sometimes arise which make it necessary
to cast away the `const`-ness of a variable. To see why, consider the inline implementation
for the `SubString` constructor that makes a `SubString` from a `String`:

```
inline SubString::SubString(const String& s,
                            unsigned pos, unsigned lgt)
{
    sp = &((String&)s)[pos];
//  if (pos+lgt >= s.len)   error
    sl = lgt;
}
```

The constructor expects a `const String& s` as its first parameter. If we used a pointer
to modify s through indirection—something we should not do to a constant—C++ will
refuse to compile code that simply sets the `SubString` pointer sp to the address of s.
Instead, we must first cast s to a non-constant as the constructor implementation shows.
This potentially subverts the compiler's attempt to prevent us from changing a constant,
for example, by altering the constructed `SubString`, which, in reality, is a part of the
`const String& s`. We have not, however, taken such a seemingly drastic step lightly.
Recall that class `SubString` is a private class whose constructors are available only
to its member functions and the member functions of the friend class `String`. Thus, a
client program cannot make a `SubString`. Indeed, a client of class `String`, as defined by `ExString.h`, has access only to `SubStrings` returned by the member functions:

```
SubString String::operator()(unsigned pos, unsigned lgt);
const SubString
    String::operator()(unsigned pos, unsigned lgt) const;
```

Since the first is a non-constant member function, the C++ compiler will not let a client
program apply it to a `const String`. A client can apply the second to a `const String`,
but it gets back a `const SubString` as a result, so the compiler will prevent unwanted
changes to a constant in this case as well.

5.3.10 Mixing `Strings` and `Substrings` with C strings

Now let us assume that we must combine `Strings` or `SubStrings` and C strings in the same expression. Although we did not have to do it in our example program, it is easy to imagine needing to do something like the following:

```
String sentence;
sentence &= ".";
```

We know the compiler will do the appropriate type conversion by interpreting this as

```
sentence.operator&=(String("."));
```

because we defined the constructor function

```
String::String(const char* cs, unsigned extra=EXTRA)
```

5.3.11 Implicit type conversion

What if we needed to use a `String` in place of a C string? The solution is to define a member function of the form `class::operator type()` which acts like the inverse of the `class::class(type)` constructor and accomplishes type conversion of a class to a built-in type or to another class. For our class `String`, we have defined

```
String::operator const char*()
```

which lets us write the following:

```
String s = "myfile.txt"
int fd = open(s,O_RDONLY);
```

This works because `stdio.h` declares `open()` to expect `const char*` as its first argument. The C++ compiler sees this and does an implicit type conversion using `operator const char*()`.

5.3.12 ADT design issues

While our class `String`, as specified in `ExString.h`, proved very useful in writing a simple example program, it needs much improvement before we would want to consider "packaging" it and releasing it for use by other programmers. For a real class `String`, such as the one included in the NIH Class Library, we should include range checking on `operator()(unsigned,unsigned)` and `operator[](unsigned)`. We should extend the functionality of class `SubString` to allow for the possibility of empty `SubStrings` and for the replacement of a `SubString` by another of different length:

```
s(s.length(),0);            // empty string
s(pos1,len1) = t(pos2,len2);  // len1 != len2
```

In place of the small handful of operators we included in ExString.h, we should provide a full complement:

```
bool operator<(const String&) const;
bool operator>(const String&) const;
bool operator<=(const String&) const;
bool operator>=(const String&) const;
bool operator==(const String&) const;
bool operator!=(const String&) const;
```

For greater efficiency, we should use optimized explicit operator definitions for various combinations of String, SubString, and char*:

```
String String::operator&(const String&) const;
String String::operator&(const SubString&) const;
String String::operator&(const char*) const;
String SubString::operator&(const String&) const;
String SubString::operator&(const SubString&) const;
String SubString::operator&(const char*) const;
String SubString::operator&(const String&) const;
friend String operator&(const char*, const String&);
friend String operator&(const char*, const SubString&);
```

Alternatively, we could define operators for only a few of the combinations as we did in ExString.h, and provide, instead, an appropriate set of class::class (*type*) and class::operator *type* () functions. Then, however, the compiler would have to do an implicit type conversion every time it encountered a combination for which no operator is defined. By providing a rich set of operators, we avoid this overhead. As an example, consider ExString.h in which we have defined only two concatenation combinations:

```
String SubString::operator&(const String&) const;
String String::operator&(const String&) const;
```

If we were to write

```
String s1 = "abcdef";
String s2 = "ghijklm";
s1 = s1 & s2(2,3);
```

the compiler would recognize that it first must invoke the constructor String(const SubString&) on s2(2,3) to convert it from a SubString to a String so that it could use the function String::operator&(const String&) to concatenate two Strings. If we provide the function String::operator&(const SubString&), the C++ compiler will use it directly and avoid the overhead of converting a SubString to a String.

Perhaps this is a good place to offer some caveats on the use of implicit type conversion and overloaded operators. C++ programmers are sometimes tempted to use operator *type* () in clever ways. For example, classes istream and ostream define `operator void*()` to return non-zero if an I/O error has occurred on a stream[2] so you can write:

```
if (cin) ... // handle error on cin
```

In our opinion, this is not as easy to understand as:

```
if (cin.fail()) ...
```

More importantly, when debugging or trying to understand a program, it is frequently useful to be able to find all the places where a given function is called. Languages like C that do not allow function name overloading make this easy because each external function has a unique name that you can search for with the UNIX `grep` command or with your favorite text editor. Overloaded C++ function names make the task more difficult, but it is still practical because most programs will have only a small number of overloaded definitions and you can usually pick out the ones of interest from local context without much difficulty. Finding all uses of an overloaded operator such as + with simple string searching becomes very difficult because most matches occur for use of the operator on fundamental types, and the uses of interest are buried in noise. Finding all uses of `operator` *type*`()` is impossible—there is nothing to search for! The same holds true for constructors and destructors since the C++ compiler often calls these implicitly to perform type conversion or to destroy auto variables as they go out of scope. For these reasons, we recommend circumspection when overloading operators and when defining implicit type conversions with `operator` *type*`()` and constructors.

Let us return now to the long list of overloaded concatenation operator definitions above. The last two, which we have declared as friend functions, accomplish another purpose in addition to efficiency: they eliminate the order dependency from concatenating `Strings` (or `SubStrings`) with C strings. Without them, we still can write

```
String s, t;
s = t & "abc";
```

and get the correct result, but, as we saw in a similar case using `BigInts`, the reverse situation

```
s = "abc" & t;
```

would be an error because the C++ compiler would try to interpret it as

```
s = "abc".operator&(t);
```

5.3.13 Summary for class `String`

Class String illustrates features typical of many ADTs that implement important, commonly used data types: we want to provide a lot of packaged functionality, and we want to allow

---

[2] The I/O stream classes define operator `void*()` for backward compatibility with the old stream I/O package provided with Release 1.2 of AT&T's C++ Translator.

applications to use that functionality by writing attractive, simple code enabled by the operator syntax. Our goal should be to make life easier and improve productivity for those who use our classes in the future by making the classes we design both effective and efficient.

5.4   ABSTRACT DATA TYPES FOR DATES AND TIMES

Another interesting and useful example of an abstract data type is one which makes it easy to handle dates similarly to other, more common data types like ints, floats, or even Strings. You probably can imagine a wealth of applications for such a type. A program might need to do calendar arithmetic, e.g., to calculate a date some number of days in the future:

```
int numberdays;
Date olddate, newdate;
newdate = olddate + numberdays;
```

or to find the number of days between two dates:

```
numberdays = date2-date1;
```

   Other possibilities include determining dates of interest, e.g., all Tuesdays in March through September of next year, or testing for dates between specified limits. For example, if we are processing invoices, and the next accounts payable cycle will not happen until after the discount date for this invoice, i.e., its date is between today and the accounts payable date, then we might "kick" it out for special handling.

   Many present day applications systems like spreadsheet packages and database managers allow their users to work with dates in some or all of these ways. A system programming language which provides the tools for including such programmer-defined abstract data types thus has obvious appeal.

5.4.1   An abstract data type for dates

Consider the following abbreviated specification for class Date (a complete class Date, like class String, would have many more functions than we show here) that implements a Gregorian calendar:

```
// Date.h - declarations for Gregorian calendar dates

typedef int bool;
typedef unsigned short dayTy;
typedef unsigned short monthTy;
typedef unsigned short yearTy;
typedef unsigned long julTy;
```

```
class Date  {
// ...
    julTy julnum;          // Julian Day Number
                           // not the same as Julian Date
// ...
public:
    Date();                // current date
    Date(int dayCount);
    Date(int dayCount, yearTy referenceYear);
    Date(dayTy newDay, const char* monthName, yearTy newYear);
    friend Date operator+(const Date& dt, int dd) {
        return Date(dt.julnum + dd);
    }
    friend Date operator+(int dd, const Date& dt) {
        return Date(dt.julnum + dd);
    }
    int operator-(const Date& dt) const;
    bool between(const Date& min, const Date& max) const;
    Date previous(const char* dayName) const;
    yearTy year() const;
    void printOn(ostream& strm =cout) const;
    void scanFrom(istream& strm);
// ...
};


extern ostream& operator<<(ostream&, const Date&);
extern istream& operator>>(istream&, const Date&);
```

This specification represents a Date as a Julian day number, and it provides three constructors which we can use to declare variables of the type Date and to initialize them to today's date or to some other date that we specify. We do not need to deal with Julian day numbers ourselves; the constructors let us specify dates in more conventional day and year or day, month, and year formats. Overloaded operator+() and operator-() functions provide calendar arithmetic; by declaring two operator+() functions as friends, we can add ints to Dates commutatively. Date::previous (const char* dayName) returns the Date of the last weekday named dayName prior to this Date. For example, the following statement will calculate the date of the last Sunday in February in the year yr:

```
cout<<(Date(1,"Mar",yr).previous("Sun");
```

One particularly interesting characteristic of class Date does not even show up in the specification: void scanFrom(istream& strm), which gets a Date from an istream, lets us represent a date using almost any reasonable notation. For example, a user entering a date from a terminal can type 14-APR-88, April 14, 1988, or 4/14/88, depending on preferences or habits, with equivalent results.

5.4.2   A simple date application

As an example of an application for class `Date`, suppose that an organization's staff director decided that future staff meetings would be held on Mondays. Staff members who attend the meetings would want whatever calendaring program they use to generate the corresponding dates for them. Example 5-7 shows how this might be done. It solicits a particular date and day of week from its user and then calculates all dates (except holidays) after that date on which the specified day of the week falls.

Example 5-7 also further emphasizes the added software reliability that results from using abstract data types in C++. Suppose that, in the body of `main()`, we declared the variable `day_of_week` as a `char*` or `char[]`. Then, the program would fail because it would attempt to use an uninitialized pointer variable. `char[N]` likewise would cause the program to fail if we attempted to enter a `day_of_week` containing more than N characters. By contrast, declaring `day_of_week` as class `String`, as we actually did, will always work because C++ will automatically invoke the constructor `String(const char*)` to initialize `day_of_week` to whatever length is needed.

```
// ex5-7.c - Find dates of working days

#include "Date.h"
#include "String.h"

bool isHoliday(const Date& day)
{
    const unsigned NUMHOLIDAYS = 10;
    int yr=day.year();
    Date holiday[NUMHOLIDAYS];

// Generate the holidays

// New Year's Day
    holiday[0] = Date(1,"Jan",yr);
// M.L. King's b'day - Third Mon, Jan.
    holiday[1] = (Date(21,"Jan",yr)).previous("Mon");
// Washington's b'day - Third Mon., Feb.
    holiday[2] = (Date(21,"Feb",yr)).previous("Mon");
// Memorial Day - Last Mon., May
    holiday[3] = (Date(31,"May",yr)).previous("Mon");
// Independence Day
    holiday[4] = Date(4,"July",yr);
// Labor Day - First Mon., Sept.
    holiday[5] = (Date(7,"Sept",yr)).previous("Mon");
// Columbus Day - Second Mon., Oct.
    holiday[6] = (Date(14,"Oct",yr)).previous("Mon");
// Veteran's Day
    holiday[7] = Date(11,"Nov",yr);
// Thanksgiving - Fourth Thurs., Nov.
```

```
    holiday[8] = (Date(28,"Nov",yr)).previous("Thur");
// Christmas
    holiday[9] = Date(25,"Dec",yr);

// See if day in question falls on a holiday

    register i;
    for (i = 0; i<=NUMHOLIDAYS-1; i++)
        if (day==holiday[i]) return YES;
    return NO;
}


/*
Find the dates for every specified day-of-the-week (e.g., Wed)
after the specified date until the end of the year.
*/
main ()
{
    Date date, day;
    String day_of_week;

    cout << "Enter date:   ";
    cin >> date;
    cout << "Enter day of week:   ";
    cin >> day_of_week;
    day = (date+7).previous(day_of_week); // Exclude specified
                                          // date
    Date end_of_year(31,"Dec",date.year());
    while(day.between(date,end_of_year)) {
        if (!isHoliday(day)) cout << day << endl;
        day = day+7;
    }
}
```

Interacting with the program might look like this:

```
Enter date:   8/27/89
Enter day of week:   Mon
28-Aug-89
11-Sep-89
18-Sep-89
25-Sep-89
 2-Oct-89
16-Oct-89
23-Oct-89
30-Oct-89
 6-Nov-89
```

```
13-Nov-89
20-Nov-89
27-Nov-89
 4-Dec-89
11-Dec-89
18-Dec-89
```

5.4.3   An abstract data type for times

Of course, we often need much more time resolution than a calendar provides. For example, a program to maintain an appointment calendar must keep track of the time of day as well as the date. A software scheduler similarly will schedule processes or tasks for future execution according to time and date. Thus, a financial system may schedule its accounts payable cycle on a monthly basis at a time when activity is low, such as midnight. Here is an abbreviated specification for class `Time`, an abstract data type that works in concert with class `Date` to provide commonly used time functions:

```
// Time.h - declarations for time

typedef int bool;
typedef unsigned short hourTy;
typedef unsigned short minuteTy;
typedef unsigned short secondTy;
typedef unsigned long clockTy;

class Time  {
// ...
    clockTy sec;        // time in seconds
// ...
public:
    Time();             // current time
    Time(const Date&, hourTy h, minuteTy m, secondTy s);
    friend Time operator+(const Time& t, long s) {
        return Time(t.sec+s);
    }
    friend Time operator+(long s, const Time& t) {
        return Time(t.sec+s);
    }
    long operator-(const Time& t) const  { return sec - t.sec; }
    Time operator-(long s) const         { return Time(sec-s); }
    bool between(const Time& a, const Time& b) const;
    bool operator<(const Time& t) const  { return sec < t.sec; }
    bool operator>=(const Time& t) const { return sec >= t.sec; }
    bool operator==(const Time& t) const { return sec == t.sec; }
// ...
};
```

The specification for class `Time` closely parallels that for class `Date`. It provides constructors that let us declare variables of type `Time` and initialize them to the current time or to some other specified time. It also gives us a set of functions for doing time arithmetic and for comparing one time to another.

5.4.4 Summary for classes `Date` and `Time`

The `Date` and `Time` classes illustrate how abstract data types, applied as reusable software components, can improve programming productivity by hiding complexity from the applications programmers who must use the them. A programmer who had to write a program like Example 5-7, but without the benefit of class `Date`, would have to work out algorithms to handle the messy calculations that calendar arithmetic involves. The resulting program probably would require at least several pages of code. Class `Date` reduces the task to a very short, easy-to-read program.

5.5 REGULAR EXPRESSIONS

Regular expressions are a useful tool for describing patterns in character strings. For instance, many text editors use regular expressions in commands that perform searches and substitutions. In this section we will describe class `Regex`, which performs pattern matching operations using regular expressions. This class is interesting not only as an example of data abstraction, but also because of the way we implemented it—we simply wrote a C++ ADT-style interface to an existing C library for handling regular expressions, thereby taking advantage of C++'s compatibility with C to save programming effort.

5.5.1 Functionality of class `Regex`

A *regular expression* (RE) is a character string that consists of ordinary characters, which match themselves, and special constructs. Some examples of special constructs are:

.   Matches any character

[*list*]   Matches any character in *list*

[^*list*]   Matches any character not in *list*

[*X–Y*]   Matches any character in range *X* to *Y*

*   Matches zero or more occurrences of the preceding RE

\ (...\)   Groups an RE in parentheses

For example, the RE ab*c describes the string pattern consisting of the character a followed by zero or more occurrences of b followed by the character c. It matches the strings ac and abbbbbbc, but it does not match ab (the pattern must end in c), bbbbbc (the pattern must begin with a), or ab*c (b* is a special construct, it does not match itself).

The constructor for class `Regex` takes an RE written as a C-style character string as an argument and converts it into an internal form that other member functions of class `Regex` can use to rapidly search a string for the pattern it describes. For example, the declaration:

```
Regex re = "ab*c";
```

constructs a `Regex` named `re` for the regular expression `ab*c`. We can use the member function `Regex::match(const String&)` to see if a particular string matches this pattern:

```
String st = "abbbc";
if (re.match(st))        // ... pattern matches ...
```

We can also use the member function `Regex::search(const String&)` to search a string for the first occurrence of this pattern:

```
String s = "xxxabbbcyyy";
re.search(s);            // ... returns 3 ...
```

The `search()` member function returns the index of the first character in the string that matches the pattern (the first character of a string has index 0), or -1 if the pattern is not found.

Usually, we also want to know where the matching pattern ends so we can extract or replace the matching substring. It may also be useful to know where various pieces of the pattern match a string. The `match()` and `search()` member functions save this information in member variables of a `Regex` object, and we can retrieve it with the function `Regex::operator[](unsigned)`.

This function returns an instance of class `Range`, another class in the NIH Class Library. Instances of class `Range` represent a range of integers by keeping track of the first integer in the range and the number of integers in the range:

```
class Range {
// ...
    int first,len;
public:
    Range(int f, int l)     { first = f; len = l; }
    int length() const      { return len; }
    int firstIndex() const  { return first; }
    int lastIndex() const   { return (first + len - 1); }
// ...
};
```

The argument to the function `operator[]()` is an integer from 0 to 9 that selects a range of character positions to return. An argument of 0 selects the range matched by the entire RE so, continuing our example:

```
Regex re = "ab*c";
String s = "xbxabbbcyyy";
if (re.search(s) != -1) {    // pattern found
    cout << re[0];           // prints "3:5"
// ...
}
```

Class `String` overloads `operator()(const Range&)` to return the substring addressed by the `Range` argument, so the expression `s(re[0])` returns the substring of `String s` matched by the `Regex re` in the last call to `match()` or `search()`:

```
Regex re = "ab*c";
String s = "xbxabbbcyyy";
if (re.search(s) != -1) {      // pattern found
    cout << s(re[0]);          // prints "abbbc"
}
```

Arguments to the function `operator[]()` between 1 and 9 select ranges matched by pieces of the RE. You define what a piece is by grouping it inside `\( ... \)`. For example, suppose, in the previous program, we wish to change the character a matched by the RE to a z and to delete all instances of the character b. We can accomplish this by writing:

```
Regex re = "\\(a\\)\\(b*\\)c";   // backslashes must be doubled
                                 // in C strings
String s = "xbxabbbcyyy";
if (re.search(s) != -1) {        // pattern found
    s(re[1]) = "z";              // replace substring matched by group 1
                                 // with a "z"
    s(re[2]) = "";               // replace substring matched by group 2
                                 // with an empty string
    cout << s;                   // prints "xbxzcyyy"
}
```

To determine the number of a group, and hence the index to use with `operator[]()` to retrieve the range it matched, number the `\(...\)` groups from left to right in the RE.

5.5.2 Implementation of class `Regex`

Class `Regex` was relatively easy to implement because we just wrote a C++ interface to the C language library functions for handling regular expressions that are part of the GNU EMACS text editor [22]. These library functions include `re_compile_pattern()`, which converts the string form of the RE into a more efficient internal form, `re_match()`, which tries to match the compiled RE to a string, and `re_search()`, which calls `re_match()` repetitively to search a string for a matching pattern. The code for these functions resides in a file named `regex.c`.

These functions use two data structures declared in the file `regex.h`: `re_pattern_buffer`, which holds the compiled form of an RE, and `re_registers`, in which `re_match()` and `re_search()` record the character positions where they found matches to groups in the RE. The file `regex.c` includes these declarations from `regex.h`.

To use the regular expression library functions with C++, we do not need to change anything in `regex.c`—we simply compile it with the C compiler and link the resulting object module with our C++ program. However, the C++ code for class `Regex` requires the declarations for `re_pattern_buffer` and `re_registers`. We could just make a copy of these declarations in the C++ file `Regex.h`, but keeping multiple copies of declarations creates a maintenance problem since we must be careful to find and update all of the copies when we want to change them. We would prefer simply to `#include regex.h` in `Regex.h`. Since C++ is almost completely compatible with C, this approach often works. In this case, however, it does not, because `regex.h` also contains C-style declarations for the library functions, which lack the argument type information that C++ requires.

We thus need to change `regex.h` so that both the C and C++ compilers will accept it. Release 2.0 of the C++ compiler defines a preprocessor symbol named `__cplusplus` that we can use to do this. We modify the library function declarations in `regex.h` as follows:

```
#ifndef __cplusplus
/* C function declarations */
extern char *re_compile_pattern ();
extern int re_match ();
extern int re_search ();
/* ... */

#else

// C++ function declarations
extern "C" {     // following functions use C (not C++) linkage
extern const char* re_compile_pattern(const char*, int size,
    struct re_pattern_buffer*);
extern int re_match(struct re_pattern_buffer*, const char*,
    int size, int pos, struct re_registers*);
extern int re_search(struct re_pattern_buffer*, const char*,
    int size, int startpos, int range, struct re_registers*);
// ...
};

#endif
```

A C compilation will not define `__cplusplus`, so it will see the C function declarations, but a C++ compilation will define `__cplusplus`, so it will compile the C++ declarations, as we intended.

Notice that we enclosed the C++ declarations in the construction `extern "C" { ... }`. We must do this because, although the library function *declarations* are intended for C++, the *implementations* of these functions are in C, so we must inform the C++ compiler to use C function naming and calling conventions when it generates code to call these functions.[3] As you can see from the long argument lists of the RE library functions, they are not as simple to use as class `Regex`, and we have omitted the most complicated functions from this example.

The resulting class declaration for `Regex` (in `Regex.h`) looks something like this:

---

[3] This is a new feature introduced in Release 2.0 of the AT&T C++ Translator—see [26].

```
#include "String.h"
#include "Range.h"
#include "regex.h"
// ...

class Regex {
// ...
    struct re_pattern_buffer pattern;
    unsigned ngroups;    // 1 + number of \( \) groups in pattern
    struct re_registers regs;
// ...
public:
    Regex(const char*, unsigned bufsize =DEFAULT_BUFSIZE);
    Regex(const Regex&);
    ~Regex();
    Range operator[](unsigned) const;
    bool match(const String&, int pos=0);
    int search(const String&, int startpos=0);
// ...
};
```

Class `Regex` provides some useful functionality, and illustrates how implementing something such as regular expressions as an abstract data type can make them easier to use. Class `Regex` is also a good example of how to build a C++ interface to an existing C function library. This is practical because C++ is highly compatible with C, to the extent that C++ will compile C data declarations the same as C does and can call functions written in C. Most languages that claim to be compatible with C really do only the latter, which is the easy part. True compatibility with C also requires a language to make it convenient for a programmer to create and interpret C data structures, as does C++. C++ is thus ideal for giving an ADT "face lift" to aging C code.

5.6   NUMERIC DATA TYPES

In this section we illustrate techniques for extending ordinary arithmetic to numeric abstract data types. A *numeric data type* (NDT) has the following characteristics:

- member variables represent fundamental numeric types (that is, `int`, `float`, `double`) or other NDTs

- member operators are declared for arithmetic operations such as addition, subtraction, multiplication, division

- arithmetic operators do computation characteristic of the data type

- arithmetic has the "look and feel" of ordinary C language arithmetic

Let us look at some numeric data types that offer functionality beyond what we can accomplish with fundamental types. NDTs like these make the time and trouble of declaring new classes well worth our while.

5.6.1   Extensions of fundamental arithmetic

The class `BigInt` introduced in Chapter 2 serves as a good example of a useful numeric data type. Class `BigInt` uses a method of representing integers that can handle whole numbers of any size. All the usual arithmetic operators are declared in class `BigInt`, and application code for `BigInt` arithmetic looks the same as ordinary C-language code. The `BigInt` numeric data type provides an application programmer with an easy way to handle large integers.

Another useful numeric data type is one that can do arithmetic with rational numbers and retain the values of a fraction's numerator and denominator separately. The NIH Class Library has a class `Fraction` that represents rational numbers. It keeps the numerator and denominator of the fraction in reduced form; that is, with no common integer divisors greater than one. Class `Fraction`, in abbreviated form, looks like this:

```
class Fraction {
// ...
    int numer;
    int denom;
// ...
public:
    Fraction(int =0, int =1);      // construct as a ratio
    Fraction(double);              // construct as truncated decimal
    operator double() const { return (double)numer/denom; }
// ...
    friend Fraction operator+(const Fraction&, const Fraction&);
    friend Fraction operator*(const Fraction&, const Fraction&);
// ...
    friend bool operator>(const Fraction&, const Fraction&);
    friend bool operator>=(const Fraction&, const Fraction&);
// ...
};
```

Using members of type `int` limits the generality of this implementation. An improved version might use a data type like `BigInt` for the numerator and denominator. This would require implementing `BigInt` member functions for multiplication and division, as well as a method to find the greatest common divisor of two `BigInt` objects.

5.6.2   Complex numbers

Stroustrup [3] describes a C++ implementation of a numeric data type for the complex numbers. Class `complex` can help to give code for performing complex arithmetic the appearance of ordinary arithmetic. For example,

```
complex z(1,2);         //  z = 1 + 2*i
complex w = (z + 1)*log(z);
```

We can illustrate class `complex` in abbreviated form:

```
class complex {
    double re, im;
public:
    complex(double r = 0.0, double i = 0.0) { re=r; im=i; }
// ...
    friend double real(const complex&);
    friend double imag(const complex&);
// ...
    friend complex log(complex);
// ...
    friend complex operator+(complex, complex);
    friend complex operator*(complex, complex);
// ...
};
```

The function `operator+()` separately adds the real and imaginary parts of the complex numbers. The function `operator*()` calculates the real and imaginary parts of the product of two complex numbers in the usual way. Functions for subtraction and division are defined similarly. The declaration for class `complex` shown here uses only friend functions and operators. We need not have declared member functions such as `real()`, `imag()`, or `log()` as friend functions, but the friend declaration allows application code to retain the familiar notation of mathematics. For instance, with `log(complex)` as a friend, we can write `complex w = log(z);` without the friend declaration, we would have to write `complex w = z.log()`. Declaring the operator members as friends similarly makes it easier to perform operations that involve several types.

A fuller implementation of class `complex` would include members for returning the conjugate and the norm, a member to test equality with another instance of class `complex`, and a number of standard functions such as `sin()` and `exp()`.

5.6.3 Vectors

The NIH Class Library contains a set of classes, `BitVec`, `ByteVec`, `ShortVec`, `IntVec`, `LongVec`, `FloatVec`, and `DoubleVec`, that provide a convenient notation for vector operations. In the following discussion, variable names consisting of a single capital letter (e.g. `V`) represent vector objects, and variables names consisting of a single lower case letter (e.g. `s`) represent scalars.

Functionality of the vector classes

The vector classes overload nearly all arithmetic operators to apply to vectors and to vectors combined with scalars.

A unary operator applied to a vector is applied to each element of the vector to produce a vector result:

```
// ex5-8.c - Vector operations

#include "IntVec.h"
```

```
static int initV[] = {1,2,3,4,5,6,7,8};
static int initW[] = {8,7,6,5,4,3,2,1};
static int initI[] = {1,3,7,2};
static int initJ[] = {-1,-2,-3,-4};


main()
{
    IntVec V(initV,sizeof(initV)/sizeof(int));
                                // V = 1 2 3 4 5 6 7 8
    IntVec W(initW,sizeof(initW)/sizeof(int));
                                // W = 8 7 6 5 4 3 2 1
    IntVec I(initI,sizeof(initI)/sizeof(int));   // I = 1 3 7 2
    IntVec J(initJ,sizeof(initJ)/sizeof(int));   // J = -1 -2 -3 -4
    cout << -V << endl;         // prints -1 -2 -3 -4 -5 -6 -7 -8
```

A binary arithmetic operator applied to two vectors, which must be of equal length, is applied to the corresponding pairs of elements of the vectors to produce a vector result:

```
cout << V-W << endl;     // prints -7 -5 -3 -1 1 3 5 7
```

A binary relational operator applied to two vectors is applied to the corresponding pairs of elements of the vectors to produce a bit vector (class BitVec) result in which a 1 indicates that the relation is true for the corresponding elements and a 0 indicates that it is false:

```
cout << (V<W) << endl;   // prints 1 1 1 1 0 0 0 0
```

A binary operator applied to a vector and a scalar is applied to each element of the vector in combination with the scalar to produce a vector result:

```
cout << V+1 << endl;            // prints 2 3 4 5 6 7 8 9
cout << (V>3) << endl;          // prints 0 0 0 1 1 1 1 1
```

A *slice* operator makes it easier to treat vectors as multidimensional arrays. A slice of a vector is defined by the starting position of the slice, the number of elements in the slice, and the *stride*, or the increment between successive elements of the slice. The slice operator of a vector V is written as: V (*position,length,stride*) . Note that vectors are indexed starting at 0, in keeping with the C and C++ convention. Thus:

```
IntVec T;
T = V(0,4,2); cout << T << endl;        // prints 1 3 5 7
T = V(2,3,1); cout << T << endl;        // prints 3 4 5
```

You can index vectors by integer scalars (type int), integer vectors (type IntVec), and bit vectors (type BitVec). Indexing a vector by an IntVec produces a vector result by selecting those elements of the vector that are indexed by the elements of the IntVec. The result thus has the same length as the index vector:

```
T = V[I]; cout << T << endl;            // prints 2 4 8 3
```

Indexing a vector by a BitVec of the same length produces a vector result by selecting those elements of the indexed vector that correspond to 1s in the BitVec index vector.

Thus the length of the result is equal to the number of 1s in the index vector. For example:

```
T = V[V>4]; cout << T << endl;   // prints 5 6 7 8
```

The slice, `IntVec` index, and `BitVec` index operators may all appear to the left of an assignment operator as well, in which case the vector elements addressed by the operator are assigned the value of the expression to the right of the assignment operator. This value may be either a scalar or a vector. If it is a vector, its length must be the same as the number of elements addressed on the left side of the assignment; if it is a scalar, all addressed elements are assigned its value. For example:

```
T = V; T(1,4,2) = I;
cout << T << endl;              // prints 1 1 3 3 5 7 7 2
T = V; T[I] = J;
cout << T << endl;             // prints 1 -1 -4 -2 5 6 7 -3
T = V; T[V>4] = 0;
cout << T << endl;             // prints 1 2 3 4 0 0 0 0
```

Implementation of the vector classes

We used private classes to provide the notational convenience of the slice, `IntVec` index, and `BitVec` index operators. For example, the `IntVec` index operator uses the private class `IntPick` to save pointers to the operand vectors:

```
class IntPick {
    IntVec* V;             // pointer to the indexed vector
    const IntVec* X;       // pointer to the index vector
    IntPick(const IntVec& v,const IntVec& x) {
        V = &(IntVec&)v;   X = &x;
    }
    IntPick(const IntPick& s)              { V = s.V; X = s.X; }
    friend IntVec;
    friend IntSlice;
// ...
public:
    void operator=(const IntVec&);
    void operator=(int);
// ...
};


class IntVec {
    int* v;                // pointer to data, NULL if empty vector
// ...
public:
    IntVec(unsigned len =0);
    IntVec(const int*, unsigned len);
    IntVec(const IntVec&);
    IntVec(const IntSlice&);
    IntPick operator[](const IntVec& I)
```

```
    {
        return IntPick(*this,I);
    }
    void operator=(const IntPick&);
    IntSlice operator()(int pos, unsigned lgt, int stride =1);
    operator IntSlice();
// ...
};
```

Thus, C++ interprets the expression V[I], where V and I are instances of class IntVec, as a call to the function IntVec::operator[](const IntVec&), which returns a result of type IntPick. The functions IntPick::operator=(const IntVec&) and IntPick::operator=(int) define assignments such as V[I] = W and V[I] = s, respectively. The function IntVec::operator=(IntPick&) defines assignments of the form W = V[I].

Class IntSlice implements the vector slice abstraction:

```
class IntSlice {
    IntVec* V;   // vector pointer
    int* p;      // slice pointer
    unsigned l;  // slice length
    int k;       // slice stride
    IntSlice(const IntVec& v,
        int pos, unsigned lgt, int stride =1);
    friend IntVec;
// ...
public:
    IntSlice(const IntPick&);
// ...
    void operator=(const IntVec&);
    void operator=(const IntPick&);
// ...
    friend IntVec operator-(const IntSlice&);
    friend IntVec operator+(const IntSlice&, const IntSlice&);
// ...
};
```

An instance of class IntSlice holds a pointer to a vector and the data needed to describe a slice of that vector: a pointer to the first element, the number of elements, and the stride. The overloaded member functions IntSlice::operator=() implement assignments to vector slices such as T(1,4,2) = I. Operator functions like IntSlice::operator+() and IntSlice::operator-(), which are friends of class IntSlice, implement all unary and binary integer vector operations as more general operations on instances of class IntSlice. As a result, the C++ compiler interprets the expression

```
V[I] + W
```

as:

```
IntVec::operator+(IntSlice(V.operator[](I)),
    IntVec::operator IntSlice(W))
```

C++ automatically supplies calls to `IntSlice::IntSlice(const IntPick&)` and `IntVec::operator IntSlice()` to convert the `IntPick V[I]` and `IntVec W` to instances of `IntSlice`.

Implementing all of these operations for a single vector class requires approximately 100 functions, or a total of about 800 functions since there are eight classes. Fortunately, many of these functions are similar, so macros can greatly reduce the required effort. For example, consider the code required to implement `operator+()` for class `IntVec` and class `FloatVec`. The two functions are the same except for the types of the arguments, the return values, and the local variables used to address the vector elements. Also, the code required to implement `operator+()` and the seven other binary arithmetic operators for a single class such as `IntVec` are all the same except for the operator name and the operator applied to the vector elements. Thus, a single code template with the type and operator parameterized can generate as many as 64 functions. For example, here is the m4 [11] macro template which generates the function definitions for all binary arithmetic operations on all types of vector slices:

```
define(FRIEND_TYPESlice_OP_TYPESlice__TYPEVec,
$1Vec operator$2(const $1Slice& u, const $1Slice& v)
// Binary arithmetic operator on two $1Vec slices
{
    i = u.length();
    if (i != v.length()) u.lengthErr(v);
    $1Vec T(i);
    const $1* up = u.pt();
    const $1* vp = v.pt();
    $1* dp = T.pt();
    uj = u.stride();
    vj = v.stride();
    while (i--) { *dp++ = *up $2 *vp; up += uj; vp += vj; }
    return T;
}
)
```

Calling this macro with the parameters `Int` and `+`

```
FRIEND_TYPESlice_OP_TYPESlice__TYPEVec(Int,+)
```

generates the definition of the function

```
IntVec operator+(const IntSlice&, const IntSlice)
```

for example. The m4 macro processor replaces occurrences of $1 in the template with the vector type (`Int` in this case) and replaces occurrences of $2 with the operator symbol (+ in this case), producing the function definition:

```
IntVec operator+(const IntSlice& u, const IntSlice& v)
// Binary arithmetic operator on two IntVec slices
```

```
{
    i = u.length();
    if (i != v.length()) u.lengthErr(v);
    IntVec T(i);
    const Int* up = u.pt();
    const Int* vp = v.pt();
    Int* dp = T.pt();
    uj = u.stride();
    vj = v.stride();
    while (i--) { *dp++ = *up + *vp; up += uj; vp += vj; }
    return T;
}
```

The type definition

```
typedef int Int;
```

generated before this function definition makes declarations such as

```
const Int* up = u.pt();
const Int* vp = v.pt();
Int* dp = T.pt();
```

compile properly.

We generate the calls to the macro templates automatically from the member and friend function declarations in the specification (.h) files for the various vector types. The UNIX sed utility [16] transforms the function declaration

```
friend IntVec operator+(const IntSlice&, const IntSlice&);
```

into the macro call shown earlier to generate the definition of operator+(), for example.

The vector classes in the NIH Class Library are still experimental—before using them for a serious project, you should be aware that current C++ compilers generate rather inefficient code for them. For example, in returning a vector result from an operator function, the entire vector is unnecessarily copied (by application of the copy constructor) from a temporary local to the function into a temporary vector supplied by the caller. However, they demonstrate the capability of and techniques for defining complicated operations in C++. The major notational inconvenience is the lack of a way to write vector constants— you cannot write a vector constructor with a variable-length argument list of the vector's elements without also supplying an additional argument to tell the constructor how many elements are present.

5.6.4 Matrices

Yet another valuable numeric data type performs the operations of matrix algebra. Packaging these operations in an NDT helps to remove many for-loops from application programs, so that we can give matrix operations the appearance of ordinary arithmetic. We can illustrate this idea with a simplified declaration for class Matrix:

```
class Matrix {
protected:
    int nrow, ncol; // no. of rows and cols
    double* _v;      // list of elements
    // ...
public:
    // constructors
    Matrix(int nr =1,int nc =1,double* =0);
    Matrix(const Matrix&);
    Matrix(int,diagonal);

    // access of elements by double index
    double& at(int irow,int icol) const
        { return *(_v+irow*(ncol)+icol); }
    double& operator()(int irow,int icol) const;

    void operator=(const Matrix&);
    int operator==(const Matrix&) const;

    // special operators: transpose and inverse
    Matrix t() const;
    Matrix operator~() const;
    // ...
};

// determinant and norm
extern double det(const Matrix&);
extern double norm(const Matrix&);

// matrix algebra
extern Matrix operator+(const Matrix&,const Matrix&);
extern Matrix operator-(const Matrix&,const Matrix&);
extern Matrix operator*(const Matrix&,const Matrix&);
extern Matrix operator-(const Matrix&);
// ...
// concatenate columns
extern Matrix operator&(const Matrix&,const Matrix&);
// ...
```

Class `Matrix` has member variables for the number of rows, the number of columns, and a pointer to a list of matrix elements. `Matrix` constructors allocate memory for the matrix elements; class `Matrix` provides several different constructors for applications programming convenience. A single member function, `at()`, implements the indexing algorithm for accessing matrix elements. Applications may also call `operator()(int i, int j)`, which does ranges checks on its arguments before attempting to access a matrix element with `at()`.

With the help of class `Matrix`, we can write application code that makes matrix algebra look like tidy mathematical statements:

```
// ex5-9.c - Matrix algebra with class Matrix

double c_1[] = { 1.1, 2.1, 3.1 };
double c_2[] = { 1.2, 2.2, 3.2 };
double c_3[] = { 1.3, 2.3, 3.3 };

// construct columns and concatenate
Matrix c1(3, 1, c_1);
Matrix c2(3, 1, c_2);
Matrix c3(3, 1, c_3);
Matrix m = c1&c2&c3;

cout << m << endl;

// extract row vector
Matrix v = m.row(1);
cout << v << endl;

// multiply matrix by column matrix
Matrix u = m*v.t();
cout << u << endl;
```

5.6.5   The automatic derivative as an ADT

Automatic differentiation is a way of computing values for derivatives without first symbolically differentiating a function and without resorting to approximation [19]. We can design an abstract data type for automatic differentiation by exploiting the idea behind the arithmetic of class `complex`. A `complex` object holds the real and imaginary parts in separate member variables and has member functions that implement the various arithmetic operators to provide an arithmetic rule for the real and imaginary members.

Suppose we have a differentiable function of a single variable, $f(x)$, and we want to compute the value of its derivative $f'(x)$ at the value $x = 0$. Using an automatic derivative data type, we can have one member variable represent the value of function, $f(0)$, and another member variable represent the value of the derivative, $f'(0)$. We can have arithmetic operators—such as $+$, $-$, $*$, and $/$—that perform ordinary arithmetic on the function value and perform the arithmetic of derivatives on the derivative value. Thus, if we know the values $f(0), f'(0)$, $g(0)$, and $g'(0)$, then we can compute:

- addition of functions

$$(f + g)(0) \;=\; f(0) + g(0)$$
$$(f + g)'(0) \;=\; f'(0) + g'(0)$$

- multiplication of functions

$$(f \cdot g)(0) \;=\; f(0) \cdot g(0)$$
$$(f \cdot g)'(0) \;=\; f(0) \cdot g'(0) + f'(0) \cdot g(0)$$

- composition of functions (Chain Rule)

$$f(g)(0) = f(g(0))$$
$$(f(g))'(0) = f'(g(0)) \cdot g'(0)$$

Rall [18] has shown how to implement an automatic derivative data type in a computer language that supports data abstraction and operator overloading. We can illustrate his idea in C++ with class `AutoDeriv`:

```
class AutoDeriv {
private:
    double u,du;
public:
    AutoDeriv(double v = 0.0,double dv = 0.0) { u=v; du=dv; }

    friend double F(const AutoDeriv& x) { return x.u; }
    friend double dF(const AutoDeriv& x) { return x.du; }

    friend AutoDeriv operator+(const AutoDeriv&,
                        const AutoDeriv&);
        { return AutoDeriv(F(x)+F(y),dF(x)+dF(y)); }
    friend AutoDeriv operator-(const AutoDeriv&,
                        const AutoDeriv&);
        { return AutoDeriv(F(x)-F(y),dF(x)-dF(y)); }
    friend AutoDeriv operator*(const AutoDeriv&,
                        const AutoDeriv&);
        { return AutoDeriv(F(x)*F(y),F(y)*dF(x)+F(x)*dF(y));}
    friend AutoDeriv operator/(const AutoDeriv&,
                        const AutoDeriv&);
        { return AutoDeriv(F(x)/F(y),
                (F(y)*dF(x)-F(x)*dF(y))/F(y)*F(y)); }

    void printOn(ostream& strm) const;
    // ...
};

inline AutoDeriv Sin(const AutoDeriv& x)
{ return AutoDeriv(sin(F(x)),dF(x)*cos(F(x))); }
// ...
```

We first use the constructors of class `AutoDeriv` to represent constant and linear functions and then build more complicated functions from these simple representations. Thus, using the constructor `AutoDeriv(double,double)`, we represent the unit constant as `AutoDeriv(1)`. Similarly, we use `AutoDeriv(0,1)` to represent the identity linear function, $f(x) = x$ and `AutoDeriv(3,2)` to represent $f(x) = 3 + 2x$. For the general linear function in one variable

$$f(x) = b + ax$$

we can evaluate the functions $f(x)$ and $f'(x)$ at the value $x = 0$ with the code:

```
AutoDeriv X(0,1);     // IDENT(x)
AutoDeriv Y = b + a*X;
```

This will result in an object Y with F(Y) returning the value b and dF(Y) returning the value a. Thus Y is equivalent to the automatic derivative, AutoDeriv(b,a).

This latter technique for representing linear functions provides the clue we need to represent more complicated algebraic and trigonometric functions using instances of class AutoDeriv. Example 5-10 shows how we can evaluate the function expressions

$$f(x) = 2 \cdot x \cdot [\sin(x) + 1] \tag{5.1}$$
$$f'(x)$$

at the values $x = 0$ and $x = \pi/2$.

```
// ex5-10 - one dimensional automatic derivatives with
//          class AutoDeriv

#include <math.h>
#include <iostream.h>
#include "AutoDeriv.h"

const double halfPI = M_PI_2; /* M_PI_2 from math.h */

main()
{
    // evaluate 2*x*(sin(x)+1) at x=0
    AutoDeriv X(0,1);
    AutoDeriv Y = 2*X*(Sin(X)+1);

    cout << "let   X = [F(X),dF(X)] = "
         << "[" << F(X)   << "," << dF(X) << "]"
         << endl;
    cout << "let   Y = 2*X*(Sin(X)+1)" << "\n"
         << "then Y = [F(Y),dF(Y)] = "
         << "[" << F(Y)   << "," << dF(Y) << "]"
         << endl<< endl;

    // evaluate 2*x*(sin(x)+1) at x=halfPI
    AutoDeriv U(halfPI,1);
    AutoDeriv V = 2*U*(Sin(U)+1);

    cout << "let   U = [F(U),dF(U)] = "
         << "[" << F(U)   << "," << dF(U) << "]"
         << endl;
    cout << "let   V = 2*U*(Sin(U)+1)" << "\n"
         << "then V = [F(V),dF(V)] = "
         << "[" << F(V)   << "," << dF(V) << "]"
         << endl;
}
```

Example 5-10 evaluates the function expressions (5.1) at $x = 0$ by using `AutoDeriv X` to represent the variable x and `AutoDeriv Y` to represent the function expression. The output statements for X and Y will produce output:

```
let  X = [F(X),dF(X)] = [0,1]
let  Y = 2*X*(Sin(X)+1)
then Y = [F(Y),dF(Y)] = [0,2]
```

We also can use class `AutoDeriv` to evaluate function expressions at any value for which they are defined by applying a linear change of variables. Thus, to evaluate function expressions (5.1) at $x = \pi/2$, we can evaluate the new expressions

$$g(x) = 2 \cdot [x + \pi/2] \cdot [\sin(x + \pi/2) + 1] \qquad (5.2)$$
$$g'(x)$$

at $x = 0$. In Example 5-10, the `AutoDeriv U` is equivalent to X+PI/2 so that evaluating X at 0 is the same as evaluating U at PI/2. Thus the representation of `AutoDeriv V` in terms of `Autoderiv U` provides an evaluation of the function expressions in (5.2) at $x = \pi/2$. The output statements for U and V in Example 5-10 will produce the output:

```
let  U = [F(U),dF(U)] = [1.5708,1]
let  V = 2*U*(Sin(U)+1)
then V = [F(V),dF(V)] = [6.28319,4]
```

More generally, we can use class `AutoDeriv` to compute the derivative values for any function representable in C++ that is chosen from the set, S, of functions which meets the following simple conditions:

- S contains the constant function $ONE(x) = 1$ for all x

- S contains the identity function $IDENT(x) = x$ for all x

- S contains standard functions with known derivative functions (e.g. sin, cos, tan, exp, log)

- S contains any function with a derivative computable by user defined software

- if $f(x)$ and $g(x)$ are in S then so is the composition $f(g(x))$

- if f is in S then $a \cdot f$ is in S where a is any constant (int, double, or float)

- if f and g are in S, then so are $f + g$, $-f$, $f \cdot g$

- if f is in S and $f(x) \neq 0$ for all x then $1/f$ is in S

5.6.6 A practical application for automatic derivatives

We can extend the concept of computing automatic derivatives with a numeric data type to include derivatives of higher order and first partial derivatives as well. We can apply the latter to the eminently practical problem of solving a system of nonlinear equations by Newton's Method. To see how to do this, consider the same system of equations as used by Rall [18]:

$$f(x,y,z) = \quad 16x^4 + 16y^4 + z^4 - 16 \quad = 0 \qquad (5.3)$$
$$g(x,y,z) = \quad x^2 + y^2 + z^2 - 3 \quad = 0$$
$$h(x,y,z) = \quad x^3 - y \quad = 0$$

Our problem is to compute the solution to equations (5.3) nearest to $(x_o, y_o, z_o) = (1, 1, 1)$, if one exists. According to Newton's Method, if we start with an approximate solution vector $X_0 = (x_0, y_0, z_0)$, then we can find a closer approximation vector

$$X_1 = (x_1, y_1, z_1) = X_0 + D$$

We obtain D, the correction vector, from the matrix equation

$$J \cdot D = - \begin{pmatrix} f(X_0) \\ g(X_0) \\ h(X_0) \end{pmatrix}$$

where J is the Jacobian matrix of partial derivatives evaluated at X_0:

$$J = \begin{pmatrix} f_x(X_0) & f_y(X_0) & f_z(X_0) \\ g_x(X_0) & g_y(X_0) & g_z(X_0) \\ h_x(X_0) & h_y(X_0) & h_z(X_0) \end{pmatrix}$$

Now that we have a new solution approximation X_1, we can use it in place of X_0 and iterate until the solution converges to the desired accuracy, if indeed we obtain convergence at all.

To approach this problem, we first need an abstract data type that will represent a function of several independent variables and its partial automatic derivative with respect to each variable. We can use the following class Partial to accomplish this objective:

```
class Partial {
    int nvar;          // number of independent variables
    double* du;        // list of partial derivatives at X=0
public:
    Partial();
    double& operator[](int k) { return du[k]; }

    friend Partial operator+(const Partial&,const Partial&);
    Partial pow(int e);    // raise to the e-th power
    // ... other arithmetic operators

    friend Partial Sin(const Partial&);
    // ... other standard functions
}
```

Class Partial has two member variables. The first, nvar, specifies the number of independent variables in the function we want to represent, and therefore the number of first partial derivatives. The second, du, points to an array containing the list of partial derivatives. Actually, the zero*th* value, *du, represents the value of the function itself, and the remaining values, `* (du+1)` to `* (du+nvar)` represent the values of the partial derivatives, all evaluated with all independent variables set to zero. We would like to use a `Partial` to represent a function with an arbitrary number of possible partial derivatives; thus we have chosen not to initialize them in the constructor. Instead, we set the value of the k*th* partial derivative by using the index operator defined by the member function, `operator[]()`. For example:

```
Partial X;
X[K] = 1.0;            // set the Kth partial derivative
double d = X[K];       // get the Kth partial derivative
```

Before we can reference the list of partial derivatives using `operator[]`, we must assure that memory for them has been allocated. The memory allocation requires that we know the number of variables in the function. For simplicity in this example, assume that the number is a static constant large enough for our application.

The member function `pow()` will raise a `Partial` to an integer power. We chose `pow()` to implement exponentiation because C++, like C, does not provide an exponentiation operator—a noticeable flaw in the language. An overloaded operator, for example, `operator^()`, would be more aesthetically pleasing, but C++ does not have a suitable operator with sufficiently high precedence for exponentiation.

We can now use an instance of class `Partial` to represent a function of several variables, but we still need a systematic method for handling multiple equations. Here, we will simply devise another class, `ArrayPartial`, to represent an array of `Partials`, that is, a system of equations:

```
class ArrayPartial {
    Partial* p;          // list of independent Partials
    int sz;              // size of list
public:
    ArrayPartial(int siz, double*);
    ArrayPartial(int siz, Partial* =0);

    Partial& operator[](int Kth);
    void operator+=(const Matrix&);

    Matrix value();      // vector of values at x=0
    Matrix jacobian();   // Jacobian matrix at x=0
    ArrayPartial operator+(const ArrayPartial&);
    friend ArrayPartial operator*(double,const ArrayPartial&);
    friend ArrayPartial operator*(const Matrix&,
                              const ArrayPartial);
};
```

In class `ArrayPartial`, the member function `value()` returns a vector of function values, while the member function `jacobian()` constructs the Jacobian matrix of partial derivatives we will need to implement Newton's Method. By using an `ArrayPartial`, we can hide all the messy details of constructing a set of initialized `Partials` to represent the system of equations we are trying to solve. We can also hide the details of the matrix operations applied to the Partials, thereby giving an easily readable, "mathematical" appearance to the application program.

The application will need these static variables to use in constructions:

```
static const int NVAR = 3;          // number of variables
static const int NEQN = 3;          // number of equations
static const int NITER = 16;        // number of iterations
static double x0[] = { 1, 1, 1 };   // trial solution
```

Of course, in this problem, the number of equations must equal the number of variables, so we have set both NVAR and NEQN to the value: 3.

Next, we will use an ArrayPartial to represent a set of three Partials for the three independent variables, initialized to (1,1,1):

```
ArrayPartial X(NVAR, x0);
```

This means that X[k] represents the Partial corresponding to the k*th* independent variable, and that the solution vector for a system of equations in these three independent variables will be (X[1][0], X[2][0], X[3][0]). By analogy, recall that we used AutoDeriv(0,1) to represent the identity function, which we subsequently used as an independent variable for AutoDerivs representing more complex functions.

Using the Matrix(int nr=1, int nc=1, double*=0) constructor from class Matrix that we introduced in Section 5.6.4, we can construct a column matrix to hold the correction vector:

```
Matrix del(NVAR  /*rows*/, 1 /*columns*/ );
```

Example 5-11 shows how we can complete the application code to solve the system (5.3) of three equations in three unknowns using Newton's Method.

```
// ex5-11.c - Using automatic derivatives
//            to solve systems of equations

#include "ArrayPartial.h"
#include "Matrix.h"

// ...

main()
{
  ArrayPartial X(NVAR, x0);
  Matrix del(NVAR/*rows*/,1/*columns*/);

  int count =0;
  while(count <=NITER) {
```

```
// ...
    // define 3 equations in 3 variables
    ArrayPartial f(NEQN);
    f[1]= 16.0*X[1].pow(4) + 16.*X[2].pow(4) + X[3].pow(4) - 16.0;
    f[2]=      X[1].pow(2) +     X[2].pow(2) + X[3].pow(2) -  3.0;
    f[3]=      X[1].pow(3) -     X[2];

// ...

    // recompute jacobian and new correction vector
    Matrix J = f.jacobian();
    Matrix v = f.value();
    del = -(~J*v);

// ...

    // compute next estimate for solution
    X += del;
    }
}
```

In Example 5-11 we declare an `ArrayPartial` f to represent the system of three equations in three unknowns. After defining the three equations, we construct the value vector for this system, (`f[1][0]`,`f[2][0]`,`f[3][0]`), returned by `f.value()`, and the Jacobian matrix, `J`, of partial derivatives for the system, return by `f.jacobian()`. The Jacobian has `J.at(i,j)` equal to `f[i][j]`. Finally, it uses matrix equations to calculate a new correction vector and the next solution approximation.

Were we to include output statements, omitted for simplicity in Example 5-11, the program would produce a solution vector containing the same values found by Rall:

```
X = 8.77965760274E-01
Y = 6.76756970518E-01
Z = 1.33085541162E+00
```

However, accuracy and precision of the results are not at issue here—they depend, among other things, on the particular algorithm for computing the inverse of the Jacobian, `J`. With this example we want to illustrate that using numeric data types to compute automatic derivatives holds promise for solving interesting computational problems.

5.7 CHAPTER SUMMARY

In this chapter we have presented examples to show how we can use data abstraction to develop reusable software components representing many diverse data types. The examples show that, in general, data abstraction results in shorter, easier-to-read, easier-to-understand programs, and that we can use abstract data types in many different kinds of applications.

- Classes `istream` and `ostream` provide a method of handling I/O operations such as the opening, closing, reading, and writing of files—something every computer program must do—in a way that is likely to become universally used by C++ programmers. You can readily extend stream input and stream output for use with classes you write yourself.

- Class `String` shows the value of developing a data type with extensive functionality for frequently used structures like the character string. The discussion of class `String` also illustrates important C++ programming concepts and techniques that you will use when you write other classes. These include private classes, forward references to class declarations, assignment to references, overloading `const` member functions, and implicit type conversion.

- Classes `Date` and `Time` not only encapsulate all the complexity of a perpetual calendar, but they allow applications to perform comparisons and arithmetic operations on dates and times as if they were ordinary numbers.

- Class `Regex` shows how we can provide a safe, easy-to-use programming interface to a complex utility written in the C-language without having to alter the original C-code.

- Numeric data types such as classes `complex`, `Vector`, `Matrix`, and `AutoDeriv` illustrate the use of abstract data types to accomplish compact, easily understood, mathematical notation in programs that solve problems in computational mathematics.

Part II
OBJECT-ORIENTED PROGRAMMING IN C++

6

OBJECT- ORIENTED
PROGRAMMING CONCEPTS

6.1 INTRODUCTION

Perhaps the most interesting and powerful features of C++ are those that support the style of programming known as *object-oriented programming*, or O-OP. Object-oriented programming is a technique for organizing related abstract data types and for exploiting their common features in order to reduce programming effort. It is characterized by:

- Encapsulation

- Inheritance

- Dynamic Binding

In earlier chapters we discussed *encapsulation*, which restricts client programs to interact with class instances only by means of a well defined set of operations, called the class's *specification*. This isolates client programs from the details of how a class represents the data it contains and the algorithms it uses, called the class's *implementation*. The results are that (correct) changes to the implementation will not cause client programs to malfunction, and programs are easier to debug and maintain because the code that deals with a class's data is localized to the class.

Inheritance simplifies the task of creating a new class that is similar to an existing class by enabling a programmer to express just the *differences* between the new class and the existing class, rather than requiring the new class to be written from the beginning.

Dynamic binding, sometimes called *late binding*, helps to make client programs more general by *hiding the differences* among a group of related classes from client programs. Dynamic binding permits each class of a group of related classes to have a different implementation of a particular function. Client programs can apply the function to an instance of one of the classes without regard for the specific class of the instance. At execution time, C++ determines the specific class of the instance and calls that class's implementation of the function.

Thus, encapsulation, inheritance, and dynamic binding work together:

- Encapsulation assures that client programs interact with objects only by calling member functions.

- Inheritance provides a means for expressing the differences among classes, while reusing the code and member variables that implement their similar features.

- Dynamic binding of the member functions called by client programs hides the differences among classes, expressed via inheritance, from the client programs.

We have already seen how C++ supports encapsulation by providing classes with private and public members. C++ supports inheritance by means of derived classes, and it supports dynamic binding by virtual member functions.

In this chapter we will introduce object-oriented programming, concentrating on inheritance and dynamic binding and the features of C++ that support them.

6.1.1   Derived classes

Suppose we have written a C++ class to realize an abstract data type, and we need another abstract data type that is similar to it. Perhaps it requires some additional member variables or functions, or a few of its member functions must do something differently. We would like to reuse the code we have already written and debugged as much as possible. C++ gives us a simple way to accomplish this: we can declare the new class as a *derived class* of the existing class, called the *base class*. The derived class *inherits* all of the member variables and functions of its base class. We can then differentiate the derived class from its base class by:

- adding member variables

- adding member functions

- re-defining member functions inherited from the base class

A base class may have more than one derived class, and a derived class may, in turn, serve as the base class for other derived classes. Thus, we can define an entire tree-structured arrangement of related classes, as shown in Figure 6.1. This gives us a coherent way to organize classes and to share common code among them.

Typically, a derived class is more specialized than its base class. Thus, classes nearer to the root of a tree of classes are more general than those farther away.

This description of derived classes may give the impression that class trees are grown by a process of specialization, in which you begin with an existing class and use it as the base class for new, more specialized derived classes. You can, however, also build a class hierarchy through a process of generalization, in which you begin with two or more related classes, recognize that they have common features, and design a base class to embody them. The related classes, which become derived classes of the new base class, then share the implementation of these common features by means of inheritance from the new base class. The example later in this chapter will illustrate the use of both of these processes during the construction of a simple class hierarchy.

6.1.2   Virtual member functions

A base class with multiple derived classes not only eliminates redundant code, but also creates an opportunity for making client programs more general. A base class, in effect, provides a uniform set of operations for manipulating instances of itself or of any of its derived classes. Client programs that use only a base class's member functions can operate on instances of any derived class of the base class as though they were actually instances

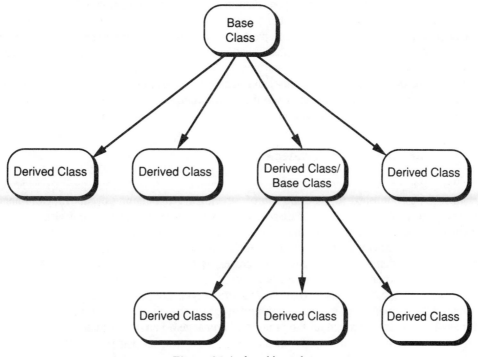

Figure 6.1 A class hierarchy

of the base class. Since such clients have no knowledge whatsoever of the derived classes, new derived classes can be added without changing client programs, or even recompiling them.

If a base class could provide only member functions of the kind we described in Part 1, inheritance would not be very interesting, because a base class could not provide many useful operations. Ordinary member functions must be implemented by the class that declares them, so a base class would have to implement all of the operations that it provides for client programs. Member functions of a base class, however, cannot readily access the member variables and functions that might be added by derived classes, so a base class usually cannot implement member functions that are useful for instances of its derived classes. Furthermore, a base class can potentially have a wide variety of derived classes, each requiring its own customized version of a particular operation. To accommodate this diversity, a member function of a base class would have to somehow determine the actual derived class of the object to which it was applied, and execute code written specifically to handle that particular class. This would result in complicated programs, and would involve the member functions of a base class so intimately with the implementation details of derived classes that it would seriously violate encapsulation. Such a scheme is also impractical because the provider of a base class cannot predict what classes might be derived from it in the future.

C++ gives us *virtual member functions* to solve these problems. A base class can declare a member function using the keyword `virtual`, signifying that the base class's implementation of the member function is only a default which will be used only when a derived class does not supply its own implementation. If a derived class does supply its own implementation of a virtual member function, then that is the implementation that C++ will use when client programs apply the member function to instances of that derived class. Since a member function of the derived class implements the operation, it has no problem accessing the member variables and other member functions of the derived class. Also, when a client applies a virtual member function to an object, C++ automatically determines which class the object belongs to at execution time, and transfers control to the correct implementation of the function. This happens even when the client program treats the object as an instance of the base class. Thus, programs remain simple and encapsulation is preserved.

6.1.3   The `switch` statement considered harmful

In 1968, Edsger W. Dijkstra's letter to the editor entitled "Go To Statement Considered Harmful" was published [6], and the Era of Structured Programming began. Programmers spurned use of the `goto` in favor of specialized single-entry/single-exit control structures such as `if-then-else`, `do-while`, and `switch`.[1] A programming style evolved in which a `struct` with a type field denoting its contents (called a *discriminated record* in some other programming languages) is processed by `switch` statements scattered around in the program wherever the `struct` is operated upon. The `switch` statements contain a `case` statement to handle each possible value of the type field; that is, each possible record variant. The problem with this programming style is that the code to deal with a particular variant is distributed throughout the program. To change a variant, or to add a new one, a programmer must find and modify all the `switch` statements that process the `struct`, which is tedious and error-prone.

In C++, you can almost always replace this use of the `switch` statement by derived classes with virtual functions. A derived class represents each record variant, and a virtual function call replaces each `switch` statement. Each `switch` statement `case` becomes a virtual member function of one of the derived classes, and dynamic binding eliminates the need for keeping a type field in the `struct`. This localizes all the code that handles a particular variant to a derived class. Adding a new variant is simply a matter of creating an additional derived class without modifying any existing programs. Suggestion 11 in Appendix C gives a detailed example of this technique.

With C++, the `switch` statement should be viewed with some of the same suspicion as the notorious `goto`.

6.2   GEOMETRY EXAMPLE

Object-oriented programming is generally useful, but is particularly suited for interactive graphics, simulation, and systems programming applications. In this chapter, we will develop a simple graphics program for drawing some two-dimensional geometric figures.

6.2.1   Class `Point`

Our example uses an abstract data type, class `Point`, for performing operations on x-y coordinate pairs:

---

[1] C programmers use the `switch` statement to realize the same control structure known as CASE in languages such as Pascal, Modula-2, and Ada.

```
// ex6-1.c - Geometry class hierarchy

class Point {
    int xc,yc;        // x-y coordinates
public:
    Point()                    { xc = yc = 0; }
    Point(int newx, int newy)  { xc=newx; yc=newy; }
    int x() const              { return xc; }
    int x(int newx)            { return xc = newx; }
    int y() const              { return yc; }
    int y(int newy)            { return yc = newy; }
    Point operator+(const Point& p) const {
        return Point(xc+p.xc, yc+p.yc);
    }
    void operator+=(const Point& p) {
        xc += p.x();
        yc += p.y();
    }
    void printOn(ostream& strm=cout) const;
};

void Point::printOn(ostream& strm) const
{
    strm << '(' << xc << ',' << yc << ')';
}

ostream& operator<<(ostream& strm, const Point& p)
{
    p.printOn(strm);
    return strm;
}
```

Class `Point` uses no features of C++ that we did not discuss in Part 1.

6.2.2 Class `Line` and class `Circle`

Our graphics program example also requires some classes for representing various geometric shapes, such as `Line`, `Triangle`, `Rectangle`, and `Circle`. All of these classes implement some of the same member functions, for example `draw()` and `move()`, and they all have a member variable, `org`, that holds the coordinates of the shape's origin. We might begin by writing representative class declarations for class `Line` and class `Circle` that look like this:

```
class Line {
    Point org;       // origin
    Point p;         // end point
```

```
public:
    Line(const Point& a, const Point& b) : org(a), p(b) {}
    void move(const Point& d);   // move Line by amount d
    void draw() const;           // draw Line from org to p
};

class Circle {
    Point org;        // origin
    int rad;          // radius of circle
public:
    Circle(const Point& c, int r) : org(c) { rad = r; }
    void move(const Point& d);   // move Line by amount d
    void draw() const;           // draw Circle with center org
                                 // and radius rad
};
```

6.2.3 Class instances as member variables

Before we develop this example further, we will discuss two features of C++ that we have
not mentioned before that classes `Line` and `Circle` illustrate. We see that an instance
of a class can be a member variable of another class: the member variables `Line::org`,
`Line::p`, and `Circle::org` are instances of class `Point`. When this occurs, the class's
constructors may need to use a special notation, called an *initializer list*, to initialize the
member variables that appear as class instances. Between the function argument list and
function body, we write the name of the member variable we wish to initialize, followed
by a list of the arguments we wish to pass to that member's constructor:

```
Line(const Point& a, const Point& b) : org(a), p(b) {}

Circle(const Point& c, int r) : org(c) { rad = r; }
```

A constructor's initializer list is processed *before* the statements in its body are executed.
We might have also written

```
Circle(const Point& c, int r)
{
    org = c;
    rad = r;
}
```

but this is probably not as efficient. Remember, if a class declares one or more constructors,
then C++ guarantees that one of them will be called to initialize every instance of the class.
Remember also that the assignment `org = c` assumes that `org` is already initialized. When
we do not explicitly specify constructor arguments when creating an instance of a class
with constructors, then C++ will call the constructor that has *no* arguments to initialize the
instance—in this situation, it is an error unless the class has a constructor with no arguments
(or, equivalently, a constructor that has defaults for all arguments). So if we "initialize" the

member variable `org` with the assignment `org = c` rather than by using the notation `: org(c)`, the C++ compiler will first call the constructor `Point::Point()`, which sets the point's x and y coordinates to 0, then immediately replace these with the values of the x and y coordinates of c. If `Point::Point()` is an inline function, as it is here, an optimizing C++ compiler may be able to eliminate the unnecessary assignments; however, if `Point::Point()` is not inline, any optimization is unlikely, so it is good practice to explicitly initialize member variables that are class instances rather than using assignment.

Thus, we see that member variables of a class may themselves be instances of other classes, and when they are, you should initialize them in a constructor's initializer list rather than in the body of a constructor.

6.2.4 Class `TransformStack`

A feature of our example graphics program is that it will keep track of a *current transformation*, which it will apply automatically to any shape we draw. For this example, the transformation is simply a distance, represented by an instance of class `Point`, by which shapes will be translated in x and y when drawn. Real graphics packages often have a similar feature to allow programmers to establish a current transformation that controls not only translation, but also scaling and rotation, but we will omit this generality to keep the example brief.

Since it is often convenient to set a new transformation, draw some shapes, and then restore whatever transformation was previously in effect, the current transformation is just the top of a stack of transformations. To set a new transformation, we push it on the transformation stack; to restore the previous transformation, we pop the stack.

It is also useful to combine a new transformation we wish to set with the transformation currently in effect, so as we push a new translation on the stack, we will add it to the current translation.

Class `TransformStack` incorporates all of these features:

```
class TransformStack {
    Point s[100];    // array to hold stack of points
    Point* top;      // current top of stack
public:
    TransformStack()         { top = s; }
    Point* current() const   { return top; }
    void push(const Point& p) {
        *++top = *top + p;
    }
    void pop()               { top-; }
};
```

The member array s holds the stack of points, and the member variable `top` points to the `Point` currently on the top of the stack. All of the points in array s are automatically initialized to (0,0) since C++ uses the default constructor, in this case `Point::Point()`, to initialize the elements of an array of class instances. The constructor for class `TransformStack` initializes `top` to point to the first `Point` of the array.

The transformation stack for our example is kept in the global variable `transform`:

```
TransformStack transform;    // shape translation stack
```

To draw a shape translated by the amount (12,34) relative to the current translation, for example, we write:

```
Point p (12,34);
transform.push(p);   // set new translation
// call draw()
transform.pop();     // restore previous translation
```

6.2.5   The member function `move()`

The member functions `Line::move()` and `Circle::move()` accept an x-y displacement represented by a `Point` as an argument, and add this to their member variables:

```
void Line::move(const Point& d)
{
    org += d;
    p += d;
}

void Circle::move(const Point& d)
{
    org += d;
}
```

6.2.6   The member function `draw()`

The implementations of the member functions of class `Line` and class `Circle` are complete except for those of `Line::draw()` and `Circle::draw()`. To keep this example short, we will not go into the details of exactly how to draw these shapes on a particular graphics device, so we will use implementations that just print the kind of shape and its coordinates:

```
void Line::draw() const
{
    cout << "Line from " << *transform.current() + org
         << " to " << *transform.current() + p << endl;
}

void Circle::draw() const
{
    cout << "Circle with center " << *transform.current() + org
         << " and radius " << rad << endl;
}
```

Both functions translate the coordinates of the shapes they draw by the amount specified by the top of the transform stack.

6.2.7 Class Shape

There are a couple of things we would like to be able to do with related classes such as Line and Circle. First, it would be useful to have an abstract data type called Picture that would be a collection of Lines, Triangles, Rectangles, and Circles. Second, we would like to be able to draw() and move() our Pictures.

It would be most elegant if class Picture were general, and contained no mention of the specific shapes. That way, we could introduce a new shape, say a Pentagon, and not have to change class Picture in any way, or even recompile it. We can do this by defining a base class Shape with derived classes Line, Triangle, and so on, as shown in Figure 6.2.

Our first version of class Shape declares functions, such as draw() and move(), that we can apply to any kind of shape as *virtual functions*, and it implements these functions to write out an error message if called:

```
class Shape {
public:
    virtual void move(const Point&);
    virtual void draw() const;
};

void Shape::move(const Point&)
{
    cerr << "Forgot to implement move()!\n";
    exit(1);
}
```

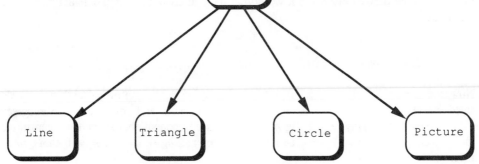

Figure 6.2 Class hierarchy for Example 6-1

```
void Shape::draw() const
{
    cerr << "Forgot to implement draw()!\n";
    exit(1);
}
```

We change the declarations of classes Line, Circle, and so on to make them derived classes of class Shape by adding the name of the base class, Shape, to the declarations of the derived classes:

```
class Line: public Shape {
    Point org;       // origin
    Point p;         // end point
public:
    Line(const Point& a, const Point& b) : org(a), p(b) {}
    virtual void move(const Point&);
    virtual void draw() const;
};
```

```
class Circle: public Shape {
    Point org;       // origin
    int rad;         // radius of circle
public:
    Circle(const Point& c, int r) : org(c) { rad = r; }
    virtual void move(const Point&);
    virtual void draw() const;
};
```

Using the keyword public before the name of the base class makes the public members of the base class public members of the derived class so that clients of the derived class may access them. If we omit the keyword public, public members of the base class become private members of the derived class, and clients of the derived class cannot access them.

We also add the keyword virtual to the declarations of the functions draw() and move() in the derived classes, but we do not have to change the implementation of these functions.[2]

6.2.8 Class Picture

Now we can write class Picture to deal only with class Shape and not its derived classes Line, Triangle, Rectangle, Circle, and so on. We can represent a Picture by an array containing pointers to its component shapes, and we can implement Picture::draw(), for example, simply by calling draw() for each shape in the picture:

---

[2] The keyword virtual is *required* only in the function declarations in the base class. It may be omitted for the functions in a derived class—we consider it good programming style because it makes it possible to tell which functions are virtual without having to look at the declarations of base classes.

```
const unsigned PICTURE_CAPACITY = 100;

class Picture: public Shape {
    Point org;                      // origin
    Shape* s[PICTURE_CAPACITY];     // array of pointers to shapes
    int n;                          // number of shapes in this Picture
public:
    Picture() : org(0,0)        { n = 0; }  // constructor
    Picture(Point& o) : org(o)  { n = 0; }  // constructor
    void add(Shape&);                       // add Shape to Picture
    virtual void move(const Point& d)    { org += d; }
    virtual void draw() const;              // draw picture;
};


void Picture::add(Shape& t)
{
    if (n == PICTURE_CAPACITY) {
        cerr << "Picture capacity exceeded\n";
        exit(1);
    }
    s[n++] = &t;          // add pointer to Shape to Picture
}


void Picture::draw() const   // draw a Picture
{
    transform.push(org);
    for (int i=0; i<n; i++) s[i]->draw();
    transform.pop();
}
```

Since draw() is a virtual function, C++ takes care of figuring out the specific class of each component Shape when the program is executed and calling the appropriate implementation of draw() for that class. This is called *dynamic binding*, in contrast to non-virtual function calls, which employ *static binding*. For example, if at execution time s[i] points to an instance of a Line, then the expression s[i]->draw() calls Line::draw(); if s[i] points to an instance of a Circle, then it calls Circle::draw(), and so on. We can demonstrate how this works with the following program:

```
main()
{
    Line l(Point(1,2),Point(3,4));  // create a Line
    Circle c(Point(5,6),1);         // create a Circle
    l.draw();                       // draw the line
    c.draw();                       // draw the circle
    Picture p;                      // create an empty Picture
    l.move(Point(1,0));             // move the line
    p.add(l);                       // add the line to the picture
```

```
    c.move(Point(1,0));            // move the circle
    p.add(c);                      // add it to the picture
    p.draw();                      // draw the picture
    p.move(Point(10,10));          // translate it by (10,10)
    p.draw();                      // draw it again
}
```

When run, this program prints:

```
Line from (1,2) to (3,4)
Circle with center (5,6) and radius 1
Line from (2,2) to (4,4)
Circle with center (6,6) and radius 1
Line from (12,12) to (14,14)
Circle with center (16,16) and radius 1
```

Dynamic binding of a virtual function call takes place only when the virtual function is applied to a pointer or a reference to an object, as in `Picture::draw()`, and not when it is applied directly to an object:

```
void drawIt(Shape& reference)
{
    Line line(Point(1,2),Point(3,4));
    Shape* pointer = &line;
    // ...
    pointer->draw();    // dynamically bound
    reference.draw();   // dynamically bound
    line.draw();        // statically bound
}
```

At execution time, the variables `pointer` and `reference` can potentially point to an instance of any derived class of `Shape`, so C++ must use dynamic binding to determine which derived class's implementation of `draw()` to call. However, the variable `line` *must* be an instance of class `Line`, so C++ can statically bind the call `line.draw()` to `Line::draw()` and avoid the overhead of dynamic binding.

6.2.9   Type compatibility

You may be wondering why the C++ compiler does not complain about an argument type mismatch on function calls like `p.add(1)` and `p.add(c)`. After all, the declaration for `Picture::add()` specifies that this function requires an argument of type `Shape&`, and the arguments for these two calls are of type `Line` and `Circle`, respectively. C++ allows this because `Line` and `Circle` are derived classes of class `Shape`. In general, C++ allows a reference or pointer to an instance of a derived class to be used in place of a reference or pointer to an instance of its base class without requiring an explicit type cast,[3] thus we call a derived class a *subtype* of its base class. Subtyping is useful, and does not compromise safety because a derived class inherits all the member variables and functions

---

[3] Unless the base class is a private base class.

of its base class; thus, a reference to any member variable or call of any member function of an instance of the base class is equally well defined for an instance of the derived class. So in this example, we think of Line, Circle, and so forth as all being different kinds (subtypes) of Shapes.

The opposite is not, however, true: C++ will not permit a reference or pointer to an instance of a base class to be used in place of a reference or pointer to an instance of a derived class. This reflects that while a Line or Circle is a kind of a Shape, a Shape is not a kind of Line or Circle.

6.2.10 Pure virtual functions

Before moving ahead, we are going to make a small improvement to the class Shape we described in Section 6.2.7. The motivation for this improvement arises from what would happen if we mistakenly forgot to implement draw() for a derived class of Shape: the class would inherit the implementation of draw() from class Shape, and when we attempted to draw that shape, Shape::draw() would be executed, printing an error message.

There are two problems with this. First, it would be better if the C++ compiler detected our omission when it compiled the program; otherwise, if we did not test it thoroughly, it might not be detected until after we delivered it to some unfortunate user! Second, it seems wasteful to be writing dummy member functions that only print out error messages. To solve these problems we can write class Shape as follows:

```
class Shape {
public:
    virtual void move(const Point&) =0;
    virtual void draw() const =0;
};
```

The =0 initializer in the declarations for move() and draw() indicates to the C++ compiler that these are *pure virtual functions*: virtual functions that a base class cannot implement, and that therefore must be defined by the derived class. There are two consequences of declaring a pure virtual function in a base class:

- The C++ compiler checks each derived class to be sure that it either implements the base class's pure virtual function, or defers its implementation again by also declaring it as a pure virtual function to be implemented by one of its derived classes.

- A class with one or more pure virtual functions is incomplete—if you applied one of its pure virtual functions to an instance of it, it would not be able to perform the function because it has no implementation to execute. To prevent this, C++ does not allow instances of classes with pure virtual functions to be constructed, except as part of a derived class. Thus, writing

```
Shape s;
```

would elicit an error message from the C++ compiler.

This solves the problems we described with our original class Shape.

6.2.11 Subpictures

Since class `Picture` has member functions `draw()` and `move()` just like class `Line` and `Circle`, we can think of a `Picture` as being just another kind of shape, so we can make it a derived class of `Shape` also. Doing this allows us to build a more complicated picture out of a number of simpler pictures:

```
main()
{
    Picture bigPic;
    Picture littlePic1, littlePic2(*new Point(10,10));
    littlePic1.add(*new Line(Point(1,1),Point(2,2)));
    littlePic1.add(*new Circle(Point(3,3),1));
    littlePic2.add(*new Line(Point(4,4),Point(5,5)));
    littlePic2.add(*new Circle(Point(3,3),2));
    littlePic2.move(Point(1,1));
    bigPic.add(littlePic1);
    bigPic.add(littlePic2);
    bigPic.draw();
}
```

Running this example prints:

```
Line from (1,1) to (2,2)
Circle with center (3,3) and radius 1
Line from (15,15) to (16,16)
Circle with center (14,14) and radius 2
```

Drawing a picture that contains subpictures utilizes the `transform` stack we described earlier.

Some readers may find it confusing that instances of class `Picture` can contain other shapes like lines and circles even though classes `Line` and `Circle` are not derived from class `Picture`. Remember, however, that the class inheritance hierarchy describes only one type of relationship between classes. One class may also be a client of another, as when one class contains a member variable that is an instance of another class, or a member variable that is a pointer to an instance of another class, and simply invokes the member functions that class provides. Class `Picture` uses pointers to instances of other classes to "contain" them, and this client relationship is independent of, and not restricted by, the inheritance hierarchy relationship. We will encounter this topic again in Chapter 9 when we discuss how to organize classes.

6.3   IMPROVED GEOMETRY EXAMPLE

In the next step in the development of our example graphics program, we take advantage of all of the derived classes of `Shape` having a common member variable, `org`. This means that we can move this member variable from the derived classes to their base class, `Shape`.

The member function Shape::move() can do something useful now, namely, adjust org, so it no longer is a pure virtual function. The base class Shape now looks like this:

```
// ex6-2.c - Improved geometry class hierarchy

class Shape {
    Point org;       // origin
public:
    Shape(const Point& p) : org(p)  {}
    Point origin() const              { return org; }
    virtual void move(const Point& d)    { org += d; }
    virtual void draw() const =0;
};
```

Since class Shape now has a member variable, we provided a constructor to initialize it and the member function origin() to read its value.

Using this definition of class Shape we can simplify derived classes Line, Circle, and Picture, since they will inherit the member variable org and the member functions origin(), move(), and draw() from class Shape:

```
class Line: public Shape {
    Point p;         // end point
public:
    Line(const Point& a, const Point& b) : Shape(a), p(b) {}
    virtual void move(const Point&);
    virtual void draw() const;
};

void Line::move(const Point& d)
{
    Shape::move(d);
    p += d;
}

void Line::draw() const
{
    cout << "Line from " << *transform.current() + origin()
         << " to " << *transform.current() + p << endl;
}

class Circle: public Shape {
    int rad;         // radius of circle
public:
    Circle(const Point& c, int r) : Shape(c) { rad = r; }
    virtual void draw() const;
};
```

```
void Circle::draw() const
{
    cout << "Circle with center "
         << *transform.current() + origin()
         << " and radius " << rad << endl;
}


const unsigned PICTURE_CAPACITY = 100;

class Picture : public Shape {
    Shape* s[PICTURE_CAPACITY]; // array of pointers to shapes
    int n;                      // number of shapes in this Picture
public:
    Picture() : Shape(Point(0,0))    { n = 0; } // constructor
    Picture(Point& org) : Shape(org) { n = 0; } // constructor
    void add(Shape&);                     // add Shape to Picture
    virtual void draw() const;            // draw picture;
};

void Picture::add(Shape& t)
{
    if (n == PICTURE_CAPACITY) {
        cerr << "Picture capacity exceeded\n";
        exit(1);
    }
    s[n++] = &t;          // add pointer to Shape to Picture
}

void Picture::draw() const  // draw a Picture
{
    transform.push(origin());
    for (int i=0; i<n; i++) s[i]->draw();
    transform.pop();
}
```

While class `Circle` can simply inherit `Shape::move()`, class `Line` cannot since it must also adjust the other end point p when moved, so it overrides the inherited `Shape::move()` by defining `Line::move()` to call `Shape::move()` to move org before it moves p.

6.3.1   Object initialization

The constructors for classes `Line`, `Circle`, and `Picture` illustrate how a derived class can pass arguments to a constructor of its base class. We write the name of the base class followed by its constructor's argument list, enclosed in parentheses, in the initializer list of the derived class's constructors:

```
Line(const Point& a, const Point& b) : Shape(a), p(b) {}

Circle(const Point& c, int r) : Shape(c) { rad = r; }

Picture() : Shape(Point(0,0))        { n = 0; }

Picture(Point& org) : Shape(org)     { n = 0; }
```

In this example, this is how the constructors of classes derived from `Shape` initialize `Shape::org` from their arguments.

The rules that determine the order in which C++ initializes the base and member variable class instances in an object are somewhat complex. The order of initialization in the case where classes have at most a single base class is:

1. the base class, if any;

2. member variables, in the order in which they are declared in the class declaration, *not* in the order they appear in the constructor's initializer list.

What complicates this is that C++ applies these rules recursively; for example, if the base class has a base class, C++ will initialize the base class's base class and any members it contains before initializing the base class. The following example shows the order in which constructors are called during the initialization of a complex object:

```
// ex6-3.c - Order of construction of base and member classes

#include <iostream.h>

class X {
    int i;
public:
    X(const char* s)    { cout << s << ' '; }
    X()                 { cout << "X::X() "; }
};

class A {
    X a1;
    X a2;
public:
    A(const char* s): a2("A::a2") { cout << s << ' '; }
};

class B: public A {
    X b1;
    X b2;
public:
    B(const char* s):
```

```
        b2("B::b2"),
        b1("B::b1"),
        A("B::A")    { cout << s << ' '; }
};

int initCi()
{
    cout << "C::i ";
    return 0;
}

int& initCr()
{
    static int n = 1;
    cout << "C::r ";
    return n;
}

class C: public B {
    const int i;
    int& r;
    X c1;
    X c2;
public:
    C(const char* s):
        B("C::B"),
        c1("C::c1"),
        r(initCr()),
        i(initCi()),
        c2("C::c2") { cout << s << endl; }
};

main()
{
    C c("c");
}
```

The output of this program is:

```
X::X() A::a2 B::A B::b1 B::b2 C::B C::i C::r C::c1 C::c2 c
```

We suggest that you take a few moments to study this example and demonstrate for yourself how the rules we just gave produce these results.

This example also shows how to initialize const and reference member variables (C::i and C::r in this case)—they *must* be initialized by the constructor's initialization list.

Multiple inheritance complicates the rules for initialization even more, but we will deal with that subject later, in Section 13.8.

6.3.2 Object finalization

The rule C++ uses to determine the order in which it calls destructors is simple: destructors are called in the reverse order of the constructors. This explains why C++ ignores the order of the members in the initialization list and uses the order of the members in the class declaration instead: a class may have several constructors, and each of those constructors could order the members in its initialization list in a different way. When it is time to destroy an object, the destructor does not know which constructor, and therefore which initialization list, was used to create the object. Using the order of the members in the class declaration avoids this problem and allows the destructors for member class instances to be called in reverse order regardless of which constructor created the object.

6.3.3 Calling virtual functions from a base class constructor

While the base class of an object is begin initialized and the constructor initialization list is being processed, the object under construction is incomplete, and this effects the behavior of virtual function calls. Consider the following example program:

```
// ex6-4.c - Calling a virtual function from a
//            base class constructor

#include <iostream.h>

class A {
public:
    virtual void vf();
};

void A::vf()    { cout << "A::vf()" << endl; }

class B: public A {
public:
    B()         { vf(); }   // Calls A::vf(), not C::vf()
};

class C: public B {
public:
    C()         { vf(); }   // Calls C::vf()
    virtual void vf();
};

void C::vf()    { cout << "B::vf()" << endl; }

main()
{
    C c;
}
```

While `B::B()` is executing, the object `c` is only partially initialized, so C++ treats it as though it were an instance of class `B` rather than an instance of class `C`. This causes the call to the virtual function `vf()` in `B::B()` to be dynamically bound to `A::vf()` instead of `C::vf()`, resulting in the following output from the program:

```
A::vf()
B::vf()
```

6.4 OBJECT-ORIENTED PROGRAMMING TERMINOLOGY

Let us take a moment to introduce some terminology for the concepts we have been discussing.

6.4.1 Single and multiple inheritance

As we mentioned earlier, a base class may have one or more derived classes, which in turn may serve as base classes for their own derived classes. This process may be repeated indefinitely, producing a hierarchical, or tree-structured, arrangement of classes, as shown in Figure 6.1. When classes have at most one base class we refer to this as *single inheritance*; i.e., a class may inherit directly from at most a single class. C++ also permits a class to have more than one base class; we refer to this as *multiple inheritance*. We will discuss multiple inheritance in Chapter 13.

Even with single inheritance, a class may inherit members from several other classes because it inherits from its base class, its base class's base class, and so on until the class at the root of the tree is reached. We call the classes from which a derived class inherits its *ancestor* classes. For example, in Example 6-3 classes A and B are class C's ancestor classes. Similarly, we refer to the classes that inherit from a base class its *descendent* classes. For example, in Example 6-3 classes B and C are class A's descendents. In C++, the descendents of a class are also subtypes of the class; that is, a pointer or reference to an instance of a descendent of a class is type-compatible with a pointer or reference to an instance of the class itself.[4]

6.4.2 Abstract classes

The only purpose of some classes is to serve as base classes—it does not make sense for client programs to construct instances of such classes. Class `Shape` is an example of this kind of class. We call classes that should be used only as base classes *abstract* classes.

Not all base classes are abstract classes, however. For example, we might implement a class for drawing circular arcs as a derived class of class `Circle`:

```
class Arc : public Circle {
    float start, stop; // starting and stopping angle of arc
```

---

[4] This description assumes public base classes—a derived class with a private base class is not a subtype of that base class.

```
public:
    Arc(const Point& c, int r, float a1, float a2) : (c,r) {
        start = a1; stop = a2;
    }
    virtual void draw();
};
```

Instances of class `Circle` are still useful themselves, even though we used `Circle` as a base class for class `Arc`.

The development of class `Arc` also illustrates how a class hierarchy can grow by the process of specialization of existing classes, which we mentioned at the beginning of this chapter.

6.4.3 Protected members

There are two ways in which we can prevent client programs from inadvertently constructing instances of an abstract class such as `Shape`:

1. we can declare a pure virtual member function in the class; or,

2. we can use a feature of C++ that we have not yet discussed and make all of an abstract class's constructors *protected members*:

```
class Shape {
    Point org;          // origin
protected:
    Shape(const Point& p) : org(p)   {}
public:
    Point origin() const                    { return org; }
    virtual void move(const Point& d)   { org += d; }
    virtual void draw() const =0;
};
```

Only members and friends of a class, or members and friends of its derived classes, can access protected members. This is just what we need in this situation: ordinary client programs cannot construct instances of class `Shape` because they are not allowed to use its constructor; however, classes derived from `Shape`, which do need to call `Shape::Shape(const Point&)` to initialize `org`, may do so because the constructor is protected.

Of course, since `Shape::draw()` is a pure virtual function, we do not really need to make `Shape::Shape()` protected in this example, as we discussed in Section 6.2.10; however, we consider it good style to do so anyway. It explicitly documents the access restriction on the constructors, and it prevents instances of an abstract class from being constructed by clients in the event that the abstract class happens to have no pure virtual member functions, or they are removed or implemented later in the class's development.

Protected members have many other uses which we will present in later chapters.

6.4.4 Polymorphism

An instance of class `Picture` is an example of a *polymorphic data structure*. We call it this because it is not restricted to containing instances of a single class, but can contain instances of any mixture of classes, as long as each of these classes has class `Shape` as an ancestor. Similarly, a virtual member function of a base class such as `Shape::draw()` is called a *polymorphic function* because we can apply it to instances of a variety of classes, not to just a single class of object. Specifically, we can apply `Shape::draw()` to an instance of any class that has class `Shape` as an ancestor. Polymorphic functions are, of course, useful when working with polymorphic data structures, as you can see from the implementation of `Picture::draw()` in our example.

Programming languages that support polymorphic data structures and polymorphic functions are said to support *polymorphism*.

6.5 CHAPTER SUMMARY

In this chapter, we introduced the concept of object-oriented programming, and described its key characteristics: encapsulation, inheritance, and dynamic binding. Next, we introduced the C++ mechanisms for inheritance and dynamic binding: derived classes and virtual functions. In the geometry example, we showed how these features are typically used to do object-oriented programming in C++. In the context of this example, we defined the following terms:

- *single inheritance*: the situation in which classes have at most one base class;

- *multiple inheritance*: the ability for a derived class to inherit member functions and variables from more than one base class;

- *ancestor classes*: the classes from which a derived class inherits member functions and variables;

- *descendent classes*: the classes which inherit member functions and variables from a base class;

- *subtypes*: the descendents of a class are also subtypes of the class, which means that a pointer or reference to an instance of a descendent of a class is type-compatible with a pointer or reference to an instance of the class itself;

- *abstract classes*: classes that can serve only as base classes;

- *pure virtual functions*: virtual functions that an abstract class does not implement, and which therefore must be implemented by a derived class;

- *protected members*: member functions and variables that only members and friends of a class and its derived classes can access;

- *polymorphic data structures*: data structures that can contain instances of a mixture of classes; and,

- *polymorphic functions*: member functions that can be applied to instances of a variety of classes.

7

AN INTRODUCTION TO THE NIH
CLASS LIBRARY

7.1 INTRODUCTION

In the previous chapter, we saw how to organize related classes into hierarchies and take advantage of their similarities by using C++ derived classes and virtual functions. Of course, once we have a collection of generally useful classes the next logical step is to place them into a library so that they can be shared by many client programs. When creating a library, it is desirable to establish some conventions so that library classes behave consistently and work together, and so that programmers who wish to write new classes for the library have guidelines to follow.

One way to achieve consistency and compatibility among classes is to define a class named, say, `Object` and make nearly *every* class a descendent of it. In class `Object` we can declare virtual functions that apply to all classes—functions for copying, printing, storing, reading, and comparing objects, for example. We then can define polymorphic data structures composed of objects and functions that operate on objects that will be useful for all classes derived from `Object`, just as class `Picture` could work with any derived class of `Shape`, as we saw in the Geometry example in the previous chapter.

The result is that all classes belong to a single tree with class `Object` as the root. We have written a library of over 60 general-purpose classes, modeled after the basic classes of the Smalltalk-80 programming language. The library, called the *NIH Class Library* (NIHCL), contains classes such as `String`, `Date`, `Time`, `Set` (hash tables), `Dictionary` (associative arrays), and `LinkedList`. We described some of the simpler classes, `String`, `Regex`, `Date`, and `Time`, in Chapter 5, and we will introduce classes to accommodate polymorphic data structures, which represent most of the more complicated classes in the NIH Class Library, in Chapter 8. Appendix A gives a complete list of the classes available in the NIH Class Library.

Writing C++ programs using a class library such as this is highly productive. The classes are general-purpose, and most programs of any size will have uses for some of them. They are flexible—if a particular class does not quite do what is needed it is usually a simple matter to derive a class that does. And the library is extensible, since it provides a framework that makes it easy to add your own custom classes and make them function along with existing ones.

7.2 GEOMETRY EXAMPLE USING NIH
LIBRARY CLASSES

As an example, let us see how the NIH Class Library can help us with the graphics package we have been discussing.

The NIH Class Library contains three classes that we can use to improve our example: `Point`, `Stack`, and `OrderedCltn`. To use these classes we include their specifications in the program source file:

```
// ex7-1.c - Geometry class hierarchy using NIH Class Library

#include "Point.h"
#include "Stack.h"
#include "OrderedCltn.h"
```

When we link any program that uses our graphics package, we will also link it with the NIH Class Library to incorporate the object modules of any NIH Library classes that we may need.

7.2.1 NIH Library class `Point`

The NIH Library class `Point` abstracts *xy* coordinates similarly to the class `Point` we introduced in Chapter 6. To use it, we include its specification and delete the version of class `Point` we have been using until now. No other changes are necessary.

7.2.2 NIH Library class `Stack`

In our original example, we implemented the `transform` stack with an array of `Point` objects, and indicated the current top of the stack with a pointer. This implementation is deficient because we did not allow for (or even check for) stack overflow. We can replace this with an instance of the NIH Library class `Stack` that holds pointers to instances of class `Point`:

```
class TransformStack {
    Stack s;
public:
    TransformStack()          { s.push(*new Point(0,0)); }
    Point* current() const    { return (Point*)s.top(); }
    void push(const Point& p) { s.push(*new Point(*current()+p)); }
    void pop()                { delete (Point*)s.pop(); }
};
```

Class `Stack` defines the member functions `push()`, `pop()`, and `top()` for pushing, popping, and referencing the top object on the stack. We have changed class `TransformStack` to use an instance of the NIH Library class `Stack` to hold the stack of `Point` objects, and we have rewritten the member functions of class `TransformStack` to call class `Stack`'s member functions. The advantage of this implementation of `TransformStack` is that class `Stack` will automatically allocate more memory for the stack if needed.

Since we properly encapsulated our transformation stack in class `TransformStack` in our first version of the example and we have not changed its specification, only its implementation, we do not need to change any of the classes that use it.

Although using the NIH Library class `Stack` to implement `TransformStack` makes it more robust, it does not simplify the code, and it is less efficient than our original version because it uses `new` and `delete` to allocate and deallocate memory for the `Point` objects kept on the stack. Class `Stack` manages pointers to objects instead of the objects themselves so it can be polymorphic, but this generality, which class `TransformStack` does not need, is achieved at a sacrifice of efficiency and complexity. In Chapter 14 we will describe *parameterized types*, a feature planned for a future release of C++ which may make it possible to design classes like `Stack`, but that are highly efficient when polymorphism is not needed.

7.2.3   NIH Library class `OrderedCltn`

Our previous implementation of class `Picture` allocated an array of fixed size to hold the pointers to its component shapes. We can use the NIH Library class `OrderedCltn` to make this a variable-length array. An `OrderedCltn` is an array of pointers to `Objects`, so we can use it to hold pointers to instances of any class derived from `Object`, just as we used an array of pointers to `Shapes` to hold pointers to `Lines`, `Triangles`, and so on. To use class `OrderedCltn` in our example, we must derive class `Shape` from class `Object`.

7.2.4   Deriving a class from class `Object`

To write a class that is a descendent of class `Object` we must declare and implement a minimum of about 20 member functions so that it behaves like an `Object` and is compatible with other NIH Library classes. This is not really difficult—the specification file for class `Object` provides several preprocessor macros that take care of about 15 of the required functions, and the rest are usually easy to write. We will describe exactly how to do this in later chapters, but for purposes of this example, we will omit most of these details since they clutter up the code. Of course, you can see the complete example in the files `ex7-1.h` and `ex7-1.c`.

To make class `Shape` a derived class of `Object`, we indicate that class `Object` is its base class by adding `: public Object` after the class name `Shape` in the class declaration:

```
class Shape: public Object {
// ...
    Point org;          // origin
protected:
    Shape(const Point& p) : org(p)   {}
public:
    Point origin() const                { return org; }
    virtual void move(const Point& d)   { org += d; }
    virtual void draw() const = 0;
// ...
};
```

7.2.5 Implementation of class `Picture` using class `OrderedCltn`

Now we can write class `Picture` as:

```
class Picture: public Shape {
// ...
    OrderedCltn s;          // collection of pointers to shapes
public:
    Picture() : Shape(Point(0,0)) {}     // constructor
    Picture(Point& org) : Shape(org) {} // constructor
    void add(Shape&);                    // add Shape to Picture
    virtual void draw() const;           // draw picture;
};
```

Class `OrderedCltn` defines member functions such as `add()`, `remove()`, `size()`, `first()`, and `last()` to let us manipulate the pointers in the array. It also overloads the subscript operator `[]` so we can subscript `OrderedCltn`s like arrays. Using these we can write the functions `Picture::add()` and `Picture::draw` as follows:

```
void Picture::add(Shape& t)
{
    s.add(t);               // calls OrderedCltn::add()
}


void Picture::draw() const       // draw a Picture
{
    transform.push(origin());
    for (int i=0; i<s.size(); i++) // s.size() is # of
                                   // objects in s
        ((Shape*)s[i])->draw();    // cast address of ith object
                                   // to Shape* and call draw()
    transform.pop();
}
```

To draw the `Shape` pointed to by the pointer at position i in the `OrderedCltn` s we cannot simply write

```
s[i]->draw();
```

because `s[i]` returns a reference to an `Object*`, and class `Object` does not have a member function `draw()`. We must cast the `Object*` to a `Shape*` before applying `draw()`:

```
((Shape*)s[i])->draw();
```

A cast of a pointer to a base class to a pointer to a descendent class, which we call a *downward cast*, is potentially dangerous—if the pointer does not really point to an instance of the class we say it does, C++ will misinterpret the member variables in that instance, usually with an undesirable outcome. However, in this example the downward cast is safe because only `Picture::add()` adds objects to s, and the type of its argument t guarantees that it only places `Shape`s in s. Often, however, there is no such assurance that a downward cast is safe, which is why the NIH Class Library provides a mechanism for checking the class of an object at execution time. We will describe this facility in Chapter 8.

By using class `OrderedCltn`, `Pictures` can have as many shapes in them as we need; class `OrderedCltn` manages the required storage for us.

Once again, proper practice of encapsulation confines the changes to class `Picture`.

7.3 COPYING OBJECTS

As we said in Section 7.1, class `Object` defines some useful operations that you can apply to any class derived from `Object`. In this section and the next, we describe two of the more complicated operations, object copying and object I/O, to illustrate how the classes in a library such as the NIH Class Library cooperate to implement them. You will see how these operations are divided among class-independent and class-dependent member functions, with class `Object` implementing the class-independent functions, and each class implementing those that are class-specific.

Class `Object` defines the functions `shallowCopy()`, and `deepCopy()`, which copy objects. Both of these functions return a pointer (an `Object*`) to a copy of the object to which they are applied. These functions construct the copy in the free store using `new`, and the client is responsible for deleting the copy.

The functions `shallowCopy()` and `deepCopy()` differ in how they copy objects that contain pointers to other objects. The function `shallowCopy()` copies only the object you apply it to. If it contains pointers to other objects the *pointers* are copied, *not* the objects they point to, which become shared by the original object and its copy, as Figure 7.1 shows. The function `deepCopy()` copies the object you apply it to, *and* any objects it might contain pointers to, *and* any objects that they might contain pointers to, and so on. The result is that the original object and its copy will share *no* objects, as Figure 7.2 shows.

The following program illustrates the operation of `shallowCopy()` and `deepCopy()` when applied to instances of class `Picture`.

```
// ex7-2.c - Improved geometry class hierarchy
//              using NIH class library

#include <fstream.h>
#include <osfcn.h>
#include "Point.h"
#include "Line.h"
#include "Circle.h"
#include "Picture.h"
#include "OIOnih.h"

main()
{
    Line l(Point(1,2),Point(3,4));
    Circle c(Point(5,6),1);
    Picture subPic;
    subPic.add(l);
    subPic.add(c);
```

```
    Picture bigPic;
    bigPic.add(*(Shape*)subPic.shallowCopy());
    bigPic.add(*(Shape*)subPic.deepCopy());
    bigPic.add(l);
    cout << "\n* Original bigPic:\n";
    bigPic.draw();

    subPic.move(Point(10,10));
    cout << "\n* After moving subPic:\n";
    bigPic.draw();

    l.move(Point(10,10));
    c.move(Point(10,10));
    cout << "\n* After moving l and c:\n";
    bigPic.draw();
// ...
}
```

When run, this program prints:

```
* Original bigPic:
Line from (1,2) to (3,4)
Circle with center (5,6) and radius 1

Line from (1,2) to (3,4)
Circle with center (5,6) and radius 1

Line from (1,2) to (3,4)

* After moving subPic:
Line from (1,2) to (3,4)
Circle with center (5,6) and radius 1

Line from (1,2) to (3,4)
Circle with center (5,6) and radius 1

Line from (1,2) to (3,4)

* After moving l and c:
Line from (11,12) to (13,14)
Circle with center (15,16) and radius 1

Line from (1,2) to (3,4)
Circle with center (5,6) and radius 1

Line from (11,12) to (13,14)
```

Before `copy = original.shallowCopy()`:

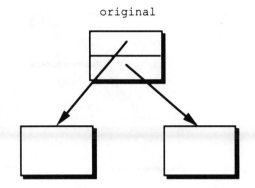

After `copy = original.shallowCopy()`:

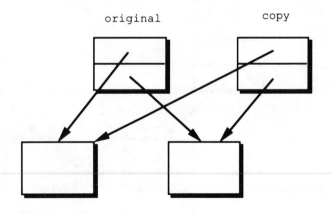

Figure 7.1 *Operation of* `shallowCopy()`

Before `copy = original.deepCopy():`

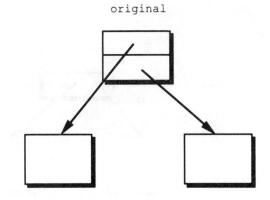

After `copy = original.deepCopy():`

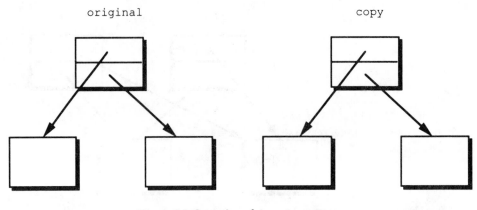

Figure 7.2 Operation of `deepCopy()`

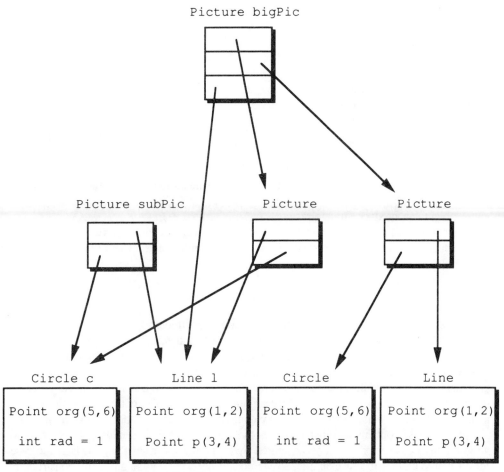

Figure 7.3 The data structure created by Example 7-2

The program in Example 7-2 creates a picture named subPic containing a line l and a circle c. It then creates another picture named bigPic and adds both a shallow and deep copy of subPic to it, along with the line l. Figure 7.3 illustrates the resulting data structure. The example shows that moving subPic, which changes only subPic.org, has no effect on bigPic because bigPic contains distinct copies of subPic; however, moving l and c does move the line and circle in the copy of subPic that shallowCopy() made and also the last line in bigPic. This demonstrates that all of these objects are indeed the same.

7.3.1 Implementation of shallowCopy()

We must use a constructor whenever we create a new object. We cannot copy an object by, for example, allocating an appropriate amount of memory and copying the original object into it byte-by-byte:

```
Object* X::badCopy()
{
    char* t = new char[sizeof(this)];
    char* dst = t;
    char* src = (char*)this;
    unsigned n = sizeof(this);
    while (n--) *dst++ = *src++;
    return (Object*)t;
}
```

This does not work in general because certain implementations of C++ maintain "hidden" pointers within objects that only constructors can properly initialize, so simply copying an entire object can produce strange results.

So how do shallowCopy() and deepCopy() work? The function shallowCopy() is a virtual function that every NIH Library class implements. The implementation of X::shallowCopy() for any class X is:

```
Object* X::shallowCopy() { return new X(*this); }
```

The expression new X(*this) calls the copy constructor X::X(const X&) (see Section 3.2.13) to construct a new instance of class X and initialize it from the argument instance. Thus, the real work of copying an object is done by the copy constructor, which C++ will automatically generate unless we provide one of our own. The copy constructor generated by C++ initializes each member variable of the new instance with the value of the corresponding member variable of the argument instance. If a member variable is itself a class instance, C++ uses that class's copy constructor to perform the initialization.

Unless a class contains member variables that are pointers, it is usually not necessary to write a copy constructor—the one generated by C++ does the right thing. This is the case for all of the classes in our example, so we do not need to provide any copy constructors for them. Furthermore, the preprocessor macros provided as part of the NIH Class Library generate the declaration and definition of shallowCopy() for each class, so we get the shallowCopy() operation without any additional effort.

7.3.2 Implementation of deepCopy()

The function deepCopy() is a non-virtual member function which class Object implements, but it relies on each class implementing the virtual function deepenShallowCopy() for its operation. First, deepCopy() calls shallowCopy() to make a shallow copy of an object, then it applies deepenShallowCopy() to the shallow copy to convert it into a deep copy.

Thus, for deepCopy() to work with our example classes, we must implement the virtual function deepenShallowCopy() for classes Shape, Line, and Picture:

```
void Shape::deepenShallowCopy()
{
    org.deepenShallowCopy();
}
```

```
void Line::deepenShallowCopy()
{
    Shape::deepenShallowCopy();
    p.deepenShallowCopy();
}

void Picture::deepenShallowCopy()
{
    Shape::deepenShallowCopy();
    s.deepenShallowCopy();
}
```

Unless a class is derived directly from class `Object`, its implementation of `deepenShallowCopy()` must first call its base class's implementation of `deepenShallowCopy()` to "deepen" the member variables of its ancestor classes. (Classes derived directly from class `Object` need not do this because class `Object` has no member variables.) Next, the function `deepenShallowCopy()` must "deepen" two kinds of member variables: those that are pointers to instances of NIH Library classes,[1] and those that are instances of NIH Library classes (since they may themselves contain pointers to instances of NIH Library classes). The function `deepenShallowCopy()` applies `deepenShallowCopy()` to member class instances to "deepen" them, as shown in the implementations for classes `Shape`, `Line`, and `Picture`, and it calls `deepCopy()` recursively to make a deep copy of class instances referenced by member pointers. Our example classes do not contain any member pointers to class instances, so here is an example of how `deepenShallowCopy()` would handle such a member:

```
class X : public Object {
    Y* p;          // Y is an NIH Library class
public:
    virtual void deepenShallowCopy();
// ...
};

void X::deepenShallowCopy()
{
    p = (Y*)p->deepCopy();   // replace pointer with
                             // pointer to copy
}
```

The function `deepCopy()` keeps a table (an instance of class `IdentDict`—see Section 8.3.11) of the addresses of all of the objects it has copied. Before actually copying an object, it consults this table to see if the object it is supposed to copy has already been copied. If so, it simply returns the address of the copy of this object from the table rather than making a

---

[1] By an NIH Library class, we mean any class that has class `Object` as an ancestor. This includes both classes in the NIH Class Library and any user-written classes derived from class `Object`.

second copy. This enables `deepCopy()` to faithfully replicate structures in which multiple pointers point to the same object, or in which objects point to one another to form a cycle.

Since class `Circle` has no member variables that are instances of NIH Library classes or pointers to instances of NIH Library classes, it does not need to implement `deepenShallowCopy()`—it can inherit it from class `Shape`.

7.3.3 Summary of object copying

The NIH Class Library provides the functions `shallowCopy()` and `deepCopy()` for making copies of objects. The function `shallowCopy()` copies only the object you apply it to—if that object contains pointers to other objects, they will be shared by the original object and its copy. The function `deepCopy()` copies an entire data structure—no objects will be shared between the original and its copy.

The implementation of the virtual function `shallowCopy()` is the same for every class. It simply uses the copy constructor for each class to construct an instance in the free storage area.

The function `deepCopy()` is implemented in class `Object`, and handles the class-independent portion of the deep copying operation—keeping track of which objects in a data structure have been copied so that multiple pointers to an object point to a single copy of that object in the copy of the data structure. However, `deepCopy()` calls the virtual function `deepenShallowCopy()`, which all derived classes must implement, to deal with member variables that are class instances or pointers to other objects. This is the class-dependent part of the deep copying operation—only a class knows which of its member variables are class instances or pointers and can access them to recursively copy them.

7.4   OBJECT I/O

One of the most powerful features of the NIH Class Library is its ability to perform object I/O: it can convert an arbitrarily complex data structure containing instances of both NIH Library classes and user-defined classes to or from a program-independent, machine-independent representation. We can store this representation of a data structure on a disk file, move it between two programs running on the same machine, or move it over a network between two programs running on different kinds of machines. This capability is particularly useful for spread sheets, forms, documents, drawings, electronic mail, and so on. The NIH Class Library also gives us a framework to use when implementing object I/O for our own classes. We do not have to spend time designing a storage format (although the storage format can be controlled if desired), or worry about such issues as what to do with the pointers in a data structure. We can use the general-purpose mechanism provided by the NIH Class Library, and concentrate on our particular application.

7.4.1   Object output

What if we wanted to save the data structure `bigPic` from the previous example on a disk file so it could be read in later and used by another program? The NIH Class Library makes this simple. We can add statements to the `main()` function in Example 7-2 that will create an output stream (an instance of class `fstream`) named `out` and write the picture to it:

```
#include <fstream.h>
#include <osfcn.h>
#include "Point.h"
#include "Line.h"
#include "Circle.h"
#include "Picture.h"
#include "OIOnih.h"

main()
{
// ...
    Picture bigPic;
// ...
    ofstream out("picturefile",ios::out,0664);
                        // UNIX protection mode 0664
    if (out.fail()) {
        cerr << "Failed to open picturefile\n";
        exit(1);
    }
    bigPic.storeOn(OIOnihout(out));
}
```

The function `storeOn()`, which is implemented in class `Object`, handles the details of finding all of the objects in `bigPic` and writing them to the output stream in a program-independent, machine-independent format that is determined by the class `OIOnihout` argument to `storeOn()`. Like the `deepCopy()` function we described in Section 7.3.2, `storeOn()` keeps a table of addresses of all objects stored. Associated with each object is an integer *object number* that uniquely identifies the object within the data structure being stored. Before storing an object, `storeOn()` consults its table to see if the object has already been stored; if so, it stores a reference to that object's number instead of another copy of the object. This allows `storeOn()` to handle complex data structures containing multiple pointers to the same object, or in which objects point to one another to form a cycle.

In addition to storing the values of an object's member variables, `storeOn()` writes out the class name of each object it stores so that the object input function, `readFrom()`, can construct the right class of object when it reads the object back in.

The `storeOn()` function calls the virtual function `storer()` to actually write out member variables. Class `Object` declares the `storer()` function, and each derived class reimplements it to write out its own member variables. All of the NIH Library classes already implement a `storer()` function, so we must write one only for our own classes that we have derived from class `Object`. Although this is straightforward to do, writing a fully functional class that is compatible with the NIH Class Library and that supports object I/O involves a lot of detail that we will postpone until Chapter 10, so we will show only the highlights now.

Here are the `storer()` functions for the classes in our example:

```
void Shape::storer(OIOout& strm) const
{
    Object::storer(strm);
    org.storeMemberOn(strm);
}

void Circle::storer(OIOout& strm) const
{
    Shape::storer(strm);
    strm << rad;
}

void Line::storer(OIOout& strm) const
{
    Shape::storer(strm);
    p.storeMemberOn(strm);
}

void Picture::storer(OIOout& strm) const
{
    Shape::storer(strm);
    s.storeMemberOn(strm);
}
```

The strategy for storing the member variables of an object is simple: first, each `storer()` function calls the `storer()` function of its base class; then, it stores its own member variables. Since *every* `storer()` function performs these two steps (except `Object::storer()`—class `Object` has no base class and no member variables to store, so it does nothing), the first step stores the member variables of *all* the ancestors of a class.

We must consider five categories of member variables in the second step. A member variable is either:

1. an instance of an NIH Library class,

2. a pointer to an instance of an NIH Library class,

3. a fundamental type, such as `int` or `float`,

4. an array of a fundamental type, or

5. a user-defined structure or non-NIH Library class.[2]

The `storer()` virtual member function stores these categories of member variables according to the following rules:

---

[2] C++ also permits member variables to be pointers to functions, pointers to member functions, or pointers to virtual member functions, but the NIH Class Library's object I/O facility does not support these types of member variables. It seems feasible to support pointers to virtual member functions, however.

- Store an instance of an NIH Library class by applying the function storeMemberOn() to it, as the example shows. Class Object supplies the implementation of storeMemberOn().

- Call storeOn() recursively to store a member variable that is a pointer to an instance of an NIH Library class.

- Store fundamental types using output operators similar to those that class ostream defines, as we described in Section 5.2.

- Store an array by storing the size of the array followed by a list of elements in the array.

- Store user-defined structures and non-NIH Library classes by individually storing the members that comprise them.

7.4.2   Class OIOout

The argument to storeOn() and the storer() functions is an instance of class OIOout, an abstract class that declares the pure virtual functions operator<<() and put(), overloaded for all the fundamental data types and arrays of fundamental data types, respectively:

```
class OIOout {
// ...
public:
    virtual OIOout& operator<<(const char*) = 0;
    virtual OIOout& operator<<(char) = 0;
    virtual OIOout& operator<<(unsigned char) = 0;
    virtual OIOout& operator<<(short) = 0;
    virtual OIOout& operator<<(unsigned short) = 0;
    virtual OIOout& operator<<(int) = 0;
    virtual OIOout& operator<<(unsigned) = 0;
    virtual OIOout& operator<<(long) = 0;
    virtual OIOout& operator<<(unsigned long) = 0;
    virtual OIOout& operator<<(float) = 0;
    virtual OIOout& operator<<(double) = 0;
    virtual OIOout& put(const char* val, unsigned size) = 0;
    virtual OIOout&
        put(const unsigned char* val, unsigned size) = 0;
    virtual OIOout& put(const short* val, unsigned size) = 0;
    virtual OIOout&
        put(const unsigned short* val, unsigned size) = 0;
    virtual OIOout& put(const int* val, unsigned size) = 0;
    virtual OIOout&
        put(const unsigned int* val, unsigned size) = 0;
    virtual OIOout& put(const long* val, unsigned size) = 0;
    virtual OIOout&
        put(const unsigned long* val, unsigned size) = 0;
```

```
    virtual OIOout& put(const float* val, unsigned size) = 0;
    virtual OIOout& put(const double* val, unsigned size) = 0;
// ...
};
```

Derived classes of OIOout, such as OIOnihout, implement these virtual functions to write out the values of the fundamental types in a specific format. This means that if you desire, you can define your own storage format, implement it in a new derived class of OIOout, and pass an instance of your class to storeOn() to cause a data structure to be stored in your new format—without needing to re-compile any existing classes.

7.4.3   Object input

To read a picture from a file in Example 7-3, we create an instance of class fstream as an input stream connected to the file we wish to read, and read the picture from it by calling the function readFrom().

```
// ex7-3.c - Object I/O readFrom()

#include <fstream.h>
#include <osfcn.h>
#include "Point.h"
#include "Line.h"
#include "Circle.h"
#include "Picture.h"
#include "OIOnih.h"

main()
{
    ifstream in("picturefile");
    if (in.fail()) {
        cerr << "Failed to open picturefile\n";
        exit(1);
    }
    Picture* bigPic = Picture::readFrom(OIOnihin(in));
    bigPic->draw();
}
```

The function readFrom() is the counterpart to storeOn(). It reads the data produced by storeOn() and maintains a table (an OrderedCltn—see Section 8.3.4) containing the addresses of all the objects it reads in. The table is indexed by the object number such that readFrom() can use it to map an object number into the object's memory address. When readFrom() encounters an object reference during the process of reading back a data structure, it uses its table to convert the object number into a pointer to the object.

When readFrom() encounters the name of a class, it creates a new instance of that class and initializes its member variables from the values that follow on the input data stream. To do this, it must use a constructor defined by each class rather than an ordinary member function so that any "hidden" pointers in the objects are properly initialized, as we described in Section 7.3.1. Here are these constructors for the classes in our example:

```
Shape::Shape(OIOin& strm) : Object(strm),org(strm) {}

Circle::Circle(OIOin& strm)
    : Shape(strm)
{
    strm >> rad;
}

Line::Line(OIOin& strm) : Shape(strm),p(strm) {}

Picture::Picture(OIOin& strm) : Shape(strm),s(strm) {}
```

The key to understanding these constructors, which we will refer to as *readFrom() constructors* because they support the `readFrom()` function, is to recall the rules C++ uses to initialize an object's base and member variable class instances. First, each `readFrom()` constructor uses the notation *baseclass*`(strm)` in its initializer list to cause C++ to call the `readFrom()` constructor of its base class. Next, it reads its own member variables. Just as we noted before when describing the `storer()` function, since *every* `readFrom()` constructor performs these two steps, the first step reads the member variables of *all* the ancestors of a class.

The `readFrom()` constructor reads the five categories of member variables according to the following rules:

- Read an instance of an NIH Library class by specifying its initialization with its `readFrom()` constructor in the initializer list; for example, the constructor `Shape::Shape(OIOistream& strm)` initializes its member variable `Point org` with the notation `org(strm)` in its initializer list.

- Call `readFrom()` recursively to read a member variable that is a pointer to an instance of an NIH Library class.

- Read fundamental types from the `OIOistream` using input operators similar to those that class `istream` defines, as we described in Section 5.2.

- Read the size of an array and allocate memory for the array if necessary. Read the required number of elements into the array.

- Read user-defined structures and non-NIH Library classes by individually reading the members that comprise them.

When writing a class's `storer()` function and its corresponding `readFrom()` constructor, we must be careful that the `readFrom()` constructor reads a class's member variables back in the same order in which the `storer()` function writes them. Since we must use a constructor in the initializer list to read member variables that are instances of NIH Library classes, and since the order in which C++ initializes member instances is determined by their order in the class declaration, we *must* store them in the order they are declared in the class declaration.

7.4.4 Class `OIOin`

The argument to `readFrom()` and the `readFrom()` constructors is an instance of class `OIOin`, which is the counterpart to class `OIOout`. Class `OIOin` is an abstract class that declares the pure virtual functions `operator>>()` and `get()`, overloaded for all the fundamental data types and arrays of fundamental data types, respectively. Derived classes of `OIOin`, such as `OIOnihin`, implement these virtual functions to read in the values of the fundamental types using the format determined by the corresponding `OIOout` derived class. You must ensure that when you read in an object, you use a derived class of `OIOin` that is compatible with the class used to store the object.

7.4.5 Static member functions

Have you noticed something unusual about the function `Picture::readFrom()` in Example 7-3? At first glance, this appears to refer to the member function `readFrom()` of class `Picture`. It is not, however, a member function like any we have discussed thus far, which you must always apply to an instance of its class. We cannot apply `readFrom()` to an instance of a `Picture` because we do not have a `Picture` until `readFrom()` has read one in!

The function `Picture::readFrom()` is an example of a *static member function*. A static member function is like other kinds of member functions in that it has access to the private members of its class and the protected members of its class's base class. Unlike other types of member functions, you do not apply it to a class instance using the `.` or `->` operators, and for this reason there is no `this` pointer implicitly defined for a static member function.

You declare a static member function in a class declaration just like an ordinary member function, but you precede the declaration with the keyword `static`

```
class Picture: public Shape {
    static Picture* readFrom(OIOin&);
// ...
```

and a static member function's definition looks like that of an ordinary member function:

```
Picture* Picture::readFrom(OIOin& strm)
// ...
```

Static member functions are very useful, and appear frequently in NIH Library classes.

So we see that each class has its own implementation of `readFrom()`, whereas only class `Object` implements `storeOn()`. The implementation of `readFrom()` is, however, the same for each class, so the NIH Class Library's preprocessor macros can generate its declaration and definition automatically—the class writer needs to provide only the `readFrom()` constructor.

7.4.6 Object input and polymorphism

To reconstruct an object from the external representation produced by `storeOn()`, we call the class's `readFrom()` function, which checks the class of the object it is reading to ensure that it is the same as that class *or is a descendent of that class*. Because of this we could just as well have read in a `Shape` in Example 7-3:

```
Shape* bigPic = Shape::readFrom(OIOnihin(in));
bigPic->draw();
```

This is possible and reasonable because of encapsulation, inheritance, and dynamic binding. A client expecting an instance of a base class will not be aware that it is actually operating on one of its derived classes.

7.4.7 Object I/O summary

Object I/O is one of the most powerful features a class library such as the NIH Class Library can provide. You can apply the function `storeOn()` to a complex data structure composed of classes derived from class `Object` to convert it into a portable representation that you can save on a disk file, or send to another program. The function `readFrom()` can read the representation and reconstruct the original data structure.

The `storeOn()` and `readFrom()` functions perform the class-independent portion of object I/O operations—translating object addresses to and from object numbers. They both rely on each class to perform the class-dependent part of object I/O—writing and reading its own member variables. We call the write function `storer()` and the read function a `readFrom()` constructor.

7.5 CHAPTER SUMMARY

In this chapter, we discussed the motivation for class libraries, and showed how using classes from the NIH Class Library improved the example program for drawing geometric figures. We described two general operations the the NIH Class Library provides: object copying and object I/O, and showed how their implementations rely on member functions provided by class `Object` and each of its derived classes.

In the object input `readFrom()` function, we encountered our first example of a *static member function*. A static member function enjoys the same access rights to members as an ordinary member function, but is called in the same manner as a non-member function; that is, it is not applied to an instance of a class using the . or -> operators.

8

PROGRAMMING WITH THE
NIH CONTAINER CLASSES

8.1 INTRODUCTION

Data structures are central to computer programming. In this chapter we describe the NIH Class Library's *container classes*, which make it easier to construct and manipulate complex data structures. We call these classes container classes because they hold, or contain, instances of NIH Library classes. Examples of container classes include implementations of classic data structures such as indexed arrays (class OrderedCltn), stacks (class Stack), singly-linked lists (class LinkedList), hash tables (class Set), and associative arrays (class Dictionary).

In the previous chapter we showed how using two of these classes, class OrderedCltn and class Stack, to implement a simple graphics package saved programming effort and resulted in a more robust program. In this chapter we take a closer look at these two classes and the other container classes in the NIH Class Library, along with various other NIH Library classes that are used with them. We show how we can use container classes to glue together instances of other library classes to form data structures that are complex, yet well organized and comprehensible.

The container classes in the NIH Class Library are polymorphic and thus useful for a wide range of applications. A container holds pointers to objects (type Object*) rather than the objects themselves and thus can hold instances of a variety of classes. A client program operates on the objects in a container using virtual functions that are dynamically bound to an implementation appropriate for each class of object in the container. But even though the container classes actually hold *pointers* to objects, we often ignore this detail when it is not important and say that a *container holds an object*, or that an *object is in a container*, even though this is not technically correct.

Since the container classes are polymorphic and can, therefore, hold instances of any descendent of class Object, a container class can hold instances of other container classes. This allows us to use them to create recursive data structures such as trees and graphs. For example, we can use instances of class OrderedCltn as interior nodes of a tree. If a particular node has leaves, we can add the leaf objects to the OrderedCltn; if a node has branches to other interior nodes, we can add other OrderedCltn objects to it to represent them. Thus, we can easily construct a polymorphic, N-way branching tree.

8.1.1 Class Object

Before discussing the container classes, let us briefly review class Object and describe those member functions that are important for understanding how the container classes operate.

The abstract class `Object` is the most general NIH Library class. It is the root of the NIH Class Library's inheritance tree, so that its member functions are inherited by all its descendents. These member functions do such things as copying, printing, storing, reading, and comparing objects—general operations that apply to any class of object. However, as we described in Chapter 7, class `Object` cannot actually implement most of these member functions itself. Each derived class is responsible for implementing those functions that depend upon accessing its member variables or that must exhibit specialized behavior. If a client program attempts to apply one of these functions to an instance of a class that does not implement it, a run-time "derived class responsibility" error occurs.

Three categories of member functions declared by class `Object` are particularly relevant to our discussion of container classes:

- identifying and testing the class of an object
- comparing objects
- printing objects

The member functions of the container classes often apply these operations to the objects they hold; thus, if you write a class of your own and you want to add instances of it to an NIH Library container class, you must make it a descendent of class `Object` and supply implementations for the virtual functions your class thereby inherits. (We will describe how you can extend the library with one of your own classes in Chapters 9 and 10.) Of course, all the NIH Library classes implement these functions, so they work properly with the container classes.

8.1.2 Identifying and testing an object's class

This section describes the member functions of class `Object` that deal with identifying and testing the class to which an object belongs.

The function `const Class* isA() const`

Every NIH Library class has a private static member variable named `classDesc` that is an instance of the class named `Class`. This *class descriptor* object contains items of information about an object's class such as its name, base class or classes, member classes, size, and version number. You can obtain a pointer to the descriptor of an object's class by applying the virtual function `isA()` to the object. For example, if p is an instance of class `Point`, then `p.isA()` returns the address of the `Class` object `Point::classDesc`. Every class implements `isA()` in a similar way. The definition of `isA()` for a class X is:

```
const Class* X::isA() const    { return &classDesc; }
```

Many of the other member functions described in this section rely on the `isA()` function for their operation.

Since `classDesc` is a *static member variable*, there is but a *single instance* of this member variable that all instances of the class share—the information in the class descriptor is the same for all instances of a particular class, so there is no point in each instance having its own copy, as would be the case if `classDesc` were an ordinary (non-static) member variable.

The function `const Class* desc()`

While you can use the `isA()` function to locate the class descriptor for an object, sometimes you already know what class you need a descriptor for, and you do not necessarily have a particular instance of that class handy to apply `isA()` to. For these situations, every NIH Library class defines the static member function `desc()`, which returns a pointer to a class's descriptor. For example, to obtain a pointer to the class descriptor for class `Point` you would write:

```
Point::desc()
```

The implementation of `desc()` follows the same pattern for every class:

```
const Class* X::desc()   { return &classDesc; }
```

The function `const char* className() const`

You can obtain a character string containing the class name of an object by applying the function `className()` to the object; for example:

```
Point p(0,1);
cout << p.className();  // prints "Point"
```

The function `bool isMemberOf(const Class&) const`

You can test to see if an object is an instance of a particular class by applying the function `isMemberOf()`. This function returns `YES` if the object it is applied to is an instance of the class described by the argument, for example:

```
Point p(0,1);
if (p.isMemberOf(*Point::desc())) ...   // YES
if (p.isMemberOf(*Object::desc())) ...  // NO
if (p.isMemberOf(*String::desc())) ...  // NO
```

Class `Object` implements `isMemberOf()` as follows:

```
bool Object::isMemberOf(const Class& cl) const
{
    return isA() == &cl;
}
```

The function `bool isKindOf(const Class& class) const`

The function `isKindOf()` is similar to `isMemberOf()`, but it returns `YES` if the object it is applied to is an instance of the class described by the argument, or if it is an instance of a descendent class, for example:

```
Point p(0,1);
if (p.isKindOf(*Point::desc())) ...      // YES
if (p.isKindOf(*Object::desc())) ...     // YES
if (p.isKindOf(*String::desc())) ...     // NO
```

The function `const Class* species() const`

This virtual function is similar to the `isA()` function. It returns a pointer to the instance of class `Class` that describes the *species* of the object it is applied to. We will give a more detailed discussion of `species()` in Section 10.3.10, but the basic notion is that the species of an object determines what classes of objects we wish to consider it comparable to. That is, when we wish to test two objects to see if they are equal, we first check that they are of the same species: two objects of different species cannot be equal. Class `Object` implements `species()` so that by default, the species of an object is the same as its class:

```
const Class* Object::species() const
{
    return isA();
}
```

Derived classes reimplement `species()` if they wish to make their instances comparable to instances of some other class.

The function `bool isSpecies(const Class&) const`

The function `isSpecies()` is similar to `isMemberOf()`, but it returns `YES` if the object it is applied to has the same species as the class described by the argument.

Class `Object` implements `isSpecies()` as follows:

```
bool Object::isSpecies(const Class& cl)
{
    return species() == &cl;
}
```

8.1.3   Comparing objects

This section describes the member functions of class `Object` that deal with comparing objects.

The function `bool isEqual(const Object&) const`

This virtual function returns `YES` if the object it is applied to equals the argument object:

```
Point a(0,1), b(0,1), c(2,3);
String s = "abc";
if (a.isEqual(b)) ...    // YES
if (a.isEqual(c)) ...    // NO
if (a.isEqual(s)) ...    // NO
```

Each class derived from `Object` is responsible for implementing `isEqual()` for its class. Usually, the implementation of `isEqual()` first calls `isSpecies()` to verify that the two objects are of comparable classes, then tests the objects for equality. For example:

```
bool Point::isEqual(const Object& p) const
{
    return p.isSpecies(classDesc) && *this == (const Point&)p;
}
```

Most classes implement `operator==()` to test for equality by comparing the member variables of instances of the class:

```
bool Point::operator==(const Point& p) const
{
    return (xc==p.xc && yc==p.yc);
}
```

If a class has member variables that are pointers to auxiliary data on the free store (like class `BigInt` described in Chapters 3 and 4) or pointers to instances of other NIH Library classes (like class `Picture` described in Section 6.2.8), the equality operator will probably need to follow these pointers and compare the data they point to rather than comparing the values of the pointers themselves.

The function `unsigned hash() const`

Container classes that insert objects in hash tables (class `Set` described in Section 6.3.8 for example) use the virtual function `hash()`. We describe the `hash()` function here because it is closely related to the `isEqual()` function. When applied to an object, the `hash()` function returns a large, unsigned integer that is computed from the same member variables that `isEqual()` uses to test objects for equality. The hashing algorithm uses this number to compute an initial guess at the location of the object in the hash table. For most classes, `hash()` simply applies the exclusive OR operation to these member variables:

```
unsigned Point::hash() const
{
    return xc ^ yc;
}
```

The hash() function must have the following property: if two objects are equal (isEqual() returns YES), then hash() must return the same value for both objects. However, if hash() returns the same value for two objects, those objects need not necessarily compare as equal with the isEqual() function.

The function bool isSame(const Object&) const

The function isSame() returns YES if the object it is applied to is the same object as the argument object; that is, the two objects reside at the same memory address:

```
Point a(0,1), b(0,1);
if (a.isSame(b)) ...     // NO
if (a.isSame(a)) ...     // YES
```

Class Object implements isSame() as follows:

```
bool Object::isSame(const Object& ob) const
{
    return this == &ob;
}
```

The function int compare(const Object&) const

This virtual function compares the object it is applied to with the argument object. It returns a negative number if the object it is applied to is *less than* the argument object, zero if the objects are *equal*, and a positive number if the object it is applied to is *greater than* the argument object. However, compare() checks that the two objects are comparable, usually by comparing their species(), and causes a run-time error if they are not. For example:

```
String a="x", b="y", c="z";
Point p(0,1);
cout << b.compare(a);    // prints 1
cout << b.compare(b);    // prints 0
cout << b.compare(c);    // prints -1
cout << b.compare(p);    // run-time error!
```

Each class derived from Object is responsible for implementing compare() for its class.

We discuss the design issues you will encounter when writing the species(), isEqual(), and compare() functions for a class in Section 10.3.10.

8.1.4 Printing objects

The function void printOn(iostream& strm =cout) const

The function void dumpOn(iostream& strm =cerr) const

Class Object declares two virtual functions for printing objects: printOn() and dumpOn(). They differ in that printOn() by default writes its output to cout, while dumpOn() writes to cerr. The dumpOn() function is intended as a debugging aid, so it typically writes out more information about an object than printOn() does, such as the name of the object's class. For example:

```
Point a(0,1);
a.printOn();     // writes "(0,1)" to cout
a.dumpOn();      // writes "Point[(0,1)]" to cerr
```

The NIH Class Library defines the function operator<<(ostream&, const Object&) to call printOn(), so writing

```
cout << a;
```

is the same as writing:

```
a.printOn(cout);
```

The container classes implement printOn() and dumpOn() to simply apply printOn() or dumpOn(), respectively, to all the objects they contain.

8.2 CLASS Patient

Most of the examples in this chapter use a class Patient which we have modeled on a primitive patient information record. Class Patient is derived from class Object, and implements all of the member functions expected of an Object. However, to save space we will show only the pertinent parts of class Patient here—the complete source code is included in the source distribution kit.

```
// Patient.h - Simple patient record class

#include "Object.h"
#include "String.h"

class Patient: public Object {
// ...
    String _name;     // last name, first name, middle initial
    String _ssn;      // social security number: ddd-dd-dddd
```

```
        int _zip;            // ZIP code : ddddd
public:
        Patient(const String& nam, const String& num, int zip);

        String name() const         { return _name; }
        String ssn() const          { return _ssn; }
        int zip() const             { return _zip; }

        bool operator==(const Patient&) const;
        bool operator!=(const Patient& a) const { return !(*this==a); }
        void operator=(const Patient&);

        virtual int compare(const Object&) const;
        virtual void deepenShallowCopy();
        virtual void dumpOn(ostream& strm =cerr) const;
        virtual unsigned hash() const;
        virtual bool isEqual(const Object&) const;
        virtual void printOn(ostream& strm =cout) const;
};
```

Two of the member variables in class Patient are instances of class String, an NIH Library class described in Section 5.3.

Two Patient objects are considered equal when their member variables are equal:

```
bool Patient::operator==(const Patient& p) const
{
        return _name == p._name
            && _ssn == p._ssn
            && _zip == p._zip;
}
```

The isEqual() function checks that its argument has species Patient, then uses operator==() to test for equality:

```
bool Patient::isEqual(const Object& p) const
{
        return p.isSpecies(classDesc) && *this==(const Patient&)p;
}
```

The hash() function forms its result by first applying hash() to the two member String variables and then applying exclusive-OR to those results and the value of the integer member variable zip:

```
unsigned Patient::hash() const
{
        return _name.hash() ^ _ssn.hash() ^ _zip;
}
```

The member function printOn() formats and writes a patient record to an output stream:

```
void Patient::printOn(ostream& strm) const
{
    strm << _name << ' ' << _ssn << ' ' << _zip;
}
```

The member function dumpOn() produces an annotated printout of a patient record:

```
void Patient::dumpOn(ostream& strm) const
{
    strm << className() << '[' << endl;
    strm << "name:\t" << _name << endl;
    strm << "ssn:\t" << _ssn << endl;
    strm << "zip:\t" << _zip << endl;
    strm << ']' << endl;
}
```

The program in Example 8-1 displays some information about a Patient object.

```
// ex8-1.c - Description of a Patient object

#include "Patient.h"

main()
{
    Patient aPatient("Doe, John","000-00-0000",12345);

    cout << "Class[" << aPatient.className() << "] "
         << "ByteSize[" << sizeof(aPatient) << "]" << endl;
    aPatient.dumpOn(cout);
}
```

The output of the example program is:

```
Class[Patient] ByteSize[46]
Patient[
name:    Doe, John
ssn:     000-00-0000
zip:     12345
]
```

8.3   THE NIH CLASS LIBRARY CONTAINER CLASSES

In this section we give you a guided tour of the NIH Class Library's container classes, and related classes that you would typically use with them. We do not describe the behavior of every member function of every class—to do so would require many additional pages—but rather we present just the highlights of each class and give an example of its use.

8.3.1   Class Collection

Object
   Collection
      ArrayOb
      Set
      SeqCltn

Class Collection is an abstract class that serves as the base class for all container classes in the NIH Class Library and declares those virtual member functions that apply to all container classes:

- add an object to a container (add())

- remove an object from a container (remove())

- convert one type of container to another

- copy objects from one container to another (addContentsTo())

- test for the presence of an object in a container (includes())

- test for an empty container (isEmpty())

- report the number of objects in a container (size())

- report the capacity of a container (capacity())

- report the number of occurrences of a particular object in a container (occurrencesOf())

A client program can thus perform these operations on a container object without needing to know specifically what kind of container it is. Class Iterator, which we describe next, is a good example of this.

8.3.2   Class Iterator

Object
   Collection
      Iterator

An application program often requires sequential access to the objects in a container. In a C language program sequential access is typically performed with a for loop:

```
int x[5];   /* array of integers */
int i;

/* sequential access to the integers in the array */
for( i=0; i<5; i++) x[i] = i;
```

Class Iterator generalizes the for loop construct to container classes in the NIH Class

Library. An `Iterator` object has a member variable pointing to the container which it will access, and it also has member variables that point to the object currently selected from the container. The `Iterator` delegates to the container the responsibility for determining which object is first, which object to select next at each step, and what to do when iteration is completed.

We are able to describe class `Iterator` now, before discussing any particular kind of container class, because an `Iterator` does not have to know the actual class of its associated container, which must be a descendent of class `Collection`. Each container class has a virtual member function `doNext()` that determines an ordering for the objects in the container. A container also has a virtual member function `doReset()` that initializes an `Iterator` such that the next call to `doNext()` returns a pointer to the first object (if any) in the container, and a virtual member function `doFinish()` that performs any cleanup necessary when an `Iterator` is destroyed. Class `Collection` declares the virtual member functions `doReset()`, `doNext()`, and `doFinish()`, and that is enough for an `Iterator` to do its job.

A client program can gain access to objects in a container by calling the member functions `Iterator::operator++()` and `Iterator::operator()()`. The function `operator++()` sets the `Iterator` to point to the next object in its associated container. The function `operator()()` will return a pointer to the same object each time it is called, until `operator++()` is called again.

Example 8-2 shows how to apply an `Iterator` to any container, even when the specific class of the container is not known. At run time, the actual argument to the `Iterator` constructor must be an instance of a derived `Collection` class that implements `doNext()`. Of course, the responsibility for implementing function `doNext()` lies with the derived `Collection` class and not the caller of the function.

```
// ex8-2.c - Use of an Iterator with container
//              for objects of unknown class

#include "OrderedCltn.h"
#include "Iterator.h"
#include "String.h"

void listContainer(ostream& strm,Collection& cltn)
{
//  Iterator knows neither
//  the actual class of cltn nor
//  the actual class of any Object in cltn
    Iterator it(cltn);
    while (it++) strm << *it() << " ";
}

main()
{
    OrderedCltn symbols;
```

```
    symbols.add(*new String("A"));
    symbols.add(*new String("C"));
    symbols.add(*new String("G"));
    symbols.add(*new String("T"));

    listContainer(cout,symbols);
    cout << endl;
}
```

The output of the program in Example 8-2 is:

```
A  C  G  T
```

An application may use two or more Iterators on a container at the same time, as Example 8-3 shows. In this example, function printPairs() prints all possible pairs of objects by a double iteration through two containers, which in this case happen to be the same container. Just as in the previous example, printPairs() does not know the class of the argument containers or the class of any object in them.

```
// ex8-3.c - Nested Iterators

#include "OrderedCltn.h"
#include "Iterator.h"
#include "String.h"

void printPairs(const Collection& c1, const Collection& c2)
{
    Iterator it1(c1), it2(c2);

    while(it1++) {
        while (it2++) {
            cout << '[' << *it1() << ',' << *it2() << "]   ";
        }
        cout << endl;
        it2.reset();
    }
}

main()
{
    OrderedCltn symbols;
    symbols.add(*new String("A"));
    symbols.add(*new String("C"));
    symbols.add(*new String("G"));
    symbols.add(*new String("T"));
    printPairs(symbols,symbols);
}
```

When run Example 8-3 prints:

```
[A,A]   [A,C]   [A,G]   [A,T]
[C,A]   [C,C]   [C,G]   [C,T]
[G,A]   [G,C]   [G,G]   [G,T]
[T,A]   [T,C]   [T,G]   [T,T]
```

Finally, a word of caution. It is a dangerous practice to add objects to or remove objects from a container while iterating through the container, because the order of the objects in the container may change. Example 8-4 demonstrates this problem:

```
// ex8-4.c - Incorrectly modifying a container during iteration

#include "OrderedCltn.h"
#include "Iterator.h"
#include "String.h"

main()
{
    OrderedCltn symbols;
    symbols.add(*new String("A"));
    symbols.add(*new String("C"));
    symbols.add(*new String("G"));
    symbols.add(*new String("T"));

    Iterator it(symbols);
    while (it++)
        if (it()->compare(String("G")) < 0) symbols.remove(*it());

    cout << symbols << endl;
}
```

The intention is to remove all strings alphabetically before "G" from the OrderedCltn symbols, but that is not what actually happens:

```
C
G
T
```

The reason is that the first iteration removes "A" from symbols, and "C" becomes the first object. The Iterator is not aware of this change, so on the second iteration it returns the second object in symbols, which is "G". Thus, the Iterator skips over "C", and it is not removed from symbols as a result.

One correct way of programming this problem is to iterate through a copy of the container while modifying the original, as Example 8-5 illustrates:

```
// ex8-5.c - Modifying a container during iteration

#include "OrderedCltn.h"
#include "Iterator.h"
#include "String.h"

main()
{
    OrderedCltn symbols;
    symbols.add(*new String("A"));
    symbols.add(*new String("C"));
    symbols.add(*new String("G"));
    symbols.add(*new String("T"));

    OrderedCltn temp = symbols;
    Iterator it(temp);
    while (it++)
        if (it()->compare(String("G")) < 0)
            symbols.removeId(*it());

    cout << symbols << endl;
}
```

The OrderedCltn temp in this example is a shallow copy of symbols; that is, it contains the same objects that symbols does, not copies. The function removeId() is like remove(), but uses isSame() instead of isEqual() to locate the object to remove. This produces the intended results, as the output shows:

```
G
T
```

8.3.3 Class SeqCltn

Object
  Collection
    SeqCltn
      LinkedList
      OrderedCltn
      Stack

Class SeqCltn is an abstract base class for containers that order their objects sequentially; that is, objects are numbered sequentially (usually beginning at 0), and can be referenced by specifying their index number. The sequentially ordered containers in the NIH Class Library include classes Stack and OrderedCltn, which we introduced in Sections 7.2.2 and 7.2.3, and class LinkedList.

The member function first() returns a pointer to the first object and the member function last() returns a pointer to the last. A SeqCltn associates an integer index with each object it contains by the pure virtual member function `at()`, which it declares as

```
virtual Object*& at(int) = 0;
virtual const Object *const& at(int) const = 0;
```

in order to prevent the unintentional modification of `const` objects, as we described in Section 5.3.8.

Member `at()` is intended to return the *i*th object for argument `i` in the range 0 to `size()-1`. Because the return value of the function `at()` is a reference to a pointer, the expression `at(i)` on the left of the assignment operator replaces the *pointer* to the *i*th object in a sequential container. For example:

```
void some_function(SeqCltn& cltn)
{
    cltn.add(*new String("A"));
    cltn.add(*new String("B"));

    int ilast = cltn.size()-1;      // index of last object

// at(ilast) points to String with value "B"
// at(ilast-1) points to String with value "A"

    cltn.at(ilast) = cltn.at(ilast-1);

// at(ilast) points to String with value "A"
// at(ilast-1) points to String with value "A"
}
```

Using Iterators, class `SeqCltn` implements `isEqual()`, `hash()`, `occurrencesOf()` and `compare()`. For example, here is how class `Iterator` implements `isEqual()`:

```
bool SeqCltn::isEqual(const Object& ob) const
{
// Check that ob isKindOf() SeqCltn
    if (!ob.isKindOf(*SeqCltn::desc())) return NO;
    if (size() != ob.size()) return NO;
    Iterator i(*this);
    Iterator j((const SeqCltn&)ob);
    Object* p;
    while (p = i++) if (!p->isEqual(*(j++))) return NO;
    return YES;
}
```

8.3.4 Class `OrderedCltn`

Object
  Collection
    SeqCltn

> **OrderedCltn**
>   SortedCltn
>   KeySortCltn

We have already encountered a use of class `OrderedCltn` in Examples 8-2 through 8-5. Class `OrderedCltn` is derived from class `SeqCltn` and implements a variable-length array of pointers to objects. The member function `add()` appends objects to the end of the array at index `size()`, and the member function `remove(const Object& ob)` removes the first object that is `isEqual()` to ob from the array.

The index operators

```
Object*& operator[](int i)
const Object *const& operator[](int i) const
```

allow you to access the object pointers in an `OrderedCltn` by their index, for example:

```
OrderedCltn c;
// ...
object* obj = c[0];      // retrieves the object at index 0
c[0] = new Point(0,1);   // stores new object pointer at index 0
```

The virtual member function `at(int i)` also provides `OrderedCltn` indexing, and its default implementation simply calls `operator[]()`.

Members `addBefore(const Object&)` and `addAfter(const Object&)` allow you to insert an object at any place in the array, either before or after the first object that is `isEqual()` to the specified object. Since additions and removals of object pointers at any position other than at the end of an `OrderedCltn` cause the remaining pointers to be moved up or down, applications using large arrays that require a lot of insertions and deletions will perform those operations more efficiently with a `LinkedList`.

Class `OrderedCltn` performs several important operations on its pointer array that make it easier to use than a simple C++ array. An `OrderedCltn` automatically resizes itself when it needs more room for pointers and its array is automatically deallocated when its destructor function is executed. Constructors for an `OrderedCltn` make an initial allocation for an array of pointers to objects. The member function `capacity()` returns the maximum number of objects the `OrderedCltn` can contain without resizing. You can add objects to an `OrderedCltn` without any further allocation of memory until `size()` equals `capacity()`, at which time the array is reallocated with a larger capacity. Calls to the memory allocator can be costly so class `OrderedCltn` allows an ample increase in capacity. You can call the member function `reSize()` directly to anticipate a certain capacity for the array, as with `reSize(best_guess_capacity)`.

Example 8-6 illustrates the use of an `OrderedCltn` as an array of pointers with automatic resizing.

```
// ex8-6.c - Sequential access to Objects in an OrderedCltn

#include "OrderedCltn.h"
#include "Iterator.h"
```

```
#include "Patient.h"

main()
{
// new Patient objects to put in OrderedCltn
    Patient* p1 =new Patient("Smith John A.","111-22-3333",22222);
    Patient* p2 =new Patient("Fried Harry I.","123-45-6789",22221);
    Patient* p3 =
      new Patient("Chavez Maria G.","444-555-6666",22223);

// add each Patient to OrderedCltn
    OrderedCltn patientlist(1);// capacity=1 (default=16)
    patientlist.add(*p1);       // at[0] in order
    patientlist.add(*p2);       // at[1] in order
    patientlist.add(*p3);       // at[2] in order

    cout << "ACCESS OBJECTS WITH operator[]():" << endl;
    for(int i=0; i<patientlist.size(); i++) {
        Patient& p = *(Patient*)patientlist[i];
        cout << p << endl;
    }

    cout << "ACCESS OBJECTS WITH Iterator:" << endl;
    Iterator it(patientlist);
    while ( it++ ) {
        Patient& p = *(Patient*)it();
        cout << p << endl;
    }
}
```

In Example 8-6 we show how to add `Patient` records to an `OrderedCltn` and access them in two ways: by means of the function `OrderedCltn::operator[]()` and by using an `Iterator`. The `for` loop accesses the `Patient` objects in `patientlist` as `patientlist[0]`, `patientlist[1]`, and `patientlist[2]`. The `while` loop accesses the `Patient` objects with an `Iterator`. Both types of access will produce the same result because the `doNext()` member defined for `OrderedCltn` follows the index ordering of an `OrderedCltn`. The output from function `printOn()` for both cases will be:

```
ACCESS OBJECTS WITH operator[]():
Smith John A. 111-22-3333 22222
Fried Harry I. 123-45-6789 22221
Chavez Maria G. 444-555-6666 22223
ACCESS OBJECTS WITH Iterator:
Smith John A. 111-22-3333 22222
Fried Harry I. 123-45-6789 22221
Chavez Maria G. 444-555-6666 22223
```

The choice between using a `for` loop or an `Iterator` for an `OrderedCltn` is often a matter of programming style, but there are several important differences:

- The function `operator[]()` allows for random access to objects contained in the `OrderedCltn` whereas an `Iterator` does not.

- The function `operator[]()` allows for the replacement of object pointers and and `Iterator` does not.

- Using an `Iterator` is more general, because you can use it on any kind of container class.

- The `operator[]()` function is faster than an `Iterator`.

8.3.5 Class `SortedCltn`

Object
  Collection
    SeqCltn
      OrderedCltn
        SortedCltn
          KeySortCltn

Class `SortedCltn` is derived from class `OrderedCltn` and implements a sorted array of object pointers. The function `SortedCltn::add()` inserts an object in sort order as it adds a pointer to the object to its array. You can access each object a `SortedCltn` contains with an integer index, like an `OrderedCltn`, but, `SortedCltn::operator[]()` returns the ith object in the sorted list, while `OrderedCltn::operator[]()` returns the ith object added to the container.

Also like an `OrderedCltn`, when you add or delete an object from a `SortedCltn`, all the object pointers after the point of insertion or deletion will be moved up or down in the array, so if your application performs many additions or removals on a large sorted container, it will be more efficient to use a linked list or balanced tree data structure rather than a `SortedCltn`.

To perform its sorting function, a `SortedCltn` must compare each new object added with the objects already in the container. A `SortedCltn` performs these comparisons by applying the virtual function `compare()` (see Section 8.1.3) to the objects it holds. Thus, although a `SortedCltn` is polymorphic in the sense that it can contain any kind of object, you must assure that all the objects you place in a `SortedCltn` are comparable. That is, you must be sure that the objects you add to a `SortedCltn` meet the comparability criteria that `compare()` requires—usually that the objects have the same species—otherwise, `compare()` will fail with a run-time error.

Example 8-7 demonstrates the behavior of the sorted container implemented by class `SortedCltn`.

```
// ex 8-7.c - Sorting Patient records by name

#include "SortedCltn.h"
```

```
#include "String.h"
#include "Patient.h"

main()
{
    SortedCltn cltn;
    cltn.add(*new Patient("Smith John A.","111-22-3333",22222));
    cltn.add(*new Patient("Fried Harry I.","123-45-6789",22221));
    cltn.add(*new Patient("Chavez Maria G.","444-555-6666",22223));

    cout << cltn << endl;
}
```

The function `Patient::compare()` determines the sort order in Example 8-7 as the sort order of the member variables `Patient::_name`:

```
int Patient::compare(const Object& p) const
{
// verify that p has species Patient
    assertArgSpecies(p,classDesc,"compare");
// compare Patient names
    return _name.compare(((const Patient&)p)._name);
}
```

Example 8-7 prints the `Patient` records on the standard output in name order:

```
Chavez Maria G. 444-555-6666 22223
Fried Harry I. 123-45-6789 22221
Smith John A. 111-22-3333 22222
```

8.3.6 Classes `KeySortCltn`, `LookupKey`, and `Assoc`

Object
  Collection
    SeqCltn
      OrderedCltn
        SortedCltn
           KeySortCltn
  LookupKey
    Assoc

Class `SortedCltn` provides a convenient means of sorting the instances of a class in a single way, but what if we need to sort objects in several different ways in a single program? For example, we just saw how to sort `Patient` records by name using a `SortedCltn`, but we have a problem if we also want a second list with the same `Patient` records sorted by ZIP code. The source of the difficulty is that class `SortedCltn` uses the virtual function `compare()` to order the objects it holds, so to change the sort key, we must change the definition of `Patient::compare()` to compare ZIP codes instead of names when making the second list—but class `Patient` provides no obvious way to do that.

We designed class `KeySortCltn` to solve this problem. Instead of sorting object pointers directly, a `KeySortCltn` sorts *associations* between *key objects* and *value objects*. An *association* is simply an object that holds:

- a pointer to a key object

- a pointer to (or the value of) a value object

Classes such as `KeySortCltn` use only the key object when performing comparisons—the value object just tags along with the key for the ride. Since the sort key is separate from the object being sorted, we can combine several different keys with the same object. For example, we can solve the problem of sorting `Patient` records by name and ZIP code by creating two associations for each `Patient` record: one with the patient's name as the key object, and another with the patient's ZIP code as the key object. Both kinds of association for a particular patient will have the same `Patient` record as the value object. Adding the name-keyed associations to a `KeySortCltn` will produce a list sorted by patient name, and adding the ZIP code-keyed associations to a second `KeySortCltn` will produce a list sorted by ZIP code.

We will present an example program that does this later on, but first we need to describe the NIH Library classes that implement associations.

Class `LookupKey`

Class `LookupKey` serves as a base class for derived classes that provide associations between key objects and value objects. A `LookupKey` holds a pointer to the key object of the association, and declares the `value()` virtual functions (which derived classes must implement) for accessing the value object of the association:

```
class LookupKey: public Object {
    Object* akey;
// ...
public:
    LookupKey(Object& newKey =*nil);
    virtual int compare(const Object&) const;
    virtual void deepenShallowCopy();
    virtual void dumpOn(ostream& strm =cerr) const;
    virtual unsigned hash() const;
    virtual bool isEqual(const Object&) const;
    virtual Object* key() const;
    virtual Object* key(Object& newkey);
    virtual void printOn(ostream& strm =cout) const;
    virtual Object* value();
    virtual const Object* value() const;
    virtual Object* value(Object& newvalue);
};
```

Class `LookupKey` implements the functions `compare()`, `isEqual()`, and `hash()` by applying the corresponding operation on the key object, `akey`; for example, `LookupKey`'s implementation of `compare()` is:

```
int LookupKey::compare(const Object& ob) const
{
    return -ob.compare(*akey);
}
```

The comparison is done in this subtle manner instead of as `akey -> compare (ob)` to correctly handle the case where `ob` is also a `LookupKey`.

Since a `LookupKey` behaves the same as its key object with respect to the functions `isEqual()`, `compare()`, and `hash()`, you can substitute an instance of a class derived from `LookupKey` in place of its key object for any of these operations.

Class `Assoc`

Class `Assoc` is derived from class `LookupKey`, and provides a pointer (an `Object*`) to the value object of an association:

```
class Assoc: public LookupKey {
    Object* avalue;
// ...
public:
    Assoc(Object& newKey =*nil, Object& newValue =*nil);
    virtual void deepenShallowCopy();
    virtual Object* value();
    virtual const Object* value() const;
    virtual Object* value(Object& newvalue);
};
```

It implements the `value()` virtual functions, declared in class `LookupKey`, to access and change the value object pointer:

```
Object* Assoc::value() { return avalue; }
const Object* Assoc::value() const { return avalue; }
Object* Assoc::value(Object& newvalue)
{
    Object* temp = avalue;
    avalue = &newvalue;
    return temp;
}
```

Classes `AssocInt` *and* `Integer`

Object
  Integer
  LookupKey
    Assoc
    AssocInt

We broke up the implementation of the abstraction of the association data type into two classes, class `LookupKey` to handle the key object and class `Assoc` to handle the value object, so that we could use `LookupKey` as a base class for more specific kinds of associations. For example, the NIH Class Library uses class `AssocInt` to provide an association between a key object and an integer value:

```
class AssocInt: public LookupKey {
    Integer avalue;
// ...
public:
    AssocInt(Object& newKey =*nil, int newValue =0);
    virtual void deepenShallowCopy();
    virtual Object* value();
    virtual const Object* value() const;
    virtual Object* value(Object& newValue);
};
```

Class `AssocInt` incorporates an instance of an `Integer` object directly as a member variable rather than using an `Object*` member variable pointing to a separately allocated value object as class `Assoc` does. This eliminates the overhead of allocating memory for a separate value object each time we construct an association with an integer.

We could not simply use an `int` member variable as the value object of an `AssocInt` because we must reimplement the virtual `value()` functions to return a pointer to an `Object`, and an `int` is a fundamental data type, not a derived class of `Object`. So we wrote the trivial `Integer` class so we would have a way of treating integers as instances of an NIH Library Class:

```
class Integer: public Object {
    long val;
// ...
public:
    Integer(long v =0)      { val = v; }
    Integer(istream&);
    long value() const       { return val; }
    long value(long newval) { return val = newval; }
// ...
};
```

That way, we could implement the `AssocInt::value()` functions as:

```
Object* AssocInt::value() { return &avalue; }
const Object* AssocInt::value() const { return &avalue; }
Object* AssocInt::value(Object& newValue)
{
// Check that newValue isKindOf Integer
    assertArgClass(newValue,*Integer::desc(),"value");
    avalue = (Integer&)newValue;
    return &avalue;
}
```

Using class `KeySortCltn`

Class `KeySortCltn` is derived from class `SortedCltn` and provides several special member functions for handling associations and their key and value objects:

```
class KeySortCltn: public SortedCltn {
// ...
public:
    KeySortCltn(int size =DEFAULT_CAPACITY);

    LookupKey* assocAt(int i);
    Object* keyAt(int i);
    Object* valueAt(int i);
    Object* atKey(Object& key);

    Assoc* addAssoc(Object& key,Object& val);
// ...
};
```

The function `addAssoc()` creates a new association for the key and value objects you specify as arguments, and adds this association to a `KeySortCltn`. Eventually, you must remember to delete the association it creates to free its storage.

The functions `assocAt(int i)`, `keyAt(int i)`, and `valueAt(int i)` allow you to index the associations in a `KeySortCltn` and retrieve a pointer to the *i*th association, key object, or value object, respectively.

Example 8-8 shows how to use a `KeySortCltn` to sort `Patient` records in three ways: by name, by Social Security Number, and by ZIP code:

```
// ex8-8.c - Sorting Patient records with a KeySortCltn

#include "Assoc.h"
#include "Integer.h"
#include "Iterator.h"
#include "KeySortCltn.h"
#include "String.h"
#include "Patient.h"

main()
{
// Build list of Patient records
    OrderedCltn cltn;
    cltn.add(*new Patient("Smith John A.","111-22-3333",22222));
    cltn.add(*new Patient("Fried Harry I.","123-45-6789",22221));
    cltn.add(*new Patient("Chavez Maria G.","444-555-6666",22223));

// Three KeySortCltn collections for three different keys
    KeySortCltn sort0(cltn.size());
```

```
        KeySortCltn sort1(cltn.size());
        KeySortCltn sort2(cltn.size());

        Iterator it(cltn);
        while ( it++ )  {
            Patient& p = *(Patient*)it();

// Sort Patient by name
            sort0.addAssoc(*new String(p.name()),p);

// Sort Patient by social security number
            sort1.addAssoc(*new String(p.ssn()),p);

// Sort Patient by zip code
            sort2.addAssoc(*new Integer(p.zip()),p);
        }

        cout << "SORT BY NAME:\n"
            << sort0 << '\n' << endl;

        cout << "SORT BY SOCIAL SECURITY NUMBER:\n"
            << sort1 << '\n' << endl;

        cout << "SORT BY ZIP CODE:\n"
            << sort2 << '\n';
}
```

Example 8-8 constructs `Patient` records for three `Patients` named "Chavez", "Fried", and "Smith". It uses three sort keys: name, Social Security Number, and ZIP code and constructs an instance of class `KeySortCltn` for each. Associations for the three `Patient` objects are added to each `KeySortCltn` and a listing of each `KeySortCltn` is written to the standard output. The resulting output is:

```
SORT BY NAME:
Chavez Maria G.=>Chavez Maria G. 444-555-6666 22223
Fried Harry I.=>Fried Harry I. 123-45-6789 22221
Smith John A.=>Smith John A. 111-22-3333 22222

SORT BY SOCIAL SECURITY NUMBER:
111-22-3333=>Smith John A. 111-22-3333 22222
123-45-6789=>Fried Harry I. 123-45-6789 22221
444-555-6666=>Chavez Maria G. 444-555-6666 22223

SORT BY ZIP CODE:
22221=>Fried Harry I. 123-45-6789 22221
22222=>Smith John A. 111-22-3333 22222
22223=>Chavez Maria G. 444-555-6666 22223
```

Multi-key sorting

We can also use a `KeySortCltn` for performing multi-key sorts by using any kind of container of key objects as the key object of an association, as long as the container class implements the virtual function `compare()`. This works because:

- Class `KeySortCltn` applies `compare()` to pairs of `Assoc` objects.

- Class `LookupKey`, from which `Assoc` inherits its implementation of `compare()`, applies `compare()` to the key objects of the pair of associations.

- A container class that implements the `compare()` function extends the comparison to apply to two ordered arrays of key objects by applying `compare()` to corresponding pairs of key objects in each array, thus performing a multi-key comparison.

Example 8-9 illustrates this by using instances of class `ArrayOb`, the simplest kind of container class, which we will describe in great detail in Chapters 9 and 10, to hold three keys for performing a multi-key sort of `Patient` records.

```
// ex8-9.c - Sorting on Multiple Keys with ArrayOb and KeySortCltn
#include "KeySortCltn.h"
#include "ArrayOb.h"
#include "Assoc.h"
#include "Patient.h"
#include "Integer.h"

void sort_Patient(KeySortCltn& c, Patient& p)
{
// Set up ArrayOb with sort keys zip,name,ss_number
    ArrayOb& key = *new ArrayOb(3);
    key[0] = new Integer(p.zip());
    key[1] = new String(p.name());
    key[2] = new String(p.ssn());
    c.addAssoc(key,p);
}
main()
{
    KeySortCltn cltn;
// Define 6 Patient records
// in parent/child pairs with the same name and zip
// and sort with ArrayOb key in a KeySortCltn
    sort_Patient(cltn,
        *new Patient("Smith John A.","333-22-1111",22223));
    sort_Patient(cltn,
        *new Patient("Smith John A.","111-22-3333",22223));
    sort_Patient(cltn,
        *new Patient("Fried Harry I.","987-65-4321",22221));
```

```
    sort_Patient(cltn,
        *new Patient("Fried Harry I.","123-45-6789",22221));
    sort_Patient(cltn,
        *new Patient("Chavez Maria G.","666-555-4444",22223));
    sort_Patient(cltn,
        *new Patient("Chavez Maria G.","444-555-6666",22223));

// Print Patient records in sorted order
    cout << "Sort by zip, name, and ssn: \n\n";

    Iterator it(cltn);
    while (it++) {
        Assoc& as = *(Assoc*)it();
        cout << *as.value() << endl;
    }
}
```

Example 8-9 declares six `Patient` records that we want to sort on three keys: ZIP code, name, and Social Security Number, in that order. To provide a good illustration in a small space, we chose the patient data to represent three pairs of individuals, with each pair a parent and child who have the same name and residence.

We construct a new `ArrayOb` of size three for each `Patient` record. The first sort key is an instance of class `Integer`. The second and third sort keys are instances of class `String`.

The example makes an association between each `Patient` object and its `ArrayOb` by invoking the function `KeySortCltn::addAssoc()`. The resulting output is a list of `Patient` records sorted first by ZIP code, next by name, and last by social security number:

```
Sort by zip, name, and ssn:

Fried Harry I. 123-45-6789 22221
Fried Harry I. 987-65-4321 22221
Chavez Maria G. 444-555-6666 22223
Chavez Maria G. 666-555-4444 22223
Smith John A. 111-22-3333 22223
Smith John A. 333-22-1111 22223
```

Summary of classes KeySortCltn, LookupKey, *and* Assoc

Class `KeySortCltn` allows you to sort objects in several different ways in a single program, and to sort objects on multiple keys. It accomplishes this by sorting *associations* (instances of class `Assoc`) between *key objects* (the objects that determine the sort order) and *value objects* (the objects you wish to sort) rather than sorting the objects directly as class `SortedCltn` does.

Class `LookupKey` serves as a base class for derived classes, such as `Assoc`, that implement associations between key and value objects. A member variable of class `LookupKey` holds a pointer to the key object, and a member variable of class `Assoc` holds a pointer to the value object. Other association classes derived from `LookupKey`, for example class `AssocInt`, implement special kinds of associations more efficiently by incorporating the value object as a member variable of the association. In the case of class `AssocInt`, the value object is an integer, represented by an instance of the NIH Library class `Integer`.

8.3.7   Class `LinkedList`

Object
  Collection
    SeqCltn
      LinkedList
  Link
    LinkOb

Class `LinkedList` implements the traditional singly-linked list data structure. It is more restrictive than most other container classes in that you can only add instances of classes derived from another NIH Library class, class `Link`, to a `LinkedList`. This is because class `Link`'s member variable provides the storage for the forward pointer to the next instance on the `LinkedList`.

Class `LinkedList` implements a number of operations typical of a linked structure, including the member functions:

- `addFirst()` and `addLast()`, which add an object to either end of the list;

- `addAfter()`, which inserts an object in the list;

- `removeFirst()` and `removeLast()`, which remove an object from either end of the list; and,

- `first()` and `last()`, which return pointers to an object at either end of the list.

Since a `Link` can be added or removed by making one or two pointer assignments instead of by moving a potentially large numbers of pointers around in an array, a `LinkedList` is more efficient for large, frequently changing lists than an `OrderedCltn`.

Class `Link`

The NIH Class Library provides two ways to link objects into a `LinkedList`: by a direct link or by an indirect link. An object is *directly linked* to a `LinkedList` when the object is an instance of a class derived from `Link` and thus has class `Link`'s inherited forward pointer embedded in it (see Figure 8.1). An object is *indirectly linked* to a `LinkedList` when the `LinkedList` contains another object, an instance of class `LinkOb`, that in turn contains a pointer to the indirectly linked object (see Figure 8.2).

In either case, the objects on a `LinkedList` are instances of classes derived from class `Link`:

```
class Link: public Object { // abstract class
    Link* next;              // pointer to next Link
  friend LinkedList;
```

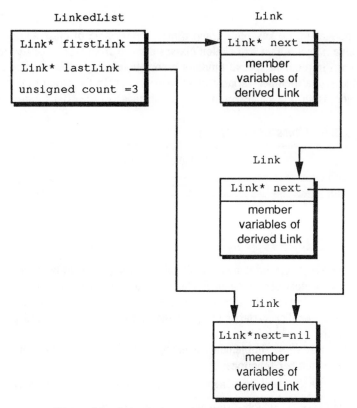

Figure 8.1 `LinkedList` *with direct links*

```
protected:
    Link()                     { next = NULL; }
    Link(Link* nextlink)       { next = nextlink; }
    Link(const Link&)          { next = NULL; }
public:
    ~Link();
    Link* nextLink() const              { return next; }
    Link* nextLink(Link* nextlink) {
        next = nextlink; return next;
    }
    bool isListEnd() const;
    virtual int compare(const Object&) const = 0;
    virtual unsigned hash() const = 0;
    virtual bool isEqual(const Object&) const = 0;
    virtual void printOn(ostream& strm =cout) const = 0;
// ...
}
```

You can read or set the `next` link with the `nextLink()` member functions. Class `LinkedList` stores a special pointer value to represent the `nextLink` of the last `Link`

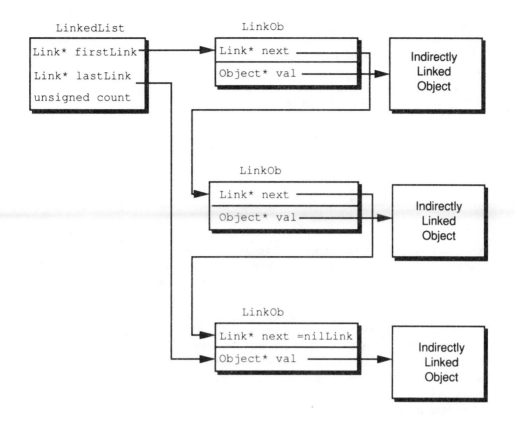

Figure 8.2 LinkedList *with indirect links*

in a LinkedList. You can check to see if you have reached the end of a LinkedList by calling isListEnd(), which looks for this special pointer.

Since there is only one next pointer in each Link, a Link can be threaded on at most one LinkedList at any time. Class Link initializes the next pointer to NULL, and class LinkedList enforces this restriction by producing a run-time error if you attempt to add a Link with a non-NULL next pointer.

With single inheritance, a directly linked object may be on at most one LinkedList at a time since class Link can only be a base class once. However, with multiple inheritance, you can write classes that inherit multiple copies of class Link, and instances of such classes can simultaneously be on as many LinkedLists as there are inherited Links. We will see how to use multiple inheritance to do this in Chapter 13.

Class LinkOb

Indirect links, which class LinkOb provides, are more flexible, but less efficient, than direct links. Class LinkOb is a derived class of Link that adds a member variable (Object* val) to point to the object on the LinkedList:

```
class LinkOb: public Link {
    Object* val;
```

```
// ...
public:
    LinkOb(Object& newval =*nil);

    virtual int compare(const Object&) const;
    virtual void dumpOn(ostream& strm =cerr) const;
    virtual unsigned hash() const;
    virtual bool isEqual(const Object&) const;
    virtual void printOn(ostream& strm =cout) const;
    virtual Object* value() const;
    virtual Object* value(Object& newval);
// ...
};
```

Since there is no limit on the number of LinkObs that can point to an object, there is no problem in indirectly linking an object on as many LinkedLists as you wish.

The value() member functions allow you to read or set the val pointer to the indirectly linked object.

Class LinkOb is reminiscent of class LookupKey (Section 8.3.6) in the way it implements the virtual member functions compare(), isEqual(), hash(), dumpOn() and printOn(): it applies the corresponding operation to the object pointed to by its member variable val. Since a LinkOb thus behaves the same as the indirectly linked object with respect to the functions isEqual(), compare(), hash(), dumpOn() and printOn(), you can substitute a LinkOb in place of its indirectly linked object for any of these operations.

Using instances of class LinkOb to indirectly link objects on a LinkedList is less efficient than directly linking objects on a LinkedList for two reasons. First, you must go through an additional pointer (which also consumes additional memory) to access the indirectly linked object. Second, allocating the memory for a separate LinkOb object requires an extra call to the memory allocator.

Example 8-10 shows how to construct and use a LinkedList with indirectly linked objects.

```
// ex8-10.c - Linking into a LinkedList

#include "LinkOb.h"
#include "LinkedList.h"
#include "String.h"

main()
{
    LinkedList list;

// Add new first link
    LinkOb* firstLink = new LinkOb(*new String("first in"));
    list.addFirst(*firstLink);
```

```
// Add new last link
   LinkOb* lastLink = new LinkOb(*new String("second in"));
   list.addLast(*lastLink);

// Insert new link in between first and last
   LinkOb* newlink = new LinkOb(*new String("third in"));
   list.addAfter(*firstLink,*newlink);

// Print the LinkedList of LinkObs
   if (list.size() > 0) {
       LinkOb* link = (LinkOb*)list.first();
       while (!link->isListEnd()) {
           cout << *link << endl;
           link = (LinkOb*)link->nextLink();
       }
   }
}
```

In Example 8-10, we use `String` objects as the indirectly linked objects. We use the member function `addFirst()` to explicitly link the `String` "first in" as the first `Link`, the member function `addLast()` to explicitly link the `String` "second in" as the last `Link`, and finally, we use the member function `addAfter()` to link the `String` "third in" into the list immediately after the first `Link` of the list. The `while` loop at the end of the program prints the indirectly linked objects on the list:

```
first in
third in
second in
```

We checked to make sure that the size of `list` was greater than zero before using `LinkedList::first()` because it is a run-time error to access the first object of an empty `LinkedList`. The `while` loop calls `isListEnd()` to test for the end of the `LinkedList` list.

8.3.8 Class `Set`

Object
  Collection
    Set
      IdentSet
      Dictionary
        IdentDict

With this section we begin our description of the *unsequenced*, or *unordered*, container classes. These classes have no notion of a "first" or "last" object, or of one object being "before" or "after" another. You cannot access an object in an unordered container by an integer index, and an `Iterator` visits the objects in an unordered container in an unpredictable sequence. These may sound like limitations, but in fact, the unordered container classes are among the most useful in the NIH Class Library.

A `Set` is a container that ignores attempts to add any object that duplicates one already in the `Set`. A `Set` considers two objects to be duplicates if they are `isEqual()` to one another.

As is the case with all container classes, you add an object to a `Set` with the function `add()` and remove it with the function `remove()`. You can test to see if an object is already in a `Set` with the function `includes()`. Since a `Set` is implemented as a hash table with open addressing [13], the `includes()` operation is fast—it does not test each object in the `Set` sequentially—making `Set`s very useful for searching. Of course, the objects used in conjunction with a `Set` must all implement the `hash()` function since class `Set`'s hash table algorithm relies on it.

Example 8-11 illustrates how to use a `Set` in a program that performs a search. The variable `weekdays` is a `Set` of `String`s of all weekday names. To see if a given date is a weekday, we apply `weekDay()` to the date to obtain a weekday number in the range 0–6, with 0 corresponding to Sunday. We then call `nameOfDay()` to convert this number to a C-style character string (a `const char*`) with the weekday name, convert this to a `String`, and use `includes()` to see if this `String` is in the `Set` `weekdays`:

```
// ex8-11.c - Test if date falls on a weekday

#include "Date.h"
#include "Set.h"
#include "String.h"

main ()
{
    Set weekdays;          // Set of weekday names
    String mon = "Monday", tue = "Tuesday", wed = "Wednesday",
        thu = "Thursday", fri = "Friday";
    weekdays.add(mon);  weekdays.add(tue);  weekdays.add(wed);
        weekdays.add(thu);  weekdays.add(fri);

    Date date;
    while (YES) {
        cout << "Enter date: ";  cin >> date;
        if (cin.eof()) break;
// Convert date to String containing name of day and
// search Set for match
        if (weekdays.includes(
            String(Date::nameOfDay(date.weekDay()))))
            cout << date << " is a weekday" << endl;
        else
            cout << date << " is not a weekday" << endl;
    }
    cout << endl;
}
```

A sample run of Example 8-11 might look like this:

```
Enter date: 8/31/89
31-Aug-89 is a weekday
Enter date: 3-SEP-89
 3-Sep-89 is not a weekday
Enter date: September 4, 1989
 4-Sep-89 is a weekday
```

Class `Set` also provides binary set comparison, intersection, union, and difference operators:

- The member functions `operator==()` and `operator!=()` compare two `Set`s. We say two `Set`s A and B are equal if they have the same number of objects, and set B `includes()` each object in set A.[1] `Set::isEqual()` uses `Set::operator==()` for its implementation.

- `Set::operator&()` returns a `Set` that is the intersection of two `Set`s; that is, the result of A & B is the set of objects that are included in both A and B.

- `Set::operator|()` returns a `Set` that is the union of two `Set`s; that is, the result of A | B is the set of all objects included in either A or B.

- `Set::operator-()` returns a `Set` that is the difference of two `Set`s; that is, the result of A − B is the set of objects that are included in A but not in B.

Example 8-12 illustrates the use of these `Set` operators.

```
// ex8-12.c - Binary Set operators

#include "Patient.h"
#include "Set.h"
#include "SortedCltn.h"

main()
{
    Patient p1("Smith John A.","111-22-3333",22222);
    Patient p2("Fried Harry I.","123-45-6789",20892);
    Patient p3("Chavez Maria G.","444-555-6666",22223);
    Patient p4("Doe, Jane B.","123-98-7654",20892);

    Set males;                  // set of all male Patients
    males.add(p1); males.add(p2);
    Set females;                // set of all female Patients
    females.add(p3); females.add(p4);
    Set washingtonResidents;    // set of all Patients living
                                // in Washington
    washingtonResidents.add(p2); washingtonResidents.add(p4);
```

---

[1] This is not the same notion as mathematical set equality. Two *different* Set containers can be "equal".

```
    cout << "All patients:\n";
    cout << (males | females).asSortedCltn() << endl;

    cout << "\nAll female patients living in Washington:\n";
    cout << (females & washingtonResidents).asSortedCltn() << endl;

    cout <<
      "\nAll female patients living outside of Washington:\n";
    cout << (females - washingtonResidents).asSortedCltn() << endl;

    cout << "\nDo all male patients live in Washington? ";
    cout << (males == (males & washingtonResidents) ? "Yes" : "No")
      << endl;
}
```

Since `Sets` are unordered container classes, if you print them they list their contents in an unpredictable order. Example 8-12 uses the function `Set::asSortedCltn()` to convert the `Sets` to `SortedCltns` before printing the results:

```
All patients:
Chavez Maria G. 444-555-6666 22223
Doe, Jane B. 123-98-7654 20892
Fried Harry I. 123-45-6789 20892
Smith John A. 111-22-3333 22222

All female patients living in Washington:
Doe, Jane B. 123-98-7654 20892

All female patients living outside of Washington:
Chavez Maria G. 444-555-6666 22223

Do all male patients live in Washington? No
```

Class `Set` is useful by itself for searching and for its binary set operators. In the following sections, we will also see how useful it is as a base class for a variety of more specialized derived classes.

8.3.9   Class `IdentSet`

Object
  Collection
    Set
      IdentSet
      Dictionary
        IdentDict

Class `IdentSet` is like class `Set`, except that an `IdentSet` uses `isSame()` to test for duplicate objects, rather than `isEqual()`. Thus, an `IdentSet` will ignore a request to add an object only if that same object is already in the IdentSet. Example 8-13 illustrates the difference in behavior between a Set and an IdentSet:

```
// ex8-13.c - Comparison of classes Set and IdentSet

#include "Set.h"
#include "IdentSet.h"
#include "String.h"
#include "SortedCltn.h"

main()
{
    String s1 = "A String";
    String s2 = "A String";
    String s3 = "Another String";

    Set s;
    s.add(s1); s.add(s2); s.add(s3); s.add(s3);
    cout << "Set:\n";
    cout << s.asSortedCltn() << endl;

    IdentSet i;
    i.add(s1); i.add(s2); i.add(s3); i.add(s3);
    cout << "\nIdentSet:\n";
    cout << i.asSortedCltn() << endl;
}
```

When you run this example it prints

```
Set:
A String
Another String

IdentSet:
A String
A String
Another String
```

because the Set s ignores the second and fourth add() operations—s1 is isEqual() to s2 and s3 is isEqual() to itself. But the IdentSet i ignores only the fourth add() operation—s2 is not the *same* String object as s1.

IdentSets are useful in conjunction with multiple inheritance and virtual base classes, as we will see later in Section 13.9.2.

8.3.10 Class Dictionary

Object
  Collection

Set
  IdentSet
  Dictionary
    IdentDict

Class Dictionary provides *associative arrays*. You can create an association between a key object and a value object and add it to a `Dictionary` by calling the member function:

```
Assoc* addAssoc(Object& key, Object& value)
```

Later, you can use a key that is `isEqual()` to the key argument you originally gave to `addAssoc()` to retrieve the associated value object by calling the function:

```
Object* atKey(const Object& key)
```

For example, you can create a `Dictionary` and add to it associations between key objects representing words and value objects representing the definitions of the words:

```
Dictionary d;
String word = "computer";
String definition =
    "an automatic electronic machine for performing calculations";
d.addAssoc(word, definition);
```

You can then retrieve the definition of one of the words from the `Dictionary`:

```
// Print the definition of "computer"
cout << *d.atKey(String("computer")) << endl;
```

This application no doubt inspired the name of class `Dictionary`.

Class `Dictionary` is implemented literally as a "set of associations": it is an instance of a derived `Set` containing `Assoc` objects. This is analogous to the way that class KeySortCltn is a `SortedCltn` of associations, as we described in Section 8.3.6. Figure 8.3 illustrates the data structure of a `Dictionary` containing three associations.

The member function addAssoc() creates a new instance of class `Assoc` with the key and value objects you specify as arguments, adds the new association to the `Dictionary`, and returns a pointer to the newly created `Assoc` object. A client program that creates an `Assoc` object in this way is responsible for destroying it.

The function atKey() generates a run-time error if the key argument cannot be matched with any key in the `Dictionary`. If you are not certain that a particular key is in a `Dictionary` and you cannot risk the occurrence of the run-time error, you can use the member function

```
bool includesKey(const Object& key) const
```

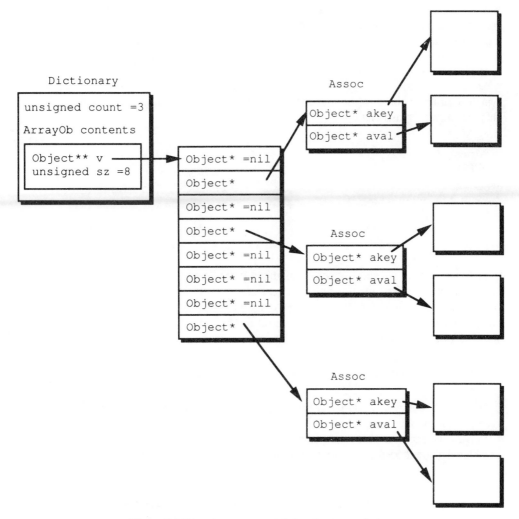

Figure 8.3 Dictionary *containing three associations*

to test the Dictionary to see if it includes the key before calling atKey(). For example:

```
Dictionary d;
String word;
// ...
cout << "Enter a word: ";  cin >> word;
if (d.includesKey(word)) cout << *d.atKey(word) << endl;
else cout << word << " not in Dictionary" << endl;
```

Using includesKey() to test for the occurrence of a key object in a Dictionary means that the Dictionary lookup is done twice for each access: once by includesKey() and once by atKey(). To avoid this, you can call the member function

```
LookupKey* assocAt(const Object& key) const
```

which returns a pointer to the association that matches the key object argument, or 0 if it finds no matching association:

```
Dictionary d;
String word;
// ...
cout << "Enter a word: ";  cin >> word;
LookupKey* lk = d.assocAt(word);
if (lk) cout << *lk->value() << endl;
else cout << word << " not in Dictionary" << endl;
```

In Example 8-14 we show how to construct a Dictionary of Patient records keyed by patient name. First, we use function addAssoc() to associate new String names with new Patient records in a Dictionary. Next, we print the patient records in sorted order by name. To do this, we add all the key objects in the Dictionary to an instance of a SortedCltn by calling the member function:

```
Collection& addKeysTo(Collection&) const
```

We then iterate over the sorted list of keys, looking up and printing the associated patient record from the Dictionary.

Finally, we enter a loop that prompts the user for a patient name and prints out the associated patient record, or prints the message "not found" if the name is not in the Dictionary.

```
// ex8-14.c - A Dictionary of Patient records keyed by name

#include "Assoc.h"
#include "Dictionary.h"
#include "Iterator.h"
#include "SortedCltn.h"
#include "String.h"
#include "Patient.h"

main()
{
// Associate key names with Patient records in a Dictionary
    Dictionary dict;
    cout << "Order of Insertion:" << endl;
    String& fried = *new String("Fried Harry I.");
```

```
    Patient& patient_fried =
        *new Patient(fried,"987-65-4321",22221);
    dict.addAssoc(fried,patient_fried);
    cout << patient_fried << endl;

    String& smith = *new String("Smith John A.");
    Patient& patient_smith =
        *new Patient(smith,"333-22-1111",22223);
    dict.addAssoc(smith,patient_smith);
    cout << patient_smith << endl;

    String& chavez = *new String("Chavez Maria G.");
    Patient& patient_chavez =
        *new Patient(chavez,"444-555-6666",22223);
    dict.addAssoc(chavez,patient_chavez);
    cout << patient_chavez << endl;
    cout << endl;

// Get sorted list of key Strings
    SortedCltn scltn;
    dict.addKeysTo(scltn);

// Print Patient records in sorted order
    cout << "Sorted by Name:" << endl;
    Iterator its(scltn);
    while (its++) {
        cout << *dict.atKey(*its()) << endl;
    }
    cout << endl;

// Process queries
    String name;
    while (YES) {
        cout << "Patient name: "; cin >> name;
        if (cin.eof()) break;
        LookupKey* lk = dict.assocAt(name);
        if (lk) cout << *lk->value() << endl;
        else cout << name << " not found" << endl;
    }
    cout << endl;
}
```

Here is a sample run of Example 8-14:

```
Order of Insertion:
Fried Harry I. 987-65-4321 22221
Smith John A. 333-22-1111 22223
Chavez Maria G. 444-555-6666 22223
```

```
Sorted by Name:
Chavez Maria G. 444-555-6666 22223
Fried Harry I. 987-65-4321 22221
Smith John A. 333-22-1111 22223

Patient name: Chavez Maria G.
Chavez Maria G. 444-555-6666 22223
Patient name: John Doe
John Doe not found
```

8.3.11   Class IdentDict

Object
  Collection
    Set
      IdentSet
      Dictionary
        IdentDict

Class IdentDict modifies the behavior of a Dictionary in the same way that class IdentSet (see Section 8.3.9) modifies the behavior of a Set: it uses isSame() to test for matching keys rather than isEqual(). Example 8-15 illustrates the difference in behavior between a Dictionary and an IdentDict.

```
// ex8-15.c - Comparison of classes Dictionary and IdentDict

include "Dictionary.h"
#include "IdentDict.h"
#include "LookupKey.h"
#include "String.h"
#include "SortedCltn.h"

main()
{
    String s1 = "A String";

    Dictionary d;
    d.addAssoc(s1,*new String("value associated with s1"));
    cout << "Dictionary:" << endl;
    LookupKey* lk = d.assocAt(String("A String"));
    if (lk) cout << *lk->value() << endl;
    else cout << "Not found" << endl;
    lk = d.assocAt(s1);
    if (lk) cout << *lk->value() << endl;
    else cout << "Not found" << endl;
    cout << endl;
```

```
        IdentDict i;
        i.addAssoc(s1,*new String("value associated with s1"));
        cout << "IdentDict:" << endl;
        lk = i.assocAt(String("A String"));
        if (lk) cout << *lk->value() << endl;
        else cout << "Not found" << endl;
        lk = i.assocAt(s1);
        if (lk) cout << *lk->value() << endl;
        else cout << "Not found" << endl;
}
```

The output of Example 8-15 is

```
Dictionary:
value associated with s1
value associated with s1

IdentDict:
Not found
value associated with s1
```

shows that while either the key "A String" or s1 is found in the Dictionary, only the key s1 is found in the IdentDict.

An IdentDict is useful for associating data with an object without using memory storage within the object itself, a technique sometimes referred to as *hash linking*. We will develop this idea in Example 8-16 with a class Property that uses hash linking to associate an owner object with a list of property objects. The list of properties is a Dictionary that associates a String name with each property object. Thus, in a single instance of class IdentDict, each owner object has its own list of properties and each property is referenced by name. The public static member function

```
Object* Property::add(Object& owner, String& name, Object& value)
```

adds the property named name with the value value to the list of properties for object owner, and returns the old value of the property if it already existed. The public static member function

```
Object* Property::get(const Object& owner, const String& name)
```

returns the property named name for object owner.

```
// ex8-16.c - Property list

#include "IdentDict.h"
#include "Dictionary.h"
```

```
#include "String.h"
#include "Date.h"
#include "Patient.h"

class Property: public NIHCL {
    static IdentDict prop;        // object property lists
public:
    static Object* add(Object& owner, String& name, Object& value);
    static Object* get(const Object& owner, const String& name);
};

IdentDict Property::prop;

Object* Property::add(
    Object& owner,       // object to receive property
    String& name,        // name of property
    Object& value)       // property value
{
    Object* oldvalue = &value;
    Dictionary* d;
    if (!prop.includesKey(owner)) {
        d = new Dictionary;
        d->addAssoc(*new String(name),value);
        prop.addAssoc(owner,*d);
    }
    else {
        d = (Dictionary*)prop.atKey(owner);
        if (d->includesKey(name))
            oldvalue = d->atKey(name,value);
        else d->addAssoc(*new String(name),value);
    }
    return oldvalue;
}


Object* Property::get(
    const Object& owner,// object with property
    const String& name) // name of property
{
    if (!prop.includesKey(owner)) return Object::nil;
    Dictionary* d = (Dictionary*)prop.atKey(owner);
    if (d->includesKey(name)) return d->atKey(name);
    else return Object::nil;
}

main()
{
```

```
// First patient
    Patient p1("Fried Harry I.","987-65-4321",22221);
    Property::add(p1,
        *new String("admission date"),*new Date(10,"Mar",86));
    Property::add(p1,
        *new String("complaint"),*new String("fever"));

// Second patient
    Patient p2("Chavez Maria G.","444-555-6666",22223);
    Property::add(p2,
        *new String("admission date"),*new Date(20,"Mar",86));
    Property::add(p2,
        *new String("complaint"),*new String("broken leg"));

// Print some properties of Patient objects
    cout << *Property::get(p1,"admission date") << endl;
    cout << *Property::get(p1,"complaint") << endl;
    cout << *Property::get(p2,"admission date") << endl;
// Non-existent property
    cout << *Property::get(p2,"birthdate") << endl;
}
```

The output of Example 8-16 is:

```
10-Mar-86
fever
20-Mar-86
NIL
```

The last line of output shows what happens if you try to get a non-existent property: `Property::get()` returns a pointer to an instance of a special class named `Nil`, which prints as `NIL`.

8.3.12   Class `Nil` and the `Nil` object

Object
  Nil

Sometimes a member function of a container class needs to use a pointer to an object when there is no appropriate object at hand. This might happen when a search fails, as happened in `Property::get()` in Example 8-16, or a place in an array of `Object` pointers that does not point to an object, for example when the array is initialized. Under similar circumstances, a C language program might use a 0 (or NULL) pointer. This can cause problems in C++ programs, because applying a member function to a 0 pointer usually results in a run-time error. To avoid this, you would need to explicitly check that the pointer is non-zero before applying a member function to the object it references. As an alternative, the NIH Class Library defines a unique instance of a class `Nil` which you can use as a "no object". Client programs always access the `Nil` object by means of the static pointer member variable `Object::nil`, which you can use wherever a pointer to an object (an

`Object*`) is needed. For example, there is no harm in looping through a list of pointers to objects and executing `ob->printOn(cout)`, because if one of the pointers is the `nil` pointer, we have arranged for `Nil::printOn()` to print `NIL`. Useful properties of class `Nil` and the `Nil` object are:

- You cannot create any other instance of class `Nil` other than the one the NIH Class Library creates at initialization and sets `Object::nil` to point to—the class declaration for class `Nil` is not even in a `.h` file.

- You cannot `copy()` or `deepCopy()` the `Nil` object—these functions return `Object::nil`.

- `Nil::dumpOn()` and `printOn()` print the character string `"NIL"`.

- `Nil::isEqual()` returns `YES` if both objects are the `Nil` object, and `NO` otherwise.

- `Nil::hash()` always returns 0.

- `Nil::compare()` returns 0 if both objects are the `Nil` object, and causes a run-time error otherwise.

- `storeOn()` and `readFrom()` implicitly consider the `Nil` object as object number 0, so `storeOn()` always stores a pointer to the `Nil` object as a reference to object number 0.

Class `Nil` inherits the rest of its behavior from its base class, `Object`.

8.4 GUIDELINES FOR USING CONTAINER CLASSES

In this section we present a number of guidelines which we recommend you follow when writing programs that use the NIH Library container classes.

8.4.1 Specializing container classes

All of the NIH Library container classes hold pointers to objects. A client program gains access to an object in a container only by calling some member function of the container that returns a pointer (reference) of type `Object*` (`Object&`). For example, in the code fragment

```
OrderedCltn cltn;
String* s = new String("object");
cltn.add(*s);
Object* ob = cltn.at(0);
```

the client, at first, knows the `String` object only as an instance of class `Object`. To apply the more specialized member functions of class `String`, the client must first cast the pointer ob to a pointer of type `String`:

```
String* ps = (String*)ob;
```

We call the cast of a base class pointer to a descendent class pointer a *downward cast*. Downward casts are potentially dangerous. If, for example, the pointer ob does not actually point to an instance of the descendent class String named in the cast, C++ will misinterpret the member variables in that instance, usually with fatal consequences for the program.

You can protect against unsafe downward casts in two ways. The best way is to encapsulate the NIH Library container class and the operations that place objects in it in another special-purpose class that assures that only a specific class of object can be added to the container. Then, we can safely cast down any Object* pointers obtained from the encapsulated container to the specific class. Class Picture, which we discussed in Section 7.2.5, is an example of this technique: the only way to place an object in a Picture is via the function Picture::add(Shape&), and function argument type checking by C++ guarantees that only a Shape object can be specified as an argument to add(). Thus, a downward cast of any Object* obtained from the OrderedCltn encapsulated by class Picture to a Shape* is safe. The advantage of this technique is that it involves no run-time overhead.

When you cannot use the static type checking of C++ to assure that a downward cast is safe, you should perform a run-time check on the class of an object before doing a downward cast. Class Object provides several useful member functions to make this easier.

```
void assertClass(const Class& expect) const
void assertSpecies(const Class& expect) const
```

These functions test the class (by calling isKindOf()) or the species (by calling isSpecies()) of the object they are applied to. If the class or species, respectively, differs from the class descriptor argument expect, they print an error message.

```
void assertArgClass(const Class& expect, const char* fname) const
void assertArgSpecies(const Class& expect, const char* fname) const
```

These functions are similar to assertClass() and assertSpecies(), but you can specify the name of the function detecting the error as the argument fname, which is included in the error message.

```
void assertArgClass(const Object& ob, const Class& expect,
    const char* fname) const
void assertArgSpecies(const Object& ob, const Class& expect,
    const char* fname) const
```

These functions are similar to assertArgClass() and assertArgSpecies(), but are intended for use within member functions. They test the class or species of the argument ob, and include the value of the this pointer in the error message.

8.4.2 Managing memory correctly

Another, perhaps more serious, consequence of a container class's holding object pointers and not the objects themselves is that we must be careful about the lifetime of the objects we place in containers. Failure to do so can cause two kinds of memory-management related problems: *dangling pointers* and *memory leaks*.

A *dangling pointer* occurs when we add an object pointer to a container, then prematurely delete the object, leaving behind a pointer to unused memory—or, if the unused memory is later allocated for another object, a pointer to the wrong object! Such problems can be hideously difficult to track down, because the fault may not come to light during program execution until long after the object was prematurely destroyed.

A *memory leak* occurs when we destroy a container without retaining pointers to the objects in the container. As a result, the program can never reclaim or reuse the memory occupied by these objects, and its storage requirement grows larger and larger as it executes. Memory leaks are usually noticed only in programs that run continuously, and are also very difficult to track down.

The following guidelines will help you to avoid these pitfalls:

- Never add temporary objects to a container:

```
#include "OrderedCltn.h"
#include "String.h"

main()
{
    OrderedCltn c;
    c.add(String("abcdef"));    // never do this!
    cout << c << endl;
}
```

The `String` in this example is a compiler-generated temporary that the compiler may delete after the statement in which it appears, leaving a dangling pointer in the container.[2]

- Never add objects that are local variables to a container that is also a local variable unless it is in the same block or in a nested block. The C++ compiler automatically destroys local objects when execution leaves the scope of the block they are declared in. If such a local object was added to a container with a longer lifetime, destruction of the local object results in a dangling pointer:

```
#include "OrderedCltn.h"
#include "String.h"

main()
{
    OrderedCltn c;
// ...
    if (c.isEmpty()) {
        String s = "abcdef";
        c.add(s);         // never do this!
    }
    cout << c << endl;
}
```

---

[2] Fortunately, Release 2.0 of the AT&T C++ Translator flags this with a "temporary used for non-const argument" warning message.

Example 8-11 (Section 8.3.8) shows how to correctly add local objects to a local container.

- Try to follow a convention when deleting objects created with new. For example, the NIH Class Library follows the convention that library classes are responsible for deleting the objects they create, and library clients are responsible for deleting the objects that they create.[3]

The most general technique for eliminating memory management problems is *automatic garbage collection*, which we discuss in Section 14.4.

8.4.3 Modifying objects while in containers

Client programs can modify objects while they are in a container. The operation of some NIH Library container classes, such as SortedCltn, KeySortCltn, Set, Dictionary, IdentDict, and IdentSet, relies on the implementations of the virtual functions compare(), isEqual(), and hash() provided by the objects they hold. If an object is modified such that the result returned by one of these functions changes from what it was when the object was originally added to the container, unexpected results may occur. For example

```
#include "SortedCltn.h"
#include "String.h"

main()
{
    SortedCltn s;
    String s1 = "A", s2 = "B", s3 = "C";
    s.add(s1); s.add(s2); s.add(s3);
    cout << s << endl;
    s2 = "Z";
    cout << "After modifying s2:\n";
    cout << s << endl;  // s is no longer sorted!
}
```

prints:

```
A
B
C
After modifying s2:
A
Z
C
```

---

[3] The function addAssoc() is a notable exception to this rule.

To avoid this, remove the object you wish to change from the container, modify it, then add it back to the container again.

8.5 CHAPTER SUMMARY

In this chapter, we described the NIH Class Library's container classes, and other classes related to their use:

- Class `Object`, which is the root of the NIH Class Library's inheritance hierarchy, declares functions for copying, printing, storing, reading, and comparing objects that all its descendent classes inherit.

- Class `Class`, whose instances describe other classes, contains information such as a class's name, its base class or classes, member classes, and the size of its instances. Every NIH Library class has a static member instance of class `Class` that describes it. The address of this class descriptor may be obtained by calling a class's static member function `classDesc()`, or by applying the virtual function `isA()` to an object.

- Class `Collection`, the base class for all container classes, declares functions for adding objects, removing objects, converting containers, testing to see if an object is in a container, and determining how many objects are in a container.

- Class `Iterator` enables a client program to sequence through the objects in a container in a general fashion.

- Class `SeqCltn`, which is the base class for containers that order their objects sequentially, declares functions for accessing the first and last objects in a sequenced container, and for indexing sequenced containers.

- Class `OrderedCltn` is a simple variable-length array of object pointers.

- Class `SortedCltn` maintains an array of object pointers in the order determined by applying the virtual function `compare()` to the objects.

- Class `KeySortCltn`, which is a `SortedCltn` of associations, is capable of sorting a group of object pointers on different keys, or of sorting object pointers on multiple keys.

- Class `LookupKey` is a base class for various kinds of associations between *key objects* and *value objects*. Class `LookupKey` provides a pointer to the key object of an association and declares virtual functions for accessing the value object, which is added by a derived class. Class `LookupKey` implements the functions `compare()`, `isEqual()`, and `hash()` by applying the corresponding operation on the key object, so a `LookupKey` can be substituted for its key object for any of these operations.

- Class `Assoc`, which is a derived class of `LookupKey`, provides a pointer (an `Object*`) to the value object of an association.

- Class `AssocInt`, which is also a derived class of `LookupKey`, implements associations with an `Integer` value objects.

- Class `Integer` allows an integer value to be treated as a class object.

- Class `LinkedList` implements singly-linked lists composed of instances of classes descended from class `Link`.

- Class `Link` provides the forward pointer in the objects on a `LinkedList`.

- Class `LinkOb` is used to indirectly link objects on a `LinkedList`.

- Class `Set` is the base class of the unsequenced, or unordered, container classes. A `Set` is a container that ignores attempts to add any object that is `isEqual()` to one already in the `Set`. Sets are implemented as hash tables, and are useful for searching.

- Class `IdentSet` modifies the behavior of a `Set` to use `isSame()` instead of `isEqual()` to test for duplicate objects.

- Class `Dictionary` is a `Set` of associations, provides *associative arrays*.

- Class `IdentDict`, which modifies the behavior of a `Dictionary` to use `isSame()` instead of `isEqual()` to test for duplicate objects, is useful for *hash linking*: a technique for associating data with an object without using memory storage within the object itself.

- Class `Nil` and the `Nil` object are used to indicate failure of a search for an object and to initialize the object pointers in empty containers.

We then presented a few guidelines for using container classes: techniques for making the *downward casts* needed when specializing containers safe, ways to help avoid *dangling pointers* and *memory leaks*, and cautions against modifying objects while in containers.

9
DESIGNING LIBRARY CLASSES

9.1 INTRODUCTION

Although it is possible to write programs that simply use existing NIH Library classes, most real programs need to define *new* classes that are customized for a particular application. In fact, some C++ programs consist almost *entirely* of classes, with only a small main() routine just to get the program started. The big advantage of a class library (such as the NIH Class Library) over a procedural library (such as the C language library) is that by defining your own derived classes and overriding virtual functions, you can easily modify the behavior of library classes to suit your needs. Thus, a class library is more flexible, and hence more reusable, than a procedural library.

In this chapter and the next we explain how to design and write classes that are compatible with the NIH Class Library so that they will work together—you can add an instance of a compatible class to an NIH Library container class, for example—and they will inherit useful functionality, such as object I/O.

New classes should follow the same design rules and programming conventions that existing NIH Library classes use, so we will describe in detail the class ArrayOb, a simple container class that manages an array of pointers to other NIH Library objects. Other NIH Library container classes, for example OrderedCltn, Stack, SharedQueue, Set, Bag, and Dictionary, use an instance of ArrayOb as one of their member variables to hold the object pointers they manage.

Class ArrayOb defines member functions for:

- constructing an instance to hold a specified number of object pointers
- initializing one instance from another (copy constructor)
- assigning one instance to another
- accessing the object pointers an instance contains by means of the subscript operator (operator[]())
- comparing two instances to see if they are equal
- determining and changing the size of an instance
- copying an instance and the objects it contains
- iterating over the contents of an instance
- storing and reading an instance to or from a stream

The program in Example 9-1 gives an idea of what class ArrayOb does:

```
// ex9-1.c - Class ArrayOb example

#include "ArrayOb.h"
#include "Point.h"
#include "String.h"
#include "Date.h"

main()
{
    ArrayOb a(3),b(3);          // two ArrayObs with size 3
    cout << "The size of a is " << a.size() << endl;
    a[0] = new Point(0,0);       // 0-origin indexing, like C
    a[1] = new Date(10,"March",1986);
    a[2] = new String("hello");
    cout << *a[2] << endl;
    b = a;
    if (a == b) cout << "a equals b, as it should\n";
    b[2] = new String("goodbye");
    if (a != b) cout << "a does not equal b any more\n";
    cout << b << endl;
}
```

When it runs, Example 9-1 prints:

```
The size of a is 3
hello
a equals b, as it should
a does not equal b any more
(0,0)
10-Mar-86
goodbye
```

Thus, you can subscript `ArrayOb` objects much like ordinary C arrays, but unlike C arrays:

- you can change the size of the array at execution time

- the array elements can be pointers to instances of a variety of NIH Library classes, not just a single type as in C

- you can perform some operations, such as assign, compare, and print, on the entire array instead of just individual elements

9.2   OBJECT-ORIENTED DESIGN

How does a programmer decide that a class such as `ArrayOb` is needed in the first place? The art of object-oriented design involves making decisions on the following issues:

- What classes does a particular application require?

- How does a particular class relate to other classes that already exist or that may also be useful in an application? Should it inherit from another class? Should it serve as the base class for other classes? Should it be a client of other classes?

- What member functions should a particular class have? Which should be virtual? Which virtual functions should be pure? Which should be inline?

- What member variables should a particular class have?

- Which members should be private, which should be protected, and which should be public?

The decisions on these issues are interdependent, and cannot be made in isolation of one another. Let us discuss each in more detail.

9.2.1 When to use classes

The most basic issue is to decide what classes an application requires and how to structure a program around them. Here are a few guidelines to help you recognize when using a class might be appropriate:

- Use classes to represent real-world concepts. This frequently arises in simulation or graphics applications. For example, if you are designing a traffic simulation, you would probably organize the program around classes such as `Vehicle`, `TrafficLight`, `TollBooth`, and so on. The distributed file system backup utility discussed in Chapter 12 is a good example of this use of classes.

- Use classes to encapsulate design decisions that are difficult to make or involve machine or system dependencies, and are therefore likely to change. This makes it easier to experiment with various designs or port the program to a different environment because the changes will be localized to the class. The NIH Library `Time` class, for example, relies on UNIX-specific system calls to obtain the current time, time zone, and Daylight Savings Time indicator. A client program can be easily ported to another operating system just by changing class `Time` to use whatever system calls are provided by the target operating system.

- Use classes to hide complexity. The `DigitStream` class described in Section 4.2.14 is a good example of this.

- Use classes to represent well known data structures or algorithms that are of general use when writing programs. This is the motivation behind most of the classes in the NIH Library, such as `LinkedList`, `Set`, `Heap`, `Stack`, and `OrderedCltn`.

- Use classes to create a more convenient, object-oriented interface to existing procedure libraries. The `Regex` class described in Section 5.5 is an example of this.

- Use classes to permit the use of a convenient notation. The `SubString` class described in Section 5.3.4 exemplifies this.

- Use classes to take advantage of constructors and destructors. Rule 9 of Appendix C has an example of using a static instance of a class with a constructor to initialize data in a library routine. You can also use a local instance of a class with a constructor and destructor to guarantee the release of a resource upon exit from a block. See Section 11.4 for an example.

- Use classes when you need more than one instance of some data. In fact, you should plan for the future and use classes even if your immediate application only requires a single instance—this may make your program easier to generalize later on.

- Use classes containing only static members to eliminate global variables and functions, as we will describe in Section 13.2. (This use of classes is more in the style of modular programming than object-oriented programming, but we mention it here for sake of completeness.)

This list of guidelines was drawn from our experiences in developing and using the NIH Class Library. For example, our motivations for creating the example class `ArrayOb` are mainly to represent a generally useful data structure, the array, and to hide the complexity of managing storage for arrays of dynamically varying size.

9.2.2   Organizing classes

Once you have decided on a tentative set of classes to use in an application, you should look for relationships among them that will help you organize them. The objectives are:

- to maximize reuse of code
- to encourage generality in programs

Two classes may be related to each other by inheritance, or one class may simply be a client of (use an instance of) another. These two relationships are not necessarily exclusive— a class may be both an heir of and a client of another class. Class `Picture`, introduced in Section 6.2.8, is both derived from and a client of class `Shape`, for example.

When you design a class, you must consider its two external interfaces: the interface it presents to its clients, which consists of its public members, and the interface it presents to derived classes, which consists of its public members plus its protected members.

Inheritance as opposed to use by client

Given two classes, how do you decide whether to derive one from the other or to make one a client of the other? The simplistic answer is to ask if the relationship between two classes is an "is-a" relationship or a "has-a" relationship. If one class "is-a" kind of the other class, then use inheritance and derive it; if one class "has-a" instance of the other class, then make it a client of the other class. This formula works best when using classes to represent real-world objects; for example, an `Automobile` "is-a" `Vehicle`, so you would derive class `Automobile` from class `Vehicle`. On the other hand, an `Automobile` "has-a" `Driver`, so you would make class `Automobile` a client of class `Driver`.

It would be nice if life were this easy, but as Meyer [17] points out, it is not, particularly when the classes in question represent relatively poorly understood abstractions rather than real-world objects. For example:

- Is an `Arc` a kind of `Circle`, or vice-versa?

- Is a `Picture` a kind of `Shape`, or does a `Picture` have a `Shape`?

- Is a `Bag` a kind of `Set` (a set of associations between objects in the set and their occurrence counts), or does a `Bag` simply have such a `Set`?

To answer such questions, you must understand the properties of inheritance versus those of use by a client, try out variations of both techniques on the classes you are considering, and see which seems to work out best. We will present an example of such an analysis in Section 9.2.2.

In C++, there is only one way that one class can inherit from another: it must specify it or one of its descendents as its base class. However, for one class to be a client of another, all the client needs is an instance of the other class to apply member functions to. A client can obtain such an instance in many ways: as an argument to one of its member functions, as the return value from a function it calls, from a global variable, or by creating one for itself, just to name a few. The commonly occurring case that interests us now is when a client incorporates an instance of another class or a pointer to an instance of another class as one of its member variables. In the following sections, we will compare the properties of the three most common ways of expressing a relationship between two classes:

- making one class a derived class of another (inheritance);

- making an instance of one class a member variable of a client class; and,

- making a pointer to an instance of one class a member variable of a client class.

The purpose of this comparison is to help you to decide when to use these three techniques.

Properties of inheritance

If we have a class X and a class Base, we can write

```
class X: public Base { // ...
```

to make X a derived class of Base. When we do this, class X inherits all of the member variables and functions of class Base,[1] and X will be a subtype of class Base, as we described in Section 6.2.9.

Although we can disable inherited member functions as we describe in Section 9.2.6, the method for doing so relies on run-time checking, which is less desirable than compile-time detection.

As we will describe in detail in Chapter 13, a class may inherit from multiple base classes

```
class X: public Base1, public Base2, public Base3 { // ...
```

in which case class X inherits all of the member variables and functions of all of the base classes.

---

[1] Descendents inherit even private member variables and functions—they just cannot access them.

Inheritance is a specialized mechanism for expressing a relation between classes. It is useful, efficient, convenient, and safe. These properties make it the preferred way of relating classes when it is appropriate.

Properties of member class instances

If we have a client class X and a class Included and we write

```
class X {
    Included a;
// ...
};
```

then instances of class X contain all of the member variables of class Included, but none of class Included's member functions become defined automatically for class X, nor will X be a subtype of class Included. Class Included cannot be the same class as class X, nor can it be a descendent of class X.

If we have a function Included::f() which we would like to be applicable to instances of class X as if class X had inherited f() from class Included, we can accomplish this as follows:

```
class X {
    Included a;
public:
    f() { return a.f(); }
// ...
};
```

Thus, the technique of including an instance of one class as a member variable of a client class is more flexible than inheritance because we can select which functions the client class "inherits" from the included class. The price we pay for this flexibility is that we must write a member function for each member function we wish to "inherit". Of course, we would need to write these additional member functions anyway if we wanted to augment them to do some additional things for the client class. For example, if we wish to implement the function X::hash() to compute the exclusive-OR of all the member variables in an object, it would look much the same whether we use inheritance or a member class instance:

```
class X: public Base {
    int i;
public:
    hash()  { return i ^ Base::hash(); }
//...
};

class X {
    Included a;
    int i;
public:
```

```
        hash()    { return i ^ a.hash(); }
    // ...
    };
```

Including a class instance as a member variable is more flexible than inheritance, but not as convenient because it usually requires writing more code. It is about as safe and efficient as inheritance, so it is the method of choice in situations where inheritance is not suitable.

Properties of member pointers to class instances

If we have a client class X and a class `Referenced` and we write

```
class X {
    Referenced* p;
// ...
};
```

then instances of class X contain none of the member variables of class `Referenced`, none of the member functions of class `Referenced` become defined automatically for class X, and X is not a subtype of class `Referenced`. A member pointer variable may point to an instance of any class, including an instance of the same class or of a descendent class. This is less restrictive than using member instances, which cannot be of the same class as, or be a descendent of, the containing class.

If we have a function `Referenced::f()` which we would like to be applicable to instances of class X as if class X had inherited `f()` from class `Referenced`, we can accomplish this by writing:

```
class X {
    Referenced* p;
public:
    f() { return p->f(); }
// ...
};
```

The technique of including a pointer to an instance of one class as a member variable of a client class is the most flexible technique of the three. As when using a class instance directly, we can select which functions the client class "inherits" from the referenced class. In addition, polymorphism is possible since member functions of the client class may use the pointer to call virtual member functions of the referenced class, causing dynamic binding to occur. Also, since the referenced instance is stored separately from the client instance, it may have a different lifetime, and it can be shared with other instances that contain pointers to it.

The price we pay for this additional flexibility is that we are responsible for creating and destroying the referenced instance, and we must manage the member pointer correctly, as we will describe in Section 9.2.3. In short, using member pointers to class instances is the most work and is prone to error.

We have discussed these techniques in order of preference for expressing a relationship. If you have two classes that seem to be related, first see if it is sensible to make the more specialized class a derived class of the other. If this does not work, consider using an instance of one class as a member variable of the other; use a member variable pointer to an instance as a last resort.

When to use inheritance

If you notice that several classes have member variables in common, you should consider creating a base class containing the common member variables and making all the classes that need these member variables derived classes. For example, the NIH Library classes `Assoc` and `AssocInt`, which associate a key object with a value object as described in Chapter 8, both require a member variable of type `Object*` to point to the key object. Rather than duplicate this member variable and the member functions that use it in both classes, we created the base class `LookupKey` with these common members and made `Assoc` and `AssocInt` derived classes of `LookupKey`. This lets `Assoc`, `AssocInt`, and other similar classes that you might add in the future share the implementations of such functions as `LookupKey::isEqual()` and `LookupKey::hash()`. Creating the base class `LookupKey` can also improve the generality of the implementation of its client classes. For example, since class `Dictionary` operates on instances of `LookupKey`, it naturally works on instances of `Assoc`, `AssocInt`, and any other class derived from `LookupKey`.

If you notice that a group of classes share a complex algorithm, you might make a base class that implements the algorithm by one or more member functions, and derive the classes that use it from this base class so that they will inherit these member functions. The NIH Library classes `Set`, `Dictionary`, and `IdentDict` provide a good example of this organization. Class `Set` implements member functions for performing operations on hash tables, which classes `Dictionary` and `IdentDict` inherit.

You should look for groups of classes that are special cases of some more general concept, and create a base class for them. We explored this line of development, for example, with the geometry classes we described in Chapter 6. As you will recall, we began with classes `Line`, `Triangle`, `Rectangle`, and `Circle`, then added the more general class `Shape` as their base class.

This works the other way around, also. You should look at each class and consider the utility of creating one or more specialized derived classes. Suppose, for example, you have created a class `Vehicle` as part of a traffic simulation. You should consider if the simulation might also require particular kinds of vehicles, such as `Car`, `Truck`, and `MotorCycle`, which you can implement as derived classes of `Vehicle`. Even if you decide that you do not need derived classes, you should plan your implementation to allow for the addition of derived classes in the future. This will simplify and encourage extensions to the program.

When not to use inheritance

How do we know when inheritance is not the appropriate choice for expressing a relationship? Here are the signs to look for:

- inheritance of unnecessary member variables
- inheritance of many (a purist would say *any*) member functions that are not useful

If a derived class exhibits these symptoms, you should consider the other alternatives we just described.

An example problem

Let us apply these guidelines to help us decide where to place class `ArrayOb` in a class hierarchy. First, we try using single inheritance to incorporate class ArrayOb into the classes that wish to utilize its functionality. Figure 9.1 shows one plausible arrangement of some of the NIH Library classes.

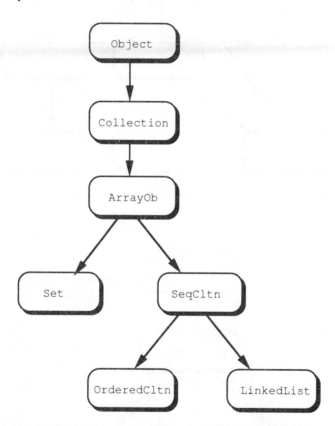

Figure 9.1 Single inheritance container hierarchy for class `ArrayOb`

The problem with this arrangement occurs when we wish to add class `LinkedList`. It should be a derived class of `SeqCltn`, but then it inherits members unnecessarily from `ArrayOb`. Two possible solutions merit consideration. The first is to use multiple inheritance, as shown in Figure 9.2.

Alternatively, we could include an instance of `ArrayOb` as a member variable in those classes that need to use it (`Set` and `OrderedCltn`) and employ only single inheritance, as shown in Figure 9.3.

Which arrangement is better? If we use multiple inheritance, classes `Set` and `OrderedCltn` will inherit both the member variables and member functions of class

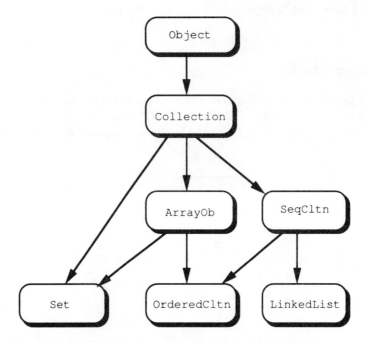

Figure 9.2 Multiple inheritance container hierarchy for class ArrayOb

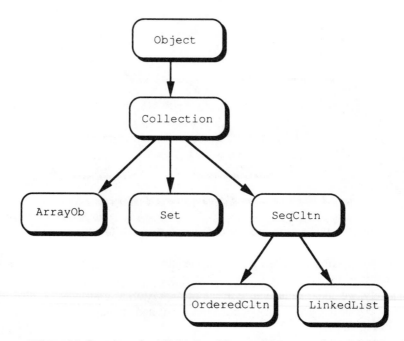

Figure 9.3 Container class hierarchy with ArrayOb *as member variable*

ArrayOb. If we just include an instance of ArrayOb as a member variable, classes Set and OrderedCltn will contain the member variables of class ArrayOb, but the member functions of ArrayOb will not be defined for instances of these classes. The question becomes one of considering the usefulness of ArrayOb's member functions to these classes.

It turns out that classes like Set and OrderedCltn cannot usefully employ most of ArrayOb's member functions: ArrayOb's functions generally operate on *all* of the objects in the array, whereas Set and OrderedCltn populate only a portion of the array with meaningful objects. For example, ArrayOb::isEqual() tests all of the objects in the array element-by-element to see if they match. Class OrderedCltn creates an ArrayOb with some initial capacity, adding objects until the ArrayOb becomes full. When the next object is added, OrderedCltn uses ArrayOb::reSize() to obtain an additional fixed amount of space, so all of the ArrayOb is not always in use, and using ArrayOb::isEqual() to compare two instances of OrderedCltn would incorrectly check the objects in the unused part. Thus, if OrderedCltn were to inherit ArrayOb::isEqual(), it would have to redefine it anyway. Similar reasoning shows that none of ArrayOb's member functions are useful when inherited by OrderedCltn, except perhaps for ArrayOb::capacity(), so in this case, we chose the second solution and made ArrayOb a member variable of client container classes rather than a base class of these classes.

Summary of guidelines for organizing classes

When we organize classes, we can employ three common ways of expressing a relationship between classes: inheritance, inclusion of an instance of a class as a member variable of a client class, and referencing an instance of a class with a member pointer variable of a client class. Inheritance is the preferred method of relating classes when it is appropriate, followed by including a class instance as a member variable of a client. Using member pointers to class instances is the method of last resort.

The following situations suggest the use of inheritance:

- If a group of classes has one or more member variables in common, consider creating a base class with the common member variables.

- If a group of classes share a complex algorithm, consider creating a base class with member functions that implement the algorithm.

- If a group of classes are special cases of a more general concept, consider creating a base class to represent the general concept.

- If a class represents a general concept, consider implementing special cases of that general concept as derived classes.

- Write every class to allow for addition of derived classes in the future.

However, if a derived class winds up inheriting unnecessary member variables or many useless member functions from the base class, this indicates that the derived class should perhaps be a client of the base class instead.

9.2.3   Member instances as opposed to member pointers to instances

For sake of discussion, let us continue with the example problem presented in Section 9.2.2 and consider two alternatives for incorporating class `ArrayOb` in client classes that need its functionality, such as `OrderedCltn`. We can use an instance of class `ArrayOb` directly as a member variable

```
class OrderedCltn : public SeqCltn {
    ArrayOb contents;
// ...
};
```

or, we can construct an instance of `ArrayOb` in the free store and keep a pointer to it as a member variable:

```
class OrderedCltn : public SeqCltn {
    ArrayOb* contents;
// ...
};
```

Which alternative is better? In general, using class instances as members, while restricting flexibility, offers more protection against errors. The C++ compiler constructs and destroys class instance members automatically, and automatically copies them on assignment and initialization. If a member instance is private, access to it is limited to members and friends of the class, as with any private member variable.

Using member pointers to class instances is not only less efficient because of the allocation and deallocation of an additional area of memory for the referenced object, is it also fraught with pitfalls. You must remember to explicitly construct and destroy the referenced object, and to initialize the pointer to it. Also, initializing and assigning objects containing pointers is tricky. Consider the program in Example 9-2.

```
// ex9-2.c - Incorrect handling of member
//           pointers to class instances

#include "String.h"

class X {
    String* s;
public:
    X(const char* t="")    { s = new String(t); }
    ~X()                   { delete s; }
    void set(const char* t) { *s = t; }
    friend ostream& operator<<(ostream& strm, X& x) {
        strm << *x.s;
        return strm;
    }
};
```

```
main()
{
    X a = "abc";
    X b = a;
    X c;
    c = a;
    a.set("xyz");
    cout << "a=" << a << endl;
    cout << "b=" << b << endl;
    cout << "c=" << c << endl;
}
```

You would expect it to print out

```
a=xyz
b=abc
c=abc
```

but it does not. It prints

```
a=xyz
b=xyz
c=xyz
```

because the initialization in the statement X b = a and the assignment c = a *copy* the member pointer variable s, not the String object that it points to. Thus, b and c both wind up pointing to the same String object that a points to, and so appear to take on whatever value a is set to. All this happens because, by default, C++ copies member variables that are pointers or other fundamental types on initialization and assignment.

To make class X behave as expected when instances are initialized or assigned, we must supply definitions of X(const X&) (the copy constructor) and operator=() that explicitly manage the pointer. The simplest technique is to copy the object that is pointed to, as in Example 9-3:

```
// ex9-3.c - Correct handling of member pointers
//              to class instances

#include "String.h"

class X {
    String* s;
public:
    X(const char* t="")     { s = new String(t); }
    X(const X& x)           { s = new String(*x.s); }
    void operator=(const X&);
    ~X()                    { delete s; }
    void set(const char* t) { *s = t; }
```

```
    friend ostream& operator<<(ostream& strm, X& x) {
        strm << *x.s;
        return strm;
    }
};

void X::operator=(const X& x)
{
    if (this == &x) return;
    delete s;
    s = new String(*x.s);
}

main()
{
    X a = "abc";
    X b = a;
    X c;
    c = a;
    a.set("xyz");
    cout << "a=" << a << endl;
    cout << "b=" << b << endl;
    cout << "c=" << c << endl;
}
```

You can also use more elaborate techniques such as reference counting and copy-on-write, but the point is that managing a pointer to an object is much more error-prone than simply making the object a member variable. If, in the previous example, s were a String instead of a String*, we would not need to define X(const X&) and operator=() because C++ would, by default, use the definitions of these functions defined for class String when initializing or copying the member variable String s contained in instances of class X.

Despite the difficulties, situations arise where you *must* use member pointers to class instances. You must use a pointer to take advantage of polymorphism; that is, when you can generalize your class to use the virtual functions declared in a base class, but the actual class of the instance will be that of a derived class and not determined until execution time. Suppose, for example, that class OrderedCltn could be implemented to use the more general notion of a Collection rather than an ArrayOb. We could not write

```
class OrderedCltn : public SeqCltn {
    Collection contents;
// ...
};
```

because Collection is an abstract class, designed to be used only as a base class. To be useful, at execution time contents would need to be an instance of a class derived from Collection. The C++ compiler must, however, reserve a fixed amount of storage for `contents` at compile time, and so allows only enough storage to hold the member variables of a `Collection`, not for those that might be added by derived classes, thus `contents` can never become an instance of a useful class. We can accomplish this with a pointer to a `Collection`:

```
class OrderedCltn : public SeqCltn {
    Collection* contents;
// ...
};
```

At some point, we will initialize `contents` to point to an instance of a class derived from `Collection`:

```
contents = new ArrayOb;
```

Another situation where you must use a member pointer is when the instance a client class needs to use may have a different lifetime; that is, when it may be created before the client class instance is constructed or must continue to exist after the client class instance is destroyed.

You should also use a member pointer to an instance when you wish to share it among several other instances of client classes. For example:

```
class X {
    String* s;
public:
    X(String* t)    { s = t; }
// ...
};

main()
{
    String* p = new String("shared text");
    X x1(p);
    X x2(p);
}
```

Objects `x1` and `x2` each have a pointer to the same instance of the `String`, which is allocated in the free storage area.

Do *not* share a member instance by supplying a member function that client programs can use to obtain a pointer to a member variable:

```
class X {
    String* s;
public:
    X(String* t)    { s = t; }
// ...
};
```

```
class Y {
    String s;
public:
    Y(const char* t) : s(t) {};
    String* f() { return &s; }   // do not do this!
};


main()
{
    Y y("shared text");
    X x(y.f());
}
```

This violates the encapsulation of class Y, since anyone can access the String member variable Y::s via the pointer returned by Y::f(), and it may also cause an error message if you attempt to do object I/O for the following reason: if you were to store a data structure containing both x and y, storeOn() may encounter x first and write out y.s without realizing that it is a member variable of y, and later write out y with a reference to it in place of y.s. The readFrom() function cannot handle this situation—when reconstructing y, it cannot move the instance of y.s it constructed earlier when reading in x to its proper place inside y because there may be pointers to y.s that it would need to change, and readFrom() does not know where they are. Fortunately, storeOn() detects this situation and issues an error message rather than quietly producing an unreadable representation of an object.

One benefit of using member pointers to instances is that you usually do not need to include the specification of the class of the referenced instance in the specification of the class with the member pointer, you only need to declare the name of the class in a class declaration. For example, if we were to change Example 9-3 to define class X in a separate header file (X.h) using an instance of class String instead of a String* for the member variable s, we would need to include the specification of class String:

```
#include <nihcl/String.h>

class X {
    String s;
public:
    X(const char* t="") : s(t) {}   // calls
                                     // String::String(const char*)
// ...
};
```

If, however, we use a String* for the member variable s and we avoid calling any member functions of class String from inline functions defined in X.h, we can eliminate including String.h:

```
class String;
```

```
class X {
    String* s;
public:
    X(const char* t="");
    X(const X& x);
// ...
};
```

This means that the specification of the referenced class, class String, may change without requiring recompilation of class X's clients. Thus, a member pointer to an instance "decouples" the specification of the referenced class from that of the class with the member pointer.

In summary, avoid member pointer variables unless you need to:

- take advantage of polymorphism

- use an instance with a different lifetime

- share an instance with other objects

- decouple specification files

Unfortunately, these situations frequently occur in real programs.

9.2.4 Member functions

What member functions should a class have? Class Object defines a minimal set:

- construct and destroy objects
- read and store objects
- copy objects
- print objects
- compare objects
- compute hash table probe
- access member variables

What the class does determines what additional member functions are appropriate. A class usually has:

manager functions These include the constructors, destructor, copy constructor (X::X(const X&)), assignment operator (operator=()), and type conversion (operator *type*()) member functions;

implementor functions These are the class's member functions that make it "do its thing", and usually modify an object's member variables.

accessor functions These are constant member functions that return information about an object's current state.

internal functions These member functions are used internally by the other member functions in a class—functions that handle error conditions are a common example. Since they are not intended for use by clients, they are usually private.

Member as opposed to non-member functions

Almost all functions should be member functions of some class. This reduces the number of global names, thereby reducing the chances of global name conflicts when you wish to combine independently developed libraries. There is no performance penalty for using static or non-virtual member functions instead of non-member functions. Calling a static member function is as fast as calling a non-member function, and calling a non-static, non-virtual member function with n arguments is as fast as calling a non-member function with $n + 1$ arguments (the `this` pointer is implicitly passed as an argument to non-static member functions).

The most notable exception to this rule are binary operator functions that have fundamental types as operands, which you must define as non-member friend functions in order to finesse the C++ compiler into performing automatic type conversion for their left operands, as we discussed in Section 4.2.16.

Whenever you notice a non-member function that has a class as an argument, you should consider eliminating this argument and making the function a member function of the class.

Virtual as opposed to non-virtual member functions

Which member functions should be virtual?[2] Virtual functions are more powerful than non-virtual member functions, but are less efficient. As we described earlier, the power of virtual functions lies in the ability of a derived class to re-implement an inherited virtual function, effectively replacing its ancestor class's implementation of that virtual function with its own. This potentially changes the behavior of client programs that use these ancestor classes without requiring their re-compilation. A derived class may also redefine inherited non-virtual member functions, but the redefinition has no effect on clients of ancestor classes.

In some cases, a base class defines non-trivial member functions that should *not* be overridden by derived classes, and hence should not be declared virtual. A good example of this is `Object::storeOn()`. This function performs class-independent operations to convert an object into an external representation, and uses data structures that are not accessible to other functions in the process; thus, derived classes cannot meaningfully override it, so class `Object` does not declare it virtual.

Table 9.1 shows the relative execution overhead of various kinds of member function calls. As the table shows, the additional overhead of calling a virtual member function as opposed to an ordinary (i.e. non-virtual, non-inline) function is small, at worst a factor of 2.9, which is not noticeable if the function performs a non-trivial computation.

---

[2] Some programming languages, such as Object Pascal and Smalltalk-80, do not give the programmer this choice—all member functions (called *methods* in these languages) use dynamic binding, and so are similar to virtual functions.

Table 9.1 Member function call execution overhead

Member Function Type	Overhead(μs)*	Ratio of Overhead to Non-virtual Member Function
non-virtual	3.6	1.0
virtual	7.6	2.1
inline virtual	7.6	2.1
virtual base class† non-virtual	4.1	1.2
virtual base class virtual	10.3	2.9

* These timings were measured on a Sun-3/50 running SunOS 3.5 and Release 2.00 of the AT&T C++ Translator.

† We discuss virtual base classes in Chapter 13.

Pure as opposed to impure virtual functions

When designing an abstract class with a virtual function that it cannot implement, you have two choices: you can declare the function to be a pure virtual function as we described in Section 6.2.10 and defer its implementation to a derived class, or you can supply a dummy implementation of the virtual function that prints out an error message or attempts some other remedial action. A pure virtual function is safer than an impure virtual function because C++ guarantees that all non-abstract descendents will implement it. If, however, a derived class neglects to implement an impure virtual function, it inherits that of the base class so that when that member function is applied to an instance of the derived class the error message is printed. Unfortunately, this type of error is not detected until execution time. The program can successfully compile and link, but we must rely on testing to uncover the omission, which does not give us the same level of confidence in the program's correctness.

On the other hand, if the abstract class has many non-abstract descendents that cannot implement the virtual function at all, it becomes a nuisance to supply each one with a dummy definition. In this case, an impure virtual function with a dummy implementation is a convenience that may be worth the small risk. A good example is the virtual function scanFrom() in the NIH Library class Object. The scanFrom() function is supposed to parse text from an input stream in a format convenient for humans, and set the instance to which it is applied to the value the text represents. It is useful for reading a value of a Date or Time, for example. We implement it in class Object so that we can write an overloaded definition of the istream extraction operator

```
inline istream& operator>>(istream& strm, Object& ob)
{
    ob.scanFrom(strm);
    return strm;
}
```

that will be applicable to all objects. Most descendents of class Object, however, cannot implement scanFrom()—it is unlikely someone would want to type in a Dictionary or Process (see Chapter 11), for example. So rather than require most derived classes to provide dummy implementations of scanFrom(), we defined it as an impure virtual function with a default dummy implementation in class Object.

Inline as opposed to non-inline

As we discussed in Section 4.2.22, small functions and functions with many arguments but little code are good candidates for inline compilation.

The more difficult decision is whether to make a trivial function virtual or inline. In theory, the C++ language allows a member function to be both virtual and inline, so it may seem that no decision is necessary. As we shall see later, however, C++ compilers often impose hidden inefficiencies that make the combination impractical.

In some cases, the overhead of calling a virtual function is unacceptable, so the only choice is to use an inline function. For example, the NIH Class Library member functions Point::x() and Point::y(), which return the X and Y coordinates of a Point object, will run at only one-tenth the speed than if they were virtual functions, and so must be inline to give acceptable performance in applications that use them heavily.

Alternatively, we can provide two different member functions, one inline and one virtual, to perform similar operations. NIH Library classes use this approach with the member functions operator==() and isEqual(), both of which test objects for equality. Classes for which the test for equality is a simple operation declare operator==() inline; otherwise, it is non-virtual. The function isEqual() is always virtual, and for most classes isEqual() calls operator==(). We describe the implementation of ArrayOb::operator==() and ArrayOb::isEqual() in detail in Chapter 10.

As we said, a member function can be both virtual and inline; however, making a virtual function inline may help or hurt the efficiency of a program depending upon the C++ compiler used and the way in which the program calls the function. The inline keyword is just a hint to the compiler, which may choose to ignore it. We can apply a member function to a class instance in four ways, and a particular C++ compiler may ignore the inline hint for any or all of them. You can compile the test program for Example 9-4 with your compiler and examine the generated code to determine which forms are expanded inline:

```
// ex9-4.c - Virtual inline function calls

class X {
    int n;
public:
    X(int i=0)          { n = i; }
    virtual void inc()  { n++; }
};

main()
{
    X x;
    X* xp = new X;
// virtual function with scope resolution applied
// to class instance
    x.X::inc();
// virtual function with scope resolution applied
// through pointer to class instance
```

```
    xp->X::inc();
// virtual function applied to class instance
    x.inc();
// virtual function applied through pointer to class instance
    xp->inc();
}
```

Most compilers will expand inline the first two forms, in which the scope resolution operator explicitly specifies the function implementation to use, but these forms occur relatively infrequently in real programs. Some C++ compilers, such as the AT&T C++ Translator Release 2.0, will expand the third form (x.inc()) inline. No compilers we currently know of optimize the fourth form (xp->inc())—you can see from Table 9.1 that an inline virtual function call of this kind is no faster than a non-inline virtual function call.

Normally, this would not be of great concern to a programmer, except that declaring a virtual function inline may incur a penalty when a compiler cannot perform the inline expansion: the compiler may generate a separate, static copy of the virtual function in each module (the result of compiling a C++ .c file) that calls the function, making the program larger than necessary.

Summary of member function design decisions

To summarize our guidelines for designing member functions:

- Classes usually have a variety of member functions, broadly categorized as manager, implementor, accessor, and internal functions.

- Most functions should be member functions of some class—this reduces pollution of the global name space, and there is no performance penalty for using static or non-virtual member functions.

- Virtual member functions are more powerful that non-virtual member functions, at a modest cost in efficiency.

- Pure virtual member functions are safer than impure virtual member functions because they force all non-abstract descendents to provide implementations.

- Small functions and functions with many arguments but little code are good candidates for inline compilation.

- Declaring virtual functions inline may provide no improvement in performance and make your programs unnecessarily larger.

9.2.5 Member variables

What member variables should a class have? This depends mostly on what the class does, but here are some general observations about member variables.

Often, a class will have *no* member variables. This usually occurs in the case of an abstract class like Object or Collection, or when a class changes the behavior of its base class in some simple way, for example `Dictionary`, `IdentDict`, and `SortedCltn`. None of these NIH Library classes have member variables.

You can declare a member variable to be `static`, in which case *all* instances of the class *share a single instance* of the static member variable. For example, if you wanted to write a class that kept a count of how many instances of itself existed, you could do this with a static member variable:

```
// In the file Counted.h:

class Counted {
    static unsigned n;
public:
    Counted()                          { n++; }
    ~Counted()                         { n--; }
    static unsigned howMany()    { return n; }
// ...
};


// In the file Counted.c:

unsigned Counted::n = 0;
```

Notice that you initialize a static member variable much as you would a global variable: with a separate definition placed in a `.c` file.

As an alternative to using a static member variable, you can declare a static, non-member variable in the `.c` file containing the implementation of the member functions of the class, for example:

```
// In the file Counted.h:

class Counted {
public:
    Counted();
    ~Counted();
    static unsigned howMany();
// ...
};


// In the file Counted.c:

static unsigned n = 0;

Counted::Counted()             { n++; }
Counted::~Counted()            { n--; }
unsigned Counted::howMany() { return n; }
```

The advantage is that if no inline functions need to access a static variable, and if you can place the definitions of all of the functions that do need to access a static variable in the same .c file, then it is better to declare the variable as a static non-member variable in the .c file rather than as a static member variable in the .h file. That way, a change to the declaration of the variable affects only the .c file—changing the declaration of a static member variable in the .h file will make it necessary to re-compile all the client programs that include the .h file in addition to the .c file.

9.2.6 Member accessibility

How accessible should we make the members of a class? That is, which members should be private, which should be protected, and which should be public? A good general policy is to restrict access to members as much as possible.

Private member variables

Member variables should almost always be private; otherwise, we do not realize the advantages of encapsulation. If you are concerned about efficiency, use a public inline member function to provide clients with read access to private member variables.

To illustrate this, let us consider these two ways of writing a class to represent a weather report:

```
class Weather {      // public member variables
public:
    float temperature;   // degrees Celsius
    float pressure;      // mm. Hg
    float humidity;      // 0-100%
// ...
};

class Weather {      // private member variables
    float temperature;   // degrees Celsius
    float pressure;      // mm. Hg
    float humidity;      // 0-100%
public:
    float temp() const  { return temperature; }
    float temp(float c) { return temperature = c; }
// ...
};
```

In the first case, where the member variables are public, client programs can access them directly:

```
Weather x;
x.temperature = 0.0;
```

In the second case, the member variables are private and class Weather provides inline member functions such as temp() to allow client programs to access them:

```
Weather x;
x.temp(0.0);
```

Encapsulating the member variables of class `Weather` so that client programs must use member functions to access them does not allow a notation as convenient as when using public member variables directly, but is just as efficient. The real advantage becomes apparent if we decide to change class `Weather` to represent the temperature in degrees Fahrenheit instead of Celsius, for example. If we had used public member variables, we would have no choice but to modify the client programs. However, if we had used public member functions to access the private member variables, we can change to degrees Fahrenheit and still provide the same interface to client programs:

```
class Weather {      // private member variables
    float temperature;  // degrees Fahrenheit
    float pressure;     // mm. Hg
    float humidity;     // 0-100%
public:
    float temp() const  { return (5.0/9.0) * (temperature-32.0); }
    float temp(float c) {
        temperature = (9.0/5.0) * c + 32.0;
        return c;
    }
// ...
};
```

Occasionally, you will find it convenient to declare some or all of a class's member variables protected so that derived classes can access them—otherwise, you might have to write many additional protected member accessor functions. This is particularly tempting when the member variable in question is a class instance, since you would need to provide a protected member function for each of that class's operations that a derived class might need. But beware! Your descendents then depend upon these implementation details of your class, which you might someday regret.

Member variables should almost never be public, however. One possible exception to this rule is public `const` member variables, since clients can't alter these.

Private member functions

You should make member functions that clients can easily misuse, or that are really only useful to other member functions private (error handling functions are a good example of this). If a few specific non-member functions must call private member functions, you can make these functions friends of the class. You also want, however, to avoid a situation that will require you to modify an existing class to make a new class or function a friend. If existing classes have to be modified when new classes are added, it often indicates that you have not decomposed your application into classes properly, suggesting you should consider other possible decompositions. This situation usually arises when the new class is derived from an existing class. Then, you can solve the problem by making the necessary member functions protected instead of private. Otherwise, consider redesigning your class to make the private member functions safe to use, and then make them public.

The class `SubString`, which we described in Section 5.3.4, illustrates a situation in which private constructor functions are useful. As you recall, we created class `SubString` solely to provide a convenient notation for extracting and replacing substrings of instances of class `String`. We referred to `SubString` as a *private class* because we wanted clients to be able to perform many of the operations defined by class `String` on substrings, but we did not want clients to be able to create named instances of class `SubString`. We accomplished this by making all of constructors of class `SubString` private, and made class `String` a friend of `SubString` so that only it could construct instances of class `SubString`.

Sometimes a derived class must disable an inherited member function. For example, the NIH Library class `SortedCltn` must disable the function `addAfter()`, inherited from class `OrderedCltn`. In a `SortedCltn` the order of the objects is determined by the virtual function `compare()`, so it does not make sense to allow a client program to explicitly specify the order of two objects with a function like `addAfter()`. Class `SortedCltn` disables `addAfter()` by making it private. If a client program attempts to apply `addAfter()` to an instance of a `SortedCltn`, the C++ compiler will produce an error message:

```
SortedCltn s;
String t = "z",  u = "a";
s.add(t);
s.addAfter(t,u);    // error - SortedCltn::addAfter() is private
```

This is not enough—friends or members of `SortedCltn` are still able to call `addAfter()`, and since `addAfter()` is a virtual function, a client may call it through a pointer with the type of an ancestor class:

```
OrderedCltn* o = new SortedCltn;
String t = "z",  u = "a";
o->add(t);
o->addAfter(t,u);   // run-time error
```

Class `SortedCltn` prevents this by reimplementing `addAfter()` to print an error message if it is called in addition to declaring it private:

```
Object* SortedCltn::addAfter(const Object&, Object& /*newob*/)
{
    shouldNotImplement("addAfter"); return 0;
}
```

The function `shouldNotImplement()` is a member function of class `Object` that prints an "Illegal function" error message. In this case it would print:

```
[ILLEGALMFCN] Illegal function address->SortedCltn::addAfter()
```

where *address* is the address of the object to which the client program attempted to apply the illegal function.

Protected member functions

The implementation of some operations on objects breaks down naturally into two parts: a general, class-independent part and a class-dependent part. The NIH Class Library's implementation of the `storeOn()` operation provides a good example of this. The function `Object::storeOn()` is a public, non-virtual member function that does the general bookkeeping, such as keeping track of multiple references to objects, calling the virtual member function `storer()` to actually store the member variables for a specific class. Each class reimplements `storer()` to first write out the member variables of its ancestor classes by calling the `storer()` function of its base class, and then to store its own member variables. Thus, only the member function implementing the general part, in this case `storeOn()`, needs to be public. The function implementing the class-dependent part, in this case `storer()`, should be called only by derived classes, and can therefore be protected, thereby preventing client programs from using it.

Another good use of protected members is to make the constructors of abstract classes protected members. This prevents client programs from creating instances of them, while still allowing the constructors of derived classes to access them. Even if a class has pure virtual functions, it is still good style to do this anyway because it explicitly documents the access restriction on the constructors, and it prevents instances of an abstract class from being constructed by clients in the event that the pure virtual functions are removed or implemented later in the class's development. We saw protected members used in this manner in class `Shape` in the geometry example of Chapter 6.

Summary of member accessibility

- Make member variables private.

- Keep member functions that client programs can misuse or have no need for private.

- Make the constructors of private classes private.

- Make inherited member functions that a class disables private.

- Make member functions that should be called only by derived classes protected.

- Make the constructors of abstract classes protected.

9.3   CHAPTER SUMMARY

In this chapter we have described some principles of good object-oriented design in C++ and we have shown how we applied these to the design of class `ArrayOb`, a typical NIH Library class. We discussed when to use C++ classes, various approaches to organizing classes in relation to one another, what member variables and functions classes should have, and when to restrict access to members.

AN EXAMPLE NIH LIBRARY CLASS

10.1 INTRODUCTION

NIH Library classes contain a lot of "boiler plate" code—code that is uninteresting to write because it varies little from class to class, yet must be present for a class to function properly with other NIH Library classes. Each NIH Library class must also implement functions to support features such as object I/O, copying, printing, comparing, and so on; these functions must adhere to certain conventions. Furthermore, both novices and experienced programmers alike find it distressing and intimidating to begin writing a program starting with an empty screen. It is always better to modify and extend a working piece of code if possible.

We have devised a pair of files, named `Template_h` and `Template_c`, that contain the specification and implementation, respectively, for a generic NIH Library class. A programmer can make some simple changes to these template files to produce the "boiler plate" code required by a new NIH Library class. The template files also contain the stubs (function definitions with empty bodies) of the support functions most NIH Library classes will need along with comments describing the conventions they must follow. Using these template files reduces the number of programming errors, and encourages programmers to implement all of the support functions expected of an NIH Library class, even if their immediate application does not require them. Appendix B contains a complete listing of the template files. This chapter describes how to use `Template_h` and `Template_c` to help write class `ArrayOb`.

10.2 WRITING THE SPECIFICATION

Here is the specification (or header file) of class `ArrayOb`, kept in the file `ArrayOb.h`. We created this file by making a copy of `Template_h`, changing all occurrences of the string `THIS_CLASS` to `ArrayOb` and `BASE_CLASS` to `Collection`, and adding the lines marked `// +`:

```
#ifndef ARRAYOB_H
#define ARRAYOB_H

// ArrayOb.h - Basic polymorphic array of objects
```

```
#include "Collection.h"
class Iterator;                                              // +
class ArrayOb: public Collection {
    DECLARE_MEMBERS(ArrayOb);
    Object** v;                                              // +
    unsigned sz;                                             // +
    void allocSizeErr() const;                              // +
    void indexRangeErr() const;                            // +
protected:                // storer() functions for object I/O
    virtual void storer(OIOofd&) const;
    virtual void storer(OIOout&) const;
public:
    ArrayOb(unsigned size =DEFAULT_CAPACITY);               // +
    ArrayOb(const ArrayOb&);                                // +
    ~ArrayOb()   { delete v; }                              // +
    void operator=(const ArrayOb&);                        // +
    bool operator==(const ArrayOb&) const;
    bool operator!=(const ArrayOb& a) const { return !(*this==a); }
    Object*& operator[](int i) {                           // +
        if ((unsigned)i >= sz) indexRangeErr();            // +
        return v[i];                                        // +
    }                                                       // +
    const Object *const& operator[](int i) const {         // +
        if ((unsigned)i >= sz) indexRangeErr();            // +
        return v[i];                                        // +
    }                                                       // +
    virtual Collection& addContentsTo(Collection&) const;  // +
    virtual Object*& at(int i);                             // +
    virtual const Object *const& at(int i) const;          // +
    virtual unsigned capacity() const;                     // +
    virtual int compare(const Object&) const;
    virtual void deepenShallowCopy();
    virtual Object* doNext(Iterator&) const;               // +
    virtual unsigned hash() const;
    virtual bool isEqual(const Object&) const;
    virtual void reSize(unsigned);                         // +
    virtual void removeAll();                              // +
    virtual unsigned size() const;                         // +
    virtual const Class* species() const;
private:                  // shouldNotImplement();
    virtual Object* add(Object&);                          // +
    virtual unsigned occurrencesOf(const Object&) const;  // +
    virtual Object* remove(const Object&);                 // +
};


#endif
```

10.2.1 Including header files and preventing multiple definitions

The header file (the .h file) for a class must #include the header files of all of its base classes and the header files for any class objects that:

- are used as member or extern variables;

- are passed by value as arguments to functions;

- are returned by value from functions; or,

- have member functions or variables that are referenced in the definitions of inline functions in the header file.

Pointers and references to class objects do not count—you can just declare these class names in class declarations such as

```
class Iterator;
```

rather than including their header files, reduce dependencies, and save some compilation time.

The header file for class ArrayOb mentions the following classes: Collection, Object*, OIOofd&, OIOout&, Iterator&, and of course ArrayOb. We must include Collection.h because it is the base class for ArrayOb. The classes OIOofd and OIOout are defined in Object.h, which is always included as a result of including the header file of *any* NIH Library class. That leaves class Iterator, which is used as a reference argument to ArrayOb::doNext(), so we only need to declare it in a class declaration.

The requirement to include the header files of the base classes means we must be careful to avoid compiling a particular header file more than once and producing multiple definition errors. The first two lines and last line of ArrayOb.h assure that the file is compiled only once even if a program includes it more than once:

```
#ifndef ARRAYOB_H
#define ARRAYOB_H
#include "Collection.h"
// ...
#endif
```

To see how this works, suppose a program requires the use of more than one NIH Library class, say ArrayOb and Set. Then it must #include ArrayOb.h and Set.h. ArrayOb.h includes Collection.h which in turn includes Object.h. When the compiler encounters the #include "ArrayOb.h" directive, the symbols ARRAYOB_H, COLLECTION_H, and OBJECT_H will be undefined; they will be defined and their respective .h files compiled. Later, when the compiler encounters #include "Set.h", which also includes Collection.h, Collection.h will not be compiled a second time because the file is wrapped by the #ifndef COLLECTION_H ... #endif, and COLLECTION_H is now defined as a consequence of ArrayOb.h including Collection.h.

10.2.2   Declaring NIH Class Library members

The DECLARE_MEMBERS preprocessor macro is defined in Object.h. You call it with the name of the class you are declaring as an argument, and it declares the following members for this class:

- the private static member variable classDesc, which is the class descriptor object for this class, as discussed in Section 8.1.2;

- the static member function desc(), which returns a const pointer to this class's descriptor;

- the static member readFrom() functions and readFrom() constructors;

- the virtual member isA() function, described in Section 8.1.2; and,

- the virtual member shallowCopy() function, described in Section 7.3.1.

The DECLARE_MEMBERS macro also declares some member functions which you need when using multiple inheritance:

- a family of castdown() functions, which you call to convert an Object* to a pointer to an instance of this class (see Section 13.10.2);

- the deepenVBase() function, which you call to deepen a shallow copy of a special type of base class called a *virtual base class* (see Section 13.10.3); and,

- the storeVBaseOn() functions, which you call to perform object I/O for virtual base classes (see Section 13.10.4).

All of these functions, except for the readFrom() constructors, are also defined, either inline by the DECLARE_MEMBERS macro or by one of the DEFINE_CLASS macros discussed in Section 10.3.4.

10.2.3   Member variables of class ArrayOb

Class ArrayOb has two private member variables:

```
Object** v;
unsigned sz;
```

The member variable v points to an array in the free storage area that holds the pointers to the objects in the ArrayOb. The member variable sz is the size of the array. You should be familiar with this technique for managing an area of free storage, since the class BigInt we described in Chapters 3 and 4 and the String class we described in Section 5.3 do something similar.

10.2.4   Private member functions of class ArrayOb

```
void allocSizeErr() const;
void indexRangeErr() const;
```

Class `ArrayOb` has two private constant member functions to print error messages: `allocSizeErr()`, which `ArrayOb(unsigned size)` and `reSize()` call when they are requested to create a zero-length `ArrayOb`, and `indexRangeErr()`, which `operator[]()` calls when it detects an out-of-range subscript.

10.2.5   Object I/O member functions of class `ArrayOb`

Class `ArrayOb` has two additional functions concerned with object I/O:

```
protected:                  // storer() functions for object I/O
    virtual void storer(OIOofd&) const;
    virtual void storer(OIOout&) const;
```

The two `storer()` functions write the information contained in the member variables of this class to the argument file descriptor or `ostream` in a format that the corresponding constructor can interpret, as we described in Section 7.4.1. Declaring the `storer()` functions `protected` prevents client programs from using them directly—only class `ArrayOb` and its derived classes can call them.

There are two `storer()` functions (and two `readFrom()` functions and two `readFrom()` constructors) because the NIH Class Library has two kinds of object I/O: *stream object I/O* and *file descriptor object I/O*, which we'll discuss later in Sections 10.3.22 and 10.3.23.

10.2.6   Public member functions of class `ArrayOb`

We now give a brief description of class `ArrayOb`'s public member functions:

```
ArrayOb(unsigned size =DEFAULT_CAPACITY)
```

Constructs an instance of an `ArrayOb` with the specified size.

```
ArrayOb(const ArrayOb&)
```

Constructs an instance of an `ArrayOb` initialized to point to the same objects contained in the argument `ArrayOb`. This is the copy constructor for class `ArrayOb`, which we need to implement because we do not want C++ to simply copy the pointer member variable v when we copy an `ArrayOb`.

```
~ArrayOb()
```

Destroys this instance of an `ArrayOb`.

```
void operator=(const ArrayOb&)
```

Assigns the object pointers contained in the argument `ArrayOb` to this `ArrayOb`.

```
bool operator==(const ArrayOb&) const
bool operator!=(const ArrayOb&) const
```

Compare two instances of `ArrayOb` to see if they are equal or not equal.

```
Object*& operator[](int i)
virtual Object*& at(int i)
```

Return a reference to the pointer to the *i*th `Object` in this `ArrayOb`.

```
const Object *const& operator[](int i) const
virtual const Object *const& at(int i) const
```

Return a reference to the constant pointer to the *i*th `Object` in this `ArrayOb`. When you index a constant `ArrayOb`, C++ will select the `const` overloading of `operator[]()` or `at()`, which protects the pointers in the `ArrayOb` against modification by returning a constant pointer result (see 5.3.8).

```
virtual Collection& addContentsTo(Collection&) const
```

Adds the objects in the `ArrayOb` to the `Collection` specified by the argument.

```
virtual unsigned capacity() const
virtual unsigned size() const
```

Return the number of object pointers in this `ArrayOb`; i.e., the value of the member variable `sz`.

```
virtual int compare(const Object&) const
```

Does a lexical comparison of this `ArrayOb` and the argument object and returns a number < 0 if this `ArrayOb` is less than the argument, = 0 if they are equal, and > 0 if this `ArrayOb` is greater than the argument. The argument object must return the address of the `ArrayOb` class descriptor as its `species()` for it to be considered a comparable class. The `compare()` function compares the individual objects in the arrays by applying `compare()` to them.

```
virtual void deepenShallowCopy()
```

Called by `Object::deepCopy()` to convert a shallow copy of an `ArrayOb` object to a deep copy; that is, the copy does not point to the same objects that were in the original, but to copies made by calling `deepCopy()`.

```
virtual Object* doNext(Iterator&) const
```

Returns a pointer to the next object in this `ArrayOb`, or 0 if no more objects remain. The `Iterator` argument maintains the current position in the `ArrayOb`.

```
virtual unsigned hash() const
```

Returns a number that class Set can use as a hash table probe. If two objects are equal; that is, if isEqual() returns YES for the objects, then the two objects must return the same value for hash().

```
virtual bool isEqual(const Object&) const
```

Returns YES if this object and the argument object are comparable and they have equal values. Two objects are comparable if they return the same class descriptor address for species(). In this case, the argument object must return the address of class ArrayOb's class descriptor for it to be considered comparable to an ArrayOb.

```
virtual void reSize(unsigned)
```

Changes the size of this ArrayOb to the size given by the argument.

```
virtual const Collection& removeAll()
```

Removes all objects from this ArrayOb.

```
virtual const Class* species() const
```

Returns the address of class ArrayOb's class descriptor.

10.3 WRITING THE IMPLEMENTATION

The file ArrayOb.c in the distribution kit contains the implementation of class ArrayOb. We created this file from the template file Template_c by making a copy of it and changing all occurrences of the string THIS_CLASS to ArrayOb and BASE_CLASS to Collection. The template file consists mostly of function definitions with empty bodies that the programmer must supply. Comments in each function indicate any rules that must be observed when implementing the function. We usually delete these comments from the actual implementation file, as we have done for ArrayOb.c in this chapter.

10.3.1 Include files

```
#include <malloc.h>
#include "ArrayOb.h"
#include "nihclIO.h"
```

These three lines include the specification (i.e. the .h file) of the class we want to implement: ArrayOb.h, the NIH Class Library header file nihclIO.h, and the system header file malloc.h. You must always include the specification of the class you are implementing, and the specifications of any other classes it uses in its implementation. The file nihclIO.h contains the declarations for functions used in the implementation of object I/O, and we include `malloc.h` because it declares the C/C++ library function `realloc()`, which the implementation of `ArrayOb::reSize()` needs.

10.3.2 THIS and BASE

```
#define THIS    ArrayOb
#define BASE    Collection
```

By convention, we define the preprocessor symbols `THIS` and `BASE` to be the names of the class we are implementing and its base class, respectively. We use these preprocessor symbols to distinguish between references to these classes made solely because of their special hierarchical relationship to the class we are implementing and references made because of the functionality of these classes. In other words, we use the preprocessor symbol `BASE` wherever we would want to refer to the base class even if we were to change its name; otherwise, we use the class name itself. The preprocessor symbol `THIS` is rarely used.

If the class we are defining has more than one base class, that is, the class utilizes multiple inheritance, we do not define the symbol `BASE`.

10.3.3 BASE_CLASSES, MEMBER_CLASSES, and VIRTUAL_BASE_CLASSES

```
#define BASE_CLASSES Collection::desc()
#define MEMBER_CLASSES
#define VIRTUAL_BASE_CLASSES
```

Before calling the `DEFINE_CLASS` macro to define the instance of class `Class` that describes `ArrayOb`, we must first define three preprocessor symbols that describe the relationship of class `ArrayOb` to other NIH Library classes.

We set the symbol `BASE_CLASSES` to a list of the addresses of the class descriptors for the base classes of the class we are defining. These must be in the same order as they appear in the class declaration.

We set the symbol `MEMBER_CLASSES` to a list of the addresses of the class descriptors for any non-static member variables of the class that are NIH Library classes. These must be in the same order as they appear in the class declaration. Since class `ArrayOb` has no members that are instances of other NIH Library classes, we define `MEMBER_CLASSES`, but give it no value.

A *virtual base class* is a special kind of base class that is useful for multiple inheritance, and which we will describe later in Chapter 13. The symbol `VIRTUAL_BASE_CLASSES` is a list of the addresses of the class descriptors for the virtual base classes of a class. Like `MEMBER_CLASSES`, class `ArrayOb` has no virtual base classes, so we define `VIRTUAL_BASE_CLASSES`, but give it no value.

The following example shows how to set these symbols in a more complicated situation:

```
class X: public A, public virtual B {
    C c;          // C is an NIH Library class
```

```
    D d;            // D is an NIH Library class
//...
};
```

```
#define BASE_CLASSES A::desc(), B::desc()
#define MEMBER_CLASSES C::desc(), D::desc()
#define VIRTUAL_BASE_CLASSES B::desc()
```

10.3.4 DEFINE_CLASS **preprocessor macro**

```
DEFINE_CLASS(ArrayOb,1,"$Header$",NULL,NULL);
```

The call to the DEFINE_CLASS preprocessor macro in the implementation of class ArrayOb defines the descriptor for class ArrayOb and generates definitions for most of the member functions declared by the DECLARE_MEMBERS macro, which we described in Section 10.2.2.

The DEFINE_CLASS macro defines the following:

- the instance of class Class that describes the class you are implementing;

- the virtual function isA();

- the virtual function shallowCopy();

- the deepenVBase() member function;

- the storeVBaseOn() member function; and,

- the virtual function _castdown().

The format of this macro call is:

DEFINE_CLASS (*classname,version,identification,initor1,initor2*)

Classname is the name of the class you are defining.

Version is the version number of the class you are defining. You should increment it whenever the format of the information written by the storer() function changes such that older versions of readFrom() can no longer interpret it correctly. A class's version number is combined with those of its ancestor and non-static member classes to form a number called the class's *signature*. When the storeOn() function writes an object, it records its class's signature along with it. The readFrom() function verifies that the signature of an object it is reading matches that in the class descriptor linked with the program, thus preventing outdated versions of objects from being read incorrectly and causing problems with object I/O that may be difficult to diagnose.

If a class has no member variables that are stored, you can set its version number to zero. Classes with a version number of zero are ignored when computing a signature, so you can insert such a class as an ancestor without changing the signatures of its derived classes and unnecessarily outdating their stored instances. This might be useful if you are adding a class to an existing class hierarchy and realize that your new class has something in common with an existing class, and so you would like to also add a class with no member variables to serve as a base class for the existing class and your new one. If you give the new base class a zero version number, stored instances of the existing class will still be readable.

Identification is a character string that identifies the revision level of the implementation of the class. It is simply stored in the class descriptor where you can retrieve it by calling the function `Object::ident()`. We usually set the identification to a special character string such as `"$Header$"` or `"%W%\t%G%"` so that a revision control system such as RCS [31] or SCCS [20] under UNIX can generate the identification information automatically.

Initor1 and *initor2* are pointers to functions you may supply to perform initialization for the class, for example, initializing static data that the class uses. These static functions take a reference to this class's class descriptor (a `const Class&`) as an argument. The constructor for class `Class` calls *initor1* just before returning, and the NIH Class Library initialization routine calls the *initor2* functions of all classes linked with a program as the last phase of initialization. Thus, you cannot predict the order in which these functions will be called except that all *initor1* functions will be called before any *initor2* functions.

In class `ArrayOb` (as in most classes), we do not need *initor1* or *initor2*, so we specify them as `NULL`.

10.3.5 `DEFINE_ABSTRACT_CLASS` **preprocessor macro**

If we were writing an abstract class, we would use a different form of the `DEFINE_CLASS` preprocessor macro named `DEFINE_ABSTRACT_CLASS`.

`DEFINE_ABSTRACT_CLASS` requires the same arguments as `DEFINE_CLASS`. The only difference between the two is that `DEFINE_ABSTRACT_CLASS` does not reference the class's `readFrom()` constructors.

10.3.6 **Symbolic error codes**

```
extern const int NIHCL_ALLOCSIZE, NIHCL_INDEXRANGE;
```

The NIH Class Library reports errors by calling the function `NIHCL::setError()` with an error code indicating the type of error. The error codes are global symbols with names beginning with `NIHCL_`, and are defined in the file `nihclerrsx.h`. Programs must import the definitions of any error codes they use by declaring them `extern` as we have done here.

10.3.7 `ArrayOb` **constructors**

```
ArrayOb::ArrayOb(unsigned size)
{
    sz = size;
    if (sz==0) allocSizeErr();
    v = new Object*[sz];
    register i = sz;
    register Object** vp = v;
    while (i--) *vp++ = nil;
}
```

This constructor function creates an instance of `ArrayOb` with the specified size. It uses `new` to allocate an array of `Object*` and initializes each element of the array with a pointer to the `Nil` object.

```
ArrayOb::ArrayOb(const ArrayOb& a)
{
    register i = a.sz;
    sz = i;
    v = new Object*[i];
    register Object** vp = v;
    register Object** av = a.v;
    while (i--) *vp++ = *av++;
}
```

The copy constructor for class `ArrayOb` makes a copy of the argument `ArrayOb`. It uses `new` to allocate an array of `Object*` of the same size and copies the pointers held by the argument `ArrayOb` into it.

10.3.8 `ArrayOb` assignment operator

```
void ArrayOb::operator=(const ArrayOb& a)
{
    if (v != a.v {
        delete v;
        v = new Object*[sz=a.sz];
        register i = a.sz;
        register Object** vp = v;
        register Object** av = a.v;
        while (i--) *vp++ = *av++;
    }
}
```

`ArrayOb`'s assignment operator functions similarly to the copy constructor in that it also makes a copy of the argument `ArrayOb`. The difference is that the destination `ArrayOb` contains a pointer to storage that must first be freed by calling `delete` before doing the copy. The function must check that an `ArrayOb` is not being assigned to itself to prevent erroneously freeing the storage used by the source argument.

10.3.9 `ArrayOb::operator==()`

```
bool ArrayOb::operator==(const ArrayOb& a) const
{
    if (sz != a.sz) return NO;
    register unsigned i = sz;
    register Object** vp = v;
    register Object** av = a.v;
```

```
        while (i--) {
            if (!((*vp++)->isEqual(**av++))) return NO;
        }
        return YES;
    }
```

The function `operator==()` compares two instances of class `ArrayOb` to determine
if they are equal. First, they must have the same size. If they do, the function loops though
the arrays of object pointers, testing each pair of objects for equality by calling the virtual
function `isEqual()` for each pair. If it finds an unequal pair, `operator==()` returns
NO; otherwise the instances of `ArrayOb` are equal and `operator==()` returns YES.

10.3.10 `ArrayOb::species()` and `isEqual()`

```
const Class* ArrayOb::species() const { return &classDesc; }

bool ArrayOb::isEqual(const Object& a) const
{
    return a.isSpecies(classDesc) && *this==(const ArrayOb&)a;
}
```

The virtual function `isEqual()` is more general than `operator==()` in that it
tests an instance of `ArrayOb` to determine if it equals an object that is not necessarily an `ArrayOb`. This equality test consists of two parts: first, `isEqual()` checks that
it makes sense to compare the argument object to an `ArrayOb`, and if it does, it calls
`ArrayOb::operator==()` to actually perform the test for equality.

A call to `Object::isSpecies()` determines if the argument object is of a comparable class by seeing if the species of the argument object is `ArrayOb`. More precisely, it
applies the virtual function `species()` to the argument object and checks that the resulting class descriptor address equals the address of `ArrayOb`'s class descriptor. The virtual
function `species()` thus establishes the species of a class. Each NIH Library class defines
`species()` to return the address of the class descriptor object of the class it wishes to
make itself comparable to. This gives a programmer flexibility in defining the meaning of
functions that compare objects such as `isEqual()` and `compare()`. Suppose we have
an abstract base class `Fruit` with derived classes `Apple` and `Orange` as in Example
10-1.

```
// ex10-1.c - Variations of isEqual()

// compile with -DSTRICT for strict equality
// compile with -DKINDOF to use isKindOf() instead of isSpecies()

#ifndef KINDOF
#define IS_SPECIES isSpecies
#else
#define IS_SPECIES isKindOf
#endif
```

```
#include "Object.h"

class Fruit: public Object {
    DECLARE_MEMBERS(Fruit);
    float weight;        // weight in grams
    float diameter;      // diameter in centimeters
protected:
    virtual void storer(OIOofd&) const;
    virtual void storer(OIOout&) const;
public:
    Fruit(float w, float d) { weight = w; diameter = d; }
    float w() const          { return weight; }
    float d() const          { return diameter; }
    bool operator==(const Fruit&) const;
    virtual bool isEqual(const Object&) const;
    virtual const Class* species() const;
// ...
};
// ...
bool Fruit::operator==(const Fruit& f) const
{
    return weight==f.weight && diameter==f.diameter;
}
const Class* Fruit::species() const { return &classDesc; }
bool Fruit::isEqual(const Object& f) const
{
    return f.IS_SPECIES(classDesc) && *this==(const Fruit&)f;
}
// ...


class Apple: public Fruit {
    DECLARE_MEMBERS(Apple);
public:
    enum appleVariety
        { MCINTOSH, JONATHAN, REDDELICIOUS, STAYMAN };
private:
    appleVariety variety;
public:
    Apple(appleVariety v, float w, float d) : Fruit(w,d) {
        variety = v;
    }
    bool operator==(const Apple&) const;
// ...
};
```

```
// ...

bool Apple::operator==(const Apple& a) const
{
    return variety==a.variety && Fruit::operator==(a);
}


// ...

class Orange: public Fruit {
    DECLARE_MEMBERS(Orange);
public:
    enum orangeVariety { NAVAL, FLORIDA, CALIFORNIA };
private:
    orangeVariety variety;
public:
    Orange(orangeVariety v, float w, float d) : Fruit(w,d) {
        variety = v;
    }
    bool operator==(const Orange&) const;
// ...
};

// ...

bool Orange::operator==(const Orange& o) const
{
    return variety==o.variety && Fruit::operator==(o);
}

// ...
```

If we wish to define isEqual() loosely (STRICT undefined), so that two instances of Fruit are equal if they have the same weight and size, regardless of other characteristics added by derived classes, then we do not define isEqual() or species() for classes Apple and Orange and allow them to inherit their definitions of these virtual functions from class Fruit. In this case, if we run the following program

```
main()
{
    Fruit f(100.0, 8.5);
    Apple a(Apple::MCINTOSH, 100.0, 8.5);
    Orange o(Orange::NAVAL, 100.0, 8.5);
// ...
    cout << "f.isEqual(a): " << (f.isEqual(a) ? "YES" : "NO")
        << endl;
    cout << "a.isEqual(f): " << (a.isEqual(f) ? "YES" : "NO")
        << endl;
```

```
    cout << "a.isEqual(o): " << (a.isEqual(o) ? "YES" : "NO")
        << endl;
}
```

it prints:

```
f.isEqual(a): YES
a.isEqual(f): YES
a.isEqual(o): YES
```

However, if we wish to define isEqual() more strictly (STRICT defined), so that two instances of Fruit are equal only if they are the same kind of fruit (both Apples or Oranges) of the same variety, weight, and size, then we define:

```
const Class* Apple::species() const { return &classDesc; }

bool Apple::isEqual(const Object& a) const
{
    return a.IS_SPECIES(classDesc) && *this==(const Apple&)a;
}

const Class* Orange::species() const { return &classDesc; }

bool Orange::isEqual(const Object& a) const
{
    return a.IS_SPECIES(classDesc) && *this==(const Orange&)a;
}
```

If we run the same main() program with these definitions for isEqual() it prints:

```
f.isEqual(a): NO
a.isEqual(f): NO
a.isEqual(o): NO
```

For a particular application, it might not make sense to create an instance of Fruit—all instances must be Apples or Oranges. In this case Fruit is an abstract class, so we protect the constructor Fruit::Fruit() so that clients cannot create them, and we define Fruit::isEqual() as a pure virtual function so that derived classes must implement it.

We can achieve other effects by using the function isKindOf() instead of isSpecies() in the definitions of isEqual() (STRICT and KINDOF both defined). This produces the following result from running main():

```
f.isEqual(a): YES
a.isEqual(f): NO
a.isEqual(o): NO
```

Note that now isEqual() is no longer commutative, because while an apple is a kind of fruit, a fruit is not a kind of apple.

10.3.11 `ArrayOb::hash()`

```
unsigned ArrayOb::hash() const
{
    register unsigned h = sz;
    register unsigned i = sz;
    register Object** vp = v
    while (i--) h^=(*vp++)->hash();
    return h;
}
```

The function `hash()` returns a number that class `Set` can use as a hash table probe. This function should be fast, so it should be kept simple. Classes whose member variables are all fundamental types usually just cast each member variable to type `unsigned` and exclusive-OR them together. `ArrayOb` computes its `hash()` function by exclusive-OR'ing the results of applying `hash()` to all the objects it contains.

10.3.12 `ArrayOb::deepenShallowCopy()`

```
void ArrayOb::deepenShallowCopy()
{
    BASE::deepenShallowCopy();
    register i = sz;
    register Object** vp = v;
    while (i--) {
        *vp = (*vp)->deepCopy();
        vp++;
    }
}
```

Clients call `Object::deepCopy()` to make a deep copy of an object, as described in Section 7.3.2. `Object::deepCopy()` in turn calls the virtual function `deepenShallowCopy()` to copy any pointers an object might contain. `ArrayOb::deepenShallowCopy()` accomplishes this by applying `deepCopy()` to all the object pointers in its array, replacing each pointer with the pointer to its copy.

10.3.13 `ArrayOb::addContentsTo()`

```
Collection& ArrayOb::addContentsTo(Collection& cltn) const
{
    register Object** vp = v;
    register unsigned i = sz;
    while (i--) cltn.add(*vp++);
    return cltn;
}
```

Class `Collection` calls `addContentsTo()` to implement the container conversion functions such as `asOrderedCltn()`, `asSet()`, and `asSortedCltn()`. An `ArrayOb` simply adds all the objects it contains to the argument `Collection`.

Class `ArrayOb` could simply inherit `addContentsTo()` from class `Collection`, but this implementation is more efficient.

10.3.14 `ArrayOb::compare()`

```
int ArrayOb::compare(const Object& arg) const
// Compare two arrays of objects.  If *this > arg return >0,
// *this == arg return 0, and if *this < arg return <0.
{
    assertArgSpecies(arg,classDesc,"compare");
    ArrayOb& a = (ArrayOb&)arg;
    for (int i=0; i<sz; i++) {
// previous elements compared equal;
// longer ArrayOb is therefore larger
        if (i == a.sz) return 1;
// compare() != 0 at any element determines ordering
        int val;
        if ((val = v[i]->compare(*a.v[i])) != 0) return val;
    }
// all elements in this ArrayOb compare() equal to arg ArrayOb
    if (sz == a.sz) return 0;
    return -1;
}
```

`ArrayOb::compare()` implements the lexical comparison of two `ArrayOb`s by applying the virtual function `compare()` to their corresponding elements. In a lexical comparison the two arrays may be of unequal lengths. If all the objects in the shorter of the two match the initial part of the longer, the shorter array is considered less than the longer.

Although `ArrayOb::compare()` uses `species()` to determine of two objects are comparable, other variations are possible for your own classes, as we described in Section 10.3.10.

10.3.15 Interface to class `Iterator`

```
Object* ArrayOb::doNext(Iterator& pos) const
{
    if (pos.index < size()) return v[pos.index++];
    return 0;
}
```

As we described in Section 8.3.2, class `Iterator` provides an abstraction for stepping through the objects in a container class. Container classes interface to class `Iterator` by implementing three virtual functions: `doReset()`, `doNext()`, and `doFinish()`. Class

`Iterator` maintains the current position in a container class in its member variables, calls `doReset()` to reset the position to the beginning of a container, calls `doNext()` to obtain a pointer to the next object in a container, and calls `doFinish()` from its destructor to give a container an opportunity to deallocate any additional objects it may have created to perform the iteration.

For a simple container class such as `ArrayOb`, the member variable `Iterator::index` suffices to keep track of the position of the next object. Class `Iterator`'s constructor and the default implementation of `doReset()` both reset `index` to 0, so we do not need to implement `ArrayOb::doReset()`. Similarly, we do not need to implement `doFinish()` because an `ArrayOb` does not need to deallocate anything when an iteration is completed.

Class `Collection` implements `addContentsTo()`, `dumpOn()`, `printOn()`, and `removeAll()`, using an `Iterator`, enabling class `ArrayOb`, and most of `Collection`'s other derived classes to inherit a working implementation of these functions.

10.3.16 ArrayOb::at()

```
Object*& ArrayOb::at(int i)              { return (*this)[i]; }
const Object *const& ArrayOb::at(int i) const
    { return (*this)[i]; }
```

The function `at()` does the same thing that `ArrayOb::operator[]()` does: it returns a reference to the pointer to the *i*th `Object`. The difference is that `at()` is a virtual function.

10.3.17 size() and capacity()

```
unsigned ArrayOb::size() const        { return sz; }
unsigned ArrayOb::capacity() const    { return sz; }
```

The functions `size()` and `capacity()` both return the size of the `ArrayOb`.

10.3.18 ArrayOb::reSize()

```
void ArrayOb::reSize(unsigned newsize)
{
    if (newsize == 0) allocSizeErr();
    v = (Object**)realloc((char*)v,newsize*sizeof(Object*));
    if (newsize > sz) {     // initialize new space to nil
        Object** vp = &v[sz];
        while (newsize > sz) {
            *vp++ = nil;
            sz++;
        }
    }
    else sz = newsize;
}
```

The purpose of the function `reSize()` is to change the size of an `ArrayOb`. It does this by calling the C library function `realloc()`, which returns a pointer to a (possibly moved) area of length `newsize` object pointers. When the size is increased, `reSize()` initializes the additional pointers to point to the `Nil` object.

Note that it is slightly dangerous to use `realloc()` on storage that new has allocated, as in this example, because this assumes that new calls `malloc()` to allocate memory. The implementation of new supplied by the standard C++ run-time library most likely does this, but this implementation of `reSize()` will not work if your particular run-time library does not use `malloc()` or if you re-implement new so that it does not use `malloc()`.

10.3.19 `ArrayOb::removeAll()`

```
void ArrayOb::removeAll()
{
    register Object** vp = v;
    register unsigned i = sz;
    while (i--) *vp++ = nil;
}
```

The function `removeAll()` removes all the objects from an `ArrayOb` by storing `nil` in all the elements of the array.

10.3.20 `ArrayOb::allocSizeErr()`

```
void ArrayOb::allocSizeErr() const
{
    setError(NIHCL_ALLOCSIZE,DEFAULT,this,className());
}
```

The private function `allocSizeErr()` calls `setError()` to report an attempt to make an `ArrayOb` with a size of zero.

10.3.21 `ArrayOb::indexRangeErr()`

```
void ArrayOb::indexRangeErr() const
{
    setError(NIHCL_INDEXRANGE,DEFAULT,this,className());
}
```

The private function `indexRangeErr()` calls `setError()` to report an attempt to subscript an `ArrayOb` with an index larger than the `ArrayOb`'s size. The function `operator[]()` calls it if its index argument is too large. The `setError()` function has a lengthy calling sequence, and `operator[]()` is an inline function, so calling `indexRangeErr()` instead of `setNIHCLerror()` saves a significant amount of inline code. We make `indexRangeErr()` private since it is not desirable for client programs to call it.

10.3.22   Stream object I/O

```
void ArrayOb::storer(OIOout& strm) const
{
    BASE::storer(strm);
    strm << sz;
    for (register unsigned i=0; i<sz; i++)
        v[i]->storeOn(strm);
}
```

The virtual function `storer()` is called by `Object::storeOn()` to write an instance
to an `ostream` in a form that `readFrom()` can later use to reconstruct the instance, as
described in Section 7.4.1. First, the `storer()` function calls its base class's implementation of `storer()` to write out the member variables of its ancestor classes. Next, it writes
out the size of the `ArrayOb`, and finally, it calls `storeOn()` (recursively) to write out
the objects this instance contains.

```
ArrayOb::ArrayOb(OIOin& strm)
    : BASE(strm)
{
    strm >> sz;
    v = new Object*[sz];
    for (register unsigned i=0; i<sz; i++)
        v[i] = Object::readFrom(strm);
}
```

The constructor `ArrayOb(OIOistream&)` reconstructs an instance of an `ArrayOb`
from the information written by `storeOn()`, as discussed in Section 7.4.3. Reconstructing
an `ArrayOb` is straightforward: we read its size into the member variable `sz`, then call
`readFrom()` to reconstruct the objects this instance contains.

10.3.23   File descriptor object I/O

```
void ArrayOb::storer(OIOofd& fd)   const
{
    Object::storer(fd);
    fd << sz;
    for (register unsigned i=0; i<sz; i++)
        v[i]->storeOn(fd);
}
```

```
ArrayOb::ArrayOb(OIOifd& fd)
    : BASE(fd)
{
    fd >> sz;
    v = new Object*[sz];
    for (register unsigned i=0; i<sz; i++ )
```

```
        v[i] = Object::readFrom(fd);
}
```

In Sections 7.4.2 and 7.4.4 we described how classes `OIOout` and `OIOin` are abstract classes that declare all the I/O functions for fundamental data types, such as `operator>>()`, `operator<<()`, `get()`, and `put()`, as pure virtual functions. This has two advantages:

- A single program can use several different object I/O formats by passing instances of various derived classes of `OIOin` and `OIOout` to `readFrom()` and `storeOn()`.

- You can define your own object storage formats by supplying classes derived from `OIOin` and `OIOout` that read and store objects in your new format, and you do not need to recompile any existing classes.

While this is very flexible, every read and write of every member variable incurs the overhead of a virtual function call. To eliminate this overhead when object I/O performance is critical, we have provided the classes `OIOifd` and `OIOofd`, which implement the same I/O functions as `OIOin` and `OIOout`, but as non-virtual inline member functions that use the more efficient C library `read()` and `write()` file descriptor I/O primitives rather than the C++ `iostream` classes. Although you can still customize the object storage format for this kind of object I/O, you must rewrite classes `OIOin` and `OIOout`, and then recompile all classes.

Thus, the "stream" object I/O using classes `OIOin` and `OIOout` is flexible, while the "file descriptor" object I/O using classes `OIOifd` and `OIOofd` is relatively efficient.

10.4 CHAPTER SUMMARY

In this chapter we have explained how to use template files as a guide to writing a new NIH Library class.

11

LIGHTWEIGHT PROCESSES

11.1 INTRODUCTION

In this chapter, we will look into a technique that uses *lightweight processes* to simulate concurrent computation in a serial processor. We will find that C++ and object-oriented programming with the NIH Class Library can provide good support for this technique.

When a serial processor performs a computational task, it executes instructions one at a time in an order dictated by a program. Yet there are times when we require a computer to complete several computational tasks in an interval of real time under conditions that preclude performing one task after the other. For instance, when computations provide each other with intermediate results, the tasks cannot be performed in serial order. Also when computations have to wait for external events, such as the completion of I/O operations, one task might use up the whole real-time period waiting for its external event and prevent subsequently scheduled tasks from meeting the deadline. One way to complete such computational tasks in an interval of time is to perform them *concurrently*, or simultaneously, on several processors. Alternatively, we might be able to perform the tasks on a single serial processor if we could *simulate concurrency* by having the tasks take turns using computing resources so that only one of them is executing at a time, but they all get something accomplished over an interval of real time.

Typically, a multiprogramming operating system such as UNIX will handle the allocation of computing resources on a serial processor. When a processor is under the control of a multiprogramming operating system, it schedules computational tasks in units called *processes*. We will say a process is *active* when it is using the computer's central processor (CPU). Many processes may be scheduled to run at the same time, but only one of them can be active at any one time. While the CPU is busy with one process, another may be using a different resource, such as a disk, or it may be waiting in a queue until the resource is available. A multiprogramming operating system will schedule the use of resources so that a number of processes can all complete their computation over an interval of real time. In this way, the operating system simulates concurrent computation with the group of processes.

11.1.1 The lightweight process data type

For some problems we require computational tasks to be very closely coupled by large or complex data structures. Unless the data are stored in a shared virtual address space, the amount of data to be exchanged may be too much of a burden for the operating system. The term *lightweight process* [2] refers to a process that shares some system resources, such as a virtual address space, with a group of other processes. By contrast, the term *heavyweight process* refers to a single process not involved in this sharing. The difference between them is that once shared resources are allocated to an entire group of lightweight processes, each individual lightweight process in the group becomes faster to start than a single heavyweight process with the same resources. Lightweight processes that share a common virtual address space can simulate separate yet concurrent computations which require high rates of data exchange.

Two common applications of lightweight processes are simulation programs and control programs. When we design software for a simulation, we build a model of real-world objects, their attributes, and their interactions. In such a model, lightweight processes correspond to concurrent activity in the real-world system. Thus, a program comprised of multiple lightweight processes, that share, compete for, and transfer data and resources among themselves, simulates complex, concurrent behavior of a real-world system. Software in a control application has some of the same modeling properties as a simulation. However, the operation of a control system will control the actual behavior of a real-world system rather than simulate its hypothetical behavior. In Chapter 12, we will present an example of such a control program as a case study in object-oriented programming which draws on tools from the NIH Class Library.

Unfortunately, many operating systems do not support lightweight processes. For example, under the UNIX operating system, each process has its own virtual address space. To simulate concurrency under this circumstance, we need to be able to perform separately scheduled computational tasks within the same heavyweight process so they can share a common address space. We can do this kind of computational scheduling with the software construct known as a *coroutine*. A coroutine is a program segment with its own computational *context*, or computational state, normally represented as a stack, a set of registers, and local variables. Typically, a program will use a separate coroutine for each computational task it must perform. The scheduling of these tasks takes the form of one coroutine saving its context and calling another coroutine, which will then continue its work using its own context.

In this chapter, we will describe a method of simulating concurrency provided by classes in the NIH Class Library.[1] Our programming environment (UNIX) does not support lightweight processes, thus we have used coroutines to implement these classes. At the same time we applied object-oriented techniques to hide the details of the coroutines and to implement an interface that uses the more attractive terminology of the lightweight process model. We will extend our use of the term *lightweight process* (LWP) to refer to objects with member variables defining a computational context and with a distinguishing constructor function implemented as a coroutine. These lightweight processes will operate within the same heavyweight process (program) and so share the resources of that process including its virtual address space, file descriptors, and signals.

11.1.2 Lightweight processes in the NIH Class Library

The NIH Class Library supports lightweight processes with the classes `Process`, `Scheduler`, `Semaphore`, and `SharedQueue`:

- A *lightweight process* is an instance of a class derived from class `Process`

- A (unique) instance of class `Scheduler` performs the *scheduling* of LWPs

---

[1] Stroustrup and Shopiro [25] describe C++ classes with similar functionality.

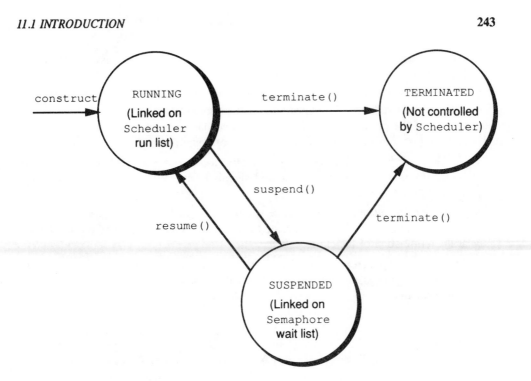

Figure 11.1 State transitions for an NIH Class Library lightweight process

- An LWP sends *signals* to another with an instance of class `Semaphore`

- An LWP *transmits objects* to another with an instance of class `SharedQueue`

The lightweight processes in the NIH Class Library have the following characteristics:

- *Any number of LWPs are allowed within a single program.* The `Processes` within a single heavyweight process share the same resources including the data segment and the same open files.

- *Each LWP has its own execution stack.* This means that each `Process` maintains its own stack of (nested) function calls, function arguments, and local variables.

- *An LWP has three states:* RUNNING, SUSPENDED, *and* TERMINATED. Once constructed, an LWP is in the RUNNING state during which time it is eligible to become the (unique) active running process executing instructions with its own stack. When in the RUNNING state, an LWP may change its state to SUSPENDED or TERMINATED. A SUSPENDED LWP gives up its control of the processor and may later be resumed to the RUNNING state by another LWP. A SUSPENDED LWP may be TERMINATED by another LWP. A TERMINATED LWP cannot change to another state. A state transition diagram of a lightweight process is shown in Figure 11.1.

- RUNNING *processes are scheduled on a first-come-first-served basis subject to a priority level.* The `Scheduler` places a newly RUNNING LWP on a scheduling queue of all lightweight processes of a given priority waiting their turn to be activated.

The `Scheduler` places a newly SUSPENDED LWP on a queue associated with a `Semaphore`.

- *The scheduling of each LWP is non-preemptive.* The `Scheduler` cannot intervene in the execution of an LWP which will continue to be active until it explicitly releases control of the processor. An LWP may suspend or terminate itself, or it may yield control to the next scheduled LWP of higher or equal priority.

- *An LWP can be scheduled to run in response to an external event such as a UNIX signal.* A signal handler relays external signals to an LWP by using an NIH Class Library `Semaphore`.

- *An LWP can control a UNIX child process by the usual UNIX fork/exec mechanism.* The LWP can wait for the child in the SUSPENDED state and resume when signaled at the termination of the child.

- *An application program is partitioned into separate lightweight processes.* In an application program using NIH Class Library Processes, all executable code is part of a member function of an instance of some `Process`.

11.2 CLASSES `Process`, `StackProc`, AND `HeapProc`

Object
    Link
        Process
            StackProc
            HeapProc
    Scheduler
    Semaphore
    SharedQueue

The NIH Class Library supports programming with lightweight processes by encapsulating a coroutine context switching mechanism in the abstract base class `Process`. A lightweight process will inherit a state from class `Process` which also has member functions to change the state:

- `Process::suspend()` will change the state of a RUNNING LWP to SUSPENDED.

- `Process::resume()` will change the state of a SUSPENDED LWP to RUNNING.

- `Process:terminate()` will change the state of a RUNNING or SUSPENDED LWP to TERMINATED.

A `Process` is implemented as a derived `Link`, so that any derived `Process` can be directly linked into a `LinkedList` (see Chapter 8). As we will see in the next section, this gives the `Scheduler` class a simple mechanism for managing the state changes of a `Process`.

The NIH Class Library also provides two abstract base classes derived from class `Process`—class `StackProc` and class `HeapProc`—which encapsulate alternate implementations for the coroutine context switching that is required for lightweight process operations.

These coroutine implementations manage memory allocation for the context—the stack and registers—associated with a lightweight process. Both implementations allocate memory for the context on the free store when an LWP process object is constructed. They differ, as their names suggest, in what happens to the context when a RUNNING lightweight process becomes active (that is, gains control of the CPU). When a HeapProc becomes active, it uses its context in place in free store (heap). In contrast, when a StackProc becomes active, the Scheduler transfers its context to the main stack; and when the StackProc becomes SUSPENDED the Scheduler saves its context on the heap again.

Clearly, a HeapProc has an advantage over a StackProc because the context is not copied on each context switch. On the other hand, a StackProc has the significant advantage that programs written with it can be effectively controlled by standard debugger programs whereas programs written using a HeapProc cannot.

In addition to the cost of computing time, there is another price to pay when programming with class StackProc. *When arguments are passed by reference to a function that switches a coroutine context, those arguments must be constructed either statically or by means of the* new *operator.* A moment's reflection will uncover the reason for this rule. When an argument is passed by reference to a C++ function—that is, the argument is either a reference to an object or a pointer to an object—it is the address of that object's memory location that is actually given to the function. If that address refers to a location on the stack, then after a lightweight process context is switched, the data in that location may have been overwritten. This rule certainly applies to every constructor function for a lightweight process object because such a constructor creates a new coroutine context. However, since we cannot easily know if a particular member function results in an LWP context switch, it will be safer to apply the argument passing restrictions to all member functions of lightweight process objects.

Use of classes StackProc and HeapProc also entails the following practical consideration. Aside from their class names, the classes HeapProc and StackProc have identical interfaces so they can be easily interchanged (and mixed) in an application. The ability to interchange these implementations aids us in using a debugger utility. However, interchanging the programming methods of passing arguments from an application program to member functions is a problem. If we intend to use class StackProc at all in a given application, we should apply the StackProc restrictions on argument passing to any HeapProc objects used in the same application.

Creating a new lightweight process

To allow portable implementations for the coroutine context switching in classes StackProc and HeapProc, the NIH Class Library requires application programs to provide some information about where the stack is located to every call to an LWP constructor function. A safe and convenient way to provide this information is to declare an overloaded static member function create() corresponding to each LWP constructor:

```
// constructing a derived StackProc with function create()

class MyProcess : public StackProc {
public:
    MyProcess(const char* name, stackTy* bot,
```

```
                    int pri =0, unsigned stacksize =1024);
       static MyProcess* create(const char* name,
                    int pri =0, unsigned stacksize =1024);
// ...
};


MyProcess* MyProcess::create(const char* name, int pri,
                             unsigned stacksize)
{
//   the next two statements must be within the same scope
//   for the address of the stack bottom to be correct
     stackTy bottom;
     return new MyProcess(name, &bottom, pri, stacksize);
}
```

Notice that in function `create()` the use of the stack bottom address is an exception to the rule about passing arguments by reference to a lightweight process. In fact, it is precisely because the object `bottom` is allocated on the stack that passing its address to the constructor function conveys information about the location of the stack.

Implementing a constructor for a lightweight process

The constructor function for a lightweight process object must be implemented in a particular way to properly establish the coroutine context. The following example shows the elements of how to write a constructor for a lightweight process in the NIH Class Library:

```
MyProcess::MyProcess(const char* name, stackTy* bot,
                     int pri, unsigned sz) :
                     StackProc(name,bot,pri,sz)
{
// parent LWP yields so that this LWP can start
    if ( FORK() ) {  Scheduler::yield(); return; }

// begin the work of this LWP
//  ...
// end the work of this LWP

// terminate to avoid return
    terminate();
}
```

In this example, the constructor function for class `MyProcess` takes as its arguments the process name, the address of the stack bottom, the process priority, and the stack size. The constructor passes the arguments to the constructor for its base class `StackProc`. The body of the `MyProcess` constructor must:

- *FORK to create the lightweight process context.* The `FORK()` macro, which must be the first statement in the body of the constructor, initializes the coroutine context for the new LWP. As with the UNIX system call `fork()`, the program returns from `FORK()` twice: a non-zero value is returned in the parent LWP context, and a zero value is returned in the new LWP context. The parent LWP must be forced to return from the constructor, whereas the new LWP will continue with the body of the constructor function. As shown in this example, the parent LWP calls `Scheduler::yield()` before returning to the scope from which the constructor function was invoked. Yielding is optional but has the advantage of allowing the new LWP to get started before the parent LWP proceeds.

- *Begin the execution of the lightweight process.* The execution may be one-pass or may contain loops. The LWP code will typically contain some statements at which the LWP suspend itself by waiting on a `Semaphore` or a `SharedQueue` until some resource is available or some condition arises.

- *Terminate the lightweight process to prevent return from the constructor.* Because the context of an LWP constructor is that of a coroutine and not a normal function call, there can be no legitimate return from the constructor function. A simple way to prevent an attempt to return after the work of the LWP constructor is completed is to terminate the LWP. Function `terminate()` will have the `Scheduler` pass control to another LWP. The current LWP will remain in the TERMINATED state until the process object is deleted or program execution is completed.

11.3 CLASS Scheduler

Object
  Link
    Process
      StackProc
      HeapProc
  Scheduler
  Semaphore
  SharedQueue

Class `Scheduler` provides the NIH Class Library policy for scheduling lightweight processes. An application program has only one instance of class `Scheduler`.

The `Scheduler` maintains each LWP in one of three states: RUNNING, SUSPENDED, or TERMINATED. Among the RUNNING LWPs only one can be active at any time. The `Scheduler` keeps member variables pointing to the currently active and the previously active LWP objects:

```
Process* Scheduler::active_process;        // currently active LWP
Process* Scheduler::previous_process;      // previously active LWP
```

The `Scheduler` holds each RUNNING lightweight process on a *run list*, implemented as a `LinkedList`, corresponding to its LWP *priority level* and saves a count of the number of RUNNING LWPs:

```
// runList[i] lists RUNNING LWP of priority i
LinkedList runList[MAXPRIORITY+1];
```

```
// number of RUNNING LWP
unsigned runcount;
```

Suspending a RUNNING LWP involves removing the LWP from the run list corresponding to its priority. Resuming a SUSPENDED LWP involves linking the LWP onto its run list. When a lightweight process enters the SUSPENDED state by waiting on a Semaphore it will be linked into the wait list of the Semaphore (see Section 11.4). Terminating a RUNNING or SUSPENDED LWP involves removing it from whatever list it is currently on. Recall that a lightweight process, as a derived Process and thus a derived Link, may be directly linked to one LinkedList at a time so that an LWP is either RUNNING (on one of the Scheduler's run lists) or SUSPENDED (on a Semaphore's wait list) or is TERMINATED (neither RUNNING nor SUSPENDED).

Any lightweight process can initiate scheduling activity in the Scheduler by calling the function Scheduler::schedule(). This scheduling activity will be *non-preemptive*. This means that once in the RUNNING state, an LWP will continue in that state until it suspends itself. An LWP may suspend itself in one of three ways: by waiting on a Semaphore, by yielding to another LWP of higher priority, or by waiting for activity on a file descriptor. An LWP yields by calling the function Scheduler::yield(), which suspends the active LWP, and searches for another RUNNING LWP of higher or equal priority to become the currently active process. If the Scheduler finds no such LWP, it returns the yielding LWP to the RUNNING state so that it again becomes the currently active process. An LWP elects to wait for activity on an open file descriptor by calling the function:

```
Process::select(FDSet& in_mask, FDSet& out_mask, FDSet& err_mask)
```

The Scheduler will suspend the calling LWP until input, output, or an error condition occurs on a file descriptor listed in the corresponding mask.

Scheduling lightweight processes with the NIH Class Library

Example 11-1 illustrates the main features of the NIH Class Library process Scheduler.

```
// ex11-1.c - Scheduling lightweight processes in the NIH Class
// Library

class TestProcess : public StackProc {
public:
    TestProcess(const char* name, stackTy* bot,
            int pri,Process* parent);
    static TestProcess* create(const char* name,
            int pri,Process* parent);
};
```

```
TestProcess::TestProcess(const char* pname,stackTy* bot,
                         int pri,Process* parent)
          : StackProc(pname,bot,pri)
{
// parent process yields to allow this process to start
    if ( FORK() ) { Scheduler::yield(); return; }

    cout << name() << pri << " start" << endl;

// yield to parent process
    if (parent) {
        parent->resume();
        Scheduler::yield();
        }
// suspend until child yields
    suspend();
    Scheduler::schedule();

    cout << name() << pri << " resume" << endl;

// terminate to avoid return
    terminate();
}

main()
{
// start Scheduler
// create main context with priority 0
    MAIN_PROCESS(0);

    Process* parent =0;
    String* pname = new String("P");
    for (register int i=MAXPRIORITY; i>=1; (i--)
        parent = TestProcess::create(*pname,i,parent);

    cout << "main Process" << endl;
    parent->resume();
    Scheduler::yield();
}
```

In Example 11-1, the `main()` context constructs a sequence of lightweight processes, one for each priority in descending order. Each LWP will do the following:

- write its name to the standard output
- yield control to the preceding `Process` of higher priority, if any

- suspend so that the `main()` context can start the LWP of next lower priority

- write its name again when resumed

- terminate

The program in Example 11-1 produces the output:

```
process P7
process P6
process P7 again
process P5
process P6 again
process P4
process P5 again
process P3
process P4 again
process P2
process P3 again
process P1
process P2 again
main Process
process P1 again
```

In each constructor `TestProcess::TestProcess()`, say for `TestProcess P6`, the statement `proc->resume()` will change the preceding `TestProcess`, P7, to the RUNNING state. By calling function `Scheduler::yield()` `TestProcess P6` gives up control to allow the `Scheduler` to activate `TestProcess P7`. When `TestProcess P7` terminates, `TestProcess P6` will be resumed because it has higher priority than the `main()` context (which has priority 0). `Process P6` will then call `suspend()` to place itself in the SUSPENDED state; the call of function `Scheduler::schedule()` will allow the `Scheduler` to activate the `main()` context so that the `TestProcess` of next lower priority can be constructed.

11.4 CLASS Semaphore

Object
  Link
    Process
      StackProc
      HeapProc
  Scheduler
  Semaphore
  SharedQueue

Class `Semaphore` provides a way to synchronize lightweight processes. A `Semaphore` has a member of type `LinkedList` that holds directly linked lightweight processes waiting to be signaled by the `Semaphore`. Typically an LWP waits for a resource to become

Table 11.1 *The states of a* Semaphore

Semaphore State	Meaning
count greater than 0	count is the number of notifications pending
count less than 0	count is the number of processes waiting for notification
count equal to 0	no notifications pending, no processes waiting

available or for some external event to take place. The nature of the resource or event and the meaning of waiting and signaling are determined by the application constructing the Semaphore. The Semaphore itself is simply a mechanism for signaling an LWP.

Class Semaphore has a member variable, count, that represents the state of the Semaphore and a constructor function that takes the count as an argument (the default is 0).

An LWP waits for a signal by calling the function Semaphore::wait(), which effectively suspends the calling LWP until a signal arrives. If a signal arrives at a Semaphore with no waiting LWPs we say the signal is *pending*. A positive value of count indicates the number of signals currently pending for the Semaphore, and thus the number of future waiting processes the Semaphore can signal without further delay. When an LWP waits on a Semaphore the Semaphore::count is decremented.

An LWP initiates a signal from a Semaphore by calling the function Semaphore:: signal(), at which time the first LWP currently waiting on the Semaphore will be signaled. If no LWPs are waiting when the signal arrives, the signal remains pending until one does wait. Signaling of an LWP takes the form of removing the LWP from the wait list of the Semaphore and resuming the LWP. A negative value of count indicates the number of future signals needed to satisfy all processes currently waiting on the Semaphore. When a signal arrives at a Semaphore the Semaphore::count is incremented.

Synchronizing a lightweight process with an external event

When initialized with the count equal to 0, a Semaphore will always keep a waiting LWP suspended until the Semaphore is signaled by another LWP.

```
// construct a Semaphore with count =0
static Semaphore externalEvent;

// ...

// suspend this LWP until
// another LWP calls externalEvent.signal()
externalEvent.wait();
```

Managing N resources

When initialized with the count equal to N, a Semaphore will allow the next N lightweight processes calling Semaphore::wait() to pass through the Semaphore without waiting. An application can interpret this behavior of the Semaphore to mean that N resources are available. To follow through, the application should signal the Semaphore every time it wants to release one of those resources.

```
// ex11-2.c - Managing N resources with a Semaphore

class TestProcess : public StackProc {
public:
    TestProcess(Semaphore*,OrderedCltn*,stackTy*);
    static TestProcess* create(Semaphore*,OrderedCltn*);
};


TestProcess::TestProcess(Semaphore* resourceAvailable,
                         OrderedCltn* resourceQ,
                         stackTy* bot)
            : StackProc("TestProcess",bot,1)
{
// parent process yields to allow this process to start
    if ( FORK() ) { Scheduler::yield(); return; }

// obtain 2 resources
    Object* resource[2];
    int i;
    for (i=0; i<2; i++) {
        resourceAvailable->wait();
        resource[i] = resourceQ->remove(*resourceQ->first());
        cout << name() << ": obtained "
            << *resource[i] << endl;
        }

// release 2 resources
    for (i=0; i<2; i++) {
        resourceQ->addLast(*resource[i]);
        resourceAvailable->signal();
        cout << name() << ": released "
            << *resource[i] << endl;
        }

// terminate to avoid return
    terminate();
}

main()
{
// start Scheduler
// create main context with priority 0
    MAIN_PROCESS(0);
```

```
// manage a resource queue of size = N
   const int N = 2;
   OrderedCltn* resourceQ = new OrderedCltn(N);
   Semaphore* resourceAvailable = new Semaphore(N);
   resourceQ->addLast(*new String("resource1"));
   resourceQ->addLast(*new String("resource2"));
   cout << "main: " << resourceQ->size()
        << " resources available" << endl;

// construct process to use resources
   TestProcess::create(resourceAvailable,resourceQ);

   do { // wait for resource to be returned
       resourceAvailable->wait();
       resourceAvailable->signal();
       cout << "main: " << resourceQ->size()
            << " resources available" << endl;
   } while (resourceQ->size()<N);
}
```

In Example 11-2, the main context adds two `String` objects to the resource queue `resourceQ` implemented, for simplicity, as an `OrderedCltn`. The `Semaphore` `resourcesAvailable` is constructed to manage N resources. The main context passes `resourceQ` and `resourcesAvailable` to a new lightweight process `TestProcess`, whose constructor function requires two resources. The `TestProcess` obtains these one at a time by first waiting on the `Semaphore` and then removing the next resource from the queue. A `TestProcess` releases the resources one at a time by adding the resource at the end of the queue and then signaling the `Semaphore`. Example 11-2 produces the output:

```
main: 2 resources available
TestProcess: obtained resource1
TestProcess: obtained resource2
TestProcess: released resource1
TestProcess: released resource2
main: 2 resources available
```

Protecting a critical section of code

When initialized with its `count` equal to 1, a `Semaphore` will allow one lightweight process at a time to pass through without waiting. An application can use such a `Semaphore` to protect a critical section of code. A *critical section* is code that an LWP must perform without interruption by another process. For instance, a section of code in which an LWP modifies a shared data object should be protected as a critical section of code. Lightweight process scheduling is non-preemptive, thus an LWP can interrupt the active LWP only when it is scheduled after the active LWP becomes suspended. An implicit assumption here is that a call to `Process::suspend()` is made sometime during the execution of the critical code. This typically happens via a call to `Semaphore::wait()`; for example, the active LWP might have to wait for some resource needed to complete the critical section. We can illustrate protection of a critical section in the following code fragment:

```
//  Protecting a critical section of code with
//  a Semaphore in state count == +1
static Semaphore protect_critical(1);
// ...

{   // begin critical section
    protect_critical.wait();

// critical code goes here
// some suspension of the active Process is assumed
// ...

    protect_critical.signal();
} // end critical section
```

To protect the critical section in this code fragment, we construct a static Semaphore with its `count` initialized to +1. Thus the first LWP to execute `protect_critical.wait()` finds `Semaphore protect_critical` in state `count==1` and immediately enters the critical section. If another LWP executes `protect_critical.wait()`, it will find `Semaphore protect_critical` in state `count==0`, and will suspend until the next call to `protect_critical().signal()` occurs. The first LWP finishes the critical section with a call to `Semaphore::signal()`, which resumes the next LWP to enter the critical section in turn.

A complication arises in the above method of protection when the critical section transfers control with a statement such as `return` or `break` and thus avoids executing the final `protect_critical.signal()`. In that situation, the protecting `Semaphore` will be left in state `count==0` thus blocking any other LWP from entering the critical section. One nice solution to this problem defines a class `AutoSignal` that provides control over the protecting `Semaphore`:

```
class AutoSignal {
    Semaphore* as;
public:
    AutoSignal(Semaphore& s) { as = &s; as.wait(); }
    ~AutoSignal() { as->signal(); }
// ...
};
```

Example 11-3 uses an improved method of protecting a critical section with an `AutoSignal`:

```
// ex11-3.c - Protecting a critical section of code with an
// AutoSignal

static Semaphore protect_critical(1);

class AutoSignal {
    Semaphore* as;
public:
    AutoSignal(Semaphore& s) { as= &s; as->wait(); }
    ~AutoSignal() { as->signal(); }
};

class TestProcess : public StackProc {
public:
    TestProcess(const char* name, stackTy* bot, int pri);
    static TestProcess* create(const char* name, int pri);
};

TestProcess::TestProcess(const char* pname,stackTy* bot,int pri)
            : StackProc(pname,bot,pri)
{
// parent process yields to allow this process to start
    if ( FORK() ) { Scheduler::yield(); return; }

    while (1) {
        // this block represents a critical section
        // although it does nothing critical
        AutoSignal autosig(protect_critical);
        cout << name() << pri << " enter critical section" << endl;
        break;
        }

// terminate to avoid return
    terminate();
}

main()
{
// start Scheduler
// create main context with priority 0
    MAIN_PROCESS(0);

String* pname = new String("P");
    for (register int i=MAXPRIORITY; i>=1; i--)
        TestProcess::create(*pname,i);

    cout << "main Process" << endl;
}
```

When a lightweight process exits the critical section, whether by a `break`, a `return`, a `goto` or by a normal sequential exit, the C++ generated code will call the destructor ~AutoSignal() which signals the Semaphore protect_critical. Just as in the first version, this will allow a second LWP to enter the critical section.

11.5 CLASS SharedQueue

Object
    Link
        Process
            StackProc
            HeapProc
    Scheduler
    Semaphore
    SharedQueue

A lightweight process transfers data to another process by adding data objects to an instance of class SharedQueue. A SharedQueue works like an ordinary first-in/first-out queue structure: an LWP can put an object at the tail end, or take the next object from the head of the queue. In addition, class SharedQueue implements a policy for what to do when an LWP attempts to put an object on a full SharedQueue or take an object from an empty SharedQueue. That policy is the same in both cases: the SharedQueue suspends the active LWP and places it on a Semaphore until the SharedQueue can complete the requested operation.

A lightweight process places an Object on a SharedQueue by calling the function SharedQueue::nextPut(Object&). The member function SharedQueue:: next() removes the Object from the head of the queue and returns a pointer to it.

Example 11-4 shows how to use a SharedQueue to pass data objects from one lightweight process to another.

```
// ex11-4.c - LWP communication with a SharedQueue

class TestProcess : public StackProc {
public:
    TestProcess(const char* name, int pri,
                SharedQueue& in, SharedQueue& out,
                stackTy* bot);
    static TestProcess* create(const char* name, int pri,
                SharedQueue& in, SharedQueue& out);
};


TestProcess::TestProcess(const char* pname, int pri,
                SharedQueue& in, SharedQueue& out,
                stackTy* bot) :
                StackProc(pname,bot,pri)
```

```
{
// parent LWP yields so this LWP can start
    if ( FORK() ) { Scheduler::yield(); return; }

    while (YES) {
        Object* msg = in.next();
        cout << className() << ": " << name()
            << " received " << *msg << endl;
        out.nextPut(*msg);
        cout << className() << ": " << name()
            << " sent " << *msg << endl;
        }
// no exit from loop so no return possible
}
TestProcess* TestProcess::create(const char* pname, int pri,
                                SharedQueue& in, SharedQueue& out)
{
    auto stackTy bottom;
    return new TestProcess(pname, pri, in, out, &bottom);
}
main()
{
// construct Scheduler
// and create main context with priority 0
    MAIN_PROCESS(0);


    SharedQueue* q0 = new SharedQueue(2);
    SharedQueue* qin = q0;
    SharedQueue* qout;

// start up lightweight processes coupled by SharedQueues:
// qout for kTH Process is qin for (k+1)TH Process
    for (register int i=1; i<=MAXPRIORITY; i++) {
        String* pname = new String("P");
        *pname &= (char)('0'+i);
        qout = new SharedQueue(2);
        TestProcess::create(*pname, i, *qin, *qout);
        qin = qout;
        }

// put a message on the first input SharedQueue
    String& inmsg = *new String("THE MESSAGE");
    cout << "process Main sending: " << inmsg << endl;
    q0->nextPut(inmsg);

// main Process waits for message on last output SharedQueue
```

```
        String& outmsg = *(String*)qout->next();
        cout << "process Main received: " << outmsg << endl;
    }
```

In Example 11-4, the main context constructs a lightweight process for each priority level and chains the LWPs together with instances of class `SharedQueue` passed as arguments to the LWP constructors. The main context puts a `String` inmsg on the first `SharedQueue`, the `String` is passed from LWP to LWP and retrieved from the last `SharedQueue` in the chain by the main context. The resulting output is:

```
process Main sending: THE MESSAGE
StackProc: P1 received THE MESSAGE
StackProc: P2 received THE MESSAGE
StackProc: P3 received THE MESSAGE
StackProc: P4 received THE MESSAGE
StackProc: P5 received THE MESSAGE
StackProc: P6 received THE MESSAGE
StackProc: P7 received THE MESSAGE
StackProc: P7 sent THE MESSAGE
StackProc: P6 sent THE MESSAGE
StackProc: P5 sent THE MESSAGE
StackProc: P4 sent THE MESSAGE
StackProc: P3 sent THE MESSAGE
StackProc: P2 sent THE MESSAGE
StackProc: P1 sent THE MESSAGE
process Main received: THE MESSAGE
```

Notice that while the `String` inmsg must have been passed along the chain of lightweight processes in order of their construction, the order in which the LWPs print their reports is not the same order in which the queue operations are actually performed. This is because as each LWP completes its call to `nextPut()` the `Scheduler` places it on the end of the run list *after* the rest of the LWPs waiting to receive an object. To eliminate this situation we would have to synchronize the lightweight processes by having each one pass the message object to a single LWP which would then distribute the message to the next `SharedQueue` in the chain. The behavior of Example 11-2 is an indication that great care is required in programming lightweight processes to produce the results intended.

11.6   CHAPTER SUMMARY

The NIH Class Library provides a lightweight process package with class `Process`, class `StackProc`, class `HeapProc`, class `Scheduler`, class `Semaphore`, and class `SharedQueue`. Scheduling of lightweight processes is non-preemptive. The package provides communication mechanisms for transferring objects between lightweight processes (class `SharedQueue`), nonblocked waiting for resources (class `Semaphore`) and for nonblocked waiting for activity on a file descriptor (`Process::select()`).

A lightweight process class for an application must be derived from either of class `StackProc` or class `HeapProc` which implement the coroutine context for the lightweight process. Applications programs using the NIH Class Library lightweight process classes should:

- use class `HeapProc` as a base class when efficiency is important
- use class `StackProc` as a base class to run with a debugger
- use a static member function `create()` to construct LWP objects as shown above
- use the new operator or a static constructor to construct any argument passed as a reference or pointer to an LWP member function
- write LWP constructor functions so they can never return

Some typical uses for a `Semaphore` are :

- Synchronizing an LWP with an external event.
- Managing N resources.
- Protecting a critical section of code.

12
AN OBJECT- ORIENTED
APPLICATION

12.1 INTRODUCTION

In this chapter we describe an application we designed and implemented using classes from the NIH Class Library. The focus of the discussion is on the modeling of a real system and the shaping of the model into an object-oriented software design using lightweight processes from the NIH Class Library and many of the NIH Library container classes as well. The application itself, a file system backup utility, will play only a supporting role and we omit most of the details of the real system and the implementation of the application. An important aspect of the discussion is the way in which the NIH Class Library affected the design of the system.

12.1.1 Background and design goals

We developed the NIH Class Library as part of a project to integrate a network of workstations with a distributed file system for campus-wide use at the National Institutes of Health. One important goal for the distributed file system is to provide centralized management of disk-to-tape backups of user files throughout the network. To complete this backup service the project needs a backup utility program that can

- reliably control disk-to-tape backups for a network of computers
- reliably control tape-to-disk restoration of files
- perform concurrent operations with distinct disks and tape drives
- maintain a database for backup tapes to support file restoration
- protect the database in case of machine and network error
- facilitate control by operators who are not programmers
- do all this in a production environment

In this discussion of the application, we will describe two of the major components of the backup system: backup control and the backup database. We will omit further mention of the restore functions, the user interface and other aspects of the production environment.

12.1.2 A model of the backup system

To present an overview of the design of the backup system, we can select certain features of the network and distributed file system and compose them into an abstract model of a backup system. The model involves the computer resources on the network, the operations of the distributed file system, as well as the backup operations.

The distributed file system, known as the Andrew File System (AFS)[10], implements additions to the standard UNIX operating system (BSD 4.3). Briefly, the idea of the AFS distributed file system is that all user and system files reside on disks of specialized computers which we call *file servers*. Each workstation class computer, which we call a *client*, connects to the file servers over a network. When a client tries to run a program or open a data file, the relevant files are copied over the network from the file server disk and are cached on the client disk. The term *cache* refers to a policy of guaranteeing the presence of a file on the client disk only as long as it is actively used. When a client closes a modified file it is copied back to the file server. The clients have 24 hour-a-day access to all files which they have permission to use, but they do not know which file server holds the files at any given time. A master set of important system files is maintained on a distinguished file server which we call the *control server*. The control server automatically distributes updates of the master files to the other file servers.

The distributed file system organizes the files into units called *volumes*. For example, a user's volume consists of all the files in the user's UNIX home directory. A volume is the unit of file management as far as the distributed file system is concerned: AFS implements operations for creating, purging, and cloning volumes.

The clone operation is of central importance to a backup system. Once every 24 hours, usually at night, the distributed file system makes a clone volume from each user volume. This *backup clone* volume is a read-only snapshot of a volume as it was at a certain time. When a user's volume is backed up, it is actually the clone volume that is copied and saved on tape. Using clone volumes has the advantage that operators can proceed with the backup without shutting down the system and without preventing users from continuing to use their volumes. Because the clone volume is a read-only volume, the data it contains cannot change during backup operations.

The backup system must perform these functions:

- *Scheduling*. Identify the volumes to get full or incremental backup.
- *Staging*. Disk-to-disk copy of volumes from file server to staging machine.
- *Taping*. Disk-to-tape copy of volumes.

The *staging machine* is a computer which runs the backup system software. It has direct connections to one or more tape drives and a number of large disks that serve as *staging disks* for the backup. During the *staging* operation, the backup system makes full or partial copies of clone volumes to a staging disk until it has gathered enough data to fill a tape.[1] During the *taping* operation, the backup system copies data from the staging disk to a magnetic tape. The backup system also maintains a database that can associate each tape serial number with identifiers for the volumes the tape contains. This information can be later used to restore volumes by copying from tapes back to the file server disks.

12.2 THE OBJECT-ORIENTED DESIGN

From the very beginning, work on the design for the backup system focused on two areas: the need for concurrent performance of staging and taping operations, and the need for

---

[1] The use of staging—disk buffering of data—is a deliberate design decision beyond the scope of this discussion.

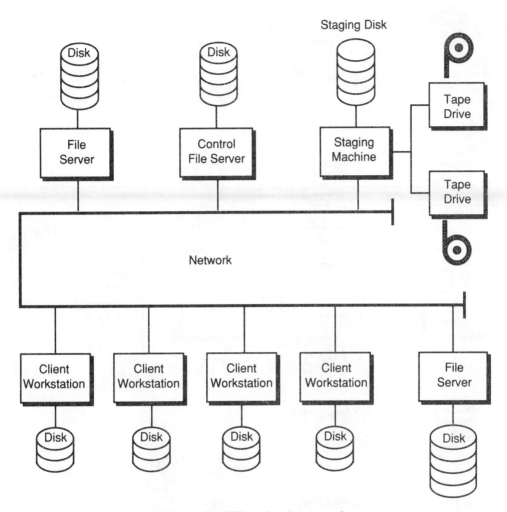

Figure 12.1 NIH workstation network

the operations to share many complex data structures, including a robust database. As we discussed in the introduction to Chapter 11, control of concurrency and shared data structures calls for lightweight processes. This design requirement, together with the presence of lightweight processes in the locally available NIH Class Library, suggested a suitable programming environment for the project: programming in C++, using the NIH Class Library. This combination promised a highly structured approach to implementing lightweight processes to provide the process control functionality of the backup system.

The design and development of the backup system, based on the models described in Figures 12.1 and 12.2, proceeded along several distinct, yet obviously interrelated, lines:

- System Configuration (what to backup? when to backup?)

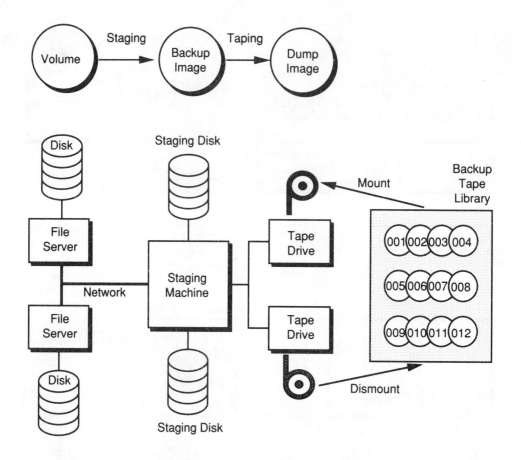

Figure 12.2 Model of backup system

- System Control Structure (concurrency with lightweight processes)

- System Resource Management (in-memory NIH Class Library containers)

- System History of Activity (database built around NIH Class Library containers)

Each of these lines of development went through several revisions as we gained experience with the actual performance of these components of the system and their interactions. Instead of trying to explain the progression through all the variations, we will describe the final object-oriented design and comment on how it improves the deficiencies of past versions. Keep in mind that the design described in this section only emerged after experience with particular implementations using C++ and the NIH Class Library. A certain amount of experimentation helped to uncover the best methods of utilizing the services of the UNIX operating system. In some cases, interactions with network software and hardware called for debugging and repairs of the software related to those areas.

12.2.1 Lightweight processes

The most puzzling issue that comes up in an object-oriented design deals with identifying those aspects of a real-world system that we want to take as the objects in the software design. That is, we must first select those real-world objects whose properties we want to represent in software. For each selected real-world object, and for some groups of objects, we design an abstract data type that represents the properties that are important for our system design. Later, during the object-oriented implementation phase, we translate those data types into C++ classes and, in this way, represent the originally selected real-world objects by C++ objects in the software.

In the case of the backup system, we need to answer the question, "Which aspects of the distributed file backup system should we represent as lightweight processes?" We first considered the lightweight processes to represent the active components of the real system: the file servers, the tape drives, and the disk drives. Whatever logical appeal this idea might have, attempts to implement it led to a dead end. The main difficulties with this approach were that it required the construction of unneeded processes and it required interprocess communication techniques that were difficult to program because they are not supported by the NIH Class Library model. A more fruitful approach emerged from turning things inside out: instead of making an object out of the active system components, we represented the activity itself as a lightweight process and the active system components as resource objects for each lightweight process to use. Thus, while the file server machines are the active agents in the real distributed file system, we chose to represent their staging and taping operations as lightweight processes, and to represent the file servers as resources needed by the staging and taping processes.

This gives a starting point for structuring our lightweight processes in the backup system, but how many kinds of lightweight processes should there be, and exactly what should they control?

Table 12.1 shows a listing of the basic operations and the system resources they require. The first column identifies operations in the backup system. We have divided system activity into three operations: scheduling, staging, and taping. The second column lists the corresponding resources. We use the term *resource* to refer to an object representing a real system component with information and/or functionality required to perform a real system operation.

The first operation in Table 12.1 deals with the scheduling of requests for backup activity. Backup administrators initiate most requests by preparing program start-up files but they may send additional requests to the backup program while it is running. A unique lightweight process we call the *Request Manager* gathers these requests and presents them in an orderly fashion to other lightweight processes in the backup system.

The second part of Table 12.1 concerns the scheduling of file server activity. We learned from experience that asking a file server to handle more than one backup operation at a time will degrade its performance. So for each file server in the real system we associate a lightweight process, called a *Server Manager*, that schedules the file server for only one backup operation at a time. The Server Manager will reserve staging disk resource and then use it to start a staging operation from its file server to the staging disk.

The third part of Table 12.1 concerns both the staging and taping operations. While staging and taping are distinctly different operations, the need to hold onto the common staging disk

Table 12.1 Backup system operations and resource requirements

Operation	Resources Required
Scheduling volume backup	volume descriptor
	request record
Staging a volume	file server
	staging disk
Taping a staging disk	staging disk
	tape drive
	tape reel

resource throughout both operations binds the two operations together very tightly. So there is another kind of lightweight process in the backup system called a *Backup Manager*. A Server Manager hands over the staging disk resource to a Backup Manager process which holds on to that staging disk until its job is completed.

In summary, a lightweight process called the Request Manager acquires requests for backup services and distributes the requests to Server Managers that schedule the backup activity of the file servers. Each Server Manager starts up a Backup Manager for every available staging disk resource, and passes along to the Backup Manager those backup requests that it received from the Request Manager. Each Backup Manager holds onto the staging disk resource until one staging/taping operation has been completed.

12.2.2   Resource management

The principal resources that the backup system has to manage are file servers, volumes, staging disks, tape drives, and tape reels. The backup system performs two resource management jobs: identification of resources in the real system, and allocation of these real resources to the real backup operations. To control these identification and allocation operations with software, we need to have some kind of software object to represent each real system resource and we need a method of distributing these (software) resource objects to any lightweight process that controls the real backup operations. We can summarize the resource management method as follows:

- *initialize* a list of available resource objects of each kind from data files
- *construct* an object to represent each real resource
- *allocate* resource objects to lightweight processes by a queuing mechanism

12.2.3   The backup database

The whole point of saving files on tape is to be able to restore selected files to disk in case of an emergency. To do so requires a practical way of finding the tapes which hold the files of interest. When many tapes are involved, we need something more than human memory or pencil and paper, for example, a computer database.

Early in the development of the backup application, we realized that we were not ready to select a commercial database package. Our alternative was to develop a special-purpose database suitable for use in the initial stages of the project. A number of factors made this a practical alternative. We expected the scale of the network to remain small—fewer than five file servers—for several years. The small scale means that we could consider retaining the entire database in memory during program execution and using object I/O to write the database to disk. Also, the time it takes to save the entire data base after each backup operation is not critical when compared to the long copying and taping sessions of the backup application, thus maintaining the database in memory relieves us of requirements for sophisticated database methods of accessing records from disk storage. We did not need record locking and other integrity features available with a commercial database because only one program needs write access to the database.

The special-purpose database had to provide:

- *Data entry and retrieval functions required by backup program.* This includes retrieval of records by key and garbage-collection of records.

- *Easy and reliable transfer between memory and disk.* The small scale permits retention of the entire database in memory.

- *Flexible, programmable interface.* The database must be both easy to use and adaptable to future changes of the application's data structures.

- *Robust performance.* The application requires protection of the integrity of data in case of program, operator, or hardware errors.

- *Rapid development.* Limits on project resources demanded this.

It turns out that an extensible, object-oriented library provides an excellent foundation with which to meet these requirements. We discuss the database in more detail in Section 12.4.

12.3   AN IMPLEMENTATION BASED ON THE NIH CLASS LIBRARY

To implement an object-oriented design we need to declare C++ classes corresponding to the various data types abstracted from the objects in the design model. Sometimes our efforts to implement abstract data types corresponding to modeled objects were not successful and we had to change the design. This was especially true on the early part of the "learning curve" while forming an understanding of what abstract data types can be practically implemented in C++. In fact, the development of the backup system did involve this kind of feedback from implementation experience to design concepts. Still, in retrospect, we can describe a pattern that emerged in the kinds of classes that were declared.

It turned out that the backup system, which is a control application with a data base, required five kinds of objects in its implementation:

- Data records
- Data record containers

- Data flow containers
- Specialized objects
- Lightweight process objects

12.3.1   Data records

A data record is a "passive" object in the sense that it minds its own business, which is primarily managing its own member variables. A typical data object, like a data base record or a resource descriptor, has member variables for data items such as names, identification numbers, and dates. A data object may have member variables pointing to other data records or member variables that are containers for attribute objects. Table 12.2 lists the classes representing the most important resource descriptors in the backup system.

Consider, for example, class `FileServer`, a C++ representation of the abstract data type for file server machines in the AFS:

```
class FileServer: public Object {
private:
    String hostname;   // host name for network
    int hostid;        // server id number for the AFS
public:
    FileServer(istream&);

    String name() { return hostname; }
    int id()      { return hostid; }

// try new connection on each call      bool inService();
// ... other members
};
```

The constructor for class `FileServer` knows how to initialize a `FileServer` object from descriptive data read from an `istream` attached to a file. The backup application can check the network connection between its host computer and the file server with member function `inService()`. All the operations pertaining to a file server machine are encapsulated in the `FileServer` data type, and a `FileServer` object knows only about one file server.

Resource data records correspond to components of the real world AFS. Another important data record in the backup system is the request record, which is used to request some service provided by a lightweight process. The abstract class `RequestRecord` implements the request record data type:

```
class RequestRecord: public Object {
    long time_of_request;
    int prio;       // request priority
    int sz;         // size of backup image in kbytes
protected:
    RequestRecord();  // abstract class
```

```
public:
    virtual String hostServer() =0; // abstract class
    long timeStamp() { return time_of_request; }
    int priority() { return prio; }
    int priority(int p) { return (prio=p); }
    int size() { return sz; }
// ... other members
};
```

Table 12.2 Classes representing backup resources

Class Name	Resource
AFSVolume	volume descriptor
FileServer	file server machine
ServerDisk	disk on file server
StageDisk	staging disk
TapeDrive	tape drive device
TapeReel	tape reel

Specific types of requests are represented by derived classes such as class `BackupRequest` and class `RestoreRequest`. It is left up to the derived class to implement a member `hostServer()` returning the name of the file server that will service the request.

12.3.2 Data object containers

To put data records to a practical use, the backup program has to gather the objects, as they are constructed, into containers from which they can be retrieved when needed. We have found that these containers can be easily fashioned from combinations of classes from the NIH Class Library. The most important example of a data record container in the backup system is the prototype data base which we describe in Section 12.4. We illustrate here several simpler examples.

The backup system uses a data dictionary implemented as an instance of a class `Locator` derived from the NIH Library class `Dictionary`. A `Locator` associates a `String` key object with one or more value objects stored in an `OrderedCltn`.

```
class Locator: public Dictionary {
public:
    Locator();

// pointer to the one and only instance
    static Locator* Ptr;
```

```
// return nth value object at key
    String* valueAtKey(const String&,int n =0) const;

// other members ...
};
```

The constructor for a `Locator` reads the data dictionary from a text file which system administrators can edit.

Another example is class `AllServers` which serves as a container for `FileServer` resource objects. An `AllServers` container is a derived `Dictionary`, each `FileServer` being keyed by a `String` holding its name.

```
class AllServers: public Dictionary {
    AllServers();
public:
// pointer to the one and only instance
    static AllServers* Ptr;

// retrieve FileServer by name
    static FileServer* serverAtKey(const String& name);

// other members ...
};

AllServers::AllServers()
{
    // open the initialization file
    // with name obtained from data dictionary
    // at key "AllServers"
    String* fname = Locator::Ptr->valueAtKey("AllServers");
    fstream istrm(fname,ios::in);

    while (1) {
      // construct FileServer from next line in istrm
      FileServer* fs = new FileServer(istrm);

      // exit loop at EOF or error
      if ( !istrm.good() ) break;

      // add FileServer to Dictionary keyed by name
      String* key = new String(fs->name());
      addAssoc(*key,*fs);
      }
}
```

The constructor `AllServers::AllServers()` opens an `istream` attached to an initialization file describing all configured file servers. The full name of the initialization file is obtained from a data dictionary at the key "AllImages". The `AllServers()` constructor constructs one instance of class `FileServer` for each line in its data file and adds the `FileServer` to its underlying `Dictionary`.

Other examples of data record containers from the backup program include:

- class `AllConfigs`, derived from class `OrderedCltn`, containing a descriptor object for each kind of backup

- class `AllStages`, derived from class `OrderedCltn`, containing a resource object for each staging disk

- class `AllTapeDrives`, derived from class `OrderedCltn`, containing a resource object for each tape drive

- class `AllVolumes`, derived from class `SortedCltn`, containing a descriptor object for each volume in the distributed file system

12.3.3 Data flow containers

A data flow container serves as a software "pipe" allowing transmission of resources between lightweight processes. All four resources for our backup system listed in Table 12.2 have two common properties that affect the behavior of the active lightweight processes:

- the resource is essential to the function of one or more lightweight processes

- the resource can be used by at most one lightweight process at a time

Thus the various lightweight processes in the backup system (Table 12.4) must compete for exclusive control of resources and we need a way to pass the resources from one LWP to another. The NIH Class Library process package provides us with class `SharedQueue` to manage the resources used by the lightweight processes. As indicated in Table 12.3, the backup system has a `SharedQueue` to manage the `StagingDisk` resources and a separate `SharedQueue` to manage the `TapeDrive` resources.

Table 12.3 Containers transmitting data between lightweight processes

Resource	Data Flow Container	
	Class	Name
StagingDisk	SharedQueue	stagingDiskQ
TapeDrive	SharedQueue	tapeDriveQ
TapeReel	LinkedList	freeTapePool
RequestRecord	LinkedList	requestQ
RequestRecord	SharedQueue	asyncQ

The `SharedQueue` structure forces a lightweight process requesting a resource to suspend its activity and wait until at least one resource object is available. The application employs this method of resource management when the requesting lightweight process has no alternative to the requested resource and cannot proceed in its activity without it. In other circumstances, when the lightweight process can take alternative actions, the application uses another kind of data flow container to queue resources. As an example, consider a request by the `BackupManager` for a `TapeReel` resource prior to starting a taping operation. A `TapeReel` falls into one of three categories: tape reels holding current backup images, tape reels holding retired backup images, and never-used tape reels. The request for a `TapeReel` resource corresponds to a request for a computer operator to mount a tape reel. The first preference is to reuse one that has been retired; if none are available for reuse, the operator is asked to mount a never-used reel. The `TapeReel` resources are held in a `LinkedList` structure, which does not require the requesting lightweight process to wait for a `TapeReel` to appear on the list. So in this case, the `BackupManager` simply takes the first `TapeReel` object from the `LinkedList` if one is available, otherwise constructs a new `TapeReel` object to represent the new reel mounted by the operator.

12.3.4 Specialized objects

A number of classes in the backup system simply encapsulate an algorithm that is essential to the application. The algorithm is probably not of general interest, and may even be used in only one place in the code, but is sufficiently complicated to warrant hiding it away in its own class implementation. The benefits obtained from using this approach, instead of including the code directly in a member function of some other class, include controlling effects of changes and convenience for testing and debugging.

Class `SelectBackup`, which selects volumes for backup from the `AllVolumes` structure based on information from the volume descriptor record and backup configuration descriptors contained in the `AllConfigs` configuration table, is an interesting example of a specialized object whose function could very well be integrated into other source code except for the reasons listed above. The straightforward approach could be achieved as follows:

```
// iterate through the list of volume descriptors
//  and save BackupRequest when appropriate
Iterator it(*AllVolumes::Ptr);
OrderedCltn requestList;
while (it++) {
    AFSVolume* v = (AFSVolume*)it();
// decide if this volume gets a backup
// ...
// add a new request to request list
    requestList.add(*new BackupRequest(/*...*/));
}
```

The method of coming to a decision about the backup of a volume is, however, complicated and would be easier to test if encapsulated in a class. We can arrange an alternative implementation by making a class `Selector`, derived from class `Iterator`, that can apply some selection criteria as it iterates through a container. For example, we can show simplified declarations for classes `Selection` and `Selector`:

```
class Selection {
public:
    Selection() {}
    virtual Object* selected(const Object&);
};

class Selector: public Iterator {
public:
    Selector(Collection&,const Selection&);

// advance to next object in container
// that is selected by the Selection object
    Object* operator++();

// other members ...
};
```

A `Selector` is an `Iterator` that applies a selection criteria supplied by the caller by means of the `Selection` object passed to the constructor function. The function `Selector::operator++()` treats the `Selection` object polymorphically in making the selection, so that the caller is free to provide an instance of any class derived from class `Selection`. In our application, we derive our class `SelectBackup` from class `Selection`, and we implement `SelectBackup::selected()` to return a pointer to the `BackupRequest` record; it returns `NULL` if the volume does not get a backup.

12.3.5 Lightweight process objects

A lightweight process is an "active" object in that its member functions simulate or control activity in a real world system. In the backup program, the lightweight processes control UNIX child processes of their parent heavyweight process, they manage the data flow in the backup system, they send signals to each other, and they respond to signals received by their parent heavyweight process.

Table 12.4 lists the lightweight process classes in the backup program, derived from the NIH Library class `Process`. Each one of these process classes manages one or more of the operations from in Table 12.1.

We can illustrate the implementation of these active manager processes with some sample code from class `RequestManager`.

```
class RequestManager: public StackProc {
// asynchronous request queue
    LinkedList requestQ;

// queue for terminated ServerManager LWPs
    SharedQueue terminatedQ;
```

Table 12.4 Classes derived from class Process *representing backup operations*

Class Name	Operation
RequestManager	backup and restore request scheduling
ServerManager	file server disk backup scheduling
BackupManager	staging (server to staging disk)
	taping (staging disk to tape)
RestoreManager	restoring disk (tape to staging disk)
	merging (staging disk to server)

```
// ServerManager keyed by file server host name
    Dictionary serverManagerTable;
public:
    RequestManager(stackTy*,SharedQueue*);

// return ServerManager* value with file server name as key
    ServerManager* serverManager(const String& name);

// remove ServerManager from serverManagerTable
    ServerManager* removeServerManager(const ServerManager&);
};
```

In addition to the member variables inherited from class Process, class RequestManager has member variables it uses to coordinate requests. The member requestQ is a LinkedList to hold RequestRecord objects. The Dictionary serverManagerTable allows the RequestManager to access ServerManager processes by name.

The constructor function for class RequestManager performs the scheduling of requests for backup and restore services. We show here a much simplified version of a RequestManager constructor to illustrate the use of NIH Class Library classes in our application:

```
RequestManager::RequestManager(
        stackTy* bot,          // stack bottom
        SharedQueue* parentQ // parent LWP's return queue
        } :                         // base class is
    CommuniProc(                    //  specialized StackProc
                "RequestManager",   // process name
                bot,                // stack bottom
                RequestManager_PRIO,  // process priority
                DEFAULT_PROCESS_STACK)// process stack allocation
{
    if ( FORK() ) { Scheduler::yield(); return; }

    terminatedQ = new SharedQueue;
```

```
// AllServers::Ptr points to a Dictionary
//    with FileServer values keyed by String names
// start up a ServerManager for each FileServer
    Iterator it(*AllServers::Ptr);
    while (it++) {
        Assoc* as = (Assoc*)it();
        String* fsname = (String*)as.key();
        FileServer* fs = (FileServer*)as.value();
        serverManagers.addAssoc(*fsname,
                            *new ServerManager(fs,terminatedQ));

    }

// distribute preconfigured backup requests to ServerManagers
// backup requests are constructed from volume descriptors
    SelectBackup selectBackup;
    Selector select(*AllVolumes::Ptr,selectBackup);
    while ( select++ ) {
        // select a backup request for the next volume
        BackupRequest* req = *(BackupRequest)select();

        // get ServerManager LWP for file server hosting backup
        ServerManager* sm = serverManager(*req->hostName());

        // put BackupRequest on ServerManager's request queue
        // ServerManager LWP will respond
// to presence of request on queue
        sm->putRequest(*req);
        }
        }

// for signals from terminated ServerManagers
// delete each
    while ( serverManagerTable.size()>0 ) {
        // suspend until next ServerManager terminates
        ServerManager* sm = (ServerManager*)terminatedQ.next();

        // remove ServerManager from table and delete LWP object
        delete removeServerManager(*sm);
        }
        }

// to exit: signal parent LWP and terminate
    parentQ.nextPut(*this);
    terminate();
}
```

The RequestManager performs three main functions. First it iterates through the AllServers dictionary of all FileServers and constructs a new ServerManager lightweight process for each `FileServer` it finds. Next, the `RequestManager` steps though a list of volume descriptors scheduled for backup services and puts a new `BackupRequest` object on the request queue of the associated `ServerManager`. Finally, the `RequestManager` waits for each `ServerManager` to place itself on the `terminatedQ`, and deletes each lightweight process in turn. The `RequestManager` finishes up by placing itself on the `SharedQueue parentQ` of the the LWP that constructed it. This mechanism of LWP communication is the same as between the `RequestManager` and each `ServerManager`.

12.3.6   The dynamics of the backup system

To illustrate the interactions among lightweight process objects, data flow containers and resource data records we have shown the dynamics of the backup system's lightweight processes in Figures 12.3 through 12.6. Boxes in the diagrams represent C++ objects. The connecting arrows represent the direction of data flow; their labels are numbered serially in the order that events take place during program execution.

In Figure 12.3 we see how request scheduling is done. When a request is configured, a `RequestRecord` is (1) *put* on the `LinkedList requestQ` of the `RequestManager`. *Put* means to add a pointer to an object to the end of a `LinkedList`. After configuring all initial requests, the `RequestManager` (2) constructs a `ServerManager` object for each `FileServer` resource, passing a new `requestQ` as an argument to the constructor. The `RequestManager` then (3) *gets* each `RequestRecord` from the `requestQ`, and (4) puts the `RequestRecord` on the `requestQ` of the `ServerManager` whose `FileServer` is the residence of the volume of files mentioned in the backup request. *Get* means to remove a pointer to an object from the beginning of a `LinkedList`. When all possible `ServerManager` LWPs have been started, the `RequestManager` waits for the termination of all of the `ServerManagers`.

Figure 12.4 shows the scheduling of backup operations for a particular `FileServer`. The `FileServer`'s `ServerManager` (5) *grabs* a `StageDisk`, used as buffer storage for the backup and restore operations, from the `SharedQueue stageQ` resource queue. *Grab* means that the LWP, in this case the `ServerManager`, must *wait* until a `Semaphore` is signaled that an `Object` is available on the `SharedQueue`, and then the LWP removes a pointer to an `Object` from the beginning of the queue. Next, the `ServerManager` (6) constructs a `BackupManager` LWP passing (pointers to) its `requestQ`, `StageDisk`, and `FileServer` objects as arguments to the constructor. Finally, the `ServerManager` (7) waits on a `Semaphore` that protects access to the `FileServer` resource. The `ServerManager` waits until the `BackupManager` (12) signals the `Semaphore` that it is finished with its `FileServer`.

Figure 12.5 shows how (13) a `BackupManager` LWP controls the staging phase of the backup. The `BackupManager` follows the strategy of copying volumes of files from its file server to the staging disk until the disk is full. The `BackupManager` is then finished with that `FileServer` and is ready to perform the taping operation. The `BackupManager` knows which volumes to backup from information in the `RequestRecord` it (8) gets from the `requestQ`. The actual staging (copying) of files from the file server to the staging disk is performed by a heavyweight (UNIX) process that is a child of the parent heavyweight process. The child process is under the control of an instance of class UnixChild (9) constructed by the BackupManager. The BackupManager (10) waits on a Semaphore until a UNIX signal is received when the UNIX child process is finished. The UnixChild has a signal handler function that relays the signal to the Semaphore on which the BackupManager is waiting. While the BackupManager is waiting on the Semaphore, other BackupManager LWPs are able to perform backup operations from other file servers to other staging disks. In this way, the lightweight processes of the backup system can control backup operations going on concurrently in different parts of the network. When the BackupManager resumes execution after receiving the (11) signal that the staging operation is completed it, in turn, (12) signals the ServerManager that it can reuse the FileServer resource.

Figure 12.6 shows how a BackupManager controls a taping operation. First, the BackupManager (13) grabs a TapeDrive resource object from the SharedQueue driveQ. The BackupManager then (14) constructs a UnixChild object to control a UNIX child process that performs the taping. The BackupManager (15) waits on a Semaphore until a (16) signal is received indicating that the taping operation is completed. At this point, the BackupManager (17) updates the backup system's database with data associating the volume backup images with their tape reels. Next, the BackupManager (18) releases the TapeDrive resource to the SharedQueue driveQ and (19) releases the StageDisk resource to the SharedQueue stageQ. *Release* means that the LWP must wait on a Semaphore until there is space available on the SharedQueue, and then it adds a pointer to an object to the end of the queue. Finally, the BackupManager (20) terminates as an LWP and is deleted as an object.

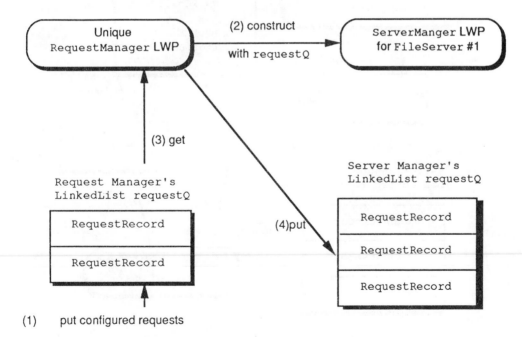

Figure 12.3 Request scheduling operations

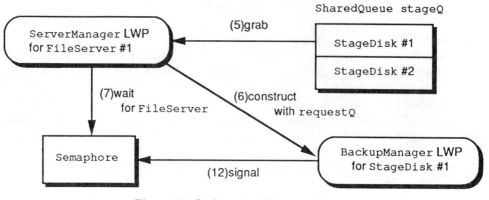

Figure 12.4 Backup scheduling operations

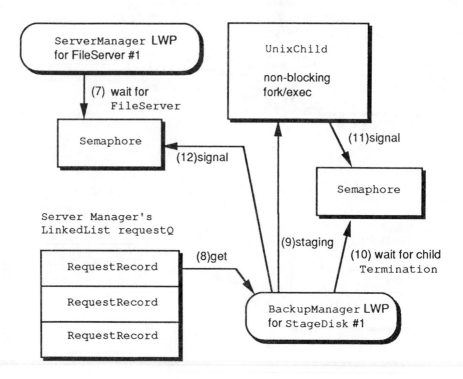

Figure 12.5 Backup staging operations

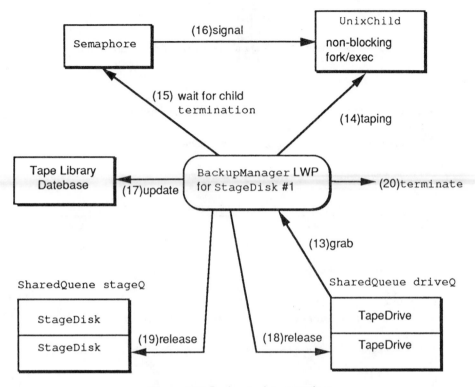

Figure 12.6 *Backup taping operations*

12.4 IMPLEMENTING A DATABASE WITH THE NIH CLASS LIBRARY

We can separate the task of developing an implementation of a backup database into three steps. First, we must identify the basic data items to be saved in the database and then invent some abstract data types to represent them. After we understand those data items, we can investigate data structures that will effectively represent the relationships among them. Finally, we can implement those data structures with C++ classes with help from the NIH Class Library.

Table 12.5 lists the basic data types from the backup system. We represent each of these data types by a C++ class with member variables reflecting the various data items. We use NIH Library containers to store instances of these classes, thus we must declare them as derived from class `Object` of the NIH Class Library (see Section 8.1.1). For example, we can represent the Volume Image data type by class `VolumeImage`:

Table 12.5 Data types from the backup system

Name	Description
Backup Identifier	specifies type of backup performed
Residence Identifier	identifies a file server and disk holding volumes
Tape Descriptor	describes an individual tape reel
Tape Identifier	identifying number of a tape reel
Time Stamp	time and date as a number of seconds
Volume Identifier	serial number and name
Volume Image	describes a backup image of a volume

```
// a class representing the Volume Image data type

class VolumeImage: public Object {
    VolumeIdent*  v_ident;    // Volume identifier
    DiskIdent*    d_ident;    // residence for this Volume
    BackupIdent*  b_ident;    // identifier for this backup
    TapeIdent*    t_indent;   // tape for this backup
    Time          backup_time;//  time of this backup
public:
    VolumeImage(const VolumeIdent&, const BackupIdent&);
    bool isEqual(const Object&);
    int compare(const Object&);
     unsigned hash();
// other members ...
};
```

Class `VolumeImage` has member variables that identify the parameters of a particular volume backup. The last member variable, `backup_time`, an instance of the NIH Library class `Time`, holds the time that the taping operation was started. Class `VolumeImage` also declares four of its member variables as pointers to derived `Object`s. The reason for using pointers has to do with the method of saving the database as a disk file. We will discuss this in more detail after describing the implementation of the data structures in the database.

To build a complete database we next must understand the relationships among the various data types in the backup system. Table 12.6 summarizes the relationships between key object and value objects in the database.

The key/value associations shown in Table 12.6 are actually four interrelated databases that together form the backup database. We describe the implementation of each of these databases below.

Table 12.6 Key/value associations for the backup database

Data Relation	Key	Value
Backup State	Volume Identifier	list of the latest Volume Image for each Backup Identifier
Residence Registry	Residence Identifier	list of all volumes that ever had given residence
Tape Catalog	Tape Identifier	set of all Volume Images with given Tape Identifier
Tape Registry	Tape Identifier	Tape Descriptor

12.4.1 Backup State database

The Backup State database saves information needed by the backup system to determine which type of backup should be performed next for a given volume. It turns out that a list of all the latest `VolumeImage` objects for a given volume, one for each backup type, can serve as a backup state when it is sorted by the backup time. To illustrate this idea, consider the sample list of `VolumeImage` objects associated with a `VolumeIdent`:

```
VolumeIdent[1762 user.anne]:

Residence[server1 /disk1]
BackupIdent[Quarterly 1 full]
BackupTime[Tue Apr 15 10:43;14 1988]

Residence[server1 /disk1]
BackupIdent[Daily 4 incr]
BackupTime[Thu May 12 16:09:39 1988]

Residence[server1 /disk1]
BackupIdent[Weekly    3 full]
BackupTime[Fri May 13 16:11:50 1988]
```

The volume in question is the volume for the user named "anne". The list indicates that Quarterly backup #1, which is a full backup, was performed on Tuesday, April 15. Daily backup #4, which is an incremental backup, was performed on Thursday May 12. Weekly backup #3, a full backup, was performed on Friday, May 13. The list is sorted by the backup time.

With prior knowledge of the container classes available in the NIH Class Library, an easy implementation for the Backup State database comes to mind. Add the selected `VolumeImage` objects to a `SortedCltn`. Then save an association between the `VolumeIdent` for the user "anne" and this `SortedCltn`. The code to do this might include the statements:

```
Dictionary backupState; // Backup State Database

// retrieve current backup state for user "anne"
VolumeIdent vid(1762,"anne");
SortedCltn* state_cltn;

if ( backupState.includesKey(vid)  )
    // get SortedCltn at key vid
    state_cltn = (SortedCltn*)backupState.atKey(vid);
  else {
    // add  new  key/value association to database
    backupState.addAssoc(*new VolumeIdent(1762,"anne"),
                    *(state_cltn=new SortedCltn));
    }

// class BackupState encapsulates the state transition method
// construct the current BackupState
// and determine the next BackupState
BackupState state(*state_cltn);

// next backup identifier
BackupIdent* b_ident = state.next();

// find the VolumeImage for b_ident  from state_cltn
VolumeImage* v_image = volumeImageFrom(b_ident,state_cltn);

// remove old VolumeImage from list
state_cltn->remove(*v_image);

// perform backup
// ...

// assign new tape and backup time  to VolumeImage
// ...

// update Backup State Database
// add new VolumeImage to list
state_cltn->add(*v_image);
```

We can take advantage of the sorting method built into SortedCltn containing the VolumeImage objects by properly implementing the compare() member function in class VolumeImage (see Section 8.3.5). We want VolumeImage objects to sort in the order of their backup times:

```
VolumeImage::compare(const Object& ob)
{
```

```
    // to be comparable ob must have actual class VolumeImage
       assertArgClass(ob, *VolumeImage::desc(),"compare");

    // cast argument to be VolumeImage
       VolumeImage& vim = (VolumeImage&)ob;

    // delegate to member variable
       return backup_time.compare(vim.backup_time);
    }
```

12.4.2   Residence Registry database

The term *residence* refers to the file server disk on which the files in a volume happen to be stored. The Residence Registry database records the list of volumes residing on each file server disk. This information is needed to be able to restore all the volumes on a file server disk. This database requires saving an association between a `ResidenceIdent` and a list of `VolumeIdent`, one for each volume residing on the disk. The implementation of the Residence Registry database is similar to that for the Backup State database.

12.4.3   Tape Catalog database

The Tape Catalog database keeps track of the contents of each tape reel in the backup tape library so that the backup system can determine when a tape reel can be reused.

How can the database know when a tape can be reused? As the example of a backup state shown above illustrates, backups are typed as "Daily", "Weekly", "Monthly", and "Quarterly". These backup types are cycled through some schedule, for example four Daily each week, three Weekly per month, three Monthly per quarter, and four Quarterly per year. When Daily #1 is repeated the next week, the volume image for the first Daily #1 is said to be *expired*. When all the volume images on a given tape reel have expired we can reuse that tape reel.

The Tape Catalog database associates with each `TapeIdent` a set of `VolumeIdent` objects corresponding to volumes that were backed up on that particular tape. This database will need an operation to add an association between `TapeIdent` and `VolumeIdent` whenever a volume is backed up on a tape. It will also need an operation to remove the association when the backup images of the volume expires. We can implement these operations very easily by using class `Set` from the NIH Class Library. The association between `TapeIdent` and `Set` can be saved in an NIH Library `Dictionary`. The implementation might look like,

```
Dictionary tapeCatalog;    // Tape Catalog Database

VolumeImage* v_image = // pointer to some VolumeImage
TapeIdent* new_tape  = // pointer to next TapeIdent

TapeIdent* old_tape = v_image->t_ident;
Set* s;
```

```
// before taping operation starts remove old association
//  between TapeIdent and VolumeImage
if ( tapeCatalog.includesKey(*old_tape) ) {
   s = (Set*)tapeCatalog.atKey(old_tape);
   s->remove(*v_image);   //  remove VolumeImage from old tape
   if (s->isEmpty()) ... //  mark TapeReel as "not busy"
   }

// taping operation
// ...

// after taping completes successfully add new association
//  between TapeIdent and VolumeImage
if ( tapeCatalog.includesKey(*new_tape) )
   // get Set of VolumeImage for new tape
   s = (Set*)tapeCatalog.atKey(new_tape);
  else
   // add new key/value association
   tapeCatalog.addAssoc(*new_tape,*(s=new Set));

//  add Volume Image to new tape set
s->add(*v_image);
```

To store the VolumeImage objects in a Set, we need to implement the hash() and isEqual() member functions to correctly distinguish the VolumeImage objects (see Section 8.3.8). These members should depend on the values of all the member variables of class VolumeImage.

```
unsigned VolumeImage::hash()
{
    return v_ident->hash()^d_ident->hash()^
          b_ident->hash()^t_ident->hash()^
          backup_time.hash();
}

bool VolumeImage::isEqual(const Object& ob)
{
// to be comparable ob must have actual class VolumeImage
    assertArgClass(ob,*VolumeImage::desc(),"isEqual");

// cast argument to class VolumeImage
    VolumeImage& v = (VolumeImage&)ob;

// compare members
    return v_ident==v.v_ident&&d_ident==v.d_ident&&
          b_ident==v.b_ident&&t_ident==v.t_ident&&
```

```
                backup_time==v.backup_time;
  }
```

12.4.4   Tape Registry database

The Tape Registry database keeps information about all the tape reels contained in the backup tape library. When a new tape reel is added to the backup tape library, a corresponding `TapeReel` record is added to the Tape Registry with the next available serial identification number. When a tape is used for a backup, the `TapeReel` records the tape as "Busy". When all the `VolumeImages` on the tape expire, the `TapeReel` records the tape reel as "not Busy" and the `TapeIdent` is put in the `tapePoolQueue` for reuse.

The Tape Registry database simply lists `TapeReel` objects in the order of their serial identification numbers. We implement this list using the NIH Library class `OrderedCltn`.

12.4.5   Implementation of the backup database

We have shown how to implement the three data relations, Backup State, Tape Catalog, and Residence Registry as instances of the class `Dictionary`. We could place these databases in the same `Dictionary` object as long as the key values for the separate `Dictionaries` do not clash. The Tape Registry database is a separate `OrderedCltn`.

As the code fragments shown for the Backup State and the Tape Catalog databases illustrate, a certain amount of noise is present in program code using NIH Class Library container classes. Such code will often introduce intermediate variables to aid readability, and will most likely have to cast pointers, returned from a container, to the actual type of the object. To avoid contaminating an application with all this noise, we can make the container a member of an envelope class which has specially designed member functions to add and extract objects. An envelope class also offers a controlled interface between an object-oriented module, in our case a database, and the application it serves. In that way, any changes to the internals of the database will have a minimal effect on the application code, thus reducing the chance for programming error. In the development of the backup system, this proved to be a valuable attribute of the object-oriented design. The database underwent several drastic changes while the interface to the application changed only slightly.

An envelope class also provides encapsulation of the operations that transfer the database between memory and disk. An important factor that led us to implement a special purpose database using the NIH Class Library was the support the library provides for object I/O. Object I/O reliably encodes the data in an NIH Library object onto an output stream in a reasonably compact format. This provides a method of storing most NIH Library objects, no matter how complex, in a disk file in such a way that the objects can later be reconstructed from the data in the file. We planned to keep the database in memory during execution of the backup program and to save it on disk at checkpoints in the program execution and before program termination. To protect the database against system failures, we also want to save database changes in a journal file and keep multiple copies of the data base on separate disks in the network. An envelope class will centralize all these operations and hide them from the application programs that use the data base.

An abbreviated declaration for the backup database envelope class is:

```
class AllImages: public Object {
    Set* objectPool;        // unique instances
    Dictionary* dataBase;   // database
public:  // only members for application interface are shown
// the one and only instance
    static AllImages::Ptr;
    AllImages();            // construct from data file
    ~AllImages();

// Backup State  database
    VolumeImage* nextVolumeImage(const GroupIdent&,
                                 const VolumeIdent&);
    void assignVolumes(const OrderedCltn&,
                       const TapeIdent&,const Time&);
    void assignVolume(VolumeImage&,const TapeIdent&,const Time&);

// Residence Registry database
    bool residence(const VolumeIdent&,String& srv,String& ptn);
    bool residenceBefore(const VolumeIdent&,const Time&,
                         String& srv,String& ptn);

// Tape Catalog and Tape Registry databases
    void installTape(int tapeid,int tapelength,long intime);
    bool recycleTape(int& tapeid, long& header_time);
    int nextTapeID();

    void reportOn(ostream&);        // formatted report
    void checkpoint();              // write to data file

    void freeTape(int tapeid);      // put tape in freeTapePool
};
```

This declaration shows only the member functions of class AllImages that are used by application programs. In fact, some 50 other member functions handle the various internal database operations, and several more overload the standard NIH Library object member's functions.

The constructor function AllImages()::AllImages() initializes the database from a data file.

```
AllImages::AllImages()
{
// the database file name is found
//   in the Locator data dictionary
    String* fname = Locator::Ptr->valueAtKey("AllImages");

// open fstream on database file
    fstream istrm(fname,ios::in);
```

```
// construct AllImages database
    if ( istrm.peek()==EOF ) {
      // first time: construct empty database
      objectPool = new Set;
      dataBase = new Dictionary;
      }
    else {
      // read existing database into temporary envelope
      OIOnihin nihinstrm(istrm);
      AllImages* temp = AllImages::readFrom(nihinstrm);
      objectPool = temp.objectPool;
      dataBase = temp.dataBase;
      delete temp;
      }

// construct Tape Registry database
    alltapes = new AllTapes();
  }
```

To make the use of the `AllImages` database in application programs as trouble free as possible, the constructor implements all the steps necessary to find the full path name of the data file, open the data file, read the data, and construct the database. When the data file is not empty, the unique `AllImages` database object is constructed by the NIH Library object I/O function `AllImages::readFrom()`.

Class `AllImages` illustrates several common object-oriented design decisions. Class `AllImages` is an envelope class for an `Dictionary`. Should we derive it from class `Dictionary` or should we declare one of its member variables as a `Dictionary`? While it is true that the `AllImages` database performs associations like a `Dictionary`, it is not a good idea to allow application programs to access the data as if it were a `Dictionary`. If, later, we were to change the design of the database, or use a different implementation of associations, the change could require extensive programming changes in any application that made calls to member functions of class `Dictionary`. A better design uses the `AllImages` envelope to completely hide the `Dictionary` from the application. The discussion in Section 9.2.2 suggests that such a decision be based on the extent to which the new class will reuse the member functions of the old class. If we do not want the user of class `AllImages` to use the `Dictionary` member functions at all, we should make the `Dictionary` a member of class `AllImages`.

Class `AllImages` also illustrates a second common object-oriented design issue. When should a member variable be a pointer and when should it be an instance of a class? According to the discussion in Section 9.2.3, criteria for making this decision include efficiency (pointers have extra allocation and deallocation costs), safety (construction and assignment of objects with pointer members must be handled properly), and flexibility (member pointers allow flexibility in polymorphism, member sharing, and lifetime of members that member instances cannot handle). None of these issues critically affect class `AllImages`. The class has only one instance in any program and its initialization is completely handled by its own constructor function. The flexibility offered by pointer members is not a consideration. Thus the choice between pointers and instances seems to be a standoff. We chose pointers for a simple cosmetic reason: the pointer arrow made the code more readable for the author than a member dot would have. This turns out to be a substantial reason when readability is important in tracking down bugs.

It is more interesting to consider the same question about the members of data objects that are stored in the `AllImages` database. Class `VolumeImage` serves as a good example. Recall that this class has four members that point to other data records involved with the `AllImages` database. Three of these members,

```
VolumeIdent*  v_ident;    //  Volume identifier
DiskIdent*    d_ident;    //  residence for this volume
TapeIdent*    t_indent;   //  tape for this backup
```

can serve as keys to the database. All of these members, including the fourth

```
BackupIdent*  b_ident;    //  identifier for this backup
```

can be shared by other `VolumeImage` objects stored in the database. Sharing member objects is a good reason to use member pointers. For example, if disk residence were to be represented by an instance variable, every `VolumeImage` for each volume on a given disk would duplicate memory allocation for the same data: file server name and disk name. Similar conclusions can be drawn about each of the other members.

The memory savings that can result from sharing of members is reason enough to do it. We can, however, also realize added efficiency in the backup application in the quantity of the output produced by the NIH Library object I/O `storeOn()` function. When writing out a container of objects with `storeOn()`, two identical objects will not necessarily be written in the same way. The `storeOn()` function knows when it stores an object accessed by a pointer, and it saves an association between that pointer and an object number. If it should encounter one of these pointers again, `storeOn()` will write the object number of the pointer instead of the full representation of the object pointed to. The number of bytes saved in the output stream can be substantial. Suppose, for example, we have an `OrderedCltn` containing `String` objects and the same `String` appears more than once in the container:

```
OrderedCltn cltn;
char* p = "a real long character array";
String* s = new String(p);
String* t = new String(p);
cltn.add(*s);  // cltn[0] == s
cltn.add(*t);  // cltn[1] == t
cltn.add(*s);  // cltn[2] == s
```

The pointers s and t both point to `String` objects with the same `String` value, p. When `storeOn()` writes the first `String` object, with address cltn[0], it will send a representation of the entire `String` object including the entire character array to the output stream. The second `String` object, with address cltn[1], will also be completely written out. The third `String` object has the same address as the first, and so `storeOn()`

will write it in abbreviated form. Considering that Strings commonly occur in programs using the NIH Class Library, and particularly in a database, the reduction of the size of the database file for Strings strongly motivated us to implement member sharing in the database.

Merely declaring a member as a pointer does not assure the memory savings offered by shared members. To share members, the application program must use the same pointer, whether VolumeIdent*, DiskIdent*, TapeIdent*, or BackupIdent*, in all VolumeImage objects that share the same data values for those entities. The programmer discipline required to guarantee this kind of uniqueness of member pointers is very difficult to achieve when working with a large software system. We need an object-oriented software mechanism to provide that discipline for us. How can we guarantee that, when referencing objects that have the same data value, we will always use the same pointer? Or, to state the problem differently, how can we guarantee that each instance of an abstract data type with particular data values is represented in the application program by a *unique* NIH Library object?

Once again we can look to the NIH Class Library for help. Class Set implements just the uniqueness guarantee we need. A Set cannot contain two NIH Library objects that are considered the same by their own isEqual() member functions. Example 7-8 shows that a Set can serve as a repository of unique objects. This is the purpose of the member variable, objectPool, declared in class AllImages. One way to guarantee uniqueness is with a member function such as:

```
Object* AllImages::UniqueCopy(const Object& ob)
{
    Object* uob = objectPool->findObjectWithKey(ob);
    if ( uob==nil )
        objectPool->add(*(uob=ob.copy()));
    return uob;
}
```

Function UniqueCopy() returns an object from the objectPool that isEqual() to the argument object. The function UniqueCopy() guarantees that whenever objects, ob1 and ob2, are matched by isEqual(), then UniqueCopy(ob1) is the same pointer as UniqueCopy(ob2). In practice, the complete solution to this uniqueness problem is a bit more complicated. If for example, the object from the object pool were to have a member pointer to another object that should be taken from the object pool, then the copy operation would not be adequate to guarantee uniqueness of the member pointer. For the backup database, this happens in the case of a VolumeIdent object which is declared as:

```
class VolumeIdent : public Object {
    String* name;
    int id;

public:
    VolumeIdent(const String& name, int id);
};
```

To guarantee uniqueness for a VolumeIdent object and its name pointer we can do something like

```
VolumeIdent vid(*UniqueCopy(String("anne")),4778564);
VolumeIdent* unique_vid = UniqueCopy(vid);
```

For an application in which the class of database objects are known ahead of time, the above method is only a minor annoyance and the database can easily handle it by implementing the uniqueness operation in a few specialized member functions. A more general solution could be achieved by developing a deep copy operation that cooperated with the unique pool of objects.

12.5 CHAPTER SUMMARY

In this chapter, we have illustrated how to use data abstraction and object-oriented programming in the practice of software development by tracing the steps from design to implementation of a real application:

- *Modeling.* Construct an informal model of a system.

- *Data Abstraction.* Describe data types of objects in the model.

- *Implement Classes.* Represent the abstract data types as C++ classes.

- *System Design.* Use classes to develop software that represents the dynamic relationships among modeled objects.

We described four categories of data types, implemented as C++ classes, from the application:

- *Passive data types* that encapsulate data items and operations on that data (e.g. database objects)

- *Data container types* that represent structures holding data objects (e.g. database and queue objects)

- *Specialized data types* that encapsulate application operations for the purpose of isolation, testing, and safety (e.g. a Selection object)

- *Active data types* that encapsulate operations involving the dynamic relationships among many other data types (e.g. lightweight processes)

Table 12.7 Class libraries in the backup application

Class Library	Size (Kbytes)	%	No. of Classes	%
Reusable	275	50	56	52
Backup database	67	13	29	27
Process control	200	37	23	21
TOTAL	542	100	108	100

Table 12.7 shows how classes in the backup application are distributed between reusable and special-purpose libraries. The special purpose classes are grouped into two types: those used with the prototype database described in Section 12.4 and those used for process control as described in Section 12.3. We have measured the size of C++ source code with all comments removed. The reusable classes make up about half of the classes in the application—including about 220 Kbytes from the NIH Class Library—and also contribute about half the source code. Among the special-purpose classes, the database classes are smaller than average, while the lightweight process classes tend to be larger than average.

13
MULTIPLE INHERITANCE

13.1 INTRODUCTION

Up to this point we have been concerned almost exclusively with single inheritance, where a derived class has only one base class. Although single inheritance is adequate for most applications, occasionally we require something more general. In this chapter, we introduce *multiple inheritance*, in which a derived class may have more than one base class, and present some examples to show how to use it. We also describe some problems that arise when using multiple inheritance, along with techniques for dealing with them. We do not present the details of how any particular C++ compiler *implements* multiple inheritance—interested readers should see [29].

The syntax for expressing multiple inheritance is simply an extension of that for single inheritance: list the names of the base classes in the class declaration. For example, if we have classes B1 and B2, and we wish to create a derived class D that has both B1 and B2 as base classes we write:

```
class D: public B1, public B2 {
    // ...
```

Class D then inherits all of the member variables and functions of both class B1 and B2, and class D is also a subtype of both classes.

13.2 MULTIPLE INHERITANCE AND MODULAR PROGRAMMING

We will start by describing how to use multiple inheritance to help practice *modular programming* techniques in C++. Modular programming is not directly related to the major themes of this book, data abstraction and object-oriented programming, but it is nonetheless a useful programming technique because it provides a way to eliminate global variable and function names. It thus reduces the chances that you will have difficulties with duplicate names when you try to use several libraries in a single program, and since it involves multiple inheritance in a very simple way, it is a good way to get our feet wet in this advanced topic.

13.2.1 What is modular programming?

Languages that support modular programming, such as Modula-2 [33] and Ada [1], support the partitioning of programs into units called *modules*. Each module comprises related constants, variables, functions (procedures), and types, which we will refer to in this discussion as a module's *components*. Each module also has two parts: a specification and an implementation. The provider of a module decides which of its components should be accessible to clients of the module and *exports* these in the module's specification. Conversely, a client may *import* for its use any or all of the components that a module exports. A module thus provides an *encapsulation* mechanism.

What then are the distinctions among modular programming, data abstraction, and object-oriented programming techniques? Modular programming, like data abstraction, supports encapsulation and the grouping of functions with the data they operate upon. However, it differs in that, from a client's point of view, modules are not data types, but must be dealt with by using language syntax that differs from that used for built-in types. There is no way to instantiate a module's data other than by instantiating its exported types, or to automatically initialize or finalize separate instances, as is possible with C++ classes. Thus, while a module provides an abstraction mechanism, the abstraction is not that of a built-in data type.

Modular programming differs from object-oriented programming in that it lacks the crucial support for inheritance and dynamic binding.

13.2.2 Practicing "modular programming" in C++

C++ cannot quite support true modular programming in the style of Modula-2 or Ada. While we can use C++ classes to encapsulate constants, variables, and functions, a C++ class cannot encapsulate a *type* as a module can. [1] We can legally place the definition of a typedef, class, or struct inside a class declaration, but the effect is the same as if we had written it outside the class, in the same scope as the class:

```
class X {
    typedef int bool;
    class Y {
        int i;
    };
};

main()
{
    bool b;      // OK
    Y y;         // OK
}
```

The function main() can use the type names bool and Y even though they are defined in the private part of class X.

Placing an enum type inside a class declaration has a mixed effect:

```
class X {
    enum color { red, green, blue };
};

main()
{
```

---

[1] Beginning with Release 2.1 of the AT & T C++ Translator, C++ *can* encapsulate types, thus eliminating most of the limitations described here.

```
color c;    // OK
c = red;    // error: red undefined
c = X::red; // error: main() cannot access X::red:
            // private member
}
```

The *name* of the enum type, `color` in this example, is not encapsulated by the class; however, the *values* of the enum type, `red`, `green`, and `blue` in this example, are encapsulated.

True modular programming languages also provide a stronger form of encapsulation, known as *opaque types*, that C++ does not support. Not only can a module encapsulate a type, but it can also export just the *name* of the type, so clients cannot even see the type definition.

Nevertheless, C++ enables us to practice a useful form of modular programming. We can use classes that have only static members as "modules". We can indicate the members we wish to "export" by making them public or protected, and other "modules" can "import" these members by specifying the "module" as one of its base classes. Multiple inheritance makes this scheme practical, for without it a class would not be able to "import" members from more than one other class.

Inheritance is not needed to import "module's" public members—any function, even a non-member function, can access these by using the "module" name with the scope resolution operator. However, you must use inheritance to "import" a "module's" protected members, and then only member and friend functions of the importing "module" and its descendents can access them.

13.2.3   Class `NIHCL` as a "module"

The NIH Class Library has a class named `NIHCL` which it uses as a "module" to encapsulate member variables and functions which would otherwise be global. This practice makes it easier to combine the NIH Class Library with other class libraries in the same program—there is less chance of duplicate global names.

```
class NIHCL {
private:            // static member variables
    static bool init;    // YES if NIHCL initialization complete
    static unsigned char char_bit_mask[sizeof(char)*8];
    static unsigned short short_bit_mask[sizeof(short)*8];
    static unsigned int int_bit_mask[sizeof(int)*8];
    static unsigned char bit_count[256];
    static unsigned char bit_reverse[256];
private:            // static member functions
    static void initTables();    // initialize tables
public:             // static member functions
    static unsigned char charBitMask(int i)
        { return char_bit_mask[i]; }
    static unsigned short shortBitMask(int i)
        { return short_bit_mask[i]; }
    static unsigned int intBitMask(int i)
        { return int_bit_mask[i]; }
```

```
      static unsigned char bitCount(unsigned i)
          { return bit_count[i]; }
      static unsigned char bitReverse(unsigned i)
          { return bit_reverse[i]; }
      static void initialize();     // library initialization
      static bool initialized()     { return init; }
      static void
          setError(int error, int sev ...); // report an error
// ...
};
```

Class `NIHCL` encapsulates an initialization flag and several private tables, and provides public member functions to access them. It also contains the `setError()` function, which NIH Library classes call to report errors. Class `Object` "imports" class `NIHCL`'s public member functions by specifying `NIHCL` as its base class:

```
class Object: public NIHCL {     // ...
```

All descendents of class `Object` can then call these "imported" functions without needing to qualify their names with the scope resolution operator. Other NIH Library classes that are not descendents of class `Object`, such as `OIOin` and `OIOout` (see Section 7.4), also "import" class `NIHCL`'s member functions.

As an example of using multiple inheritance as an "import" mechanism, suppose we wish to write a new class called `MyClass` that has member functions that must call `NIHCL::setError()`. Further, let us suppose that `MyClass` also uses another class library named `OtherLib`, and the author of `OtherLib` had the foresight to encapsulate that library's `initialize()` function along with another function, `finish()`, in a "module" named `OtherCL`, thus avoiding a potential conflicts with other functions with the same names. Here is how we could write `MyClass` and its member function `f()`:

```
#include "Object.h"
#include "OtherLib.h"

class MyClass: public NIHCL, public OtherCL {
// ...
    void f();
};

void MyClass::f()
{
// Following is ambiguous: NIHCL::initialize() or
// OtherCL::initialize()?
//   initialize();
    OtherCL::initialize();
    setError(NIHCL_ALLOCFAIL,DEFAULT);   // calls NIHCL::setError()
    finish();                            // calls OtherLib::finish()
// ...
}
```

The function f() can reference the members of either NIHCL or OtherCL without the scope resolution operator, as long as the member names by themselves are not ambiguous.

13.2.4 Private base classes

Suppose we wished to derive another class, MyDerived, from MyClass,

```
class MyDerived: public MyClass {   // ...
```

and MyDerived also needed to call NIHCL::setError(), but it has no business calling any member functions of OtherCL. As we have declared MyClass, MyDerived will inherit OtherCL's member functions. We can restrict the "import" of OtherCl's members to only MyClass and its friends by making OtherCL a *private base class* of MyClass:

```
class MyClass: public NIHCL, private OtherCL {   // ...
```

```
class MyDerived: public MyClass {
// ...
    void g();
};

void MyDerived::g()
{
    OtherCL::initialize();   // error: cannot access initialize()
    setError(NIHCL_ALLOCFAIL,DEFAULT);   // calls NIHCL::setError()
    finish();                // error: cannot access finish()
// ...
}
```

This makes the members that MyClass "imports" from OtherCL private members of MyClass, even if they are public or protected members of OtherCL.

13.3 MULTIPLE LINKED LIST EXAMPLE

Let us suppose we are writing an event-driven traffic simulation program and we are using a class Vehicle to represent the cars, trucks, motorcycles, and so on in the simulation. Suppose that we wish to maintain a LinkedList of all of the vehicles in the simulation, and we also wish to use a LinkedList to model the queue of vehicles that forms at a stop light. We will need to place a Vehicle object on two LinkedLists at the same time if it is waiting at a stop light: the LinkedList of all vehicles and the LinkedList of vehicles in the stop light queue. Although we could do this by using LinkOb objects to link the Vehicle objects indirectly as we described in Section 8.3.7, let us suppose that we wish to link Vehicle objects directly on these lists to avoid the overhead of allocating the LinkOb objects and dereferencing the pointers they contain. To do this, class Vehicle will somehow have to incorporate two instances of class Link, one to hold the link for each of the two LinkedLists.

Declaring two instances of class Link as member variables of class Vehicle

```
class Vehicle: public Object {
    Link allLink, qLink;
```

```
// ...
};
```

does not work because an object must be a descendent of class `Link` to be placed on a
`LinkedList`. Class `Link` is an abstract class, so all of its constructors are protected and
the C++ compiler will flag the declaration of `allLink` and `qLink` as an error.

Nor can we write

```
class Vehicle : public Link, public Link {
// ...
```

to inherit two copies of class `Link` because no class name may appear more than once in
the list of base classes. C++ prohibits this because we must use the name of the base class
to distinguish the names of inherited members when ambiguities arise—something we could
not do if a base class name was not unique. Instead, as Example 13-1 shows, we introduce
class `AllLink`, which is the `Link` we use for `allVehicles`, the `LinkedList` of all
vehicles, and class `QLink`, which is the `Link` we use for `stopLightQ`, the stop light
queue `LinkedList`.

Example 13-1 shows how to use multiple inheritance to create a class `Vehicle` that has
two instances of class `Link`.

```
// ex13-1.c - Class Vehicle with multiple links

#include <iostream.h>

// ...

class AllLink: public Link {
protected:
    AllLink() {};
    virtual void printOn(ostream& strm =cout) const =0;
};

class QLink: public Link {
protected:
    QLink() {};
    virtual void printOn(ostream& strm =cout) const =0;
};

class Vehicle: public AllLink, public QLink {
    static unsigned vehicleID;
    static LinkedList allVehicles;
    unsigned id;
public:
    Vehicle() {
        id = ++vehicleID;
        allVehicles.add(*(AllLink*)this);
    }
```

```
    static void printAll(ostream& strm =cout) {
        allVehicles.printOn(strm);
    }
    virtual void printOn(ostream& strm =cout) const;
};

unsigned Vehicle::vehicleID = 0;
LinkedList Vehicle::allVehicles;

void Vehicle::printOn(ostream& strm) const
{
    strm << id;
}


LinkedList stopLightQ[2];

main()
{
    stopLightQ[0].add(*(QLink*)new Vehicle);
    stopLightQ[1].add(*(QLink*)new Vehicle);
    stopLightQ[0].add(*(QLink*)new Vehicle);
    stopLightQ[1].add(*(QLink*)new Vehicle);
    cout << "allVehicles: "; Vehicle::printAll();
    cout << "stopLightQ[0]: "; stopLightQ[0].printOn();
    cout << "stopLightQ[1]: "; stopLightQ[1].printOn();
}
```

The output from Example 13-1 is:

```
allVehicles: 1 2 3 4
stopLightQ[0]: 1 3
stopLightQ[1]: 2 4
```

which shows that `allVehicles` contains a list of all vehicles (1–4), `stopLightQ[0]`
contains vehicles 1 and 3, and `stopLightQ[1]` contains vehicles 2 and 4.

13.3.1 Inheritance diagrams

Figure 13.1 shows an inheritance diagram for class `Vehicle`. While the inheritance diagram
for a group of classes related by single inheritance is a tree, when we use multiple inheritance
the inheritance diagram is a more general structure known as a *directed acyclic graph*, or
DAG. In the context of inheritance, a directed graph is a set of vertices representing classes
connected by a set of arrows representing the relationship between a base class and a derived
class. An arrow is drawn with the tail at a base class and the head at the derived class. In
a directed acyclic graph, there are no cycles; that is, for any vertex of a DAG, there is no
way to trace a path in the direction of the arrows that returns to that same vertex.

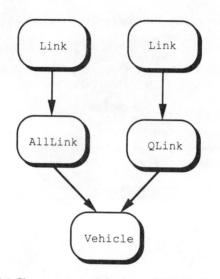

Figure 13.1 *Class* Vehicle *inheritance DAG for Example 13-1*

13.3.2   Improved vehicle linked lists

When we call LinkedList::add() to add a Vehicle object to a LinkedList, we must be careful to use the correct Link base class. We do this by casting the pointer to the Vehicle object to a pointer to either an AllLink or a QLink, depending upon the LinkedList. Thus, for allVehicles.add() we use the cast (AllLink*), and for stopLightQ[i].add() we use the cast (QLink*).

In one sense, these casts are safe because classes AllLink and Qlink are ancestors of class Vehicle; that is, class Vehicle is a subtype of classes AllLink and QLink. In fact, C++ would normally be happy to accept a Vehicle* as a Link* argument, except that in this case there is an ambiguity as to which Link to use. Thus, the only purpose of the casts is to resolve this ambiguity.

The casts to (AllLink*) and (QLink*) are still undesirable, however, because we could accidentally cast a Vehicle* to a pointer to any class descended from class Object and thereby commit an error that the C++ compiler would not detect. We can eliminate them by introducing two more classes, AllVehicles and VehicleQ, which we derive from class LinkedList, and by defining the member functions AllVehicles::addVehicle(AllLink&) and VehicleQ::addVehicle(QLink&) as shown in Example 13-2.

```
// ex13-2.c - Improved vehicle linked lists

#include <iostream.h>

// ...

class AllLink: public Link {
```

```
protected:
    AllLink() {};
    virtual void printOn(ostream& strm =cout) const =0;
};

class QLink: public Link {
protected:
    QLink() {};
    virtual void printOn(ostream& strm =cout) const =0;
};

class AllVehicles: public LinkedList {
public:
    virtual void addVehicle(AllLink&);
};

void AllVehicles::addVehicle(AllLink& l)     { add(l); }

class VehicleQ: public LinkedList {
public:
    virtual void addVehicle(QLink&);
};

void VehicleQ::addVehicle(QLink& l)          { add(l); }

class Vehicle: public AllLink, public QLink {
    static unsigned vehicleID;
    static AllVehicles allVehicles;
    unsigned id;
public:
    Vehicle() {
        id = ++vehicleID;
        allVehicles.addVehicle(*this);
    }
    static void printAll(ostream& strm =cout){
        allVehicles.printOn(strm);
    }
    virtual void printOn(ostream& strm =cout) const;
};

unsigned Vehicle::vehicleID = 0;
AllVehicles Vehicle::allVehicles;

void Vehicle::printOn(ostream& strm) const
{
    strm << id;
}
```

```
VehicleQ stopLightQ[2];

main()
{
    stopLightQ[0].addVehicle(*new Vehicle);
    stopLightQ[1].addVehicle(*new Vehicle);
    stopLightQ[0].addVehicle(*new Vehicle);
    stopLightQ[1].addVehicle(*new Vehicle);
    cout << "allVehicles: "; Vehicle::printAll();
    cout << "stopLightQ[0]: "; stopLightQ[0].printOn();
    cout << "stopLightQ[1]: "; stopLightQ[1].printOn();
}
```

Since classes `AllLink` and `QLink` are ancestors of class `Vehicle`, C++ will accept a `Vehicle` as an argument to `addVehicle()`, selecting the correct `Link` object automatically and eliminating the need for any type casts.

13.4   RESOLVING AMBIGUITIES

When two or more ancestors of a class define members with the same name, the C++ compiler must be able to determine exactly which member we mean when we use the member's name in a derived class. This is not a problem when using single inheritance—when we use the name of an inherited member in a derived class, C++ interprets it as the member of the closest ancestor class unless we explicitly state otherwise with the scope resolution operator. For example:

```
class A {
public:
    char* f();
// ...
};

class B: public A {
public:
    int f();
// ...
};

class C: public B {
// ...
};

main()
{
    C c;
    c.f();        // calls B::f()
```

```
    c.B::f();
    c.A::f();
}
```

However, this simple rule does not work when using multiple inheritance because a derived class can inherit members with the same name from two or more base classes (or their ancestors), as in the following example:

```
class A {
public:
    char* f();
// ...
};

class B {
public:
    int f();
// ...
};

class C: public A, public B {
// ...
};

main()
{
    C c;
    c.f();   // call to A::f() or B::f()?
}
```

The problem is that the derived class C inherits two member functions named f(), one from the base class A and one from the base class B. When we try to apply f() to an instance of class C, the C++ compiler cannot determine which f() we intend, so it issues an error diagnostic.

One way to resolve an ambiguity like this is to use the name of the base class with the scope resolution operator to specify the member name:

```
main()
{
    C c;
    c.A::f();    // calls A::f()
    c.B::f();    // calls B::f()
}
```

Another way uses the member function C::f() to call either A::f() or B::f() or both, as desired:

```
class C: public A, public B {
public:
    int f() {
        // specific code for class C
        A::f();
        return B::f();
    }
// ...
};


main()
{
    C c;
    c.f();   // calls C::f()
}
```

This technique resolves the ambiguity without requiring client programs to use the scope resolution operator.

13.5   VIRTUAL FUNCTIONS AND MULTIPLE INHERITANCE

Virtual functions work with multiple inheritance in a way similar to the way they work with single inheritance. That is, a call to a virtual function invokes the implementation provided by the whatever class is closest to the bottom of the object's inheritance DAG. For example:

```
// ex13-3.c - Virtual functions and multiple inheritance

#include <iostream.h>

class A {
public:
    virtual void f()    { cout << "A::f()" << endl; }
};

class B {
public:
    virtual void f()    { cout << "B::f()" << endl; }
};

class C: public A, public B {
public:
    virtual void f()    { cout << "C::f()" << endl; }
};


main()
```

```
{
    A* pa = new C;
    B* pb = new C;
    C* pc = new C;
    pa->f();        // calls C::f()
    pb->f();        // calls C::f()
    pc->f();        // calls C::f()
}
```

Applying the virtual function f() to a C object through any type of pointer always results in calling C::f() because the virtual function call dynamically binds to the implementation provided by the class closest to the bottom of the object's inheritance DAG, which in this case is class C.

13.6 VIRTUAL BASE CLASSES

Now let us expand the traffic simulation program of Example 13-2. Suppose that we wish to simulate the traffic in a city that has a boat harbor, a river, and a drawbridge, and so we wish to include the river traffic in our simulation to see how it interacts with the street traffic at the drawbridge. The following is an outline of the changes we need to make to Example 13-2.

13.6.1 Changes to class Vehicle

We make class Vehicle an abstract class, and add the member variables that we need to describe all kinds of vehicles, such as the height (tall vehicles cannot travel under the low bridges over some streets) and length (we want to calculate the length of queues) of the vehicle. The constructor for class Vehicle initializes these member variables from its arguments.

13.6.2 Classes LandVhcl and WaterVhcl

We create two new derived classes of the base class Vehicle named LandVhcl and WaterVhcl to represent vehicles that travel on the street and on the water, respectively. A LandVhcl is like a Vehicle, except that it has an additional member variable axles so we can calculate the toll the vehicle will pay at a tollbooth. A WaterVhcl is also like a Vehicle, except that it has an additional member variable draft—a deep-draft WaterVhcl won't be able float on our city's river at low tide. The constructors for these new classes use class Vehicle's constructor to initialize the vehicle's height and length, then initialize their own member variables.

13.6.3 Classes StopLightQ and DrawBridgeQ

Since we now have two kinds of vehicles, it is a good idea to create two new specialized kinds of VehicleQ, which we call StopLightQ and DrawBridgeQ. A StopLightQ is like a VehicleQ, except that it will add only a LandVhcl to the queue (a VehicleQ will add any kind of Vehicle to its queue). A DrawBridgeQ is also like a VehicleQ, except that it will add only a `WaterVhcl` to the queue. Using these classes prevents us from accidentally placing a `WaterVhcl` on a `StopLightQ` or a `LandVhcl` on a `DrawBridgeQ`. Figure 13.2 shows the inheritance DAGs for these classes.

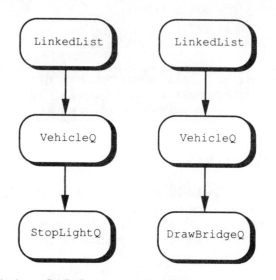

Figure 13.2 Inheritance DAGs for `StopLightQ` *and* `DrawBridgeQ` *in Example 13-4*

13.6.4 Class `AmphibVhcl`

Thus far, the changes we have described to Example 13-2 have involved simple extensions by means of single inheritance. To make the example interesting, let us imagine that we wish to include *amphibious* vehicles—vehicles that can travel on either land or water—in our simulation. Clearly, an amphibious vehicle has the properties of both a `LandVhcl` and a `WaterVhcl`, so we might try to create a class `AmphibVhcl` using multiple inheritance from the base classes `LandVhcl` and `WaterVhcl`:

```
class AmphibVhcl: public LandVhcl, public WaterVhcl { // ...
```

This may seem reasonable at first glance, but we have the following problem: both class `LandVhcl` and `WaterVhcl` inherit a copy of class `Vehicle`'s member variables, and since class `AmphibVhcl` would inherit all of the member variables of both `LandVhcl` and `WaterVhcl`, it would have *two* copies of `Vehicle::id`, `Vehicle::height`, and `Vehicle::length`, and *four* copies of class `Link`'s member variable.

C++ provides us with *virtual base classes* to deal with this problem. A derived class can specify that a base class is virtual. When two or more classes that have specified the same virtual base class are themselves used as base classes by a derived class, the member variables of the virtual base classes are merged into a single copy, and are therefore shared. In our example, we make class `Vehicle` a virtual base class of classes `LandVhcl` and `WaterVhcl` as follows:

```
class LandVhcl: public virtual Vehicle {     // ...
class WaterVhcl: public virtual Vehicle {    // ...
```

We can then declare class AmphibVhcl just as we did before, and it will inherit a single copy of the virtual base class Vehicle's member variables that is shared by classes LandVhcl and WaterVhcl. Figure 13.3 shows the resulting inheritance DAG.

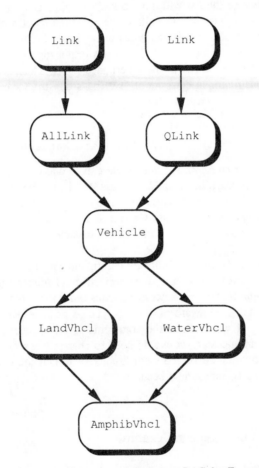

Figure 13.3 *Class* AmphibVhcl *Inheritance DAG for Example 13-4*

The two arrows emerging from the vertex representing class Vehicle indicate that classes LandVhcl and WaterVhcl share a single instance of Vehicle.

13.6.5   Virtual base class constructors

Initializing a shared instance of a virtual base class requires special consideration. The constructors of class LandVhcl and class WaterVhcl both call the constructor of their virtual base class Vehicle—that is how class Vehicle's member variables get initialized when we construct a `LandVhcl` or a `WaterVhcl`. Consider what happens when we construct an `AmphibVhcl`. Since an `AmphibVhcl` includes an instance of both a `LandVhcl` and a `WaterVhcl`, it calls the constructors of both of these base classes to initialize them. However, if the `LandVhcl` and `WaterVhcl` constructors both call class `Vehicle`'s constructor, the member variables in the instance of `Vehicle` they share will be initialized *twice*. This would be disastrous in this example—class `Vehicle`'s constructor calls `addVehicle()` to add the vehicle to the `addVehicles` list, and adding the same vehicle more than once to the list will not work.

To prevent this, C++ *suppresses* the calls to the constructors of virtual base classes made from the constructors of derived classes when those derived classes are also base classes, and makes the constructor of the most-derived class responsible for calling the constructors of *all* ancestor virtual base classes in the inheritance DAG. Thus, we must place a call to class `Vehicle`'s constructor in class `AmphibVhcl`'s constructor even though `Vehicle` is not a direct base class of `AmphibVhcl`:

```
AmphibVhcl(float h, float l, float d, unsigned a=2)
    : Vehicle(h,l), LandVhcl(h,l,a), WaterVhcl(h,l,d) {}
```

When we create an `AmphibVhcl`, this single call to class `Vehicle`'s constructor initializes the shared instance of the virtual base class `Vehicle`, because C++ has suppressed the calls to class `Vehicle` constructors in `LandVhcl` and `WaterVhcl`. If we do not explicitly specify a constructor for class `Vehicle` in `AmphibVhcl`'s constructor initialization list, C++ uses class `Vehicle`'s default constructor to initialize the shared instance of the virtual base class `Vehicle`.

Unfortunately, placing the responsibility for calling the constructors of all ancestor virtual base classes on the constructor of the most-derived class makes this class depend upon knowledge of its *distant ancestors*—ancestor classes other than its immediate base classes. Class `AmphibVhcl` must be aware of class `Vehicle` and the parameters its constructor requires, for example. If we changed the arguments to this constructor, or added another virtual base class as an ancestor, we would need to change class `AmphibVhcl` to supply the new arguments to class `Vehicle`'s constructor or to call the constructors of the new virtual base class. This is undesirable because we prefer such changes to be localized to a single class.

13.6.6   Virtual base class example

Example 13-4 modifies Example 13-2 to incorporate the expanded traffic simulation we have just described.

```
// ex13-4 - Class AmphibVhcl with virtual base class

#include <iostream.h>

// ...

class AllLink: public Link {
protected:
```

```
    AllLink() {};
    virtual void printOn(ostream& strm =cout) const =0;
};

class QLink: public Link {
protected:
    QLink() {};
    virtual void printOn(ostream& strm =cout) const =0;
};

class AllVehicles: public LinkedList {
public:
    virtual void addVehicle(AllLink&);
};

void AllVehicles::addVehicle(AllLink& l)     { add(l); }

class VehicleQ: public LinkedList {
public:
    virtual void addVehicle(QLink&);
};

void VehicleQ::addVehicle(QLink& l)     { add(l); }

class Vehicle: public AllLink, public QLink {
    static unsigned vehicleID;
    static AllVehicles allVehicles;
    unsigned id;
    float height;
    float length;
protected:
    Vehicle(float h = 0.0, float l = 0.0) {
        id = ++vehicleID;
        height = h; length = l;
        allVehicles.addVehicle(*this);
    }
public:
    static void printAll(ostream& strm =cout) {
        allVehicles.printOn(strm);
    }
    virtual void printOn(ostream& strm =cout) const;
// ...
};

unsigned Vehicle::vehicleID = 0;
AllVehicles Vehicle::allVehicles;
void Vehicle::printOn(ostream& strm) const
```

```
{
    strm << '#' << id << " height " << height << "  length "
        << length;
}

class LandVhcl: public virtual Vehicle {
    unsigned axles;
public:
    LandVhcl(float h, float l, unsigned a =2) : Vehicle(h,l)
        { axles = a; }
    virtual void printOn(ostream& strm =cout) const;
// ...
};

void LandVhcl::printOn(ostream& strm) const
{
    Vehicle::printOn(strm);
    strm << "  axles " << axles;
}

class WaterVhcl: public virtual Vehicle {
    float draft;
public:
    WaterVhcl(float h, float l, float d) : Vehicle(h,l)
        { draft = d; }
    virtual void printOn(ostream& strm =cout) const;
// ...
};

void WaterVhcl::printOn(ostream& strm) const
{
    Vehicle::printOn(strm);
    strm << "  draft " << draft;
}

class AmphibVhcl: public LandVhcl, public WaterVhcl {
public:
    AmphibVhcl(float h, float l, float d, unsigned a=2)
        : Vehicle(h,l), LandVhcl(h,l,a), WaterVhcl(h,l,d) {}
    virtual void printOn(ostream& strm =cout) const;
// ...
};

void AmphibVhcl::printOn(ostream& strm) const
{
    LandVhcl::printOn(strm);
    WaterVhcl::printOn(strm);
}
```

```
class StopLightQ: public VehicleQ {
public:
    virtual void addVehicle(LandVhcl&);
};

void StopLightQ::addVehicle(LandVhcl& v)
{
    VehicleQ::addVehicle(v);
}

class DrawBridgeQ: public VehicleQ {
public:
    virtual void addVehicle(WaterVhcl&);
};

void DrawBridgeQ::addVehicle(WaterVhcl& v)
{
    VehicleQ::addVehicle(v);
}

StopLightQ stopLightQ[2];
DrawBridgeQ drawBridgeQ;

main()
{
    stopLightQ[0].addVehicle(*new LandVhcl(4.1, 12.0));
    stopLightQ[1].addVehicle(*new LandVhcl(4.2, 12.0));
    stopLightQ[0].addVehicle(*new LandVhcl(4.3, 12.0));
    stopLightQ[1].addVehicle(*new LandVhcl(4.4, 12.0));
    drawBridgeQ.addVehicle(*new WaterVhcl(21.0, 19.0, 3.5));
    drawBridgeQ.addVehicle(*new WaterVhcl(10.0, 30.0, 2.0));
    stopLightQ[0].addVehicle(*new AmphibVhcl(5.0, 15.0, 3.0));
    drawBridgeQ.addVehicle(*new AmphibVhcl(5.1, 15.0, 3.0));
    cout << "allVehicles:\n"; Vehicle::printAll();
    cout << endl;
    cout << "stopLightQ[0]:\n"; stopLightQ[0].printOn();
    cout << endl;
    cout << "stopLightQ[1]:\n"; stopLightQ[1].printOn();
    cout << endl;
    cout << "drawBridgeQ:\n"; drawBridgeQ.printOn();
    cout << endl;
}
```

When run, Example 13-4 prints:

```
allVehicles:
#1 height 4.1   length 12   axles 2
#2 height 4.2   length 12   axles 2
#3 height 4.3   length 12   axles 2
#4 height 4.4   length 12   axles 2
```

```
#5 height 21   length 19   draft 3.5
#6 height 10   length 30   draft 2
#7 height 5   length 15   axles 2#7 height 5   length 15   draft 3
#8 height 5.1   length 15   axles 2#8 height 5.1   length 15   draft 3
stopLightQ[0]:
#1 height 4.1   length 12   axles 2
#3 height 4.3   length 12   axles 2
#7 height 5   length 15   axles 2#7 height 5   length 15   draft 3
stopLightQ[1]:
#2 height 4.2   length 12   axles 2
#4 height 4.4   length 12   axles 2
drawBridgeQ:
#5 height 21   length 19   draft 3.5
#6 height 10   length 30   draft 2
#8 height 5.1   length 15   axles 2#8 height 5.1   length 15   draft 3
```

The output illustrates one of the pitfalls in programming with virtual base classes: the ID number, height, and length of amphibious vehicles are printed twice because both LandVhcl::printOn() and WaterVhcl::printOn() call Vehicle::printOn(). We will present two techniques for eliminating extraneous calls of member functions of virtual base classes in Section 13.9.

13.7   VIRTUAL BASE CLASSES AND VIRTUAL FUNCTIONS

As we noted in Section 13.5, when you apply a virtual function to an object such that dynamic binding occurs, the application invokes the implementation provided by whatever class is closest to the bottom of the object's inheritance DAG. Although the same is true when an inheritance DAG contains virtual base classes, you may not expect the consequences. It is possible that calling an inherited virtual function will invoke an implementation defined in a class that is in a different path of the inheritance DAG. Figure 13.4 illustrates an inheritance DAG where this occurs, and Example 13-5 demonstrates this behavior.

```
// ex13-5.c - Virtual base classes and virtual functions

#include <iostream.h>

class V {
public:
    virtual void vf();
};

void V::vf()     { cout << "V::vf()" << endl; }

class A: public virtual V {
public:
    virtual void vf();
};
```

```
void A::vf()      { cout << "A::vf()" << endl; }

class B: public virtual V {
public:
    void fb()     { vf(); }
};

class C: public A, public B {
};

class D: public A, public B {
public:
    virtual void vf();
};

void D::vf()      { cout << "D::vf()" << endl; }

main()
{
    B b;
    b.fb();  // B::fb() calls V::vf()
    C c;
    c.fb(); // B::fb() calls A::vf() -- on another path of the DAG
    D d;
    d.fb();  // B::fb() calls D::vf()
}
```

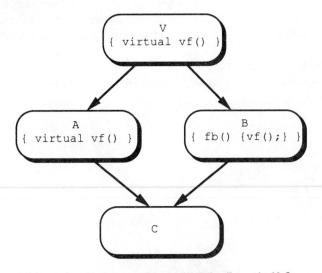

Figure 13.4 Class C *inheritance DAG for Example 13-5*

Applying `fb()` to an instance of class C calls `B::fb()`, which class C inherits from its base class B. `B::fb()` calls `vf()`, which class B inherits from its virtual base class V. Since `vf()` is a virtual function, this call invokes the implementation of `vf()` that the class closest to the bottom of class C's inheritance DAG provides. If you examine Fig. 13.4, you will see that this is `A::vf()`.

13.8   OBJECT INITIALIZATION AND MULTIPLE INHERITANCE

In Section 6.3.1, we gave two rules for determining the order in which C++ initializes the base and member variables in an object in the case of single inheritance. For multiple inheritance we must expand these rules to accommodate multiple base classes and virtual base classes. The order of initialization is:

1. virtual base classes, in the order they are encountered on a depth-first, left-to-right traversal of the inheritance DAG, starting at the bottommost class and proceeding in the direction opposite to the arrows (see [9]);

2. non-virtual base classes, in the order specified in the class declaration, *not* in the order they appear in the constructor's initializer list;

3. member variables, in the order in which they are declared in the class declaration, *not* in the order they appear in the constructor's initializer list.

C++ uses the constructor with no arguments (the default constructor) to initialize base classes and member class instances not explicitly mentioned in the constructor's initializer list.

C++ applies these rules recursively: if the base class has a base class, C++ will initialize it by applying these same rules before initializing the base class. Example 13-6 shows the order in which constructors are called during the initialization of a complex object.

```
// ex13-6.c - Order of construction of multiple base,
//            virtual base, and member classes

#include <iostream.h>

class X {
public:
    X(const char* s)     { cout << s << ' '; }
    X()                  { cout << "X::X() "; }
};

class V: public X {
public:
    V(const char* s = "default"):
        X("V::X")        { cout << s << ' '; }
};
```

```
class A {
    X a1;
    X a2;
public:
    A(const char* s): a2("A::a2") { cout << s << ' '; }
};

class B1: public A, public virtual V {
    X b1;
    X b2;
public:
    B1(const char* s):
        b2("B1::b2"),
        b1("B1::b1"),
        V("B1::V"),
        A("B1::A")        { cout << s << ' '; }
};

class B2: public virtual V, public A {
    X b1;
    X b2;
public:
    B2(const char* s):
        b1("B2::b1"),
        b2("B2::b2"),
        A("B2::A"),
        V("B2::V")        .{ cout << s << ' '; }
};

class C: public B1, public B2 {
    int i;
    X c1;
    X c2;
public:
    C(const char* s):
        B2("C::B2"),
        c1("C::c1"),
        i((cout << "C::i ",0)),
        B1("C::B1"),
        V("C::V"),
        c2("C::c2")       { cout << s << endl; }
};

main()
{
    C c("c");
}
```

The output of Example 13-6 is:

```
V::X C::V X::X() A::a2 B1::A B1::b1 B1::b2 C::B1 X::X() A::a2 B2::A
    B2::b1 B2::b2 C::B2 C::i C::c1 C::c2 c
```

Figure 13.5 shows the inheritance DAG for Example 13-6. We suggest that you take a few moments to study this example and demonstrate for yourself how the rules we have just given produce these results.

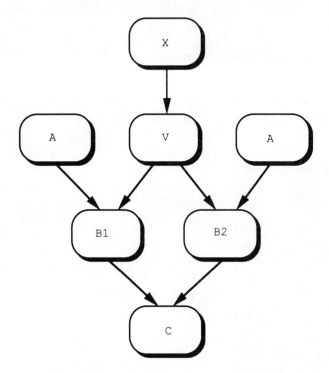

Figure 13.5 Inheritance DAG for Example 13-6

13.8.1   Object finalization

The rule C++ uses to determine the order in which it calls destructors in the case of multiple inheritance is the same as we described in Section 6.3.2: destructors are called in the reverse order of the constructors.

13.8.2   Calling virtual functions from a base class constructor

As we saw in Example 6-4 (Section 6.3.3), calling a virtual function from a constructor of a base class may not work as you expect because the object under construction is incomplete. With multiple inheritance, you may find the results particularly surprising because a derived class that is neither an ancestor nor descendent of the class you are constructing can redefine a virtual function. Consider the program in Example 13-7.

```
// ex13-7.c - Calling a virtual function from a
//              base class constructor

#include <iostream.h>

class V {
public:
    virtual void vf();
};


void V::vf()     { cout << "V::vf()" << endl; }

class A: public virtual V {
public:
    A()              { /* ... */ }
    virtual void vf();
};


void A::vf()     { cout << "A::vf()" << endl; }

class B: public virtual V {
public:
    B()              { vf(); }    // Calls A::vf(), not
                                  // V::vf() or C::vf()
};


class C: public A, public B {
public:
    C()              { vf(); }    // Calls C::vf()
    virtual void vf();
};


void C::vf()     { cout << "C::vf()" << endl; }

main()
{
    C c;
}
```

Figure 13.6 shows the inheritance DAG for Example 13-7, and the output of this example is:

```
A::vf()
C::vf()
```

The call to vf() in B::B() is dynamically bound to A::vf()—the implementation of vf() provided by class B's *sibling*. Classes A and B share a common parent, V, and A redefines the virtual function vf() that V declares. During the construction of a C object,

A::A() is executed before B::B() because A precedes B in C's base class list; thus A::A() activates the implementation of A::vf(), then B::B() calls vf(). After both A::A() and B::B() have executed, C::C() activates C::vf() as the implementation of vf(), and that is the effective implementation of vf() if you apply vf() to a C object.

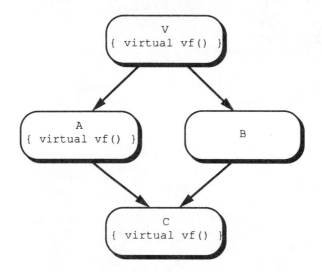

Figure 13.6 Inheritance DAG for Example 13-7

13.9   PROGRAMMING WITH VIRTUAL BASE CLASSES

As we saw in Section 13.6.6, one of the pitfalls of using virtual base classes is that unless we are careful, member functions of derived classes call member functions of the virtual base class more times than intended. This is the reason that printing an instance of an AmphibVhcl in Example 13-4 causes the ID number, height, and length to be printed twice. In the next section, we will show you a technique, first described by Stroustrup [28], for avoiding unwanted multiple calls to member functions of virtual base classes. We will call this the *static* method, since it relies simply on splitting each member function into two, and incurs no run-time overhead. In Section 13.9.2, we will present a *dynamic* method, which at run-time uses an IdentSet to keep track of which member functions have already been called as an operation on a complex object with virtual base classes progresses.

13.9.1   Static method for eliminating multiple function calls

As we said earlier, the problem with the AmphibVhcl::printOn() function in Example 13-4 is that it calls LandVhcl::printOn() and WaterVhcl::printOn() to print out the member variables of its base classes. These functions in turn both call

`Vehicle::printOn()` to do the same, causing class `Vehicle`'s member variables to get printed twice. We cannot simply eliminate the call to `Vehicle::printOn()` from either `LandVhcl` or `WaterVhcl`, because if we then applied `printOn()` to an instance of the class we removed it from, class `Vehicle`'s member variables would not be printed at all.

To employ the static method for eliminating the undesired member function calls, we implement a pair of member functions to perform the desired operation for each class comprising the complex object:

- a protected member function that deals only with performing the part of the operation for its own class; and,

- a public member function that performs the operation for the entire object, utilizing the protected member function to perform the operation once on each of its ancestor classes.

Applying this method to Example 13-4, we implement a protected member function `_printOn()` for each of the classes `Vehicle`, `LandVhcl`, `WaterVhcl`, and `AmphibVhcl` that prints only the member variables of its own class. We then implement a public member function `printOn()` for the same classes that prints out its own member variables and those of its ancestor classes by calling the `_printOn()` functions. Example 13-8 shows the result of this modification:

```
// ex13-8.c - Static method for avoiding undesired multiple calls
//            to member functions of virtual base classes

#include <stdio.h>
#include <iostream.h>

// ...

class Vehicle: public AllLink, public QLink {
    static unsigned vehicleID;
    static AllVehicles allVehicles;
    unsigned id;
    float height;
    float length;
protected:
    Vehicle(float h = 0.0, float l = 0.0) {
        id = ++vehicleID;
        height = h; length = l;
        allVehicles.addVehicle(*this);
    }
    virtual void _printOn(ostream& strm =cout) const;
public:
    static void printAll(ostream& strm =cout) {
        allVehicles.printOn(strm);
    }
```

```
        virtual void printOn(ostream& strm =cout) const;
// ...
};

void Vehicle::_printOn(ostream& strm) const
{
    strm << '#' << id << " height " << height << "  length "
        << length;
}

void Vehicle::printOn(ostream& strm) const
{
    _printOn(strm);
}

class LandVhcl: public virtual Vehicle {
    unsigned axles;
protected:
    virtual void _printOn(ostream& strm =cout) const;
public:
    LandVhcl(float h, float l, unsigned a =2) : Vehicle(h,l)
        { axles = a; }
    virtual void printOn(ostream& strm =cout) const;
// ...
};

void LandVhcl::_printOn(ostream& strm) const
{
    strm << "  axles " << axles;
}

void LandVhcl::printOn(ostream& strm) const
{
    Vehicle::_printOn(strm);
    _printOn(strm);
}

class WaterVhcl: public virtual Vehicle {
    float draft;
protected:
    virtual void _printOn(ostream& strm =cout) const;
public:
    WaterVhcl(float h, float l, float d) : Vehicle(h,l)
        { draft = d; }
    virtual void printOn(ostream& strm =cout) const;
// ...
};

void WaterVhcl::_printOn(ostream& strm) const
```

```
{
    strm << "  draft " << draft;
}


void WaterVhcl::printOn(ostream& strm) const
{
    Vehicle::_printOn(strm);
    _printOn(strm);
}


class AmphibVhcl: public LandVhcl, public WaterVhcl {
protected:
    virtual void _printOn(ostream& strm =cout) const;
public:
    AmphibVhcl(float h, float l, float d, unsigned a=2)
        : Vehicle(h,l), LandVhcl(h,l,a), WaterVhcl(h,l,d) {}
    virtual void printOn(ostream& strm =cout) const;
// ...
};


void AmphibVhcl::_printOn(ostream& strm) const {}


void AmphibVhcl::printOn(ostream& strm) const
{
    Vehicle::_printOn(strm);
    LandVhcl::_printOn(strm);
    WaterVhcl::_printOn(strm);
    _printOn(strm);
}


// ...


main()
{
    stopLightQ[0].addVehicle(*new LandVhcl(4.1, 12.0));
    stopLightQ[1].addVehicle(*new LandVhcl(4.2, 12.0));
    stopLightQ[0].addVehicle(*new LandVhcl(4.3, 12.0));
    stopLightQ[1].addVehicle(*new LandVhcl(4.4, 12.0));
    drawBridgeQ.addVehicle(*new WaterVhcl(21.0, 19.0, 3.5));
    drawBridgeQ.addVehicle(*new WaterVhcl(10.0, 30.0, 2.0));
    stopLightQ[0].addVehicle(*new AmphibVhcl(5.0, 15.0, 3.0));
    drawBridgeQ.addVehicle(*new AmphibVhcl(5.1, 15.0, 3.0));
    cout << "allVehicles:\n"; Vehicle::printAll();
    cout << endl;
    cout << "stopLightQ[0]:\n"; stopLightQ[0].printOn();
    cout << endl;
```

```
      cout << "stopLightQ[1]:\n"; stopLightQ[1].printOn();
      cout << endl;
      cout << "drawBridgeQ:\n"; drawBridgeQ.printOn();
      cout << endl;
}
```

Running Example 13-8 produces the output desired:

```
allVehicles:
#1 height 4.1   length 12   axles 2
#2 height 4.2   length 12   axles 2
#3 height 4.3   length 12   axles 2
#4 height 4.4   length 12   axles 2
#5 height 21   length 19   draft 3.5
#6 height 10   length 30   draft 2
#7 height 5   length 15   axles 2   draft 3
#8 height 5.1   length 15   axles 2   draft 3
stopLightQ[0]:
#1 height 4.1   length 12   axles 2
#3 height 4.3   length 12   axles 2
#7 height 5   length 15   axles 2   draft 3
stopLightQ[1]:
#2 height 4.2   length 12   axles 2
#4 height 4.4   length 12   axles 2
drawBridgeQ:
#5 height 21   length 19   draft 3.5
#6 height 10   length 30   draft 2
#8 height 5.1   length 15   axles 2   draft 3
```

While this approach is efficient, it has the following disadvantages:

- We had to double the number of class-specific member functions involved in the printing operation.

- The implementation of a member function for a particular class depends upon knowledge of its distant ancestors. In this example, the implementation of `AmphibVhcl::printOn()` calls `Vehicle::_printOn()`, a member function of a distant ancestor. If we rearranged the inheritance DAG anywhere above class `AmphibVhcl`, for example by adding another base to to class `Vehicle`, we would need to reflect this change in `AmphibVhcl::printOn()`.

The second disadvantage is mitigated somewhat because `AmphibVhcl`'s constructor must already be aware of all distant ancestors that are virtual base classes in order to call their constructors.

13.9.2 Dynamic method for eliminating multiple function calls

Example 13-9, a variation of the traffic simulation example, which we describe in greater detail in Section 13.10, illustrates an alternative approach that preserves localization, but at a cost of some run-time overhead. The idea here is to define for each class a single protected virtual function that performs the operation we wish to implement ("printOn" in this example) on its own class, and also on each of its ancestor classes by calling their implementations of the same function. However, any class designed to serve as a virtual base class implements this function in a special way. Before performing the operation, it checks to see if an `IdentSet` (see Section 8.3.9) includes the instance of the virtual base class that its `this` pointer references. If so, it returns without performing the operation; otherwise, it adds the `this` pointer to the `IdentSet` before performing the operation. Thus, the `IdentSet` keeps track of which virtual base class instances within a complex object have been operated on so that attempts to operate on the same virtual base class instance more than once can be ignored.

In Example 13-9, we call the protected virtual function `_printOn()` and we make the `IdentSet` a static member of class `Vehicle`:

```
class Vehicle: public AllLink, public QLink {
    static IdentSet v;                      // used by printOn()
// ...
protected:
    virtual void _printOn(ostream& strm =cout) const;
// ...
public:
    virtual void printOn(ostream& strm =cout) const;
// ...
};
```

Clients call the public member function `Vehicle::printOn()` to print instances of class `Vehicle`'s descendents. `Vehicle::printOn()` empties the `IdentSet` v, then calls `_printOn()` to actually do the printing:

```
void Vehicle::printOn(ostream& strm) const
{
    v.removeAll();
    _printOn(strm);
}
```

Here are the implementations of `_printOn()` for all relevant classes:

```
void Vehicle::_printOn(ostream& strm) const
{
    if (v.includes(*(Object*)(void*)this))
        return;         // members already printed
    v.add(*(Object*)(void*)this);
    strm << '#' << id << " height " << height << "  length "
        << length;
}


void LandVhcl::_printOn(ostream& strm) const
{
    Vehicle::_printOn(strm);
    strm << "  axles " << axles;
}
```

```
void WaterVhcl::_printOn(ostream& strm) const
{
    Vehicle::_printOn(strm);
    strm << "  draft " << draft;
}

void AmphibVhcl::_printOn(ostream& strm) const
{
    LandVhcl::_printOn(strm);
    WaterVhcl::_printOn(strm);
}
```

Notice how `Vehicle::_printOn()` first casts `this` to a `void*`, then to an `Object*` when using `this` as an argument to `IdentSet::includes()` or `IdentSet::add()`. It does so to make sure that the value is distinct for each class in an object's inheritance DAG. If instead we wrote

```
if (v.includes(*this)) return;   // members already printed
v.add(*this);
```

C++ would automatically convert `*this` to refer to the entire object as an `Object&`, the argument type that `includes()` and `add()` require. This conversion must be unique—if it were not, C++ would indicate it as an error. Thus, the conversion of `*this` to an `Object&` produces the *same* value for all the classes in an object's inheritance DAG, and is therefore not useful for distinguishing which classes have been printed. By casting `this` to `void*`, we are forcing a pointer to something that really is not an `Object` into the `IdentSet`, and we can expect trouble should the `IdentSet` ever actually try to apply a member function through one of these non-`Object` pointers. This technique works in this case because we know that the functions `IdentSet::includes()`, `IdentSet::add()`, and `IdentSet::removeAll()` do not try to use the pointers.[2]

The dynamic method for eliminating multiple function calls requires only one additional class-specific member function, and each class requires knowledge of only its immediate ancestors. The disadvantage is the run-time overhead that results from emptying, searching, and adding pointers to an `IdentSet`. When the operation involved is already time-consuming, such as the `printOn()` operation we discussed in this section, or the NIH Class Library's `storeOn()` operation which we will discuss in Section 13.10.4, the extra overhead of the dynamic method is not significant. Thus, the convenience and ease of maintenance of the dynamic method makes it the technique of choice in these situations.

13.9.3   Summary of programming with virtual base classes

We discussed a common problem that arises when using virtual base classes: the member functions of derived classes may call the member functions of virtual base classes too many times. We described two approaches to dealing with this problem in a general and extensible way: a static method and a dynamic method. The static method implements two versions

---

[2] A safer method is to derive a class from `IdentSet` that disables all the dangerous member functions (see Section 9.2.6).

of the member function for each class. One version is a protected member function that operates only on the member variables of its own class, and the other is a public member function that calls the protected functions to perform the desired operation on its ancestor class instances and on its own member variables. This approach is efficient, but doubles the number of class-specific member functions involved and makes the implementations of the public functions dependent upon the organization of distant ancestor classes.

The dynamic method uses a table (an `IdentSet`) to keep track of which virtual base class instances have been operated on so that multiple calls can be avoided by checking the table. The disadvantage of this approach is the run-time overhead it involves.

13.10 MULTIPLE INHERITANCE AND THE NIH CLASS LIBRARY

The classes in the various traffic simulation examples we have presented thus far in this chapter (Examples 13-1, 13-2, 13-4, and 13-8) are not compatible with the NIH Class Library, and the `LinkedList` and `Link` classes these examples use are not the NIH Library classes we described in Section 8.3.7. None of the NIH Library classes currently use multiple inheritance, but the library does optionally support multiple inheritance—you can write classes that inherit from a mixture of NIH Library classes and your own NIH Library compatible base classes. For example, you might wish to create a new class `AssocDate` to implement associations between `Object` keys and `Date` values for use with a `Dictionary` or `KeySortCltn`. You would derive class `AssocDate` from the NIH Library classes `LookupKey` and `Date`:

```
class AssocDate: public LookupKey, public Date {
// ...
```

As another example, you might need a directly-linked `LinkedList` of `Strings`, so you could write a new class `LinkString`:

```
class LinkString: public Link, public String {
// ...
```

However, when you use multiple inheritance with the NIH Class Library, you must use the special techniques that we describe in this section. We will present yet another version of the traffic simulation classes that are compatible with the NIH Class Library and support object I/O. Figure 13.7 illustrates the inheritance DAG for these classes.

Example 13-9 demonstrates these traffic simulation classes:

```
// ex13-9.c - MI with the NIH Class Library

#include "LandVhcl.h"
#include "WaterVhcl.h"
#include "AmphibVhcl.h"
#include "StopLightQ.h"
#include "DrawBridgeQ.h"

StopLightQ stopLightQ[2];
DrawBridgeQ drawBridgeQ;
```

```
main()
{
    stopLightQ[0].addVehicle(*new LandVhcl(4.1, 12.0));
    stopLightQ[1].addVehicle(*new LandVhcl(4.2, 12.0));
    stopLightQ[0].addVehicle(*new LandVhcl(4.3, 12.0));
    stopLightQ[1].addVehicle(*new LandVhcl(4.4, 12.0));
    drawBridgeQ.addVehicle(*new WaterVhcl(21.0, 19.0, 3.5));
    drawBridgeQ.addVehicle(*new WaterVhcl(10.0, 30.0, 2.0));
    stopLightQ[0].addVehicle(*new AmphibVhcl(5.0, 15.0, 3.0));
    drawBridgeQ.addVehicle(*new AmphibVhcl(5.1, 15.0, 3.0));

    cout << "allVehicles:\n"; Vehicle::printAll();
    cout << endl;
    cout << "stopLightQ[0]:\n"; stopLightQ[0].printOn();
    cout << endl;
    cout << "stopLightQ[1]:\n"; stopLightQ[1].printOn();
    cout << endl;
    cout << "drawBridgeQ:\n"; drawBridgeQ.printOn();
    cout << endl;
// ...
}
```

For this example, we have placed the specifications and implementations of classes Vehicle, LandVhcl, WaterVhcl, AmphibVhcl, AllVehicles, VehicleQ, StopLightQ, and DrawBridgeQ in their own individual .h and .c files. We will show excerpts from these files later in this section.

Supporting multiple inheritance introduces a significant amount of overhead, so we have made it an option that you enable by compiling the NIH Class Library and your own classes that include NIH Class Library header files with the preprocessor symbol MI defined. Defining MI causes the following to occur:

- Class Object becomes a virtual base class of all classes derived directly from it.

- The static member castdown() functions, which you must use to cast a pointer to an Object* to a pointer to a descendent class, become operative. With MI disabled, these functions simply perform an ordinary type cast.

- The readFrom() constructors of all classes not directly derived from class Object call class Object's readFrom() constructor in their initializer lists.

These changes affect all classes, even those that do not have multiple base classes anywhere among their ancestors, as a consequence of class Object being a virtual base class. A class that has multiple base classes must:

- use the DEFINE_CLASS_MI or DEFINE_ABSTRACT_CLASS_MI preprocessor macro instead of DEFINE_CLASS or DEFINE_ABSTRACT_CLASS; and,

- provide an implementation of the member function _castdown(), a function used by the castdown() member functions.

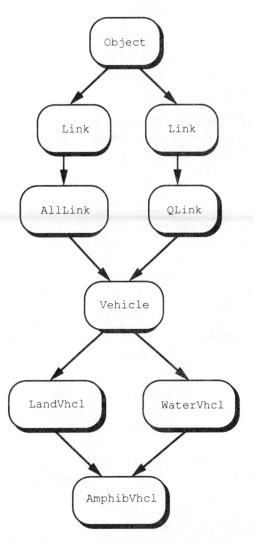

Figure 13.7 Inheritance DAG for Example 13-9

A class that has virtual base classes must:

- call the member function
  base::deepenVBase()
  instead of
  base::deepenShallowCopy()
  in the implementation of its deepenShallowCopy() function to deepen instances
  of virtual base classes;

- call the member function
  base::storeVBaseOn()
  instead of

base::storer()

in the implementation of its storer() function to store instances of virtual base classes; and,

- call the readFrom() constructors of all ancestor virtual base classes in the initializer list of its readFrom() constructors.

The following sections discuss the motivation for these changes and rules, and illustrate them with sections of code from the versions of the traffic simulation classes that we have made compatible with the NIH Class Library.

13.10.1 Object **as a virtual base class**

Enabling multiple inheritance makes Object a virtual base class. Otherwise, ambiguities would occur whenever you used a pointer or reference to an instance of a descendent class in place of a pointer or reference to an Object, and that descendent had multiple base classes among its ancestors. Such uses would be ambiguous because each descendent would inherit multiple instances of class Object, and C++ would not know which one the Object pointer or reference should refer to.

For example, if class Object were not a virtual base class, the inheritance DAG for class AmphibVhcl in Example 13-9 would appear as shown in Figure 13.8. If you tried to add an AmphibVhcl to a container class

```
OrderedCltn c;
AmphibVhcl* v;
// ...
c.add(*v);        // ambiguous - AllLink's Object or QLink's Object?
```

the C++ compiler would flag the statement as ambiguous because it could not tell whether to convert the AmphibVhcl* to a pointer to the instance of Object that is AllLink's ancestor, or to convert it to point to the instance of Object that is QLink's ancestor.

Making class Object a virtual base class resolves the ambiguity, since there is then a single, shared instance of class Object to point to.

Defining the preprocessor symbol MI causes Object.h to define the preprocessor symbol VIRTUAL as virtual; otherwise, it is empty. So you should write the declaration for a class X that is directly derived from class Object as

```
class X: public VIRTUAL Object {        // ...
```

to cause Object to be a virtual base class if MI is defined, and a non-virtual base class if MI isn't defined.

13.10.2 **Downward casts from a virtual base class**

Making class Object a virtual base class solves one problem, but creates another—due to a limitation, C++ prohibits downward casts from (or through) a virtual base class to a descendent class. In the context of Example 13-9, for instance, it is illegal to write:

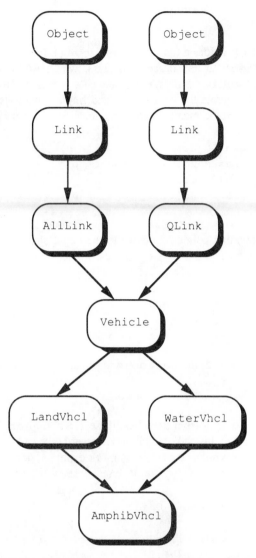

Figure 13.8 Non-virtual Object *inheritance DAG for Example 13-9*

```
bool Vehicle::isEqual(const Object& v) const
{
// error: cast: Object* ->derived Vehicle*; Object is virtual base
    return v.isSpecies(classDesc) && *this == (const Vehicle&)v;
}
```

As we have seen in many previous examples, such casts are necessary when working with polymorphic data structures and functions.

The castdown() *functions*

The NIH Class Library provides a family of castdown() functions to perform downward casts from class Object to any descendent class, which we will call the *target class*. The DECLARE_MEMBERS, DEFINE_CLASS, and DEFINE_ABSTRACT class preprocessor macros automatically generate the declarations and implementations of the castdown() functions. These are the static member functions declared for every class X:

```
static X& castdown(Object& p)
static const X& castdown(const Object& p)
static X* castdown(Object* p)
static const X* castdown(const Object* p)
```

The four functions cast every combination of constant/non-constant pointer/reference to class Object to a corresponding pointer/reference to the target class X. When MI is undefined, the castdown() functions do a simple type cast inline:

```
static X& castdown(Object& p)               { return (X&)p; }
static const X& castdown(const Object& p)   { return (const X&)p; }
static X* castdown(Object* p)               { return (X*)p; }
static const X* castdown(const Object* p)   { return (const X*)p; }
```

However, when MI is defined, the castdown() functions call the virtual function

```
virtual void* _castdown(const Class& target) const
```

to perform the downward cast from the virtual base class Object.

If you use castdown() instead of explicit downward type casts, you can write programs that will compile with or without the MI option. For example, here are the implementations of compare() and isEqual() for the Vehicle class of Example 13-9:

```
int Vehicle::compare(const Object& v) const
{
    assertArgSpecies(v,classDesc,"compare");
    return id - castdown(v).id;
}

bool Vehicle::isEqual(const Object& v) const
{
    return v.isSpecies(classDesc) && *this == castdown(v);
}
```

Even though the argument to castdown() is an Object* or Object&, you can use these functions to cast down a pointer (or reference) between *any* two descendents of Object—provided, of course, that the two classes are related. You can pass a pointer or reference to a descendent of class Object as the argument to one of the castdown() functions, which can then cast it down to the desired class. You will need to explicitly cast a non-constant object pointer or reference to type `Object*` or `Object&`; otherwise C++ will flag the call to `castdown()` as ambiguous, since a non-constant argument matches both the constant and non-constant forms of `castdown()`:

```
const Vehicle* cv;
// convert cv to a const Object* and cast it down to
// a const LandVhcl*
const LandVhcl* clv = LandVhcl::castdown(cv);

Vehicle* v;
// convert v to an Object* and cast it down to a LandVhcl*
LandVhcl* lv = LandVhcl::castdown((Object*)v);
```

How _castdown() works

The magic of `castdown()` lies in the virtual function `_castdown()`. How does this function work?

The `castdown()` functions call `_castdown()` with the class descriptor address (see Section 8.1.2) of the target class as an argument, and expect `_castdown()` to return the value of the `this` pointer for the target class. Since `_castdown()` is a virtual function which every class must implement, this call dynamically binds to the definition of `_castdown()` in the bottommost class in the inheritance DAG of the object `castdown()` was applied to. For example, if we write

```
Object* o = new AmphibVhcl(5.0, 15.0, 3.0);
Vehicle* v = Vehicle::castdown(o);
```

to cast down the `Object*` o to a `Vehicle*`, `Vehicle::castdown()` calls `_castdown()` with class `Vehicle`'s class descriptor as the argument:

```
o->_castdown(*Vehicle::desc());
```

Since in this case o is an instance of class `AmphibVhcl`, this virtual function call will execute `AmphibVhcl::_castdown()`.

Every class's implementation of `_castdown()` compares the class descriptor address of the target class to the class descriptor address of its own class. If they are equal, then this particular `_castdown()` belongs to the target class, so it returns the value of `this` cast to a `void*` as its result.

If `_castdown()` finds that it isn't a member of the target class, then it calls the implementation of `_castdown()` for each of its base classes. Since *every* class's `_castdown()` does the same, this effectively searches the object's entire inheritance DAG to locate the target class and obtain the value of its `this` pointer. The nested calls terminate whenever `Object::_castdown()` is called, which returns 0 if `Object` is not the target class:

```
void* Object::_castdown(const Class& target) const
{
    if (&target == desc()) return (void*)this;
    return 0;
}
```

The implementations of _castdown() for all classes having only one base class are similar, so the DEFINE_CLASS and DEFINE_ABSTRACT_CLASS preprocessor macros can generate them automatically:

```
void* X::_castdown(const Class& target) const
{
    if (&target == desc()) return (void*)this;
    return BASE::_castdown(target);
}
```

Writing _castdown() *for classes with multiple base classes*

However, classes with multiple base classes require a more complicated implementation of _castdown(), so you must provide a definition. That is why you must use the DEFINE_CLASS_MI or DEFINE_ABSTRACT_CLASS_MI preprocessor macros for classes with multiple bases—these macros do not generate a definition for _castdown() so you can supply your own.

Let us take a look at the definitions of _castdown() for class Vehicle and class AmphibVhcl from Example 13-9:

```
void* Vehicle::_castdown(const Class& target) const
{
    if (&target == desc()) return (void*)this;
    void* p = AllLink::_castdown(target);
    void* q = p;
    if (p = QLink::_castdown(target)) ambigCheck(p,q,target);
    return q;
}
```

```
void* AmphibVhcl::_castdown(const Class& target) const
{
    if (&target == desc()) return (void*)this;
    void* p = LandVhcl::_castdown(target);
    void* q = p;
    if (p = WaterVhcl::_castdown(target)) ambigCheck(p,q,target);
    return q;
}
```

As you can see, they are similar. First, they check to see if they belong to the target class, and return the value of `this` if so; otherwise, they call `_castdown()` for each of their base classes. However, after searching the first base class and its ancestors, they call `ambigCheck()` for each subsequent base class to detect an attempt to cast down a pointer to a class for which the inheritance DAG contains more than one instance. For example, the following downward cast is ambiguous

```
Object* o = new AmphibVhcl(5.0, 15.0, 3.0);
Link* l = Link::castdown(o);
```

because an `AmphibVhcl` has two instances of class `Link` as ancestors: the `Link` that is the base class of `AllLink` and the `Link` that is the base class of `QLink`.

However, the downward cast we used as an example earlier in this section

```
Object* o = new AmphibVhcl(5.0, 15.0, 3.0);
Vehicle* v = Vehicle::castdown(o);
```

is not ambiguous even though the calls to

```
LandVhcl::_castdown()
```

and

```
WaterVhcl::_castdown()
```

both find the target class `Vehicle` and return a non-zero result. In this case, both calls return the *same* value, because they both find the same shared instance of the virtual base class `Vehicle`.

Used in the way we have just described, `_castdown()` will produce one of three possible outcomes:

1. `_castdown()` will return 0, indicating that it did not locate the target class among itself or any of its ancestors. If `_castdown()` returns 0 to `castdown()`, `castdown()` reports an "invalid downward cast" error.

2. `ambigCheck()` will detect that a second instance of the target class with a different `this` pointer has been found, in which case it reports an "ambiguous downward cast" error.

3. `_castdown()` will locate a unique instance of the target class among itself and its ancestors and return the value of that instance's `this` pointer.

The `Template_c` file listed in Appendix B shows how to write the `_castdown()` function for an NIH Library class with multiple base classes. The pattern follows that of `Vehicle::_castdown()` and `AmphibVhcl::_castdown()`. For each base class `BASEi` after the first, add a line that reads:

```
if (p = BASEi::_castdown(target)) ambigCheck(p,q,target);
```

Summary of downward casts from a virtual base class

If class `Object` is a virtual base class, we cannot use the type cast operator to convert a
pointer or reference to an `Object` into one to a descendent class—something we need to do
when working with polymorphic data structures and functions. Instead, we provide a family
of static member `castdown()` functions in the NIH Class Library to let us to do this. These
functions rely on the virtual member function `_castdown()`, which every class must implement, to search the inheritance DAG of an object, find a unique instance of the target class,
and return the value of its `this` pointer. The `DECLARE_MEMBERS`, `DEFINE_CLASS`, and
`DEFINE_ABSTRACT_CLASS` preprocessor macros generate the declaration and implementation of `_castdown()` automatically for classes that have one base class, but we must
use an `MI` version of these macros and provide the implementation of `_castdown()` ourselves for classes with multiple base classes. The file `Template_c` listed in Appendix B
shows how to do this.

13.10.3   Multiple inheritance and `deepCopy()`

You may recall from Section 7.3.2 that every NIH Library class implements the virtual
function `deepenShallowCopy()` to support the `deepCopy()` operation provided by
class `Object`. Defining `deepenShallowCopy()` for classes with multiple base classes
is a straightforward extension of the definition for a single base class: simply call each base
class's implementation of `deepenShallowCopy()` to "deepen" the member variables of
all ancestor classes. However, classes with virtual base classes encounter the problem we
described in Section 13.9 in their implementation of `deepenShallowCopy()`: derived
classes will unintentionally call `deepenShallowCopy()` more than once for the instance
of the virtual base class they share.

The NIH Class Library defines the member function `deepenVBase()` for each
class to help eliminate undesired multiple calls. Classes with virtual base classes define `deepenShallowCopy()` to call their virtual base class's implementation of
`deepenVBase()` instead of `deepenShallowCopy()`, as these definitions for the
classes used in Example 13-9 illustrate:

```
void Vehicle::deepenShallowCopy()
{
    AllLink::deepenShallowCopy();
    QLink::deepenShallowCopy();
    allVehicles.addVehicle(*this);   // add to list of all Vehicles
}


void LandVhcl::deepenShallowCopy()
{
    Vehicle::deepenVBase();
}


void WaterVhcl::deepenShallowCopy()
{
    Vehicle::deepenVBase();
}
```

```
void AmphibVhcl::deepenShallowCopy()
{
    LandVhcl::deepenShallowCopy();
    WaterVhcl::deepenShallowCopy();
}
```

Example 13-9 demonstrates the application of deepCopy() to an instance of an AmphibVhcl:

```
// ex13-9.c - MI with the NIH Class Library

#include "LandVhcl.h"
#include "WaterVhcl.h"
#include "AmphibVhcl.h"
#include "StopLightQ.h"
#include "DrawBridgeQ.h"


StopLightQ stopLightQ[2];
DrawBridgeQ drawBridgeQ;


main()
{
    stopLightQ[0].addVehicle(*new LandVhcl(4.1, 12.0));
    stopLightQ[1].addVehicle(*new LandVhcl(4.2, 12.0));
    stopLightQ[0].addVehicle(*new LandVhcl(4.3, 12.0));
    stopLightQ[1].addVehicle(*new LandVhcl(4.4, 12.0));
    drawBridgeQ.addVehicle(*new WaterVhcl(21.0, 19.0, 3.5));
    drawBridgeQ.addVehicle(*new WaterVhcl(10.0, 30.0, 2.0));
    stopLightQ[0].addVehicle(*new AmphibVhcl(5.0, 15.0, 3.0));
    drawBridgeQ.addVehicle(*new AmphibVhcl(5.1, 15.0, 3.0));

    cout << "allVehicles:\n"; Vehicle::printAll();
    cout << endl;
    cout << "stopLightQ[0]:\n"; stopLightQ[0].printOn();
    cout << endl;
    cout << "stopLightQ[1]:\n"; stopLightQ[1].printOn();
    cout << endl;
    cout << "drawBridgeQ:\n"; drawBridgeQ.printOn();
    cout << endl;

    cout << "Test deepCopy()" << endl;
    Vehicle* copy =
        Vehicle::castdown(drawBridgeQ.last()->deepCopy());
    cout << *copy << endl;
    cout << "allVehicles:\n"; Vehicle::printAll(); cout << endl;
    delete copy;
```

```
      cout << "allVehicles:\n"; Vehicle::printAll(); cout << endl;
// ...
}
```

The output from Example 13-9 shows that the deepCopy() of AmphibVhcl #8 appears once on the allVehicles list, indicating that Vehicle:: deepenShallowCopy() was called only once:

```
allVehicles:
#1 height 4.1  length 12  axles 2
#2 height 4.2  length 12  axles 2
#3 height 4.3  length 12  axles 2
#4 height 4.4  length 12  axles 2
#5 height 21  length 19  draft 3.5
#6 height 10  length 30  draft 2
#7 height 5  length 15  axles 2  draft 3
#8 height 5.1  length 15  axles 2  draft 3
stopLightQ[0]:
#1 height 4.1  length 12  axles 2
#3 height 4.3  length 12  axles 2
#7 height 5  length 15  axles 2  draft 3
stopLightQ[1]:
#2 height 4.2  length 12  axles 2
#4 height 4.4  length 12  axles 2
drawBridgeQ:
#5 height 21  length 19  draft 3.5
#6 height 10  length 30  draft 2
#8 height 5.1  length 15  axles 2  draft 3
Test deepCopy()
#8 height 5.1  length 15  axles 2  draft 3
allVehicles:
#1 height 4.1  length 12  axles 2
#2 height 4.2  length 12  axles 2
#3 height 4.3  length 12  axles 2
#4 height 4.4  length 12  axles 2
#5 height 21  length 19  draft 3.5
#6 height 10  length 30  draft 2
#7 height 5  length 15  axles 2  draft 3
#8 height 5.1  length 15  axles 2  draft 3
#8 height 5.1  length 15  axles 2  draft 3
allVehicles:
#1 height 4.1  length 12  axles 2
#2 height 4.2  length 12  axles 2
#3 height 4.3  length 12  axles 2
#4 height 4.4  length 12  axles 2
#5 height 21  length 19  draft 3.5
#6 height 10  length 30  draft 2
```

```
#7 height 5    length 15   axles 2   draft 3
#8 height 5.1  length 15   axles 2   draft 3
```

The `Template_c` file listed in Appendix B gives complete details for implementing `deepenShallowCopy()` when using multiple inheritance.

The `deepCopy()` and `deepenVBase()` member functions utilize the dynamic method for eliminating undesired multiple calls of `deepenShallowCopy()` that we described in Section 13.9.2.

13.10.4   Multiple inheritance and object I/O

To make the `storeOn()` and `readFrom()` object I/O functions work properly on instances of classes with multiple and/or virtual base classes, we must observe a few additional conventions when writing the `storer()` member functions and `readFrom()` constructors for the class (see Section 7.4).

Multiple inheritance and `storer()` *functions*

As we described in Section 7.4, every NIH Library class implements a pair of `storer()` functions to support the `storeOn()` operation. Implementing the `storer()` functions for a class with multiple base classes is straightforward: call the `storer()` function for each non-virtual base class, *in the order listed in the class declaration*, to store the member variables of all ancestor classes, then store the member variables for the class itself. For example, here are the implementations of the `storer()` functions for the `Vehicle` class used in Example 13-9:

```
void Vehicle::storer(OIOout& strm) const
{
    AllLink::storer(strm);
    QLink::storer(strm);
    strm << id << height << length;
}

void Vehicle::storer(OIOofd& fd) const
{
    AllLink::storer(fd);
    QLink::storer(fd);
    fd << id << height << length;
}
```

Writing the `storer()` functions for a class with a virtual base class requires the usual care to be sure that derived classes call the virtual base class's `storer()` function only once so that its member variables are stored only once. The NIH Class Library defines the functions `storeVBaseOn(OIOout&)` and `storeVBaseOn(OIOofd&)` for this purpose. The `storer()` function for a class with a virtual base class must:

- call `storeVBaseOn()` instead of `storer()` for virtual base classes

- store all virtual base classes before the first non-virtual base class

- store the virtual base classes *in the order in which they will be intialized by a constructor* (see Section 13.8).

The implementations of the storer() functions for the LandVhcl, WaterVhcl, and AmphibVhcl classes used in Example 13-9 illustrate this:

```
void LandVhcl::storer(OIOout& strm) const
{
    Vehicle::storeVBaseOn(strm);
    strm << axles;
}


void LandVhcl::storer(OIOofd& fd) const
{
    Vehicle::storeVBaseOn(fd);
    fd << axles;
}


void WaterVhcl::storer(OIOout& strm) const
{
    Vehicle::storeVBaseOn(strm);
    strm << draft;
}


void WaterVhcl::storer(OIOofd& fd) const
{
    Vehicle::storeVBaseOn(fd);
    fd << draft;
}


void AmphibVhcl::storer(OIOout& strm) const
{
    Vehicle::storeVBaseOn(strm);
    LandVhcl::storer(strm);
    WaterVhcl::storer(strm);
}


void AmphibVhcl::storer(OIOofd& fd) const
{
    Vehicle::storeVBaseOn(fd);
    LandVhcl::storer(fd);
    WaterVhcl::storer(fd);
}
```

The storeOn() and storeVBaseOn() member functions also utilize the dynamic method for eliminating undesired multiple calls of storer() (see Section 13.9.2).

Multiple inheritance and readFrom() *constructors*

To support the readFrom() operation, as we described in Section 7.4.3, we must provide each class with definitions of readFrom() constructors. For a class with multiple base classes, we call the readFrom() constructors for each base class by specifying them in the initializer list of the readFrom() constructor we are writing. In addition, we must also call the readFrom() constructors of all *ancestor* virtual base classes to prevent C++ from initializing them by calling their default constructors instead, as we explained in Section 13.6.5. Since class Object is an ancestor virtual base class of every class when MI is defined, the readFrom() constructor initialization lists of all classes—even those without multiple or virtual base classes—must include class Object's readFrom() constructor. For example, here are the readFrom() contructors for the classes used in Example 13-9:

```
Vehicle::Vehicle(OIOin& strm) :
    Object(strm),
    AllLink(strm),
    QLink(strm)
{
    strm >> id >> height >> length;
    allVehicles.addVehicle(*this);   // add to list of all Vehicles
}

Vehicle::Vehicle(OIOifd& fd) :
    Object(fd),
    AllLink(fd),
    QLink(fd)
{
    fd >> id >> height >> length;
    allVehicles.addVehicle(*this);   // add to list of all Vehicles
}

LandVhcl::LandVhcl(OIOin& strm) :
    Object(strm),
    BASE(strm)
{
    strm >> axles;
}

LandVhcl::LandVhcl(OIOifd& fd) :
    Object(fd),
    BASE(fd)
{
    fd >> axles;
}

WaterVhcl::WaterVhcl(OIOin& strm) :
```

```
        Object(strm),
        BASE(strm)
    {

        strm >> draft;
    }


WaterVhcl::WaterVhcl(OIOifd& fd) :
        Object(fd),
        BASE(fd)
    {

        fd >> draft;
    }


AmphibVhcl::AmphibVhcl(OIOin& strm) :
        Object(strm),
        Vehicle(strm),
        LandVhcl(strm),
        WaterVhcl(strm)
    {
    }


AmphibVhcl::AmphibVhcl(OIOifd& fd) :
        Object(fd),
        Vehicle(fd),
        LandVhcl(fd),
        WaterVhcl(fd)
    {
    }
```

The order of the classes in the constructor initialization lists does not matter, because C++ will call the constructors according to the rules we presented in Section 13.8, which depend only on the order of the base classes in the class *declarations* involved.[3] Since we must write out the base class's member variables in the same order that they will be read, we must take care to call the storer() functions in the same order that C++ will invoke the readFrom() constructors.

See the Template_c file listed in Appendix B for a summary of how to write the storer() functions and readFrom() constructors for classes when using multiple inheritance.

Example 13-9 demonstrates storing all the vehicle queues in a simulation on a file:

```
// ex13-9.c - MI with the NIH Class Library

// ...


StopLightQ stopLightQ[2];
```

---

[3] For clarity, we recommend that you order the base classes in a constructor initialization list in the same order that they appear in the declaration of the constructor's class.

```
DrawBridgeQ drawBridgeQ;
main()
{
    stopLightQ[0].addVehicle(*new LandVhcl(4.1, 12.0));
    stopLightQ[1].addVehicle(*new LandVhcl(4.2, 12.0));
    stopLightQ[0].addVehicle(*new LandVhcl(4.3, 12.0));
    stopLightQ[1].addVehicle(*new LandVhcl(4.4, 12.0));
    drawBridgeQ.addVehicle(*new WaterVhcl(21.0, 19.0, 3.5));
    drawBridgeQ.addVehicle(*new WaterVhcl(10.0, 30.0, 2.0));
    stopLightQ[0].addVehicle(*new AmphibVhcl(5.0, 15.0, 3.0));
    drawBridgeQ.addVehicle(*new AmphibVhcl(5.1, 15.0, 3.0));
//  ...
    Vehicle::saveQueues("trafficfile",
        &stopLightQ[0], &stopLightQ[1], &drawBridgeQ, 0);
}
```

The function `Vehicle::saveQueues()` adds the `allVehicles` queue and all `VehicleQs` specified in its argument list to the `OrderedCltn allQueues`, which it then saves by applying `storeOn()`. Using a single `storeOn()` operation writes out any vehicles that appear on more than one queue only once, and stores object references for subsequent appearances.

`Vehicle::saveQueues()` also illustrates how to portably process a variable-length argument list by using the macros defined in `stdarg.h` (see [12]):

```
#include <stdarg.h>
//  ...
void Vehicle::saveQueues(const char* fname, ...)
{
    ofstream out(fname,ios::out,0664);   // UNIX protection
                                         // mode 0664
    if (out.fail()) {
        cerr << "Failed to open " << fname << endl;
        exit(1);
    }
    OrderedCltn allQueues;
    allQueues.add(allVehicles);        // allVehicles is allQueues[0]
    va_list ap;
    va_start(ap, fname);
    VehicleQ* q;
    while (q = va_arg(ap, VehicleQ*)) allQueues.add(*q);
    va_end(ap);
    allQueues.storeOn(OIOnihout(out));
}
```

Example 13-10 shows how to read in the file written by Example 13-9:

```
// ex13-10.c - MI and Object I/O readFrom()

#include <fstream.h>
#include <osfcn.h>
#include "LandVhcl.h"
#include "WaterVhcl.h"
#include "AmphibVhcl.h"
#include "StopLightQ.h"
#include "DrawBridgeQ.h"
#include "OrderedCltn.h"
#include "OIOnih.h"

StopLightQ* stopLightQ[2];
DrawBridgeQ* drawBridgeQ;

main()
{
    ifstream in("trafficfile");
    if (in.fail()) {
        cerr << "Failed to open trafficfile\n";
        exit(1);
    }
    OrderedCltn& allQueues = *OrderedCltn::readFrom(OIOnihin(in));
    stopLightQ[0] = StopLightQ::castdown(allQueues[1]);
    stopLightQ[1] = StopLightQ::castdown(allQueues[2]);
    drawBridgeQ = DrawBridgeQ::castdown(allQueues[3]);


    cout << "allVehicles:\n"; Vehicle::printAll();
    cout << endl;
    cout << "stopLightQ[0]:\n"; stopLightQ[0]->printOn();
    cout << endl;
    cout << "stopLightQ[1]:\n"; stopLightQ[1]->printOn();
    cout << endl;
    cout << "drawBridgeQ:\n"; drawBridgeQ->printOn();
    cout << endl;
}
```

The output from Example 13-10 demonstrates the faithful reproduction of the vehicle queues:

```
allVehicles:
#1 height 4.1   length 12   axles 2
#2 height 4.2   length 12   axles 2
#3 height 4.3   length 12   axles 2
#4 height 4.4   length 12   axles 2
#5 height 21    length 19   draft 3.5
#6 height 10    length 30   draft 2
```

```
#7  height  5    length  15   axles  2   draft  3
#8  height  5.1  length  15   axles  2   draft  3
stopLightQ[0]:
#1  height  4.1  length  12   axles  2
#3  height  4.3  length  12   axles  2
#7  height  5    length  15   axles  2   draft  3
stopLightQ[1]:
#2  height  4.2  length  12   axles  2
#4  height  4.4  length  12   axles  2
drawBridgeQ:
#5  height  21   length  19   draft  3.5
#6  height  10   length  30   draft  2
#8  height  5.1  length  15   axles  2   draft  3
```

Note that since class `Vehicle`'s `readFrom()` constructor adds each vehicle it reads to the `allVehicles` queue, there is no need to explicitly initialize `allVehicles` from `allQueues[0]`.

13.10.5   Methods for resolving ambiguous downward casts

In Example 13-9, classes `VehicleQ`, `AllVehicles`, `StopLightQ`, and `DrawBridgeQ` are descendants of the NIH Library class `LinkedList`. Using class `LinkedList` with multiple inheritance and the `castdown()` function raises a few problems with ambiguous downward casts that we discuss in this section.

Normally, the NIH Library's container classes operate exclusively on pointers or references to `Object`s. For example, class `Collection` declares the virtual function:

```
virtual Object* add(Object&) = 0;
```

to add an `Object` to a container. Class `LinkedList` implements `add(Object&)` to add an `Object` to a `LinkedList`. However, as we explained in Section 8.3.7, the object in this case must be a descendant of class `Link`, so `LinkedList::add(Object&)` verifies this and calls `Link::castdown()` to convert the `Object&` argument into a `Link&`.

Now consider the virtual member function `addVehicle()` in Example 13-9's class `VehicleQ`:

```
void VehicleQ::addVehicle(QLink& l) { add(l); }
```

This function calls `LinkedList::add()` to add a `Vehicle` to a `LinkedList` using its `QLink` link, for example:

```
VehicleQ q;
q.addVehicle(*new LandVhcl(4.1, 12.0));
```

The problem is that `LinkedList::add(Object&)`'s call to `Link::castdown()` will fail because it is ambiguous. C++ converts the `QLink&` argument to `add(Object&)`

to an Object&, and then Link::castdown() attempts to convert it to a Link&. This fails because there are two Link objects in a Vehicle—our intention of using the Link that is the base class of QLink is lost when C++ converts the QLink& to an Object&.

Our solution is to overload LinkedList::add(), and all other member functions with Object& arguments (addAfter(), addFirst(), addLast(), and remove()) to also accept a Link& argument. These versions have no need to apply castdown() to their arguments. For the call to LinkedList::add() in VehicleQ, C++ selects add(Link&) instead of add(Object&) because class Link is a closer ancestor of QLink than is class Object; thus, we eliminate the troublesome call to Link::castdown() altogether.

A tougher problem arises when we try to use an Iterator on a LinkedList containing Vehicles. Class Iterator (see Section 8.3.2) provides a member variable of type Object* for the doNext() function of a container class to use to maintain the current object. LinkedList::doNext() must convert this pointer to a Link* in order to follow it to the next object on the LinkedList. If it were to call Link::castdown() to perform this conversion on a Vehicle, the conversion would be ambiguous.

To solve this problem, we implemented LinkedList::doNext() to call the protected virtual function

```
virtual Link& linkCastdown(Object&) const;
```

instead of calling Link::castdown() directly. Class LinkedList implements linkCastDown() as follows

```
Link& LinkedList::linkCastdown(Object& p) const
{
    return Link::castdown(p);
}
```

and derived classes, for example AllVehicles and VehicleQ in Example 13-9, reimplement it to cast down to the appropriate, more specific, class:

```
Link& AllVehicles::linkCastdown(Object& p) const
{
    return AllLink::castdown(p);
}
```

```
Link& VehicleQ::linkCastdown(Object& p) const
{
    return QLink::castdown(p);
}
```

Both of these problems arise because converting a pointer (or reference) to a base class of which there are multiple non-virtual instances to type Object* (or type Object&) loses information. This points out a limitation of the NIH Class Library's object I/O mechanism: if you store a data structure containing such a pointer, you will not be able to to read the data structure back. The storeOn() function converts all pointers to type Object*, and readFrom() uses castdown() to convert them back to the original type. This conversion will fail with an "ambiguous downward cast" error in this situation, as the following example illustrates:

```
// ex13-11.c - Limitation of Object I/O


#include <fstream.h>
#include <osfcn.h>
#include "QLink.h"
#include "LandVhcl.h"
#include "OIOnih.h"

main()
{
    QLink* qlp = new LandVhcl(4.1, 12.0);
    Link* lp = (QLink*) new LandVhcl(4.2, 12.0);
    ofstream outstrm("badfile",ios::out,0664);   // UNIX protection
                                                 // mode 0664
    if (outstrm.fail()) {
        cerr << "Failed to open badfile";
        exit(1);
    }
    OIOnihout out(outstrm);
    qlp->storeOn(out);
    lp->storeOn(out);
    outstrm.close();
    LandVhcl* t = LandVhcl::castdown((Object*)qlp);
    delete t;
    t = LandVhcl::castdown((Object*)lp);
    delete t;

    ifstream instrm("badfile");
    if (instrm.fail()) {
        cerr << "Failed to open badfile\n";
        exit(1);
    }
    OIOnihin in(instrm);
    qlp = QLink::readFrom(in);   // OK
    cout << *qlp << endl;
    lp = Link::readFrom(in);     // error: ambiguous downward cast
}
```

13.10.6 Summary of multiple inheritance and the NIH Class Library

In this section we described how multiple inheritance impacts NIH Library classes. When NIH Library classes are compiled with the MI (multiple inheritance support) option enabled:

- Class `Object` is a virtual base class.

- Since class `Object` is a virtual base class, downward casts from type `Object*` or `Object&` are illegal, and you must use the `castdown()` functions instead.

- All `readFrom()` constructors must call class `Object`'s `readFrom()` constructor in their constructor initialization lists.

Virtual base classes require special care:

- The implementation of `deepenShallowCopy()` must call *base*::`deepenVBase()` instead of *base*::`deepenShallowCopy()` to "deepen" the member variables of virtual base classes.

- The implementation of `storer()` must call *base*::`storeVBaseOn()` instead of *base*::`storer()` to store the member variables of virtual base classes.

Finally, we described the ambiguities that can arise when using the `castdown()` function on objects multiple non-virtual instances of the same base class, and some methods for resolving these.

13.11   CHAPTER SUMMARY

In this chapter we introduced multiple inheritance, in which a derived class may have more than one base class. We showed how to use multiple inheritance in a simple way, as an import mechanism to enable the practice of modular programming techniques in C++. Examples 13-1 and 13-2 showed how to use multiple inheritance to incorporate multiple instances of class `Link` in an object so that it could be threaded onto several linked lists simultaneously. We then described the ambiguities that can arise when a derived class inherits member functions with the same name from more than one base class, and we presented ways to resolve these ambiguities.

Example 13-4 introduced the use of virtual base classes, which is a mechanism for sharing a single instance of an ancestor class's member variables when it would otherwise result in multiple instances. We then described the more elaborate rules C++ uses to initialize instances of virtual base classes and classes that use multiple inheritance. Next, we discussed the problem of unintentional multiple calls to member functions of virtual base classes and presented two techniques to eliminate them: a static method and a dynamic method. The static method breaks up each member function into two, a protected member function to operate only on the members of its own class, and a public member function that uses the protected function to perform the operation once on itself and on each of its ancestor classes. The dynamic method uses an instance of an `IdentSet` to record which member functions have already been called so they can ignore subsequent calls.

Finally, we discussed how the NIH Class Library accommodates multiple inheritance. When NIH Library classes are compiled with the preprocessor symbol `MI` defined, class `Object` becomes a virtual base class, and you must then use a special `castdown()` function to perform downward type casts. Classes with virtual base classes can use the `deepenVBase()` function to eliminate undesired multiple calls to `deepenShallowCopy()` during a `deepCopy()` operation, and the similar function `storeVBaseOn()` to eliminate extraneous calls to `storer()` during a `storeOn()` operation. Examples 13-9 and 13-10 illustrated the use of these functions, and highlighted some special considerations that arise when using class `LinkedList` and multiple inheritance.

14
FUTURE DIRECTIONS

14.1 INTRODUCTION

No programming language is perfect. In the course of this book, we have occasionally pointed out problems or deficiencies we have encountered while trying to use C++. In this chapter, we discuss the most significant of these in depth, and describe some potential solutions.

14.2 EXCEPTION HANDLING

Let us take another look at the function `Property::get()` from Example 8-16 in Section 8.3.11:

```
Object* Property::get(
    const Object& ob,   // object with property
    const String& name) // name of property
{
    if (!prop.includesKey(ob)) return Object::nil;
    Dictionary* d = (Dictionary*)prop.atKey(ob);
    if (d->includesKey(name)) return d->atKey(name);
    else return Object::nil;
}
```

The calls to the functions `includesKey()` and `atKey()` illustrate a problem with searching a `Dictionary`: if we're not sure in advance that a particular key is already included, we may wind up searching the `Dictionary` twice. The function `atKey()` is supposed to return the value object associated with the specified key object. But what if the key is not in the `Dictionary`? In that case, `atKey()` prints out an appropriate error message and terminates the program. We do not want that to happen in `Property::get()`, so we must first call `includesKey()`, which searches the `Dictionary`, and only if `includesKey()` returns `YES` do we call `atKey()` to actually retrieve the associated value object, which searches the `Dictionary` a second time for the same key. This is needlessly inefficient.

We would like to have a uniform way of coping with such "exceptional" circumstances. We would like to have an exception handling mechanism with the following characteristics:

First, the exception handling mechanism should not *require* cooperation of the client program to detect an occurrence of an error. For example, if we had written `Dictionary::atKey()` to return a distinctive value such as 0 when it could not locate the key, a client program such as `Property::get()` would have to cooperate and check for this value:

```
Object* Property::get(
    const Object& ob,    // object with property
    const String& name) // name of property
{
    Dictionary* d = (Dictionary*)prop.atKey(ob);
    if (d == 0) return Object::nil; // if key "ob" not found
    Object* value = d->atKey(name);
    if (value) return value;         // if key "name" not found
    else return Object::nil;
}
```

If it did not do this, the zero pointer would be propagated to other parts of the program until it caused an error later on, when it might be difficult to trace back the problem to its source. So a good exception handling mechanism should by default abort the client program with an error message if an error occurs that the client chose not (or forgot) to check for.

Second, the exception handling mechanism should permit the *caller* to handle the exception when desired, since only the caller knows why the operation was done and how to recover from its failure. For example, no useful purpose would be served by having `Dictionary::atKey()` call a user-supplied error handling routine when it cannot locate a key. Such an error handling routine would have no practical way of knowing whether failure to find a key is cause to abort the program, or whether it is an expected result. Even if it could make this decision, say by examining global data set up by the caller, the error handling routine has few options as to what it can do about it. It can either abort the program or return to its caller, possibly leaving some information about what happened in global variables that a cooperative client program would have to examine.

Last, since we are talking about C++, the exception handling mechanism should be *efficient*. It should impose negligible overhead in the normal situation, and the overhead when an exception actually occurs should be reasonable.

14.2.1   A hypothetical exception handling mechanism for C++

Koenig and Stroustrup [14] have proposed an exception handling mechanism for C++ that has these characteristics. Our example function `Property::get()` might look something like this if this mechanism were actually implemented:

```
Object* Property::get(
    const Object& ob,    // object with property
    const String& name) // name of property
{
    try {
        return ((Dictionary*)prop.atKey(ob))->atKey(name);
    }
    catch (keyNotFound) {
        return Object::nil;
    }
}
```

The function atKey() would contain a statement similar to the following:

```
if ( /* key not found */ ) keyNotFound.raise();
```

The name keyNotFound refers to an instance of a special built-in C++ class named exception. Our example program might define keyNotFound as a global variable:

```
exception keyNotFound;
```

Applying the member function exception::raise() to an instance of class exception raises an exception.

The try statement establishes exception handling for the block of code that immediately follows it. Should an exception be raised during the execution of that block, it will cause control to pass to one of the catch statements that follow it. Each catch statement consists of a list of the exceptions it is intended to handle, and a block of code to be executed when one of the exceptions listed occurs. You can also write a *default* catch statement, one that will handle any exceptions not handled by any previous catch statements, by omitting the list of exceptions. For example:

```
try {
    return ((Dictionary*)prop.atKey(ob))->atKey(name);
}
catch (keyNotFound) {
    return Object::nil; // handle keyNotFound exceptions
}
catch {
// Handle all other exceptions here ...
}
```

What happens if the exception raised isn't listed in any catch statement and there is no default catch statement? Execution does not simply continue with the statement following the last catch statement, but instead control passes to the next-most-recently established exception handler to give it a similar opportunity to handle the exception. C++ establishes an outermost exception handler to catch any exceptions that are not otherwise handled by the program.

In our example, the try statement in Property::get() establishes exception handling for the block that follows it. If either call to atKey() in that block raises a keyNotFound exception, control will pass to the catch (keyNotFound) statement, its code block will be executed, and Property::get() will return the pointer to the Nil object as a result. This illustrates how a program can arrange to handle exceptions that occur in the functions it calls.

Now imagine that someone replaces the implementation of atKey() with an experimental version that has a bug in it. Let us suppose that under certain circumstances this bug causes atKey() to attempt to index an ArrayOb with an invalid subscript, so ArrayOb::operator[]() raises an indexRange exception. What happens in our example program in this situation?

When `ArrayOb::operator[]()` raises the `indexRange` exception, control passes out of the block following the `try` statement as before. But this time, there is no `catch` statement to handle the `indexRange` exception, so control will pass out of `Property::get()` to the `catch` statements in the next-most-recently established exception handler. If the program has not established any handler for `indexRange` exceptions, control will eventually go to the outermost handler established automatically by C++, which will print a diagnostic message and abort the program. Thus, we see that something reasonable happens even when a client program makes no effort to handle an exception.

14.2.2   Exception handling in the NIH Class Library

The NIH Class Library has an experimental exception handling mechanism similar to the hypothetical one we just described. We do not recommend using it because it is unsafe and inefficient, but you could program the function `Property::get()` as shown in Example 14-1.

```
// ex14-1.c - Exception handling in the NIH Class Library

Object* Property::get(
    const Object& ob,   // object with property
    const String& name) // name of property
{
    RaiseException x(NIHCL__KEYNOTFOUND);
    BEGINX
        return ((Dictionary*)prop.atKey(ob))->atKey(name);
    EXCEPTION
        case NIHCL__KEYNOTFOUND: return Object::nil;
        default: RAISE(EXCEPTION_CODE);
    ENDX
}
```

Normally, NIH library classes handle errors by printing a diagnostic message and aborting the program. You can change this behavior by declaring a `RaiseException` object as we did in `Property::get()`. Executing the constructor for this object causes the NIH library classes to raise an exception for KEYNOTFOUND errors rather than aborting the program. Executing the destructor for this object, which happens when control leaves the block in which it is declared, causes the NIH library classes to revert to handling KEYNOTFOUND errors as they were when the `RaiseException` object was constructed.

The BEGINX ... EXCEPTION ... ENDX construct behaves in some ways like the `try` ... `catch` exception handling mechanism we described in the previous section. However, it differs in that:

- the exception is an `int` rather than an instance of class `exception`,
- the body of the EXCEPTION ... ENDX construct is the same as that of a `switch` statement, with the integer value of the raised exception controlling which `case` is executed; and,

- control passes to the statement following the ENDX rather than to the next-most-recently established exception handler when the exception does not match any case label.

This last difference means we must add a default label and reraise the exception explicitly by performing RAISE(EXCEPTION_CODE) to mimic the behavior of the hypothetical try … catch exception handling mechanism. The EXCEPTION_CODE preprocessor macro returns the value of the exception code that caused execution of the EXCEPTION block.

Why is this mechanism so unsafe and inefficient that we do not recommend its use? Without exception handling support from the C++ compiler, a programmer has no automatic and efficient way to arrange for calling the destructors of any class instances that go out of scope when an exception is raised. For example, suppose the function atKey() looks like this:

```
Object* Dictionary::atKey(const Object& key)
{
    OrderedCltn a;
// ...
    if ( /* key not found */ ) RAISE(NIHCL__KEYNOTFOUND);
}
```

We implemented RAISE using the C library functions setjmp() and longjmp() to transfer control to the most recently established exception handler. These functions do not know anything about C++ instances and destructors, so they simply throw away the stack space for the OrderedCltn a without calling its destructor. This violates the C++ guarantee concerning destructors, and is therefore unacceptable.

In an attempt to solve this problem, the NIH Class Library provides a class named Catch. Programmers wishing to use an auto instance of a class with a destructor are supposed to derive a new class that includes an instance of class Catch as a member variable, and use an instance of the derived class instead. The constructor for class Catch threads the instance on a doubly-linked list. When a program raises an exception, destructors are called for any objects on this list that will go out of scope as a result of doing the longjmp() to the exception handler. The destructor for class Catch must also unlink an object from this list when it dies of natural causes.

This solution requires too much programming effort and cooperation of the client, and the overhead of maintaining the linked list of auto class instances is too great to make this a practical method of handling exceptions. The implementation of a practical exception handling mechanism requires the support of the C++ compiler, and this will almost surely be added in the near future.

14.3 PARAMETERIZED TYPES

You may recall how we used the NIH library class Stack to implement class TransformStack in Example 7-1:

```
class TransformStack {
    Stack s;
public:
    TransformStack()          { s.push(*new Point(0,0)); }
    Point* current() const    { return (Point*)s.top(); }
    void push(const Point& p) { s.push(*new Point(*current()+p)); }
    void pop()                { delete (Point*)s.pop(); }
};
```

At the time, we criticized this implementation as being less efficient and in some ways more complex than the implementation of class `TransformStack` in Example 6-1, which does not use class `Stack`:

```
class TransformStack {
    Point s[100];    // array to hold stack of points
    Point* top;      // current top of stack
public:
    TransformStack()          { top = s; }
    Point* current() const    { return top; }
    void push(const Point& p) {
        *++top = *top + p;
    }
    void pop()                { top--; }
};
```

We designed class `Stack` to be as general as possible. To permit the use of polymorphism, it holds pointers to the objects in the stack rather than the objects themselves. When we do not need polymorphism, such as in the case of class `TransformStack`, we are paying a price for generality that we are not using. *Parameterized types* offer a solution to this problem.

14.3.1 A hypothetical parameterized type facility for C++

Stroustrup [30] has proposed an implementation of parameterized types for C++ that would permit us to write a generic class `Stack`. Instead of being a stack of pointers to objects (type `Object*`), it would allow the client to specify the type of the data in the stack as a parameter. So if we needed, for example, a stack of `Point` objects and a stack of pointers to `Shape` objects we could write:

```
#include "StackOb.h"
#include "StackObPt.h"
#include "Point.h"
#include "Shape.h"

StackOb<Point> translationStack;   // efficient!
```

```
StackObPt<Shape> shapeStack;        // polymorphic!

void drawStack(StackObPt<Shape>& s, Point t)
// Draw all the shapes on stack s translated by t
{
    translationStack.push(t);
    while (!s.empty()) {
        s.top()->draw();
        s.pop();
    }
    translationStack.pop();
}
```

Using the proposed parameterized type feature of C++, we could write a *class template*
for a generic class `Stack` which we could then instantiate for any particular fundamental
data type:

```
template<class T> class Stack {
    int alloc;   // current stack allocation
protected:
    T* s;        // array to hold stack of elements
    T* t;        // current top of stack
public:
    Stack(int n=10)      { t = s = new T[alloc = n]; t--; }
    ~Stack()             { delete [alloc] s; }
    bool empty() const   { return t == s-1; }
    void push(T x)       { *++t = x; }
    T& top() const       { return *t; }
    T pop()              { return *t--; }
    virtual unsigned hash() const;
};
```

Similarly, we could define generic member functions to implement a generic class `Stack`
by writing *member function templates*. For example, we could write a member function
template for `hash()` as follows:

```
template<class T> unsigned Stack<T>::hash() const
{
    unsigned h = 0;
    for (T* p=s; p <= t; p++) {
        h ^= (unsigned)*p;
    }
    return h;
}
```

A declaration such as:

```
Stack<int> stackOfInts;
```

substitutes type int for the parameter T in the class template for class Stack, resulting in a stack of ints named stackOfInts.

In the previous example, we needed a stack of Point objects, so why could we not instantiate one with the declaration:

```
Stack<Point> translationStack;
```

The reason is that C++ requires different notation for dealing with instances of fundamental data types, instances of classes, and pointers to instances of classes. Consider the expansion of the member function template for hash() if we substitute class Point for the type parameter T:

```
unsigned Stack<Point>::hash() const
{
    unsigned h = 0;
    for (Point* p=s; p <= t; p++) {
        h ^= (unsigned)*p;
    }
    return h;
}
```

The statement:

```
h ^= (unsigned)*p;
```

would not compile because the cast of a Point to type unsigned is undefined. For instances of NIH library classes we would need an implementation of hash() that executes the statement:

```
h ^= p->hash();
```

instead. We need another generic class that is like the generic Stack class, except that it has this different implementation of hash(). This suggests that we write a *derived class template*:

```
template<class T> class StackOb : public Stack<T> {
public:
    StackOb(int n=10) : (n) {}
    virtual unsigned hash() const;
};

template<class T> unsigned StackOb<T>::hash() const
{
    unsigned h = 0;
    for (T* p=s; p <= t; p++) {
        h ^= p->hash();
    }
    return h;
}
```

The class template for class StackOb instantiates its base class Stack for the same type, and redefines the member function hash().

We encounter a similar, but more severe problem if we try to instantiate the class template for class Stack or StackOb to obtain a stack of pointers to Shape objects:

```
StackOb<Shape*> shapeStack;
```

In this case, the statement:

```
h ^= p->hash();
```

in the expansion of the member function template for hash() will not compile because p-> has type Shape*, not type Shape as we need. We need an implementation of hash() containing the statement:

```
h ^= (*p)->hash();
```

We also have a problem with the member function push(). When we instantiate its template for type Shape* we obtain a function that takes an argument of type Shape*:

```
void push(Shape* x) { *++t = x; }
```

For consistency with other NIH library classes, we would like the argument to push() to be a reference instead of a pointer:

```
void push(Shape& x) { *++t = x; }
```

We could solve both these problems by writing a template for a new class StackObPt, which is a stack of pointers to NIH Class Library objects:

```
template<class T> class StackObPt : public Stack<Object*> {
public:
    StackObPt(int n=10) : (n) {}
    void push(T& x)        { *++t = &x; }
    virtual unsigned hash() const;
};

template<class T> unsigned StackObPt<T>::hash() const
{
    unsigned h = 0;
    for (T* p=s; p <= t; p++) {
        h ^= (*p)->hash();
    }
    return h;
}
```

To allow us to make the argument to push() a reference, and to guarantee that the stack is in fact a stack of pointers, the template for class StackObPt takes a class as the parameter, not a pointer to a class, and adds the * itself. By deriving class StackObPt from class Stack<Object*>, we can reuse its member variables and the implementations of ~Stack(), empty(), top(), and pop().

Another refinement to our generic Stack class would be possible under the proposed parameterized type scheme. Consider what the expansion of the member function template for hash() would be for type char:

```
unsigned Stack<char>::hash() const
{
    unsigned h = 0;
    for (char* p=s; p <= t; p++) {
        h ^= (unsigned)*p;
    }
    return h;
}
```

Although this works, it produces only an 8-bit hash number and requires one loop iteration for each character on the stack. We might wish to optimize Stack<char>::hash() to treat the char stack as an unsigned int stack, thus producing a 32-bit hash number and hashing four characters at a time on 32-bit machines. The proposed parameterized type scheme would allow us to provide a member function definition for a particular type, which the C++ compiler would use only when its class template was instantiated for that type:

```
unsigned Stack<char>::hash() const
{
    unsigned h = 0;
    unsigned i = (t-s)/sizeof(unsigned);
    unsigned* q = (unsigned*)s;
    while (i--) h ^= *q++;
    if ((i = (t-s)%sizeof(unsigned)) != 0)
        h ^= *q & mask[i];   // mask[i] masks i chars from word
    return h;
}
```

Thus, this optimized version of hash() would be used when class Stack was instantiated with type char; otherwise, the C++ compiler would use the generic implementation Stack<T>::hash().

14.3.2   Parameterized types in the NIH Class Library

Until parameterized types are implemented in C++, you can simulate them by using a macro preprocessor. The NIH library generic Array class is an example of one way of accomplishing this. Initially, we implemented it using the #define macro facility of cpp, the standard C and C++ preprocessor, but we switched to using the UNIX m4 macro processor [11] when we discovered that long #define macros made the cpp on our system do strange things, apparently because the long macros caused an internal table to overflow.

The generic `Array` class is functionally similar to the NIH Library class `ArrayOb` we described in Chapters 9 and 10, except its elements must be one of the fundamental data types `char`, `int`, `short`, `long`, `unsigned`, `float`, or `double`. The file `Array_h.m4` contains an m4 macro named ARRAYDECLARE, which you use to generate the specification (`.h`) file for an `Array` of a specific fundamental data type. The file `Array_c.m4` contains an m4 macro named ARRAYIMPLEMENT, which you use to generate the corresponding implementation (`.c`) file.

The ARRAYDECLARE macro has three parameters: the name of the class you wish to generate, the type of the elements you wish it to contain (this is the parameterized type), and an optional list of classes that you want to declare as friends. For example, you can generate the specification file for class `Arraychar`, an `Array` of type `char` with the UNIX command:

```
echo "ARRAYDECLARE(Arraychar,char)" | m4 Array_h.m4 - >Arraychar.h
```

This command runs the m4 macro processor, which first reads the definition of ARRAYDECLARE from the file `Array_h.m4`, then it reads the string `"ARRAYDECLARE(Arraychar,char)"` from its standard input. This causes m4 to expand the ARRAYDECLARE macro with the specified parameters and write the result to its standard output file, which is redirected to the file `Arraychar.h`.

To give you and idea of what the ARRAYDECLARE macro looks like, here are some fragments of it from the file `Array_h.m4`:

```
define(ARRAYDECLARE,
``#ifndef" $1_H
``#define" $1_H

``#include" "Collection.h"

class $1: public Collection {
    DECLARE_MEMBERS($1);
    $2* v;          // pointer to array in free store
    unsigned sz;    // number of elements in array
// ...
// friends go here
    $3
protected:          // storer() functions for object I/O
    virtual void storer(OIOofd&) const;
    virtual void storer(OIOout&) const;
public:
    $1(unsigned size =DEFAULT_CAPACITY);
    $1(const $1&);

    ~$1();
    $2& elem(int i)          { return v[i]; }
    const $2& elem(int i) const { return v[i]; }
    bool operator!=(const $1& a) const { return !(*this==a); }
```

```
    void operator=(const $1&);
    bool operator==(const $1&) const;
    $2& operator[](int i) {
// ...
    $2 operator[](int i) const {
// ...
};


``#endif"
)
```

As you can see, it resembles the specification for class `ArrayOb` in the file `ArrayOb.h`. The notation `$1` refers to the first parameter (the class name), `$2` refers to the second parameter (the type), and `$3` refers to the third parameter (the `friend` declarations). Expanding the macro is simply a matter of string substitution.

Generating the implementation involves a bit more work because the implementation of some functions depends upon the specific type, and so does not lend itself to being parameterized. For example, we might want the member function `Arrayint::printOn()` to print the integers in the array in decimal separated by tab characters, while we might want the member function `Arraychar::printOn()` to print the characters in the array as a string of characters with no separators:

```
void Arrayint::printOn(ostream& strm) const
{
    for (unsigned i=0; i<sz; i++) { strm << v[i] << "\t"; }
}

void Arraychar::printOn(ostream& strm) const
{
    for (unsigned i=0; i<sz; i++) { strm << v[i]; }
}
```

The difference between these two implementations of `printOn()` is not simply a matter of substituting one type for another.

We solve this problem by placing the implementations of the type-specific functions such as `printOn()` and `hash()` in a separate file, along with a call to the ARRAYIMPLEMENT macro. For class `Arraychar` we named this file `Arraychar.p`. The file `Array_c.m4` contains the definition of the ARRAYIMPLEMENT macro, which generates the implementations of the rest of a class's member functions, the ones which are type-independent. The ARRAYIMPLEMENT macro has two parameters: the name of the class you wish to generate, and the type parameter. For example, for class `Arraychar` the file `Arraychar.p` contains the call:

```
ARRAYIMPLEMENT(Arraychar,char)
```

Thus, the UNIX command

```
m4 Array_c.m4 Arraychar.p >Arraychar.c
```

generates the implementation file for class `Arraychar` by running the m4 macro processor, which first reads the definition of `ARRAYIMPLEMENT` from the file `Array_c.m4`, then reads the type-specific part of the implementation and the call to `ARRAYIMPLEMENT`. The end result is the complete implementation of class `Arraychar` in the file `Arraychar.c`.

14.3.3 Summary of parameterized types

Parameterized types offer a way to write classes that are even more general than is now possible. They can make programming safer by eliminating the need for type casts, as is now required when using NIH library container classes, and they can improve efficiency by allowing container classes to hold objects themselves, rather than pointers to objects as the NIH library classes do now. The addition of parameterized types to C++ will have a profound effect on the design of class libraries and the programs that use them. In the meantime, you can realize some of the benefits of parameterized types by using macros.

14.4 GARBAGE COLLECTION

As we mentioned in Section 8.4.2, mismanagement of memory allocated with the new operator is, in our experience, the most frequent cause of serious programming errors when using C++ classes. It is simply too easy to delete an object prematurely and then attempt to reference the deallocated memory with a "dangling" pointer, or to forget to delete it altogether, creating a "memory leak". These types of errors can be extremely difficult to track down.

From a programmer's point of view, the best remedy to this problem is *automatic garbage collection*, where the language compiler (or interpreter) handles objects in such a manner that a run-time routine, called a garbage collector, can identify those objects that are in use (active objects) and those that are not (inactive objects). When a program requires more memory than is available, the garbage collector marks all the active objects and frees the memory occupied by those that are inactive. Managing memory in a language that has automatic garbage collection is easy—you simply allocate an object when you need one, and you do not have to worry about deleting it.

Unfortunately, automatic garbage collection does not fit in well with two of the design goals of C++: compatibility with C and efficiency. Compatibility with C is very useful due to the large amount of existing C code available, so many programs are a mixture of the two languages. Since C does not support garbage collection, it makes it difficult to add it to C++ and still retain this compatibility. Also, C++ is designed to be efficient, and the code generated by a compiler that supports automatic garbage collection is necessarily less efficient than that generated by one that does not. Thus, adding automatic garbage collection to C++ would make it too inefficient for many applications.

14.4.1 Counted pointers

Shopiro [24] has devised an approach to this problem known as *counted pointers*. The idea is to keep a count of how many pointers in a program refer to a particular object, and to delete the object when this count becomes zero. To maintain this count for objects of class

Patient, as in Example 14-2, we create a counted pointer class named `Patient_CP`
which behaves like a pointer to an Patient (a Patient*), but it also updates the
reference count.

```
// ex14-2.c - Counted pointers

#include "Patient.h"
#include "IdentDict.h"
#include "AssocInt.h"

class RefCountTable: public NIHCL {
    static IdentDict t;
public:
    static unsigned inc(const Object*);
    static unsigned dec(const Object*);
    static void printOn(ostream& strm =cout) {
        t.printOn(strm); strm << endl;
    }
};

unsigned RefCountTable::inc(const Object* p)
{
// Find ref count
    AssocInt* a =
        AssocInt::castdown((Object*)t.assocAt(*p));
    if (!a) {                                  // no ref count for p
        t.add(*new AssocInt(*(Object*)p,1));   // create entry,
        return 1;                              // ref count=1
    }
    Integer& refct = *Integer::castdown(a->value());
    return refct.value(refct.value()+1);    // increment ref count
}

unsigned RefCountTable::dec(const Object* p)
{
    Integer& refct = *Integer::castdown(t.atKey(*p));
    unsigned n = refct.value(refct.value()-1);
    if (n == 0) delete t.removeKey(*p);
    return n;
}

IdentDict RefCountTable::t;

class Patient_CP: public NIHCL {
    Patient* p;
public:
    Patient_CP(Patient* pt)      { RefCountTable::inc(p = pt); }
```

```
        Patient_CP(const Patient_CP& cp)
            { RefCountTable::inc(p = cp.p); }
        ~Patient_CP()
            { if (RefCountTable::dec(p)==0) delete p; }
        Patient_CP& operator=(const Patient_CP&);
        Patient& operator*()         { return *p; }
        Patient& operator[](int i)   { return p[i]; }
        Patient* operator->()        { return p; }
    };

    Patient_CP& Patient_CP::operator=(const Patient_CP& cp)
    {
        RefCountTable::inc(cp.p);
        if (RefCountTable::dec(p) == 0) delete p;
        p = cp.p;
        return *this;
    }
```

The class `RefCountTable` holds the reference counts for objects with counted pointers. Its member function `inc()` increments the reference count for an object, and its member function `dec()` decrements it. We implemented class `RefCountTable` with an `IdentDict` containing `AssocInt` objects to associate an `int` reference count with an object's memory address.

Using the member functions `inc()` and `dec()` to maintain the reference count in class `Patient_CP` is straightforward—it is a matter of calling `inc()` when a counted pointer is constructed and calling `dec()` when one is destroyed. Assigning one counted pointer to another involves decrementing the reference count of the old object it points to and incrementing the reference count of the new.

Since counted pointers must behave like ordinary pointers, class `Patient_CP` overloads `operator*()`, the pointer dereference operator, and `operator->()`, the structure pointer operator.[1] This makes it possible to write programs such as:

```
main()
{
    Patient_CP cp1 =
        new Patient("Doe, John E","123-45-6789",20892);
    Patient_CP cp2 =
        new Patient("Doe, Jane F","987-65-4321",20892);
    Patient_CP* cpp = new Patient_CP(cp1);

    cout << "Initial RefCountTable:" << endl;
    RefCountTable::printOn(); cout << endl;
```

---

[1] The ability to overload the structure pointer operator (`operator->()`) is a new feature first introduced in Release 2.0 of the AT&T C++ Translator.

```
    cp1->printOn(); cout << endl;
    (*cp2).printOn(); cout << endl;
    (*cpp)->printOn(); cout << endl;

    cout << endl;
    cp2 = cp1;
    cp2->printOn(); cout << endl;
    cout << "\nRefCountTable after cp2 = cp1:" << endl;
    RefCountTable::printOn();

    delete cpp;
    cout << "\nRefCountTable after delete cpp:" << endl;
    RefCountTable::printOn();
}
```

and get these results:

```
Initial RefCountTable:
Doe, John E 123-45-6789 20892=>2
Doe, Jane F 987-65-4321 20892=>1

Doe, John E 123-45-6789 20892
Doe, Jane F 987-65-4321 20892
Doe, John E 123-45-6789 20892

Doe, John E 123-45-6789 20892

RefCountTable after cp2 = cp1:
Doe, John E 123-45-6789 20892=>3

RefCountTable after delete cpp:
Doe, John E 123-45-6789 20892=>2
```

The advantage of the counted pointer technique is that you can maintain efficiency by being selective about the classes you use it with. The disadvantages are:

- The client program must cooperate by not using ordinary pointers to reference objects which are being managed by counted pointers.

- You must create one counted pointer class for each class you want to manage using this technique, potentially doubling the number of classes in a program. If you created a polymorphic counted pointer class (Object_CP), you would need to do a lot of error-prone type casts; for example:

```
    Object_CP sp = new Circle(Point(1,1),2);
    ((Shape*)sp)->draw()
```

The expression sp->draw() would not work because Object::draw() is undefined. Note, however, that parameterized types would solve this problem, since you could define a counted pointer class template that you could use as follows:

```
CP<Shape> sp = new Circle(Point(1,1),2);
sp->draw();
```

- If objects contain counted pointers such that the references form a cycle, the storage for the objects will not be reclaimed because the reference count will never reach zero.

Nevertheless, counted pointers represent a promising technique for dealing with memory management in C++.

14.4.2 Garbage-collecting versions of `malloc()`

Both Caplinger [4] and Boehm and Demers [3] have described garbage-collecting versions of `malloc()`, the standard C library memory allocator function. Could one of these provide automatic garbage collection for C++?

Both of these use a similar technique to identify which blocks of memory are in use: they search every word of a program's data, including the data and stack segments and the processor's registers, looking for any bit pattern that *might* be a pointer to an allocated block. If such a pattern is found, the block it points to is marked active. Then, `malloc()` reclaims the storage of all inactive blocks. If, by accident, a bit pattern just happens to look like a valid pointer, it will cause no harm—it will just cause the storage of the block at which it points to remain allocated.

Two problems arise when adapting this method of automatic garbage collection to a C++ environment. First, this method assumes that the client program keeps a pointer to the first word of an active block, which could contain an object under C++. This is not necessarily true if we are using multiple inheritance:

```
class Object { // ...
class Point: public virtual Object { // ...

Object* p = new Point(0,1);
```

Under current versions of C++, p would point to the interior of the block holding the `Point` object, not to the first word. So a C++ garbage collector would also need to consider bit patterns that looked like pointers to the interior of a block as indicating that the block was in use.

Second, if an inactive block contains a C++ object, the garbage collector would need to call that object's destructor function before freeing the storage. Thus, `malloc()` would need a way to know if a block contains a C++ object, and it also would need a way to determine the address of an object's destructor. For a class library such as the NIH Class Library, where all classes are descendents of class `Object`, we can solve these problems by making some changes to class `Object`.

For example, the garbage-collection version of `malloc()` described by Boehm and Demers has the following interface functions:

- `char* gc_malloc(unsigned n)`, which allocates a block of n bytes, and
- `extern void gc_free(char*)`, which explicitly deallocates a block allocated

by `gc_malloc()`. You can call this function to improve performance in situations where you are certain the block is inactive.

To adapt this to a C++ environment, we need to add a third function, `gc_malloc_object()`, which we would use to allocate blocks containing C++ objects having destructors. The function `gc_malloc_object()` does what `gc_malloc()` does, but also sets a flag in the block to indicate that the object's destructor must be called when the block is reclaimed.

To make the C++ new and delete operators call these functions, we can redefine `operator new()` and `operator delete()`:

```
extern "C" {
    extern char* gc_malloc(unsigned);
    extern char* gc_malloc_object(unsigned);
    extern void gc_free(char*);
}

inline void* operator new(size_t n)      { return gc_malloc(n); }
inline void operator delete(void* p)     { gc_free((char*)p); }
```

The `extern "C" { ... }` declaration signifies to the C++ compiler that the functions declared follow C, not C++, linkage conventions.

With new and delete redeclared in this fashion, we can now use them to manage the allocation of arrays of fundamental data types, for example new `char[100]`, just as before. What about objects with destructors? We must arrange for new `String(100)`, for example, to use `gc_malloc_object()` instead of `gc_malloc()`, and we must provide a way for the garbage collector to call the object's destructor function when it reclaims its storage. We can accomplish this with the following changes to class `Object`:

```
class Object {
public:
    void* operator new(size_t nbytes) {
        return gc_malloc_object(nbytes);
    }
    void operator delete(void*) {}
    virtual ~Object() {}
// ...
};
```

Defining the member function `operator new()` overrides the new operator for a particular class and, because of inheritance, for all its descendents. So, by defining `Object::operator new()` to call `gc_malloc_object()`, we make the new operator use `gc_malloc_object()` to allocate storage for instances of all classes in the NIH Class Library as desired.

Similarly, defining the member function `operator delete()` overrides the delete operator for a particular class and its descendents. By defining `Object::operator delete()` as an empty function, we prevent the delete operator from free-

ing the storage for NIH Class Library objects, but it will still call destructor functions because C++ generates the code to do this automatically, even when operator delete()
contains no user-written code. Thus, when using this scheme for automatic garbage collection, we must be careful not to use delete on objects with destructors. We define
Object::operator delete() in this manner so we can modify the garbage collector to use it to call the destructors for inactive objects whose storage it is about to reclaim.

Since the garbage collector does not know the specific class of any object it is deleting,
we must make the destructors of all NIH library classes virtual functions so that the dynamic
binding mechanism will cause delete to execute the appropriate destructor. We do this
by defining Object::~Object() as virtual.

A destructor for an inactive object might not *ever* be called because the garbage collector
thinks that some random bit pattern in the program is actually a pointer to it. As we have
seen, destructors with side effects such as buffer flushing and resource release are very
useful, so we would like to guarantee that the destructors for all objects are ultimately
called. We can accomplish this by assuming that all blocks containing objects are to be
freed when the program exits, and activating the garbage collector in a special mode that
does this when the program calls exit().

Thus, we see that implementing automatic garbage collection for C++ is feasible, although
the overhead of examining all of a program's data for possible pointers to objects may be
too inefficient for some applications.

14.5   DYNAMIC LINKING

Consider the following program which uses the classes we developed for Example 7-2:

```
#include <fstream.h>
#include <osfcn.h>
#include "Picture.h"
#include "OIOnih.h"

main()
{
    ifstream in("picturefile");
    if (in.fail()) {
        cerr << "Failed to open picturefile\n";
        exit(1);
    }
    Picture* bigPic = Picture::readFrom(OIOnihin(in));
    bigPic->draw();
}
```

Suppose picturefile was created by another program and contains a Picture object
which includes an instance of a Line. What will happen when we run this program?

Currently, the call to readFrom() will fail with the error message:

```
[RDUNKCLASS] Tried to read object of unknown class Line
```

because we did not link the code for class `Line` in with the program—we did not
`#include` the header file `Line.h`. Often, the error messages produced by a program
can lead to interesting ideas for extensions. Is there some way to make this program work?

We could if we had an implementation of C++ that supported *dynamic linking*—the ability
to incorporate additional code into a running program. We could modify `readFrom()` to
not give up so easily when it encounters an object of a class that is not linked with the
program. Instead, it could search a list of directories or libraries where it might find the
code for the unknown class. If the search was successful, `readFrom()` could then use
dynamic linking to load the code for the new class. Once loaded, `readFrom()` could
resume reading the object in the usual way.

Dynamic linking is a powerful concept because it would allow us to write open-ended
programs—programs that could extend themselves automatically. Imagine writing an interactive drawing editor using geometric shape classes like those in Example 7-2. We could
implement such an editor as a virtual function, `Shape::edit()`, which would allow a
user to modify the size and location of a shape by using a pointing device such as a mouse.
We could provide a command to permit users to paste another shape into an existing picture,
and implement it by calling `Shape::readFrom()` to read the shape to be added from a
file.

To extend our editor to handle a new shape, say a circular arc, we would write a new
class, `Arc`, which would reimplement or inherit class `Shape`'s virtual functions, including
`edit()`. Next, we would prepare a dynamically linkable version of the code for class `Arc`
and place it in a directory or library where `readFrom()` could find it. Then, we would
write a small program that uses `storeOn()` to produce a template file for the `Arc` shape:

```
#include <fstream.h>
#include "Arc.h"
#include "OIOnih.h"

main()
{
    ofstream out("arc.template",ios::out,0664); // UNIX protection
                                                // mode 0664
    if (out.fail()) {
        cerr << "Failed to open arc.template\n";
        exit(1);
    }
    Arc arc(Point(0,0),1,0.0,90.0); // quarter circle at (0,0)
                                    // and radius 1
    arc.storeOn(OIOnihout(out));
}
```

We could then paste `arc.template` into a drawing. When our editor attempted to
read the `Arc` object from the template file, `readFrom()` would dynamically link in the
code for class `Arc`, thereby extending the editor to handle a previously unknown shape. We
would then be able to edit `Arc` shapes as though they had been built into the editor from
the beginning.

Our drawing editor could save this picture in a file by calling `storeOn()`. If our computer was part of a network of machines that shared a common distributed file system, copies of our editor running on other machines would also be able to locate and dynamically link the code for class `Arc`, so they too could display and edit the file containing our picture with a circular arc.

Another advantage of dynamic linking is that programs can potentially be smaller, since they only need to link the classes they need for a particular situation.

14.6 CHAPTER SUMMARY

In this chapter we discussed some possible extensions to C++ and to the NIH Class Library:

- *exception handling*, which we showed must be supported by C++ in order to be efficient, safe, flexible, and easy to use;

- *parameterized types*, which will provide a way to write classes that are more efficient when polymorphism is not needed and which will eliminate some of the need for explicit type casts;

- *garbage collection*, which would reduce the number of programming errors due to memory mismanagement, the most frequent source of programming errors when using C++ classes; and,

- *dynamic linking*, which would make open-ended programs possible.

NIH CLASS LIBRARY HIERARCHY

NIHCL—Library Static Member Variables and Functions
  Object—Root of the NIH Class Library Inheritance Tree
    Bitset—Set of Small Integers (like Pascal's type SET)
    Class—Class Descriptor
    Collection—Abstract Class for Collections
      Arraychar—Byte Array
      ArrayOb—Array of Object Pointers
      Bag—Unordered Collection of Objects
      SeqCltn—Abstract Class for Ordered, Indexed Collections
        Heap—Min-Max Heap of Object Pointers
        LinkedList—Singly-Linked List
        OrderedCltn—Ordered Collection of Object Pointers
          SortedCltn—Sorted Collection
            KeySortCltn—Keyed Sorted Collection
        Stack—Stack of Object Pointers
      Set—Unordered Collection of Non-Duplicate Objects
        Dictionary—Set of Associations
          IdentDict—Dictionary Keyed by Object Address
        IdentSet—Set Keyed by Object Address
    Date—Gregorian Calendar Date
    FDSet—Set of File Descriptors for Use with select(2) System Call
    Float—Floating Point Number
    Fraction—Rational Arithmetic
    Integer—Integer Number Object
    Iterator—Collection Iterator
    Link—Abstract Class for LinkedList Links
      LinkOb—Link Containing Object Pointer
      Process—Co-routine Process Object
        HeapProc—Process with Stack in Free Store
        StackProc—Process with Stack on main() Stack
  LookupKey—Abstract Class for Dictionary Associations
    Assoc—Association of Object Pointers
    AssocInt—Association of Object Pointer with Integer

`Nil`—The Nil Object
`Point`—X-Y Coordinate Pair
`Random`—Random Number Generator
`Range`—Range of Integers
`Rectangle`—Rectangle Object
`Semaphore`—Process Synchronization
`SharedQueue`—Shared Queue of Objects
`String`—Character String
  `Regex`—Regular Expression
`Time`—Time of Day
`Vector`—Abstract Class for Vectors
  `BitVec`—Bit Vector
  `ByteVec`—Byte Vector
  `ShortVec`—Short Integer Vector
  `IntVec`—Integer Vector
  `LongVec`—Long Integer Vector
  `FloatVec`—Floating Point Vector
  `DoubleVec`—Double-Precision Floating Point Vector
`ReadFromTbl`—Tables used by Object I/O `readFrom()`
  `OIOifd`—File Descriptor Object I/O `readFrom()` Formatting
  `OIOin`—Abstract Class for Object I/O `readFrom()` Formatting
    `OIOistream`—Abstract Class for Stream Object I/O `readFrom()` Formatting
      `OIOnihin`—Stream Object I/O `readFrom()` Formatting
`Scheduler`—Co-routine Process Scheduler
`StoreOnTbl`—Tables used by Object I/O `storeOn()`
  `OIOofd`—File Descriptor Object I/O `storeOn()` Formatting
  `OIOout`—Abstract Class for Object I/O `storeOn()` Formatting
    `OIOostream`—Abstract Class for Stream Object I/O `storeOn()` Formatting
      `OIOnihout`—Stream Object I/O `storeOn()` Formatting

NIH CLASS LIBRARY
TEMPLATE FILES

This is a listing of the NIH Class Library template file for writing the specifications of a library class, Template.h:

```
#ifndef THIS_CLASS_H
#define THIS_CLASS_H

/*$Header$*/

/* Template.h - example header file for an NIH Library class

Author:

Modification History:

$Log$

*/

// Define "MI" if this class uses multiple inheritance:
//#ifndef MI
//#define MI
//#endif

#include "BASE_CLASS.h"
// #include .h files for other classes used
// Insert only class declarations for classes accessed by pointer
// and reference ONLY


// If BASE_CLASS is Object:
// class THIS_CLASS: public VIRTUAL Object {

class THIS_CLASS: public BASE_CLASS {
    DECLARE_MEMBERS(THIS_CLASS);
// member variables here
```

```
protected:        // storer() functions for object I/O
    virtual void storer(OIOofd&) const;
    virtual void storer(OIOout&) const;
public:
    bool operator==(const THIS_CLASS&) const;
    bool operator!=(const THIS_CLASS& a) const
        { return !(*this==a); }
    virtual int compare(const Object&) const;
    virtual Object* copy() const;  // shallowCopy() default
                                   // if not defined
    virtual void deepenShallowCopy();
    virtual unsigned hash() const;
    virtual bool isEqual(const Object&) const;
    virtual void printOn(ostream& strm =cout) const;
    virtual const Class* species() const;
};
```

```
#endif
```

This is a listing of the NIH Class Library template file for writing the implementation of a
library class, `Template.c`:

```
/* Template.c  - example implementation of an NIH Library class

Author:

Function:

Modification History:

$Log$

*/

#include "THIS_CLASS.h"
#include "nihclIO.h"
// #include .h files for other classes used

#define THIS    THIS_CLASS
// Define BASE only for classes with one base class
#define BASE    BASE_CLASS
// Define list of addresses of descriptors of all base classes:
#define BASE_CLASSES BASE::desc()
// Define list of addresses of descriptors of all member classes:
#define MEMBER_CLASSES
// Define list of addresses of descriptors of all virtual base
// classes:
#define VIRTUAL_BASE_CLASSES
```

```
DEFINE_CLASS(THIS_CLASS,1,"$Header$",NULL,NULL);
// For abstract classes:
//DEFINE_ABSTRACT_CLASS(THIS_CLASS,1,"$Header$",NULL,NULL);
// For non-abstract classes with multiple base classes:
//DEFINE_CLASS_MI(THIS_CLASS,1,"$Header$",NULL,NULL);
// For abstract classes with multiple base classes:
//DEFINE_ABSTRACT_CLASS_MI(THIS_CLASS,1,"$Header$",NULL,NULL);
extern const int // error codes

/* _castdown() for classes with multiple base classes:

void* THIS_CLASS::_castdown(const Class& target) const
// (Probably a good candidate for memoization.)
{
    if (&target == desc()) return (void*)this;
    void* p = BASE1::_castdown(target);
    void* q = p;
    if (p = BASE2::_castdown(target)) ambigCheck(p,q,target);
// ...
    if (p = BASEn::_castdown(target)) ambigCheck(p,q,target);
    return q;
}

*/

bool THIS_CLASS::operator==(const THIS_CLASS& a) const
// Test two instances of THIS_CLASS for equality
{
}

const Class* THIS_CLASS::species() const
// Return a pointer to the descriptor of the species of this class
{
    return &classDesc;
}

bool THIS_CLASS::isEqual(const Object& p) const
// Test two objects for equality
{
    return p.isSpecies(classDesc) && *this==castdown(p);
}

unsigned THIS_CLASS::hash() const
```

```
// If two objects are equal (i.e., isEqual) they must have
// the same hash
{
}


int THIS_CLASS::compare(const Object& p) const
// Compare two objects.  If *this > p return >0,
// *this == p return 0, and if *this < p return <0.
{
    assertArgSpecies(p,classDesc,"compare");
}


void THIS_CLASS::deepenShallowCopy()
// Called by deepCopy() to convert a shallow copy to a deep copy.
// deepCopy() makes the shallow copy by calling the copy
// constructor.
{
/*
Deepen base classes in order specified in class declaration.

Deepen virtual base classes (VBase):
    VBase::deepenVBase();        // do not do this for class Object

Deepen non-virtual base classes (BASE):
    BASE::deepenShallowCopy();   // do not do this for class Object

Nothing need be done for member variables that are fundamental
types.  Copy a member variable o that is an NIHCL object:
    o.deepenShallowCopy();

Copy a member variable p that is a pointer to an NIHCL object of
class CLASS:
    p = (CLASS*)p->deepCopy();
*/
}


void THIS_CLASS::printOn(ostream& strm) const
// Print this object on an ostream
{
}


// Object I/O


/*
Member class instances are constructed in the order they are
declared in the class declaration, regardless of the order they
appear in the constructor initialization list, so they must be
```

```
stored in this order.  Note that member class instances are
constructed before body of constructor is executed.
*/

// Construct an object from OIOin "strm".
THIS_CLASS::THIS_CLASS(OIOin& strm)
:
#ifdef MI
    Object(strm),
#endif
/*
Call readFrom() constructors of all ancestor virtual base classes:
    VBase(strm),
*/
    BASE(strm)
/*
Read a member variable o that is an instance of an NIHCL class:
    o(strm)
{
Read a member variable f that is a fundamental type using ">>":
    strm >> f;

Read a member variable p that is a pointer to an instance of
the NIHCL class CLASS:
    p = CLASS::readFrom(strm);

Read member variables in the same order that they are stored.
*/
}

void THIS_CLASS::storer(OIOout& strm) const
// Store the member variables of this object on OIOout "strm".
{
/*
Store virtual base classes (VBase) in inheritance DAG order:
    VBase::storeVBaseOn(strm);

Store non-virtual base classes in order specified in class
declaration:
    BASE::storer(strm);

Store a member variable f that is a fundamental type using "<<":
    strm << f;

Store a member variable o that is an instance of the NIHCL class
CLASS:
    o.storeMemberOn(strm);
```

```
Store a member variable p that is a pointer to an instance of an
NIHCL class:
    p->storeOn(strm);

Store member variables in the same order that they are read.
*/
}

// Construct an object from file descriptor "fd".
THIS_CLASS::THIS_CLASS(OIOifd& fd)
:
#ifdef MI
    Object(fd),
#endif
/*
Call readFrom() constructors of all ancestor virtual base classes:
    VBase(fd),
*/
    BASE(fd)
/*
Read a member variable o that is an instance of an NIHCL class:
    o(fd)
{
Read a member variable f that is a fundamental type:
    fd >> f;

Read a member variable a that is a pointer to an array of length l:
    fd.get(a,l);

Read a member variable p that is a pointer to an instance of the
NIHCL class CLASS:
    p = CLASS::readFrom(fd);

Read member variables in the same order that they are stored.
*/
}

void THIS_CLASS::storer(OIOofd& fd) const
// Store an object on file descriptor "fd".
{
/*
Store virtual base classes (VBase) in inheritance DAG order:
    VBase::storeVBaseOn(fd);

Store non-virtual base classes in order specified in class
declaration:
```

```
    BASE::storer(fd);

Store a member variable f that is a fundamental type:
    fd << f;

Store a member variable a that is a pointer to an array
of length l:
    fd.put(a,l);

Store a member variable o that is an instance of the NIHCL class
CLASS:
    o.storeMemberOn(fd);

Store a member variable p that is a pointer to an instance of an
NIHCL class:
    p->storeOn(fd);

Store member variables in the same order that they are read.
*/
}
```

TIPS FOR C PROGRAMMERS

C++ provides better ways of doing certain things than its predecessor C. Programmers accustomed to programming in C may have to break some habits if they are to benefit from these improvements. This Appendix presents some common C programming conventions that the C++ programmer should abandon in favor of the preferred C++ conventions described.

1. Use const instead of #define to declare program constants.
   C:

```
#define PI 3.14159265358979323846
#define MAX_INT 0x7FFFFFFF
#define MAX_UNSIGNED 0xFFFFFFFF
```

   C++:

```
const double PI = 3.14159265358979323846;
const int MAX_INT = 0x7FFFFFFF;
const unsigned MAX_UNSIGNED = 0xFFFFFFFF;
```

Names declared with #define are untyped and unrestricted in scope; names declared with const are typed and follow C++ scope rules. The type information may help the C++ compiler detect errors and produce better code, and restricting the scope of names makes the programmer's intentions clear and prevents naming conflicts.

You must still use #define in C++ to declare names to be used in preprocessor commands such as #if and #ifdef:

```
#define DEBUG
#ifdef  DEBUG
// ...
#endif
```

You must also use #define to declare names that are not values, for example, the names of classes:

```
#define THIS    Rectangle
#define BASE    Object
void THIS::storer(OIOout& strm)
{
    BASE::storer(strm);      // call storer() of base class
    // ...
```

In other words, use #define where text substitution is required.

2. Use inline functions instead of preprocessor macros.
   C:

```
#define MAX(a,b)      ( (a) >= (b) ? (a) : (b) )
```

   C++:

```
inline int MAX(int a,int b) { return a >= b ? a : b; }
```

You will make fewer errors using inline functions than with #define. The compiler checks the types of the arguments and return value, you do not need to enclose the arguments in parentheses to assure the intended order of evaluation (consider MAX(x=y,z)), and arguments with side effects are correctly evaluated (consider MAX(x++,y)).

There are still some relatively infrequent uses for #define preprocessor macros in C++, however:

- Using a type as a parameter:

```
#define DECLARE_MAX(type) \
    inline type MAX(type a,type b) \
        { return a >= b ? a : b; }
DECLARE_MAX(int);
DECLARE_MAX(unsigned);
DECLARE_MAX(double);
```

- Control structures:

```
#define DO_FOREVER while(1)
```

- Declarations:

```
#define SIGNAL_DISABLE \
    int prior_signal_state = setpri(127)
#define SIGNAL_ENABLE    setpri(prior_signal_state)

void Semaphore::signal()
{
    SIGNAL_DISABLE;       // disable signals
    // ...
    SIGNAL_ENABLE;        // enable signals
}
```

3. Be careful to distinguish between int and unsigned.
   Unlike C, C++ distinguishes between int and unsigned int. This is particularly important when using overloaded functions:

```
#include <iostream.h>
inline void f(int)      {cout << "f(int) called\n";}
inline void f(unsigned) {cout << "f(unsigned) called\n";}
```

```
main()
{
    f(1);        // calls f(int)
    f(1U);       // calls f(unsigned)
}
```

4. Consider using references instead of pointers as function arguments.
   C:

```
void getScreenSize(height,width)
unsigned *height, *width;
/* ... */
unsigned height,width;
getScreenSize(&height, &width);
```

   C++:

```
void getScreenSize(unsigned& height, unsigned& width);
// ...
unsigned height,width;
getScreenSize(height, width);
```

   You do not need to remember to take the address of reference arguments each time you write a call to the function.

5. Declare reference or pointer arguments that are not modified by a function as const.
   C:

```
void doesNotChangeBigStruct(big_struct)
BigStruct* big_struct;   /* passed as pointer for efficiency */

int strlen(string)
char *string;
```

   C++:

```
void doesNotChangeBigStruct(const BigStruct& big_struct);

int strlen(const char* string);
```

   This prevents the function from making an assignment to the arguments declared const, and it allows callers to use const values as arguments.

6. Use overloaded function names instead of different function names to distinguish between functions that perform the same operations on different data types.
   C:

```
int abs(x)       /* absolute value of int */
int x;

double fabs(x)   /* absolute value of double */
double x;
```

C++:

```
int abs(int x);           // absolute value of int
double abs(double x);     // absolute value of double
```

This results in shorter, clearer function names and makes programs more general because they depend less on specific data types.

7. Use new and delete instead of malloc() and free().
   C:

```
struct Patient {
    char name[20];
    char sex;
    unsigned id;
};

struct Patient *p;
p = (struct Patient*)malloc(sizeof(Patient));
/* ... */
free(p);
```

C++:

```
struct Patient {
    char name[20];
    char sex;
    unsigned id;
};

struct Patient *p;
p = new Patient;
// ...
delete p;
```

The new and delete operators are more concise and, when used to allo-cate/deallocate instances of a class with a constructor/destructor, they guarantee that the instance is initialized/finalized.

8. Use << and >> instead of printf() and scanf().
   C:

```
scanf("%f",&x);
printf("The answer is %f\n",x);
fprintf(stderr,"Invalid command\n");
```

C++:

```
cin >> x;
cout << "The answer is " << x << endl;
cerr << "Invalid command\n";
```

The << and >> stream I/O operators are type-safe (you cannot accidentally read an int as a float, for example) and extensible (see Section 5.2).

9. Use static constructors/destructors instead of explicitly calling initialization/finalization functions.

Suppose we wish to write a library function evenParity() that appends an even parity bit to a character; that is, bit 7 of the character is set such that there are an even number of 1 bits. We want this library function to be as fast as possible, so we implement it using a pre-computed table of 128 characters in which the ith element holds the character with value i plus the parity bit. The function evenParity() simply masks off the low 7 bits of its argument character, uses it as an index into the table, and returns the value stored there. But how do we initialize the table?

In C, we might define a separate initialization function parityTableInit() to do this, but then a programmer who wishes to use evenParity() must remember to call parityTableInit() beforehand:

```c
static unsigned char eptable[128]; /* initialized by
                                     parityTableInit() */

void parityTableInit()
{
    unsigned i;
    for (i = 0; i < 128; i++) {
        unsigned n = 0; /* number of 1's in i */
        unsigned j = i;
        while (j != 0) {
            n++;
            j &= j-1; /* clear rightmost 1 bit */
        }
        eptable[i] = i | ( (n&1) << 7 );
    }
}

unsigned char evenParity(c)
char c;
{
    return eptable[c & 127];
}

#include <stdio.h>

main() {
    int i;
    parityTableInit(); /* must remember to do this! */
    for (i=0; i<128; i++) {
        if ( (i&7) == 0 ) printf("\n");
        printf("%.2x  %.2x      ",i,evenParity(i));
    }
}
```

In C++, we can use a static constructor to initialize the table:

```
struct EvenParityTable {
    unsigned char pchar[128];
    EvenParityTable();
};


EvenParityTable::EvenParityTable()
{
    for (unsigned i = 0; i < 128; i++) {
        unsigned n = 0;      // number of 1's in i
        unsigned j = i;
        while (j != 0) {
            n++;
            j &= j-1;          // clear rightmost 1 bit
        }
        pchar[i] = i | ( (n&1) << 7 );
    }
}


static EvenParityTable eptable; // initialized by
                                // static constructor

unsigned char evenParity(char c)
{
    return eptable.pchar[c & 127];
}


#include <iostream.h>

main() {
    cout.width(2);
    cout.fill('0');
    cout << hex;
    for (int i = 0; i<128; i++) {
        if ( (i&7) == 0 ) cout << '\n';
        cout << i << "  " << (int)evenParity(i) << '\t';
    }
}
```

The user of the C++ version of evenParity() cannot make a mistake by forgetting to initialize the table. A word of caution, however: other static constructors cannot reliably call evenParity() because it may have not been initialized—C++ does not specify the order in which static constructors are executed!

10. Declare variables near the place where they are used, and initialize variables in their declarations.
    C:

```
void assign(dst, src)
char *dst, *src;
{
    int len;
    int i;
    if (src == dst) return;
    if (dst != 0) free(dst);
    len = strlen(src);
    dst = (char*)malloc(len+1);
    for (i=0; i<len; i++) dst[i] = src[i];
    return;
}
```

C++:

```
#include <string.h>

void assign(char* dst, const char* src)
{
    if (src == dst) return;
    if (dst != 0) delete dst;
    int len = strlen(src);
    dst = new char[len+1];
    for (int i=0; i<len; i++) dst[i] = src[i];
    return;
}
```

In C++, declarations are statements that you can place anywhere, not just at the beginning of a block as in C. Often, using this feature to declare variables near the place they are used makes the program easier to understand.

Also, C++ allows you to initialize auto aggregates (classes, structs, unions, and arrays) in their declarations, resulting in shorter programs.

11. Use derived classes with virtual functions rather than switch statements on type members.
C:

```
#include <stdio.h>
#include <math.h>
enum shapeTy { triangle, rectangle, circle };
struct Triangle {
    float x1,y1,x2,y2,x3,y3;
};
struct Rectangle {
    float x1,y1,x2,y2;
};
struct Circle {
    float x,y,r;
};
```

```c
struct Shape {
    enum shapeTy shape;
    union {
        struct Triangle t;
        struct Rectangle r;
        struct Circle c;
    } u;
};

float area(s)
struct Shape *s;
{
    switch (s->shape) {
        case triangle:  {
            struct Triangle *p = &s->u.t;
            return fabs(p->x1*p->y2 - p->x2*p->y1
                + p->x2*p->y3 - p->x3*p->y2
                + p->x3*p->y1 - p->x1*p->y3)/2;
        }
        case rectangle: {
            struct Rectangle *p = &s->u.r;
            return fabs((p->x1 - p->x2)
                *(p->y1 - p->y2));
        }
        case circle: {
            struct Circle *p = &s->u.c;
            return M_PI * p->r * p->r;
        }
        default: {
            fprintf(stderr,"Invalid shape\n");
            abort();
        }
    }
}
```

C++:

```cpp
#include <iostream.h>
#include <math.h>

class Shape {
public:
    Shape() {};
    virtual float area() const =0;
};

class Triangle: public Shape {
    float x1,y1,x2,y2,x3,y3;
```

```
public:
    Triangle(float X1, float Y1, float X2, float Y2,
        float X3, float Y3);  // implementation of
                              // constructor not shown
    virtual float area() const;
};

float Triangle::area() const
{
    return fabs(x1*y2-x2*y1+x2*y3-x3*y2+x3*y1-x1*y3)/2.0;
}

class Rectangle: public Shape {
    float x1,y1,x2,y2;
public:
    Rectangle(float X1, float Y1,
        float X2, float Y2);    // implementation of
                                // constructor not shown
    virtual float area() const;
};

float Rectangle::area() const
{
    return fabs((x1-x2)*(y1-y2));
}

class Circle: public Shape {
    float x,y,r;
public:
    Circle(float X, float Y, float R);  // implementation of
                                        // constructor not
                                        // shown
    virtual float area() const;
};

float Circle::area() const
{
    return M_PI*r*r;
}
```

Using C++ derived classes and virtual functions is more readable, general, and flexible than using structs with type fields and switch statements in C. To add a new kind of shape, say a Pentagon, to the C example, you would need to add the identifier Pentagon to enum shapeTy, define struct Pentagon, add a struct Pentagon to the union in struct Shape, and add another case to the function area(). These modifications are not localized, and the changes to struct Shape would necessitate recompilation of all programs that used it.

To add a `Pentagon` to the C++ example, you would need only to define class `Pentagon` as a derived class of `Shape` and define its constructor and member function `area()`—no modifications to existing code are needed, and you would not need to recompile any programs.

12. Use static member variables and functions instead of global variables and functions, and place `enum` types in class declarations.
    C:

```
#include <stdio.h>

enum colorTy { red, green, blue };
enum colorTy color = red;
unsigned char evenParity();

main()
{
    color = green;
    printf("%.2x\n",evenParity('Z'));
}
```

    C++:

```
#include <iostream.h>

class MyLib {
public:
    enum colorTy { red, green, blue };
    static colorTy color;
    static unsigned char evenParity(char c);
};

colorTy MyLib::color = red;

main()
{
    MyLib::color = MyLib::green;
    cout << hex << (int)MyLib::evenParity('Z') << endl;
}
```

This avoids polluting the global name space with identifiers, making name conflicts much less likely when libraries written by different programmers are combined in the same program. Furthermore, access to static member variables and functions can be controlled by making them private or protected members.

13. Use anonymous unions to eliminate unnecessary identifiers.
    C:

```
unsigned hash(val)
double val;
/* Hash a double into an unsigned int */
```

```
    {
        static union {
            unsigned asint[2];
            double asdouble;
        } u;
        u.asdouble = val;
        return u.asint[0] ^ u.asint[1];
    }
```

C++:

```
unsigned hash(double val)
// Hash a double into an unsigned int
    {
        static union {
            unsigned asint[2];
            double asdouble;
        };
        asdouble = val;
        return asint[0] ^ asint[1];
    }
```

The C++ example eliminates the unnecessary identifier u and is shorter.

REFERENCES

[1] J. G. P. Barnes, *Programming in Ada*, Addison-Wesley, Reading, Massachusetts, 1982.

[2] J. M. Barton, and J. C. Wagner, 'Enhanced Resource Sharing in UNIX', *Computing Systems*, **1**(2), 111–133 (1988).

[3] H. -J. Boehm and M. Weiser, 'Garbage Collection in an Uncooperative Environment', *Software—Practice and Experience*, **18**(9), 807–820 (1988).

[4] M. Caplinger, 'A Memory Allocator with Garbage Collection for C', in *Proceedings of the Winter 1988 Usenix Conference*, Rob Kolstad ed. pp. 325–330 USENIX Association, Berkeley, California, 1988.

[5] O-J. Dahl, B. Myrhaug, and K. Nygaard, *SIMULA Common Base Language*, Norwegian Computing Center S-22, Oslo, Norway, 1970.

[6] E. W. Dijkstra, 'Go To Statement Considered Harmful', *Communications of the ACM*, **11**(3), 147–148 (1968).

[7] A. Goldberg and D. Robson, *Smalltalk-80 The Language and its Implementation*, Addison-Wesley, Reading, Massachusetts, 1983.

[8] K. Gorlen, 'An Object-Oriented Class Library for C++ Programs', *Software—Practice and Experience*, **17**(12), 899–922 (1987).

[9] E. Horowitz and S. Sahni, *Fundamentals of Computer Algorithms*, Computer Science Press, Inc., Potomac, Maryland, 1978.

[10] J. H. Howard, M. L. Kazar, S. G. Menees, D. A. Nichols, M. Satyanarayanan, R. N. Sidebotham, and M. J. West, 'Scale and Performance in a Distributed File System', *ACM Transactions on Computer Systems*, **6**(1), 51–81 (1988).

[11] B. W. Kernighan and D. M. Ritchie, 'The M4 Macro Processor', in *UNIX Programmer's Supplementary Documents Volume 1*, University of California, Berkeley, California, 1986.

[12] B. W. Kernighan and D. M. Ritchie, *The C Programming Language*, 2nd edition, Prentice-Hall, Englewood Cliffs, NJ, 1988.

[13] D. E. Knuth, *The Art of Computer Programming, Vol. 3*, Addison-Wesley, Reading, Massachusetts, 1973.

[14] A. Koenig and B. Stroustrup, 'Exception Handling for C++', in *Proceedings of the C++ at Work Conference*, Tyngsboro, Massachusetts, November 1989.

[15] S. B. Lippman, *C++ Primer*, Addison-Wesley, Reading, Massachusetts, 1989.

[16] L. E. McMahon, 'SED—A Non-interactive TextEditor', in *UNIX User's Supplementary Documents*, University of California, Berkeley, California, 1986.

[17] B. Meyer, *Object-Oriented Software Construction*, Prentice-Hall, New York, New York, 1988.

[18] L. B. Rall, 'Differentiation in Pascal-SC: Type Gradient', *ACM Transactions on Mathematical Software*, **10**(2), 161–184 (1984).

[19] L. B. Rall, 'The Arithmetic of Differentiation', *Mathematics Magazine*, **59**(5), 275–282 (1986).

[20] M. J. Rochkind, 'The Source Code Control System', *IEEE Transactions on Software Engineering*, **SE-1**(4), 364–370 (1975).

[21] J. Schwarz, 'Iostream Examples', in *AT&T C++ Language System Release 2. 0 Library Manual* (Select Code 307-145), AT&T Customer Information Center, Indianapolis, Indiana, 1989.

[22] R. Stallman, *GNU EMACS Reference Manual*, Free Software Foundation, Cambridge, Massachusetts, 1986.

[23] B. Stroustrup, *The C++ Programming Language*, Addison-Wesley, Reading, Massachusetts, 1986.

[24] B. Stroustrup, 'Possible Directions for C++', in *Proceedings of the USENIX C++ Workshop*, Keith Gorlen ed. pp. 399–416 USENIX Association, Berkeley, California, 1987.

[25] B. Stroustrup and J. Shopiro, 'A Set of C++ Classes for Co-routine Style Programming', in *Proceedings of the USENIX C++ Workshop*, Keith Gorlen ed. pp. 417–439 USENIX Association, Berkeley, California, 1987.

[26] B. Stroustrup, 'Type-safe Linkage for C++', *Computing Systems*, 1(4), 371–403 (1988).

[27] B. Stroustrup, 'What is "Object-Oriented Programming"?', *IEEE Software*, **5**(3), 10–20 (1988).

[28] B. Stroustrup, 'The Evolution of C++: 1985 to 1989', in *AT&T C++ Language System Release 2. 0 Selected Readings* (Select Code 307-144), AT&T Customer Information Center, Indianapolis, Indiana, 1989.

[29] B. Stroustrup, 'Multiple Inheritance for C++', *Computing Systems*, **2**(4), 367–397 (1989).

[30] B. Stroustrup, 'Parameterized Types in C++', *Journal of Object-Oriented Programming*, 1(5), 5–16 (1989).

[31] W. F. Tichy, 'Design, Implementation, and Evaluation of a Revision Control System', in *Proceedings of the 6th International Conference on Software Engineering*, IEEE, Tokyo, 1982.

[32] *UNIX Programmer's Reference Manual*, University of California, Berkeley, California, 1986.

[33] N. Wirth, *Programming in Modula-2*, Springer-Verlag, Berlin, Germany, 1982.

INDEX

!= inequality operator
   in class Set, 175
() function call operator
   in class String, 61
- subtraction operator
   in class Set, 175
-> structure pointer, 363
:: scope resolution operator, 34, 33–35,
      295–297, 302–304
<< left shift operator, 53
= assignment operator, 46–47, 230
   in class ArrayOb, 230
== equality operator, 150, 224, 230
   in class ArrayOb, 224, 230
   in class Set, 175
>> right shift operator, 54
[] indexing operator, 224
   in class ArrayOb, 224
   in class OrderedCltn, 158
   in class Regex, 78
   in class SortedCltn, 160
   in class String, 67
& bitwise AND operator
   in class Set, 175
   in class String, 70
&= operator
   in class String, 61
_cplusplus preprocessor symbol, 80
_castdown(), 326, 331–333
| bitwise OR operator
   in class Set, 175

abstract class, 120–121, 122, 152, 156, 228,
      298
   member variables, 213
   protected constructors, 121, 218
   virtual member functions, 211
abstract data type, 2, 11
   and class, 2
   implementation, 16, 16–18, 33–50
   packaging for re-use, 69–71
   specification, 16, 16–31

accessor function, 210, 213, 216
Ada, i, 16, 17, 293
add(), 152, 158
   in class Set, 174
   in class SortedCltn, 160
addAfter(), 158
   in class LinkedList, 169
addAssoc()
   Dictionary, 178
   in class KeySortCltn, 165
addBefore(), 158
addContentsTo(), 152, 224, 234–235
   in class ArrayOb, 224, 234–235
addFirst()
   in class LinkedList, 169
addKeysTo()
   Dictionary, 180
addLast()
   in class LinkedList, 169
ADT, see abstract data type
Algol, 3
allocSizeErr(), 222, 237
   in class ArrayOb, 237
ancestor class, 120, 122
   distant, 308
   with multiple inheritance, 302–303, 308,
      319, 322, 324–326, 328, 334, 337, 339,
      346
   virtual functions, 210
ARRAYDECLARE macro, 359
ARRAYIMPLEMENT macro, 359, 361
ArrayOb class, 193–194, 219–239
   addContentsTo(), 224, 234–235
   allocSizeErr(), 237
   at(), 224, 236
   capacity(), 224, 236
   compare(), 224, 235
   constructors, 223, 228–230
   copy constructor, 228–230
   deepCopy(), 224
   deepenShallowCopy(), 234
   destructor, 223

ArrayOb class (*cont.*)
  doFinish(), 235–236
  doNext(), 224, 235–236
  doReset(), 235–236
  file descriptor I/O, 239
  hash(), 225, 234
  indexRangeErr(), 237–238
  isEqual(), 225, 230–233
  member variables, 222
  object I/O, 223, 238–239
  operator=(), 230
  operator==(), 224, 230
  operator[](), 224
  public member functions, 223–225
  readFrom() constructor, 238–239
  removeAll(), 225, 237
  reSize(), 225, 236–237
  size(), 224, 236
  species(), 225, 230–233
  storer(), 238–239
asOrderedCltn()
  in class Collection, 235
assertArgClass(), 187
assertArgSpecies(), 187
assertClass(), 187
assertSpecies(), 187
asSet()
  in class Collection, 235
Assoc class, 163, 178
assocAt()
  in class Dictionary, 180
  in class KeySortCltn, 165
associative array, 180–182
AssocInt class, 164
asSortedCltn(), 176
  in class Collection, 235
at(), 224, 236
  in class ArrayOb, 224, 236
  in class OrderedCltn, 158
atKey()
  in class Dictionary, 178
attach(), 59
automatic derivative, 90, 90–97

base class, 5, 102–104, 112, 120, 126,
    140–141, 144, 186, 195, 197, 200–203,
    206, 211, 221, 222, 226–228
BASE macro, 226
BASE_CLASS macro, 219, 225
BASE_CLASSES macro, 226–227
BEGINX macro, 352
BigInt example
  printOn(), 47
  constructor, 33–36, 39, 42–43
  copy constructor, 39
  data type, 14–15

  destructor, 47–48
  DigitStream class, 43–44
  and Fraction class, 82
  implementation, 33–50
  operator+(), 41–42
  operator=(), 46–47
  scanChunk(), 56–58
  specification, 19–30
BitVec class, 83–85
ByteVec class, 83

C, i, 1, 15, 51, 60
  call by value, 3
  function argument checking, 3, 40
  lacks call by reference, 3, 39–40
  type checking, 3
C++, i, 1–7, 51, 60
  and C, 3–4
  class, 2
  class member, 17
  and data abstraction, 4–5, 17–18
  declarations in blocks, 38–39
  heritage, 3
  lacks class library, 6
  modular programming, support for, 294–295
  and object-oriented programming, 4–5
  reference type, 39–41
  treatment of data types, 6
call by reference, 3–4, 39–41, 245
call by value, 3
capacity(), 152, 224, 236
  in class ArrayOb, 224, 236
cast, *see* type casting
castdown(), 222, 326, 328–334
cin stream, 54
Circle example, 105–106
class, 5, 17
  abstract, 120–121, 122
  and abstract data type, 2
  forward reference, 66
Class class, 144–146
class declaration, 20
class descriptor, 144, 144–146, 225–228, 230,
    331
  and object I/O, 227
class implementation template, 219, 225–239,
    333
  #include files, 225–226
  BASE macro, 226
  BASE_CLASSES macro, 226–227
  constructors, 228–230
  DEFINE_ABSTRACT_CLASS macro, 228
  DEFINE_CLASS macro, 227–228
  file descriptor I/O, 239
  MEMBER_CLASSES macro, 226–227
  object I/O, 238–239

symbolic error codes, 228
Template_c file, 219
THIS macro, 226
VIRTUAL_BASE_CLASSES macro, 226–227
class specification template, 219, 219–225
  #include files, 221
  declaring NIHCL members, 222
  object I/O, 223
  preventing multiple definitions, 221
  Template_h file, 219
class template, 355, 355–361
classDesc member, 144
classDesc(), 190
className(), 145
client class, 195, 196
client program, 1
Collection class, 152–153
  asOrderedCltn(), 235
  asSet(), 235
  asSortedCltn(), 235
  doFinish(), 153
  doNext(), 153
  doReset(), 153
compare(), 148, 224, 235
  in class ArrayOb, 224, 235
  in class LinkOb, 172
  in class LookupKey, 163
comparing objects, 146–148
complex class, 82, 90
const function, 36–37, 67–68
const keyword, 35–36
constant member function, 33, 36–37
constant type, 33, 35–36
constructor function, 17, 25–29, 39, 42–43
  and initialization, 28–29
  protected in abstract class, 121, 218
  static, 26–27
  and type conversion, 27–28
container class, 143, 143–191
  dangerous operations, 155–156
  guidelines for use, 186–190
  iteration, 153–156
  Iterator vs for-loop, 159–160
  linked, 169–173
  memory management, 187–189
  modifying contents, 189–190
  nested iteration, 154–155
  polymorphism, 143
  sequenced, 156, 156–157
  sorted, 160–169
  specialized containers, 186–187
  unsequenced, 174, 173–186
copy constructor, 29, 39, 46–47, 66, 88, 132, 193, 209
  in class ArrayOb, 230

copy(), 186
coroutine, 242
coroutine context, 242, 244, 246–247, 258
counted pointers, 362, 362–365
cout stream, 52–53
cpp macro processor, 358
create(), 245
critical section, 253, 253–256

DAG, *see* directed acyclic graph
dangling pointer, 187, 187–189, 361
data abstraction, 1, 1–2, 11–18
  in C++, 17–18
data hiding, 16, 18, 66, 77, 95, 195, 196, 242, 273, 285
data type
  abstract, 2, 11
  fundamental, 11
  instance of, 11
Date class, 6, 72–77
declarations in blocks, 38–39
DECLARE_MEMBERS macro, 222, 330, 334
deepCopy(), 224, 334
  in class ArrayOb, 224
ShallowCopy(), 334
deepenShallowCopy(), 234
  in class ArrayOb, 234
deepenVBase(), 222, 327, 334–337
default constructor function, 26
default function argument, 24, 31
DEFINE_ABSTRACT macro, 330
DEFINE_ABSTRACT_CLASS macro, 228, 332, 334
DEFINE_ABSTRACT_CLASS_MI macro, 332
DEFINE_CLASS macro, 222, 226–228, 326, 330, 332, 334
DEFINE_CLASS_MI macro, 332
delete operator, 33, 366–367
derived class, 5, 102–104, 112, 120, 141
derived class responsibility, 144
deriving from class Object, 125, 149–151
desc(), 145, 222
descendent class, 120, 122, 126, 186, 295–296, 298, 323, 326, 328, 330, 334, 365, 366
destructor function, 17, 30, 47–48, 365–367
  static, 30
Dictionary class, 6, 177–182
  addAssoc(), 178
  addKeysTo(), 180
  assocAt(), 180
  atKey(), 178
  includesKey(), 178
Dictionary example, 180–182
Dijkstra, Edsger W., 104
direct link, 169, 169–171

directed acyclic graph, <u>299</u>
discriminated record, 104
distant ancestor class, <u>308</u>, 322, 325
doFinish(), 153, 235–236
  in class ArrayOb, 235–236
doNext(), 153, 224, 235–236
  in class ArrayOb, 224, 235–236
doReset(), 153, 235–236
  in class ArrayOb, 235–236
DoubleVec class, 83
downward cast, <u>186</u>, 186–187, 300, 326,
    328–334, 343–345
dumpOn(), 151
dynamic binding, 2, 5, 101–102, <u>111</u>, 141,
    199, 210, 294, 312, 367
dynamic character strings, 59–72
dynamic linking, <u>368</u>, 367–369

EMACS, GNU, 79
encapsulation, <u>17</u>, 20–21, 31, 101, 295
  C++ support for, 17
  class based, 44–45
  in module, 294
  object based, 44–45
endl manipulator, 53
ENDX macro, 352
exception handling
  in C++, 349–353
  in NIHCL, 352–353
EXCEPTION macro, 352
EXCEPTION_CODE macro, 353

finalization, of object, 119
first()
  in class LinkedList, 169
FloatVec class, 83
flush manipulator, 54
FORK(), 247
Fraction class, 82
friend keyword, 33, 45, 71, 83, 121, 204,
    210, 216
fstream class, 59
function argument
  default, 24
  type checking, 22–23
function argument type checking, 31
function name overloading, 31
function overloading, 5, 17, 23–24, 344
fundamental data type, <u>1</u>, 5

garbage collection in C++, 361–367
  using malloc(), 365–367
  with counted pointers, 362–365
geometry example, 104–120, 123–127
  Picture class, 126–127
  TransformStack class, 123–125

global name space, 210, 213
goto, 104

hash linking example, 183–185
hash table example, 174–175
hash(), 147–148, 150, 225, 234
  in class ArrayOb, 225, 234
  in class LinkOb, 172
  in class LookupKey, 163
  in class Set, 174
HeapProc class, 244–245
heavyweight process, <u>241</u>

IdentDict class, 182–186
IdentSet class, 176–177
implementation of data type, <u>16</u>, 16–18
implementor function, <u>210</u>, 213
implicit member operator, 37–38
implicit member reference, 33
implicit type conversion, 31, 69–70
impure virtual function, 211, 213
includes(), 152
  in class Set, 174–175
includesKey()
  Dictionary, 178
INDEXRANGE error, 351
indexRangeErr(), 222, 237–238
  in class ArrayOb, 237–238
indirect link, <u>169</u>, 171–173
inheritance, 101–104, 120, 197–198, 200–203
  multiple, *see* multiple inheritance
  single, *see* single inheritance
inheritance diagram, 299–300
initialization, of object, 116–119
initializer list, 106, 107, 116, 117, 139, 314,
    326, 328, 339
inline function, 195
inline keyword, 33, 48–50, 212–213
input, *see* stream I/O
  see also
    object I/O,
    scanFrom(),
instance of a class, 20–31
instance of a data type, <u>11</u>
Integer class, 164
internal function, <u>210</u>, 213
IntPick class, 85
IntVec class, 83–88
isA(), 144–145, 222
isEmpty(), 152
isEqual(), 147, 150, 158, 178, 225,
    230–233
  in class ArrayOb, 225, 230–233
  in class LinkOb, 172
  in class LookupKey, 163
  in class Set, 174, 175

isKindOf(), 146
isListEnd(), 171
isMemberOf(), 145
isSame(), 148
isSpecies(), 146
istream class, 56–58
istream class, 52, 54
iterating through a container, 153–156
   dangerous operations, 155–156
   nested iteration, 154–155
Iterator class, 152–156
   operator()(), 153
   operator++(), 153

keyAt()
   in class KeySortCltn, 165
KEYNOTFOUND error, 351
KeySortCltn class, 161–162, 165–169
   multi-key sorting, 167–168

last()
   in class LinkedList, 169
late binding, *see* dynamic binding
lightweight process, 241, 241–259
   active, 241
   and control programs, 242
   data type for, 241–242
   NIHCL implementation, 242–244, 259
   RUNNING state, 243, 244
   and simulations, 242
   SUSPENDED state, 243, 244
   TERMINATED state, 243, 244
Line example, 105–106
Link class, 169–171, 297, 298
   isListEnd(), 171
   next link, 170
   nextLink(), 170
LinkedList, 158
LinkedList class, 6, 156, 169–173, 297, 298
   addAfter(), 169
   addFirst(), 169
   addLast(), 169
   direct link, 169–171
   first(), 169
   indirect link, 171–173
   last(), 169
   removeFirst(), 169
   removeLast(), 169
LinkOb
   compare(), 172
   hash(), 172
   isEqual(), 172
   value(), 172
LinkOb class, 171–173, 297
LongVec class, 83

LookupKey class, 162–163
LWP, *see* lightweight process

m4 macro processor, 358
manager function, 210, 213
manipulator, 53
match(), 78
mathematical set, 175–176
Matrix class, 88–90
member class, 198–199
member function, 5, 21–22, 24–25, 210–213
member operator, 37–38
member pointer, 199–200
member variable, 5, 20, 21, 106–107
MEMBER_CLASSES macro, 226–227
memory leak, 187–189, 361
method, 210
MI, 326
Modula-2, i, 15–17, 293
modular programming, 1, 293–297
   in C++, 294–295
   and data abstraction, 294
   export, 295
   import, 295
   module, 293
   module component, 293
   module export, 294
   module implementation, 294
   module import, 294
   module specification, 293
   with multiple inheritance, 293–297
   and object-oriented programming, 294
multiple base classes, 197
multiple inheritance, 120, 122, 171, 293, 293–347
   ambiguous downward casts, 343–345
      resolved by linkCastdown(), 344
      resolved by overloading, 343
   base class ambiguity, 300–304
      resolved by casting, 300
      resolved by encapsulation, 300–302
      resolved by operator::(), 302–303
      resolved by overloading, 303–304
   base class constructor and virtual
      functions, 316–318
   list of base classes, 293, 298
   and modular programming, 293–297
   object finalization, 316
   object initialization, 314–316
   syntax, 293
   virtual base class, 305–314, 318–325
      constructors, 307–308
      resolving multiple calls, dynamic method, 322–324
      resolving multiple calls, static method, 318–322

multiple inheritance (*cont.*)
  virtual base class (*cont.*)
    and virtual functions, 312–314
  and virtual functions, 304–305
multiple inheritance in NIHCL, 325–343
  castdown(), 326, 328–334
  copying objects, 334–337
  deepenVBase(), 327, 334–337
  DEFINE_ABSTRACT_CLASS_MI macro,
    326
  DEFINE_CLASS_MI macro, 326
  MI macro, 326
  Object as virtual base class, 326, 328
  object I/O, 337–343
  object I/O limitation, 344
  readFrom(), 326, 339–343
  storer() functions, 337–338
  storeVBaseOn(), 327, 337–338
multiply linked list example, 297–302

new operator, 33, 366
new() operator, 38
next(), 256–258
next link, 170
nextLink(), 170
nextPut(), 256–258
NIH Class Library, 6, 123–141
  polymorphic functions, 140–141
  programming environment, 7–8
  Smalltalk heritage, 6, 123
  source distribution kit, 7
  see also
    class implementation template,
    class specification template,
    exception handling in NIHCL,
    multiple inheritance in NIHCL,
    parametrized types in NIHCL,
NIH Library class, 133
NIHCL, *see* NIH Class Library
NIHCL class, 295–297
  setError(), 296
NIHCL_ prefix, 228
nihclerrsx.h header file, 228
nihclIO.h header file, 225
Nil object, 185–186
nil pointer, 185–186
non-member function, 23, 45, 141, 210, 295
numeric data type, 81–97

Object class, 125, 143–151
  className(), 145
  compare(), 148
  desc(), 145
  dumpOn(), 149
  hash(), 147–148
  isA(), 144–145

isEqual(), 147
isKindOf(), 146
isMemberOf(), 145
isSame(), 148
isSpecies(), 146
printOn(), 149
species(), 146
object copy in NIHCL, 127–134
  deepCopy(), 127–134
  deepenShallowCopy(), 132–134
  shallowCopy(), 127–132, 134
object finalization, 119
object I/O, 6, 134–141
  OIOin class, 140
  OIOnihin class, 140
  OIOnihout class, 138
  OIOout class, 137–138
  readFrom(), 138–140
  readFrom() constructor, 139, 139–140,
    223, 238–239
  storeMemberOn(), 136–137
  storeOn(), 134–137
  storer(), 135–137, 141, 223, 238–239
object initialization, 116–119
object instance of data type, 2
object number, 135, 138, 141, 186, 288
object-oriented design, 193–218, 261–291
  case study, 261–291
  class inheritance, 200–203
  class organization, 196, 202–203
  classes, inheritance vs. client, 196–197
  classes, when to use, 195–196
  data flow containers, 272–273
  data record containers, 270–272
  data records, 269–270
  database, 267–268, 279–290
  design issues, 194–195
  functions, 209–213
    inline vs. non-inline, 212–213
    member vs. non-member, 210
    pure vs. impure virtual, 211
    virtual vs. non-virtual, 210–211
  lightweight process, 266–267, 274–279
  member accessibility, 215–218
  private functions, 216–217
  private variables, 215–216
  protected functions, 218
  resource management, 267
  specialized classes, 273–274
  variables, 213–215
  variables, instance vs. pointer, 204–209
object-oriented programming, 1–3, 101–122
  and C++, 4–6
  compared with
    conventional programming, 2
    modular programming, 294

heritage, 2
  Smalltalk supports, 6, 210
occurrencesOf(), 152
OIOifd class, 239
OIOin class, 140
OIOistream class, 139
OIOnihin class, 140
OIOnihout class, 135, 138
OIOofd class, 239
OIOout class, 137–138
opaque type, 295
operator overloading, 5, 17, 29–30, 70–71, 224
OrderedCltn class, 6, 125–127, 156–160
  add(), 158
  addAfter(), 158
  addBefore(), 158
  at(), 158
  automatic resizing, 158
  capacity(), 158
  isEqual(), 158
  operator[](), 158
  remove(), 158
  reSize(), 158
  size(), 158
ostream class, 52–55
output, *see* stream I/O
  see also
    dumpOn(),
    object I/O,
    printOn(),
overloaded function, 5, 17, 23–24, 344
overloaded operator, 5, 17, 29–30, 70–71, 224

parameterized types
  in C++, 353–361
  in NIHCL, 358–361
Pascal, i, 1, 15, 210
Patient example, 149–151
Picture example, 110–112
Point class, 104–105, 123
polymorphic data structure, 122
polymorphic function, 122, 140–141
polymorphism, 122, 199, 206
printing objects, 149
printOn(), 47, 151
private base class, 297
private class, 65–66
private keyword, 17
private member, 21, 102, 110, 140, 195
private member function, 17, 216–217
private member variable, 17, 21, 204, 215–216
procedural programming, 1
Process class, 6, 242, 244–245
protected keyword, 121–122

protected member, 195
protected member function, 218
public class, 110
public keyword, 17, 21, 110
public member, 102, 110, 195
public member function, 21
pure virtual function, 114, 122, 211, 213

RAISE macro, 353
Range class, 6, 78–79
readFrom(), 138–140, 339–343
readFrom() constructor, 139, 139–140, 222–223, 326
  in class ArrayOb, 223, 238–239
reference type, 39–41
  assignment to, 67
Regex class, 77–81
regular expression, *see* Regex class
remove(), 152, 158
  in class OrderedCltn, 156
removeAll(), 225, 237
  in class ArrayOb, 225, 237
removeFirst()
  in class LinkedList, 169
removeId()
  in class OrderedCltn, 156
removeLast()
  in class LinkedList, 169
resizable array example, 158–159
reSize(), 225, 236–237
  in class ArrayOb, 225, 236–237
resume(), 244
return keyword, 46

scanFrom(), 57, 211
schedule(), 248
Scheduler class, 6, 242, 247–250
scope resolution operator, 34, 33–35, 295–297, 302–304
search(), 78
select(), 248
Selector class, 274
Semaphore class, 6, 242, 250–256
SeqCltn class, 156–157
  at(), 157
  first(), 156
  isEqual(), 157
  last(), 156
sequenced container, 156, 156–157
Set class, 6, 173–176
  add(), 174
  as hash table, 174–175
  as mathematical set, 175–176
  as unsequenced container, 173, 176
  hash(), 174
  includes(), 174, 175

Set class (*cont.*)
  isEqual(), 174, 175
  operator!=(), 175
  operator-(), 175
  operator==(), 175
  operator&(), 175
  operator|(), 175
setError()
  in class NIHCL, 296
shallowCopy(), 222
Shape example, 109–110
SharedQueue class, 6, 242, 256–258
ShortVec class, 83
shouldNotImplement(), 217
signal(), 251–256
Simula, 2, 3
single inheritance, 120, <u>122</u>, 171, 196, 201,
    299, 302, 304
size(), 152, 158, 224, 236
  in class ArrayOb, 224, 236
slice operator, 84
Smalltalk, i, 2, 44, 210
sorted container, 160–169
  external sort keys, 161–162
  multi-key sorting, 167–168
SortedCltn class, 160–169
  add(), 160
  compare(), 160
  external sort keys, 161–162, 165–169
  operator[](), 160
species(), 146, 225, 230–233
  in class ArrayOb, 225, 230–233
specification of data type, <u>16</u>, 16–18
Stack class, 123–125, 156
StackProc class, 244–245
static binding, <u>111</u>
static constructor function, 26–27
static destructor function, 30
static keyword, 140
static member function, 140–141, 196,
    210, 295
static member variable, 196, 214, 215, 295
storeMemberOn(), 136–137
storeOn(), 134–137
storer(), 135–137, 223, 337–338
  in class ArrayOb, 223, 238–239
storeVBaseOn(), 222, 327, 337–338
stream I/O, 51–59
  attaching an open file, 58–59
  and C-language I/O library, 51
  cerr stream, 52
  cin stream, 52, 54
  cout stream, 52–53
  extending to abstract data types, 54–55
  header file, 52
  ifstream class, 58

  istream class, 56–58
  istream class, 52
  ofstream class, 58–59
  ostream class, 52
  standard error, 52
  standard input, 52, 54, 56–58
  standard output, 52–53
  stream reassignment, 52
stride of a vector, 84
String class, 6, 59–72
  operator()(), 61
  operator[](), 67
  operator&(), 70
  operator&=(), 61
  SubString class, 62–65
Stroustrup, Bjarne, 3, 4, 318, 350, 354
subtype, 112, <u>120</u>
suspend(), 244
switch statement, 104
symbolic constants, 35

Template_c file, *see* class implementation
    template
Template_h file, *see* class specification
    template
terminate(), 244
THIS macro, 226
this pointer, 45–46
THIS_CLASS macro, 219, 225
Time class, 6, 72–77
traffic simulation example, 297–302, 305–346
TransformStack example, 107–108
type casting, 126, 186–187, 222, 234, 361,
    364, 369
  const objects, 37, 68
  explicit, 112
  implicit, 70–71
  and multiple inheritance, 300, 326, 328–334
type checking, 22–23, 40, 187
type compatibility, 112–113
type conversion, 5, 17, 18, 27–28, 45, 69–71,
    209
type conversion operator, 209

UNIX, 7, 12, 71, 241, 242, 244, 247, 262,
    265, 274, 277, 278, 358, 359, 361
unsequenced container, <u>174</u>, 173–186

value()
  in class Assoc, 163
  in class AssocInt, 164
  in class Integer, 164
  in class LinkOb, 172
  in class LookupKey, 162
vector classes, 6, 83–88
  macro template, 87–88

as parameterized type, 87–88
slice operator, 84
stride, 84
see also
   BitVec class,
   ByteVec class,
   DoubleVec class,
   FloatVec class,
   IntVec class,
   LongVec class,
   ShortVec class,
Vehicle example, 297–346

virtual function, 5, 102–104, 210–211, 213
   and base class constructor, 119–120
   in abstract class, 211
   pure, 113, 113–114, 122
virtual keyword, 110, 328
VIRTUAL macro, 328
virtual member function, 102
VIRTUAL_BASE_CLASSES macro, 226–227

wait(), 251–256

yield(), 247